Simulation Modelling

While simulation has a vast area of application, this textbook focuses on the use of simulation to analyse business processes. It provides an up-to-date coverage of all stages of the discrete-event simulation (DES) process, covering important areas such as conceptual modelling, modelling input data, verification and validation and simulation output analysis.

The book is comprehensive yet uncomplicated, covering the theoretical aspects of the subject and the practical elements of a typical simulation project, demonstrated by cases, examples and exercises. It also shows how simulation relates to new developments in machine learning, big data analytics and conceptual modelling techniques. Guidance is provided on how to build DES models using the Arena, Simio and Simul8 simulation software, and tutorials for using the software are incorporated throughout.

Simulation Modelling offers a uniquely practical and end-to-end overview of the subject, which makes it perfect required or recommended reading for advanced undergraduate and postgraduate students studying business simulation and simulation modelling as part of operations research, business analytics, supply chain management and computer science courses.

Andrew Greasley is Lecturer in Supply Chain Analytics and Modelling in the School of Infrastructure and Sustainable Engineering at Aston University, Birmingham, UK.

Simulation Modelling

Concepts, Tools and Practical Business Applications

Andrew Greasley

Routledge
Taylor & Francis Group

LONDON AND NEW YORK

Cover image: Maria Pavledis The Owl Sanctuary, drawing with smoke
www.mariapavledis.com

First published 2023
by Routledge
4 Park Square, Milton Park, Abingdon, Oxon OX14 4RN

and by Routledge
605 Third Avenue, New York, NY 10158

Routledge is an imprint of the Taylor & Francis Group, an informa business

British Library Cataloguing-in-Publication Data
A catalogue record for this book is available from the British Library

Library of Congress Cataloging-in-Publication Data
Names: Greasley, Andrew, author.
Title: Simulation modelling : concepts, tools and practical business applications /
    Andrew Greasley.
Description: Abingdon, Oxon ; New York, NY : Routledge, 2023. | Includes
    bibliographical references and index.
Identifiers: LCCN 2022013149 | ISBN 9780367643515 (hbk) | ISBN 9780367643539
    (pbk) | ISBN 9781003124092 (ebk)
Subjects: LCSH: Business—Data processing. | Decision making—Simulation methods.
Classification: LCC HF5548.2 .G639 2023 | DDC 658.4/032—dc23/eng/20220715
LC record available at https://lccn.loc.gov/2022013149

ISBN: 978-0-367-64351-5 (hbk)
ISBN: 978-0-367-64353-9 (pbk)
ISBN: 978-1-003-12409-2 (ebk)

DOI: 10.4324/9781003124092

Typeset in Times New Roman
by Apex CoVantage, LLC

Contents

1 Introduction

Introduction

This chapter introduces simulation modelling as an important method for analysing organisational systems. Simulation modelling is explained in terms of its use of a combination of explanatory and descriptive modelling approaches and its characteristic as a dynamic mathematical model which allows changes in system attributes to be derived as a function of time. The simulation modelling approaches of discrete-event simulation, agent-based simulation and system dynamics (henceforth referred to as DES, ABS and SD, respectively) are then covered with a particular emphasis on the key features of DES. The relevance of DES to analysing organisational systems is established, and example application areas of the method are outlined.

Why Simulation Modelling?

Simulation modelling is an extremely powerful and important method, widely used in consulting, industry and the public sector. But why is simulation modelling so useful?

One reason is that we need to make decisions for an uncertain future. For organisations, uncertainty can be caused by a wide variety of reasons, such as shorter product/service life cycles, increasing system complexity with the use of IT systems and the increasing use of performance metrics, and when managing innovation, firms must make many decisions, such as whether to invest in new products for markets that do not yet exist. Thus, in order to make decisions about the future, we need to be able to predict the future as best we can.

Another reason is that often 'strategic aims' are put forward in organisations without any real notion of how they will be implemented in practice. Simulation can help convert these aims into reality by providing specific workable implementations of change at an operational level. Simulation can help specify how work should be done to successfully operate a system and specify what tasks and what resources are needed. Addressing the operational issue of how work will be done enables specific, workable implementations to be designed. Simulation can even address issues at the design stage, before a system exists, so that problems that might have appeared later (with greater time and cost) are dealt with.

What Is a Simulation Model?

A model is intended to represent a real system, either existing or planned. The major advantages of a model are that it succinctly represents the real system (this helps us interpret the output of the model), and it allows one to discover things about the real system by

DOI: 10.4324/9781003124092-1

investigating the model (this should be much quicker and less costly than experimenting with the real system). A computer is not needed to build a model, but the models we are concerned with here are built using a computer and may be referred to as computational models. These types of models are formulated as computer programs in which the program itself represents the processes in the real world. Simulation refers to the process of conducting experiments with the model to understand the behaviour of the system and/or evaluate various strategies for the operation of the system. This text considers the whole process of moving from a real-world problem to the use of a simulation model to provide understanding and/or solutions to that problem. For details on the history of simulation, see Goldsman et al. (2010). In this text, for brevity, the term 'simulation' may be used instead of the term 'simulation modelling'. In fact, simulation may be defined as subsuming the modelling activity and defined as establishing a model in a computational environment and allowing us to experiment with that model to solidify our understanding in a dynamic environment (Ören et al., 2018). This text is focused on the use of simulation to analyse organisational systems, but simulation is used across many disciplines to support scientific research. For example, computational sciences, such as computational physics, computational biology and computational social science, are the execution of scientific models on a computer, which is simulation (Tolk, 2018).

What Are We Simulating? The Systems View

In order to understand the simulation modelling approach, we need to understand the concept of a system. A system can be defined as a collection of interrelated components that work together towards a collective goal. The function of a system is to receive inputs and transform these into outputs (figure 1.1).

Thus, the systems view is based on an understanding that in an organised system, the behaviour of any part of that system ultimately has some effect on every other part. The

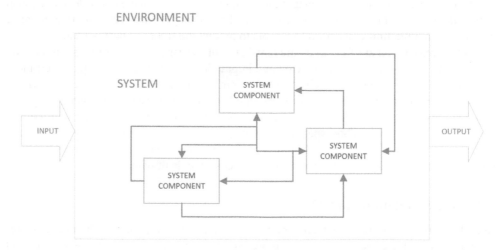

Figure 1.1 A system as a collection of interrelated components which receive inputs and transform these into outputs

following selection of characteristics of systems is presented to demonstrate their complexity and thus the need for tools such as simulation to analyse and improve their performance.

- Environment

  Systems do not operate in complete isolation. They are contained within an environment that contains other systems and external agencies. The scope of a system is defined by its boundary. Everything outside of the boundary is part of the system's environment; everything within the boundary forms part of the system itself. The boundary also marks the interface between a system and its environment. The interface describes exchanges between a system and the environment or other systems.

- Organisation

  The components of a system work towards a collective goal. This is known as the system's objective. The objective of a system is normally very specific and can often be expressed in a single sentence. As an example, the objective of a car might be expressed simply as to transport people and goods to a specified location.

- Interdependency

  Systems are made up of subsystems (components) that may themselves be made up of other subsystems. From this, one should realise that the parts of a system are dependent on one another in some way. This interdependence means that a change to one part of a system leads to or results from changes to one or more other parts.

While analytics techniques stress observation of data and description of behaviour, simulation is an attempt to look inside the physical boundary of a system at the components which drives their dynamics and thus determines their behaviour. For understanding a complex organisational setting using a systems view, the real system is subdivided into individual components, and the interdependencies or connections between them are defined. However, not all of these effects are significant, so the approach is about identifying significant interactions in the system. From a systems perspective, simulation involves providing a static representation of the real system by defining the relevant components (subsystems) of the system and the connections between them. The relevant components are identified by reference to the specific purpose of the model. The next stage involves providing a dynamic representation of the real system so that the state of the system at a particular point in time can be defined.

Systems occur in both the natural world, such as weather systems and disease transmission, as well as with human systems of cities and organisational systems, such as manufacturing and service operations. This text is focused on the use of simulation in an organisational context, but simulation is employed to imitate many different types of systems. Thus, simulation is used to predict the behaviour of physical, biological and other systems and is seen as a computational means to solve analytically intractable equations. In this context, it is often referred to as computational modelling or computational science, where models can be seen in a wider sense as a documentation of current knowledge about some aspect of the world.

How Can We Simulate? Descriptive and Explanatory Modelling

There are two main modelling methods for simulating or imitating the behaviour of a system. A descriptive modelling approach is based on measuring observed behaviour. If a system shows a certain regularity in behaviour, then future behaviour may be predicted under the same conditions. The statement 'under the same conditions' is an important caveat, and applying a descriptive modelling approach when conditions differ significantly from the conditions of observation is not valid. Although descriptive modelling is characterised by extensive and consuming data collection and parameter estimation, it only captures a small part of the potential behaviour of the system because, even with big data, we will not be able to collect all of the data that was ever generated or could be generated by a system. For example, the descriptive approach is used in many econometric models which use a parameter-fitting approach, repeated as new data becomes available. This is then used to update predictions of future trends based on the trends of the recent past. The actual processes of the economic system are not represented in the model, and so a valid prediction of new or unforeseen events is simply not possible. The descriptive modelling approach is shown in figure 1.2. where a regression analysis may be used to express the real system input-output behaviour as a mathematical relationship. Here, the descriptive modelling method provides, in essence, a data-fitting approach which is not able to reflect the variety of the individual process behaviour that an explanatory model can by reflecting the system structure.

Simulation is considered in this text as an explanatory modelling approach. Here, we take a systems view and represent the real system structure in what is termed an explanatory model. By representing the structure of the real system, the simulation model is able to produce dynamic behaviour similar to that of the real system (figure 1.3). When building an explanatory model, the emphasis is on the identification of those processes that are decisive

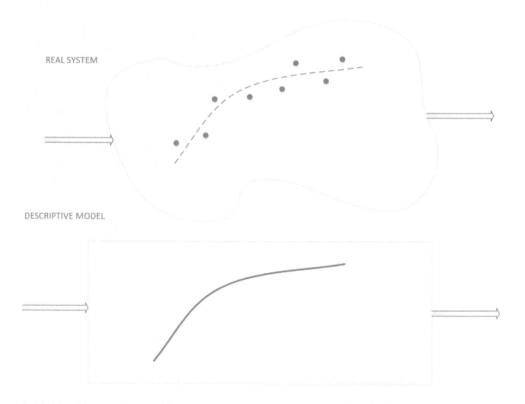

Figure 1.2 Descriptive model representing the essential behaviour of the real system

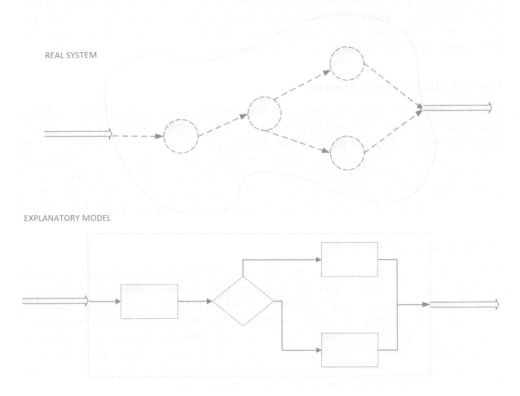

Figure 1.3 Explanatory model representing the essential structure of the real system

for system behaviour. The modeller investigates the structure and function of the system with experts who are familiar with the system and its operation. More detail on building the explanatory model in a simulation study is in chapter 4. The validity of the model is independent of historical observations of behaviour, and so behaviour may be represented under circumstances that have not yet been observed in reality, hence the ability to conduct what-if or scenario analysis. This does not mean, however, that an explanatory model can always accurately predict the future. For example, weather forecasts are based on explanatory models, and while they may be able to generate scenarios of future weather behaviour in the short term, it is not possible to provide accurate forecasts of the weather over more than a few days because the weather is chaotic and not fully predictable.

Explanatory models usually depend on descriptive sub-models to describe individual relationships in an aggregated form, and this is the case with DES. Inputs to the system and individual components are modelled by either parameter-fitting of theoretical or empirical distributions or other descriptive modelling methods such as mathematical equations (see chapter 5).

In summary, while analytics techniques stress observation of data and description of behaviour, the simulation methods considered in this text attempt to look inside the physical boundary of a system at the processes which drives their dynamics and thus determines their behaviour. From a systems perspective, simulation involves providing a static representation of the real system by defining the relevant components (subsystems) of the system and the connections between them. The relevant components are identified by reference to the specific purpose of the model. The next stage involves providing a dynamic representation of the real system so that the state of the system at a particular point in time can be defined.

Types of Mathematical Models

Before we discuss the different types of simulation methods in detail, we will look at the different types of mathematical models to which simulation belongs. There are many different approaches to modelling, but mathematical models represent a system as a number of mathematical variables (termed state variables) with mathematical equations used to describe how these state variables change over time. An important distinction between mathematical models is the classification between static (fixed in time) and dynamic (change over time), with dynamics systems being modelled using a continuous or discrete approach (figure 1.4).

Static Mathematical Models

Static models include the use of a computer spreadsheet, which is an example of a static numerical model in which relationships can be constructed and studied for different scenarios. Another example of a static numerical model is the Monte Carlo simulation method. This consists of experimental sampling with random numbers and deriving results based on these. Although random numbers are being used, the problems that are being solved are essentially determinate. The Monte Carlo method is widely used in risk analysis for assessing the risks and benefits of decisions. Linear programming is a modelling method that seeks defined goals when a set of variables and constraints are given.

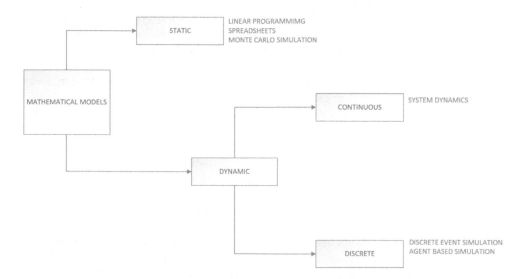

Figure 1.4 Categories of mathematical models

Dynamic Mathematical Models

A dynamic mathematical model allows changes in system attributes to be derived as a function of time. A classification is made between continuous and discrete model types. A discrete system changes only at separate points in time. For example, the number of customers in a service system is dependent on individual arrivals and departures of customers at discrete points in time. Continuous systems vary over time; for example, the amount of petrol in a tanker being emptied varies continuously over time and is thus classified as a continuous system. In practice, most continuous systems can be modelled as discrete and vice versa at different levels of detail. Also, systems will usually have a mixture of both discrete and continuous elements. In general, continuous models are used at a high level of abstraction – for example, investigating cause-and-effect linkages in organisational systems, while discrete models are used to model business processes. The SD approach is described as an example of a continuous mathematical model, while DES is described as a discrete mathematical modelling approach.

Deterministic and Stochastic Models

Another way of classifying models is between deterministic and stochastic models. A deterministic model does not represent uncertainty, and so for a given set of conditions, parameters will always produce the same outcome. This implies that given a well enough detailed snapshot of a system, we should be able to forecast the system's dynamic behaviour perfectly. Thus, these types of models are analytically tractable and may be expressed as mathematical formulae. Stochastic models include some random components, such as variable demand rate or variation of processing rates due to natural variability. The inclusion of stochasticity typically makes even simple models intractable but increases their realism. This is because few systems show no variation over time or can be perfectly understood and measured. However, a stochastic model only allows us to quote a probability of a future prediction.

A Framework for Modelling and Simulation

Zeigler et al. (2019) present a theory for simulation that is based on general systems theory, and a reference modelling formalism termed the discrete-event system specification (DEVS). In terms of the theory for simulation, simulation systems follow an architecture defined as three components of the source system, models and simulators. The source system is the real or virtual environment we are interested in modelling, and the data that has been gathered from observing or otherwise experimenting with a system is called the system behaviour database. An experimental frame is a specification of the conditions under which the system is observed or experimented with and is the operational formulation of the objectives that motivate a simulation project. The source system has a modelling relation with the model, which is a set of instructions, rules, equations, or constraints for generating input/output behaviour. The simulator then complements the model by adding a simulation relation to it. The simulator serves as a computational device and executes the model.

Simulation Modelling Methods

There now follows a brief overview of the three main methods of dynamic simulation modelling. These are system dynamics (SD), agent-based simulation (ABS) and discrete-event simulation (DES). The three methods have their own philosophies, communities of users and main areas of application. A hybrid simulation study consists of at least two of the three main methods of ABS, SD and DES. Hybrid simulation is covered in chapter 12. Hybrid modelling can refer to the use of simulation in combination with other analytical techniques. Hybrid modelling is covered in chapter 13.

System Dynamics (SD)

SD is an approach that attempts to understand the world as a system. The method was originally developed by Professor Jay Forrester when it was known as industrial dynamics. SD attempts to describe systems in terms of feedback and delays. Negative feedback loops provide a control mechanism that compares the output of a system against a target and adjusts the input to eliminate the difference. Instead of reducing this variance between actual output and target output, positive feedback adds the variance to the output value and thus increases the overall variance. Most systems consist of a number of positive and negative feedback cycles, which make them difficult to understand. Adding to this dynamic complexity is the time delay that will occur between the identification of the variation and action taken to eliminate it and the taking of that action and its effect on output. What often occurs is a cycle of overshooting and undershooting the target value until the variance is eliminated.

SD studies are usually, but not always, used when we understand the behaviour of a system but do not understand why the behaviour occurs. SD has been used extensively in a wide range of application areas, such as economics, supply chain, ecology and population dynamics, to name a few. SD has a well-developed methodology in which the main stages and phases of the construction of a model are defined. The SD methodology covers a number of areas, such as problem restructuring, causal loop diagramming and SD simulation models.

Problem restructuring is about determining the context of the problem. This involves relating a problem situation to previous experience of the simulation modeller but also seeing what from their perspective is unique or new about the problem. See chapter 3, defining the problem situation for more detail on this topic.

Causal loop diagrams can be used to understand the broad structure of a system. Figure 1.5 shows a causal loop diagram for a simple population model. The elements are linked

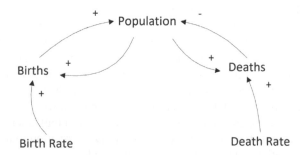

Figure 1.5 Causal loop diagram for a population model

by arrows which indicate the direction of causality of the link. A positive sign next to the arrow indicates that a change in the factor associated with the link will cause the factor at the head of the link arrow to change in the same direction, other factors remaining constant. For example, an increase in birth rate will lead to an increase in births. A negative sign indicates that the change will be in the opposite direction.

A type of causal loop diagram termed a system archetype provides a template of common behaviour in systems. For example, we know that expediting orders causes missed delivery dates in a production system but don't know exactly how the two events interact. We could link the two by mapping the underlying structure of the system to a system archetype. The potential advantage of this approach is that it provides a way of understanding the underlying dynamics to explain behaviour. See the case study 'Using System Dynamics in a Discrete-Event Simulation Study of a Manufacturing Plant' in chapter 3 for an example of the use of a system archetype.

SD simulation models involve the construction of a dynamic simulation model. In SD models, stocks of variables are connected together via flows. The SD simulation model can be implemented using computer software such as Stella II, Vensim and iThink. A system is represented by a number of stocks (also termed levels) and flows (also termed rates). A stock is an accumulation of a resource, such as materials, and a flow is the movement of this resource that leads to the stock rising, falling or remaining constant. A characteristic of stocks is that they will remain in the system even if flow rates drop to zero and they act to decouple flow rates. An example is a safety stock of finished goods, which provides a buffer between a production system which manufactures them at a constant rate and fluctuating external customer demand for the goods. An SD flow diagram maps out the relationships between stocks and flows. In Stella II, resource flows are represented by a double arrow, and information flows by a single arrow. Stocks are represented by rectangles. Converters, which are used for a variety of tasks, such as combining flows, are represented by a circle. Figure 1.6 shows an SD model of a simple population model in Stella II format.

Once the diagram is entered, it is necessary to enter first-order difference equations that compute the changes of a time slice represented by the time increment *dt*. There are stock, flow and convertor equations.

- Stock Equations

    At the current time point (*t*) the stock value *Lev(t)* is calculated by the software as follows:

    Lev(t) = Lev (t − dt) + (InRate − OutRate) × dt

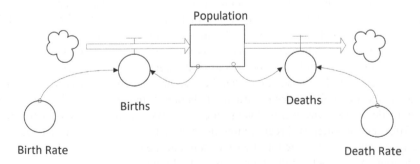

Figure 1.6 System dynamics diagram for a population model

This equation translates to the current stock value as a function of the previously calculated stock value plus the net flow over the time interval since the last calculation. For the population model, the following equation could be used to express the population stock value:

Population (t) = Population (t − dt) + (Births − Deaths) × dt

- Flow Equations

  Flow equations are generally the policy statements in the system and reflect the rate at which the system will change during the simulation time increment (*dt*). For the population model:

  Deaths = Population × Death rate
  Births = Population × Birth rate

- Convertor Equations

  Convertors can be intermediate variables or constants in our model. In the population model, two constants are provided. The value of these constants could be changed to observe the sensitivity of the model to these values. For the population model, the constants are as follows:

  Death rate
  Birth rate

SD simulation models show statistics of measures at an aggregate level and plots to observe and understand the behaviour of the system over long time periods. This is due to the extended time scales that feedback loops may operate in strategic systems.

SD is a form of *continuous simulation* in that it models the system as it changes continuously through time as distinct from DES, which 'slices' time into discrete steps. In reality, of course, a computer is a digital artefact and must represent a continuous change by approximation as a number of small discrete time steps. However, continuous simulation is useful if a 'flow' approach to modelling is required, either applied in tools such as SD or for modelling flows such as liquids directly as differential equations. Many DES software tools such as Arena and Simio incorporate continuous simulation capabilities. Pidd (2004) provides an introduction to building SD models.

Agent-Based Simulation (ABS)

The use of agents in the design of simulation models has its origins in the complexity of science and game theory. Agents are components in a system that have a set of rules or behaviour that controls how they take in information, process that information and effect change in their environment. ABS refers to the study of the behaviour of agents from the bottom up. This means that agent behaviours are defined, and then the agents are released into the environment of study. The behaviour of the agents then emerges as a consequence of their interaction. In this sense, the system behaviour is an emergent property of the agent interactions, and the main source of structural change in the system itself is in the form of the relationship between the agents. Agents interact by passing messages to each other which contain information, such as direct communication. These messages can contain information regarding other agents, such as their location, and be used to detect the effects of other agents' actions. Agents act within an environment which may represent a concept, such as a geographical space, in which case the ABS is termed a spatial model. The environment may be configured to have a range of effects on the agents depending on the application. Agents may have the following characteristics:

- They can perceive their environment, possibly including the presence of other agents in their vicinity.
- They have a set of behaviours which may include moving through the space in their environment, sending and receiving messages from other agents and interacting with their environment. Communication between agents is often through the environment as the environment can be used as a buffer to hold all the messages from one agent to another.
- They have a memory which records previous states and actions.
- They have a production rule system which consists of a set of rules that determines their future behaviour depending on their past history and current situation.
- Some agents can, over time, learn more effective rules and change their behaviour as a result of that learning. This may be implemented by agents that engage in reinforcement learning (RL). See chapter 13 for more details on RL.
- Objects in the environment can also be programmed in a similar way to agents, but they do not need to react to their surroundings. The environment can incorporate terrains from real landscapes by integrating a geographical information system (GIS) into the model.

In general, in an ABS, time is modelled in discrete time steps of the same duration, termed fixed-increment time advance (FITA) (Law, 2015). Here, all agents are checked for action in turn at a fixed time interval. As an alternative, a next-event time advance (NETA) approach can be adopted as used in DES. Here, any future actions are placed on a future event list, and simulation time jumps to the time of the next event. This can provide a more efficient execution. More details of this method can be found in the section on DES in this chapter.

One issue to consider when the simulation is moving through time is termed synchronicity. This relates to the fact that the computer model cannot update all agents simultaneously at each time step but must process the updates in sequence. The question arises: what sequence should the update of each agent's status occur? Three possible approaches to the issue of the execution order of agents at a point in time are as follows.

Sequential Asynchronous Execution

This involves invoking each agent in sequential order (agent A, agent B, agent C . . .), but this order can influence the performance of the simulation.

Random Asynchronous Execution

This involves invoking the agents in random order. The effect of the ordering can be investigated by running the simulation multiple times.

Simulated Synchronous Execution

This invokes agents in any convenient order. However, all inputs to agents are completed before all outputs.

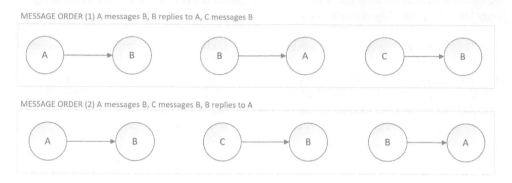

Figure 1.7 Alternative message ordering between three agents

Consider figure 1.7, showing an alternative ordering of messaging between three agents. In message order (1), agent B immediately replies to the message from agent A before being messaged by agent C. In message order (2), agent B receives messages from agents A and C before messaging/replying to agent A. Thus, it is clear that the outcome of these messages may be quite different depending on their execution sequence over time. Simulated synchronous execution is equivalent to 'message order (2)' in figure 1.7, where both the A and C message inputs to B are considered before the B output message to A. This approach is considered the closest to synchronous execution but can be difficult to implement in some models.

ABS has been applied across a wide area, such as economics, human behaviour, supply chains, emergency evacuation, transport and healthcare. A particular class of agent-based systems termed multi-agent simulations are concerned with modelling both individual agents (with autonomy and interactivity) and also the emergent system behaviour that is a consequence of the agent's collective actions and interactions. Unified Modelling Language (UML) is a modelling language which incorporates a collection of diagram types, such as use case, state diagrams, activity diagrams, class diagrams and object diagrams that can be used to document and design an agent-based model. Software implementations include object-oriented programming languages, such as Java in Anylogic and NetLogo. ABSs can also be programmed in object-oriented DES packages, such as Simio (see chapter on Hybrid Simulation). Railsback and Grimm (2019) provide an introduction to building ABS using NetLogo.

There has been an increasing interest in the use of ABS and some discussion of the relative merits of this approach as compared to DES. The two different methods have their own philosophies, communities, conferences and main areas of application. DES has typically been applied heavily in manufacturing and process type areas and services. Its process orientation means that it is a natural fit for people interested in process improvement and optimisation. On the other hand, ABS has emerged from the behavioural science and social sciences and, therefore, the domain of application has been more in that area. There are differing views on whether an ABS offers capabilities that discrete-event cannot provide or whether all agent-based applications can at least, in theory, be undertaken using a discrete-event approach. Some authors view ABS simply as a variation of DES (Law, 2015). However, as discussed, DES and ABS users are generally from different backgrounds, and a panel discussion on why this might be the case and why more DES practitioners are not using ABS is contained in Siebers et al. (2010).

Cellular Automata

Cellular automata are simple agent-based systems that consist of a number of identical cells that are arranged in a grid, usually in the form of a rectangular or 3D cube structure. Each cell may be in one defined state (such as 'on' or 'off') that is determined by a set of rules that specify how that state depends on its previous state and the states of the cell's immediate neighbours. The same rules are used to update the state of every cell in the grid. Thus, the method is best used to model local interactions, which are governed by rules that are homogeneous with respect to the cell population. Most types of agent-based systems now have actors that are freed from their cells with the ability to perform autonomous and goal-directed behaviour.

Discrete-Event Simulation (DES)

DES is defined by Law (2015) as 'the modelling of a system as it evolves over time by a representation in which the state variables change instantaneously at separate points in time. These points in time are the ones at which an event occurs, where an event is defined as an instantaneous occurrence that may change the state of the system'. A DES is defined by Collins et al. (2021) as one that breaks down the dynamic changes in a system into discrete events and resolves each event one at a time; this resolution might result in new events being created. To understand how DES works in detail, we need to understand how it represents a real system as it moves through time. Figure 1.8 and table 1.1 show the main features of a DES.

Explanatory Modelling (Process View)

DES involves building models of systems that consist of a number of building blocks, including processes, entities and resources (Pidd, 2004), and so is particularly suited to a process orientation. Using systems theory as a means of analysing and improving business processes, the process view considers the transformation of materials, information and customers into goods and services. This transformation is undertaken by processes that require the allocation of resources, such as staff and facilities (figure 1.9).

When constructing a DES, the system being simulated is seen as consisting of a number of flow units, termed entities (customers, materials, information), that are generated as inputs and flow through a network of processes. Examples of entities that are within the main classifications of customers, materials and information include transaction data from an IT system, customers for a supermarket and components for a manufacturer. Outputs from the process are classified as finished goods and services. Each individual process (which may be termed an activity) may use a resource in some form, such as staff or facilities. The amount and timing of resource availability may be specified by the model user. Entities may wait in a buffer, termed a queue, if a resource is not available when required. Each entity may have several attributes associated with it, such as a component type or person identification. Within the network, processes are linked so that the output of one process becomes an input into another, often through an intermediate buffer. Thus, the process can be viewed as a network of sub-processes (activities) and buffers. The relationship that defines the linkages

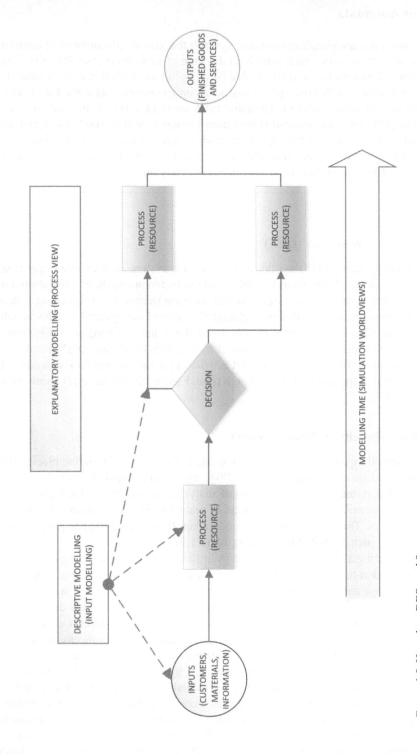

Figure 1.8 How does DES work?

Table 1.1 Features of a DES

Feature	Approach
Explanatory Modelling (Process View)	The transformation of entities flow through a network of processes which consume resources.
Descriptive Modelling (Input Modelling)	Parameter-fitting and other descriptive modelling approaches are used to represent process variability and individual process behaviour.
Modelling Time	Simulation worldviews provide a mechanism for moving the model through time.

Figure 1.9 The process view of an organisation

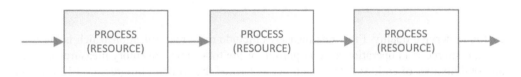

Figure 1.10 Serial relationship of processes

between processes can be either serial (figure 1.10) or parallel (figure 1.11). Most process networks are made up of a number of serial and parallel relationships with different entity types moving through different routes through the process, with the routes for each entity determined by decision points. Thus, the network structure has a large influence on the performance of the process, and one of the uses of simulation is to investigate the effect of different network structure designs on overall process performance. The definition of the model content in terms of entities, processes, resources, queues and decisions is covered in chapter 3. Explanatory modelling using diagrammatic techniques for the mapping of the transformation process is covered in chapter 4

The DES can be used to measure the success of this transformation process from inputs to outputs by providing measures including the cost and speed of the process. Process performance measures include flow time measures, flow rate measures and inventory measures. Flow time measures include the lead time, which is the time taken to undertake the steps in the process. This can relate to the speed of delivering goods and services to customers. Another flow time measure is queue time, which is the time taken between being ready to be processed and the resource undertaking the processing to become available and processing to commence. In a service operation, we need to minimise queue time to ensure

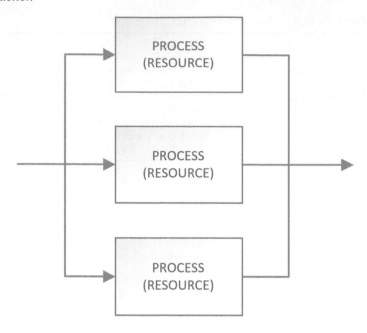

Figure 1.11 Parallel relationship of processes

customer service quality. Flow rate measures include resource utilisation which is the time that a resource is in operation as a proportion of the total time. Inventory measures include the total number of entities within the process, termed the work-in-progress (WIP). Process performance measures for DES are covered in chapter 3.

Descriptive Modelling (Input Modelling)

Arrival rates, individual process durations, decision conditions, breakdown events and other elements are modelled by either parameter-fitting of theoretical or empirical distributions or other descriptive modelling methods, such as mathematical equations. Descriptive modelling, also termed input modelling in simulation studies, is covered in chapter 5.

Modelling Time

In terms of moving the model through time, the simplest method is the use of time steps of the same duration as is often employed in ABSs. This method, though, is inefficient as many time steps are redundant as there has been no change in the system since the previous step. It may be difficult to increase the size of the time step to improve efficiency as process times may vary greatly (from seconds to years) and, in any case, will be unlikely to be whole numbers (for example, 1.23 minutes) and so will require small time steps to be resolved correctly. DES addresses these issues by only moving through time at the points at which the state of the system changes. Thus, in DES, time is moved forward in discrete chunks from event to event, ignoring any time between those events. This is termed next-event time advance

(NETA) (Law, 2015). There are three main approaches or worldviews to how simulation moves through time.

- In an *event-based* simulation, the simulation needs to keep a record of when future events will occur and activate them in time order. These event timings are kept on what is termed the simulation calendar, also known as the future event list. In the first phase of the approach, the executive program simply advances the simulation clock to the time of the next event. In the second phase, all events at that particular clock time are then executed. Any new events that are derived from these events are added to the simulation calendar. When all events have been executed at the current time, the executive program advances the simulation clock to the time of the next event and the loop repeats. The simulation continues until no events remain on the simulation calendar or a termination event is executed.
- The *activity-based* approach works by scanning activities at a fixed time interval, and activities that satisfy the necessary conditions are immediately scheduled. Unlike the event-based approach, the activity scanning method does not require event lists to be maintained. However, the method is relatively inefficient and therefore slow because of the number of unnecessary scans that are needed when no events may be occurring. Also, an event may be scheduled between two consecutive scans and thus will not be activated at the correct time.
- Most commercial software uses the *process-based* approach, with simulation as a series of process flows that detail the events through which a class of entity will pass. The use of entity attributes allows decision points to be incorporated into the flowchart, providing alternative process routes for entity classes. In each process, there is either a predetermined delay time, termed an unconditional delay, or if the delay time is not known – for example, waiting in a queue – it is termed a conditional delay.

Whatever worldview is employed, the loop behaviour of executing all events at a particular time and then advancing the simulation clock is controlled by the control program or executive of the simulation. A popular method of control is the three-phase approach that combines the event-based and activity-based methods. The three phases are shown in figure 1.12 and described as follows:

- The A phase advances the simulation clock to the next event time. The simulation calendar is inspected, and the clock jumps directly to the event with the time closest to the current simulation clock time. The clock is held constant during the three phases until the next A phase.
- The B phase executes all activities whose future time is known (bound events). The simulation takes all bound events that are due to occur at the current simulation time from the calendar and executes them. The execution of bound events may cause further events to occur. These are placed on the simulation calendar to be activated at the appropriate time.
- The C phase executes all activities whose future time depends on other events (conditional events termed C-events). For each C phase, all conditional events are checked to see if the conditions determining whether they can be executed are met. If the conditions are met, the conditional event is executed. The execution of a C-event may cause other C-event conditions to be met. For this reason, the C-events are repeatedly scanned until all C-event conditions are not met at this time point.

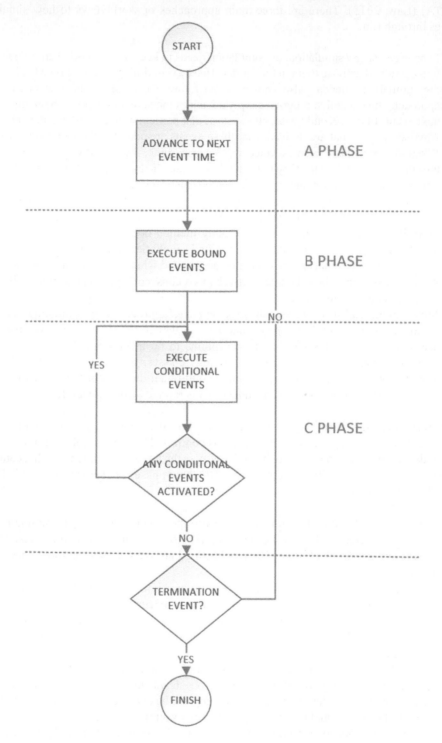

Figure 1.12 The three-phase executive

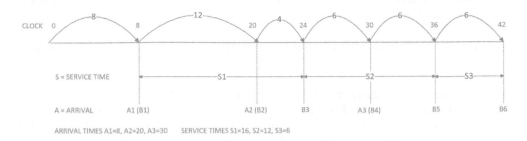

Figure 1.13 Operation of the three-phase approach

In general, bound events are events such as the end of a process when time can be predicted by simply adding the current simulation time to the process duration. Conditional events are occurrences that are dependent on resource availability whose future timing cannot be predicted (e.g. the time when a customer will receive service while in a queue at a bank). The three-phase approach simply scans all conditional events after the bound events have been executed to check if the simulation state allows the conditional event to take place.

The operation of the three-phase discrete-event method can be shown by studying the actions of the next event mechanism on the simulation clock (figure 1.13).

Figure 1.13 demonstrates how the next-event time mechanism increments the simulation clock to the next (in time order) event on the calendar. At this point, the system status is updated, and future event times are calculated. The time between each advance will vary depending on the pattern of future events. Arrival times (A1, A2, . . .) and service times (S1, S2, . . .) will normally be random variables taken from a suitable distribution. The discrete-event system operates as follows.

- At time 8, the simulation clock advances to the first event. This is an arrival event (A1) where entity 1 arrives at the resource. At this time, the resource is available ('idle') and so is immediately serviced for 16 time units (S1). During this period, the server status is set to 'busy'. The completion time is calculated as the current time + service time (8 + 16 = 24), and a completion event is entered on the calendar at this time.
- At time 20, entity 2 arrives (A2). Because the server is currently in the 'busy' state, the entity waits at the server queue until the server becomes available. At each future event, the status of the server is checked using a conditional (C) event.
- At time 24, the entity 1 completes service and thus changes the server status from 'busy' to 'idle'. Entity 2 will now leave the queue and commence service, changing the server status back from 'idle' to 'busy'. The completion time is calculated as the current time + service time (24 + 12 = 36), and a completion event is entered on the calendar at this time.
- At time 30, entity 3 arrives (A3). Again, the server is busy, so the entity waits at the server queue. At each future event, the status of the server is checked using a conditional (C) event.
- At time 36, entity 2 completes service and thus changes the server status from 'busy' to 'idle'. Entity 3 will now leave the queue and commence service, changing the server

status back from 'idle' to 'busy'. The completion time is calculated as the current time + service time (36 + 6 = 42), and a completion event is entered on the calendar at this time.
- At time 42, entity 3 completes service. The simulation continues until a termination state is reached.

Table 1.2 shows the bound events, or those events whose times that they occur we know – in this case, arrival times and finish activity times. Table 1.3 shows the conditional events, or those events whose times that they will occur we do not know as they are conditional – that is, they are dependent on a condition – in this case, the resource state being idle.

The time in the system for each entity can be calculated by the addition of the queuing time and service time (table 1.4).

To demonstrate how DES models time, a spreadsheet simulation is presented in Greasley (1998). The spreadsheet DES model is based on the three-phase version of the activity-based approach and is implemented on an Excel spreadsheet using the Microsoft Visual Basic for Applications (VBA) development environment. The spreadsheet simulation calendar screen is shown in figure 1.14.

Table 1.2 B-Events

Time	Event	Type	Description	Future Event Scheduled
8	B1	Arrival (A1)	Entity 1 arrives	A1
20	B2	Arrival (A2)	Entity 2 arrives	A2
24	B3	Finish Activity	Entity 1 finishes	-
30	B4	Arrival (A3)	Entity 3 arrives	A3
36	B5	Finish Activity	Entity 2 finishes	-
42	B6	Finish Activity	Entity 3 finishes	-

Table 1.3 C-Events

Time	Event	Type	Condition	Future Event Scheduled
8	C1	Start Activity	Resource Idle	B3
24	C2	Start Activity	Resource Idle	B5
36	C3	Start Activity	Resource Idle	B6

Table 1.4 Queue and Service Times for Entities

Entity	Queue Time	Service Time	Time in the System
1	0	16	16
2	4	12	16
3	6	6	12

	A	B	C	D	E
1	ENTITY NUMBER	BOUND EVENT TIME	BOUND EVENT NUMBER	BOUND EVENT DESCRIPTION	SIMULATION TIME
2	1436	480.984	4	Finished at Till 1	480.984
3	1449	481.000	50	Collect Statistics	
4	1441	481.243	5	Finished at Till 2	
5	1443	481.534	6	Finished at Till 3	
6	1444	481.636	2	Basket Arrival	
7	1448	483.354	8	Trolley Arrival	
8					

Figure 1.14 A spreadsheet DES model calendar screen

It is hard to estimate the number of global users of DES, but there is little doubt that of the three types of simulation outlined here, DES has the largest user base. Evidence for this is provided by the biannual simulation survey carried out by OR/MS Today, which demonstrates the wide range of applications for which DES has been used. The 2021 results are at https://pubsonline.informs.org/magazine/orms-today/2021-simulation-software-survey. The main areas of application are manufacturing, supply chain and logistics, military and, more recently, healthcare.

Why Is DES Needed to Model Organisational Systems?

The focus of this book is the use of DES to model organisational systems. So why is DES needed to do this? Well, when studying organisational systems, we are studying a dynamic system – one that changes over time and reacts to its environment and thus shows both structure and behaviour. This means that the model must also be dynamic, and there are two aspects of dynamic systems that are addressed by DES: variability and interdependence.

Variability

Most business systems contain variability in both the demand on the system (e.g. customer arrivals) and in durations (e.g. customer service times) of activities within the system. The use of fixed (e.g. average) values will provide some indication of performance, but simulation permits the incorporation of statistical distributions and thus provides an indication of both the range and variability of the performance of the system. This is important in customer-based systems when not only is the average performance relevant, but performance should also not drop below a certain level (e.g. customer service time), or customers will be lost. In service systems, two widely used performance measures are an estimate of the maximum queuing time for customers and the utilisation (i.e. percentage time occupied) for the staff serving the customer. If there is no variability, there will be no queues as long as the arrival rate is less than or equal to the service time. However, figure 1.15 shows that the higher the variability, the higher the average queue time for a given utilisation. At point A, with high

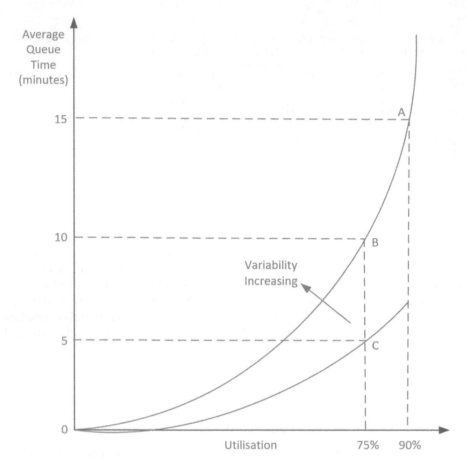

Figure 1.15 Average number in queue against utilisation and variability

variability and 90% utilisation, we have a queue time of 15 minutes. This can be reduced by reducing utilisation (moving from A to B) to 75%, and queue time is now 10 minutes. Queue time can be reduced further by decreasing variability (moving from B to C) to 5 minutes. In most systems, it is difficult to eliminate variability entirely (or we might even accept strategic variability), so rather than aim for the 'highest' efficiency of 100% utilisation, it is recommended to keep utilisation below around 80%. The increasing effect of utilisation on queue time can be estimated using the equation of utilisation factor (uf) = utilisation / (1 − utilisation). So for 75% utilisation, uf = 0.75 / (1 − 0.75) = 3, for 90% utilisation, uf = 0.9 / (1 − 0.9) = 9, for 99% utilisation, uf = 0.99 / (1 − 0.99) = 99. This means for a level of variability, giving a queue time of 5 minutes at 75% utilisation would increase to a queue time of 15 minutes at 90% utilisation and a queue time of 165 minutes at 99% utilisation!

Variability can be classified into customer-introduced variability and internal process variability. Customer-introduced variability includes the fact that customers don't arrive uniformly to a service, and customers will require different services with different service times. Also, not all customers appreciate the same thing in a service; some like self-service and some do not. In addition, variability from internal process variability can arise from internal processes within the organisation; for example, variability in staff performance can be caused by staff (this includes both the variability between different people's performance and the variability in the execution of process performance by one person over time). Variability can also be caused by equipment and material variations.

Most manufacturing and particularly service processes have variability in their operation both in terms of interarrival variability and process variability. This is sometimes referred to as stochastic variability to distinguish it from more predictable changes over longer periods of time, such as seasonal variability. Variability is important as even when the average process rate (capacity) of a process is greater than the demand for the process (arrival rate), there may still be delays and queues in the system. This is because the variability in process times is independent of the variability in arrival times, and so short interarrival times cannot be synchronised with short processing times. This means even when overall capacity is sufficient, there will be a queue form when, for example, short interarrival events occur at the same time as long process times. The main types of variability in DES are the following.

Interarrival Variability

- Entities (customers, materials, information) don't arrive uniformly. For example, the time between individual customer arrivals to a retail shop may vary throughout the day.

Process Variability

- Entities require different service times – for example, some customers may have lower skill levels or lack engagement in the service delivery process, leading to longer service times.
- Entities require different aspects of the service – for example, a single process duration may encompass many variations to the basic service, depending on individual customer requirements.
- Resources show variability in performance – for example, the different skill levels and experience of staff members will affect process variability. Individual staff performance may vary during the day or over different days. Resources such as equipment show variability from being poorly maintained or faulty.

Measuring Variability

We can measure variability using the standard deviation measure, which indicates the amount of dispersion around the mean value of a metric such as queue time. However, although a higher standard deviation represents an increased variability, we need to consider the amount of variability in terms of the mean value itself. For example, a standard deviation of 2 minutes around a mean value of 5 minutes represents significantly more variability than a standard deviation of 2 minutes around a mean value of 50 minutes. For this reason, we may wish to use an alternative to the standard deviation, which is the coefficient of variation – the ratio of the standard deviation to the mean.

Dysfunctional and Strategic Variability

Variability is not necessarily a problem for an organisation. Suri (2010) distinguishes between dysfunctional variability caused by errors and ineffective systems. Examples of dysfunctional variability are rework, constantly changing due dates and 'lumpy' demand due to a poor interface between sales and customers. Strategic variability is what firms use to maintain a competitive edge in the market. This includes coping with unexpected changes in demand and offering a large number of options to customers.

Interdependence

Most systems contain a number of connected activities that affect the overall performance of the system. The knock-on effect of many interdependent activities over time can be assessed using the model's ability to show system behaviour over time. The nature of the interdependence in a system will depend on both the combinatorial complexity – the number of activities within the system and the dynamic complexity – the nature of the interaction between the activities. For combinatorial complexity, when we have activities that have a two-way relationship with every other activity, the number of interconnections can be calculated by $n(n-1)$ where *n* is the number of activities. Thus, two activities will have two connections (activity 1 → activity 2 and activity 2 → activity 1), but this rises quickly as the number of activities increases. So for five activities, there will be $5(5-1) = 20$ interconnections, increasing complexity. Dynamic complexity can arise in systems due to feedback and delays, such as, time delays between cause and effect. The 'fixes that fail' archetype that demonstrates unintended consequences is another example of dynamic complexity. See the case study 'Using System Dynamics in a Discrete-Event Simulation Study of a Manufacturing Plant' in chapter 3 for more details. The section on SD in this chapter includes more detail on dynamic complexity in systems.

A Small Shop Model

If a system contains uncertain inputs, it can be very misleading to build a deterministic model by using the means of the inputs to predict an output – this is termed 'the flaw of averages'. To show the effect of variability on systems, a simple example will be presented. An owner of a small shop wishes to predict how long customers wait for service during a typical day. The owner has identified two types of customers, who have different amounts of shopping and so take different amounts of time to serve. Type A customers account for 70% of custom and take on average 10 minutes to serve. Type B customers account for 30% of custom and take on average 5 minutes to serve. The owner has estimated that during an 8-hour day, on average the shop will serve 40 customers. The owner then calculates the serve time during a particular day:

Customer A = 0.7 × 40 × 10 minutes = 280 minutes
Customer B = 0.3 × 40 × 5 minutes = 60 minutes

Therefore, the total service time = 340 minutes and gives a utilisation of the shop till of 340/480 × 100 = 71%

Thus, the owner is confident that all customers can be served promptly during a typical day. A simulation model was constructed for this system to estimate the service time for customers. Using a fixed time between customer arrivals of 480 / 40 = 12 minutes and with a 70% probability of a 10-minute service time and a 30% probability of a 5-minute service time, the overall service time for customers (including queuing time) has a range of between 5 and 10 minutes, and no queues are present in this system.

Service Time for Customer (minutes)
Average   8.5
Minimum   5
Maximum   10

However, in reality, customers will not arrive equally spaced at 12-minute intervals but will arrive randomly with an average interval of 12 minutes. The simulation is altered to show a time between arrivals following an exponential distribution (the exponential distribution is often used to mimic the behaviour of customer arrivals) with a mean of 12 minutes. The owner was surprised by the simulation results:

Service Time for Customer (minutes)
Average   17
Minimum   5
Maximum   46

The average service time for a customer had doubled to 17 minutes, with a maximum of 46 minutes!

The example demonstrates how the performance of even simple systems can be affected by randomness. Here, variability in the process times is independent of the variability in arrival times, and so short interarrival times are not synchronised with short processing times. This means even though overall capacity is sufficient, queues have formed when short interarrival events occur together. Variability would also be present in this system in other areas, such as customer service times and the mix of customer types over time. Simulation is able to incorporate all of these sources of variability to provide a more realistic picture of system performance.

Application Areas for DES

Simulation modelling is a flexible tool and is capable of analysing most aspects of an organisation. The two main areas of operations are the design and management of processes. In terms of design, simulation has an obvious role in the testing of system designs for systems that do not yet exist. Simulation can also be used for the design of existing systems where it can be used to assess a number of design options without disruption to the real system. One of the advantages of thoroughly testing processes at the design stage is that errors found at this stage will generally be much more costly to rectify at later stages of installation and operation. Simulation is often used to assess large capital investments such as equipment and plant, where it can reduce the risk of implementation at a relatively small cost. Simulation is increasingly being used to model computer software processes (García-García et al., 2020). Simulation can also be used in the management of business processes. For example, a service operation may wish to ensure continued good customer service while meeting increased demand. Making decisions around aspects such as staffing levels and job priorities to meet increased demand requires the ability to predict changes in these areas of performance. Simulation can be used to provide a predictive capability to help make better decisions and ensure future service levels are maintained.

To ensure the maximum value is gained from using the DES method, it is necessary to define the areas of the organisation that are key to overall performance and select feasible options for the method in these areas. Some examples of simulation use are given in the next sections with reference to decision areas that are applicable to simulation analysis. Some examples of Industrial case studies undertaken by the author are briefly described. More details of these studies can be found in Greasley (2019).

Manufacturing Systems

In order to remain competitive, manufacturing organisations must ensure their systems can meet changing market needs in terms of product mix and capacity levels while achieving efficient use of resources. Because of the complex nature of these systems with many interdependent parts, simulation is used extensively to optimise performance. Design decision areas in manufacturing include estimating required resource capacity, layout design, bottleneck analysis, machine setup time reduction, implementation of automation and production lead time estimation. Management decision areas in manufacturing include estimating batch size, determining parts sequencing, workforce scheduling and assessing preventative maintenance policies.

The case study 'A simulation of a snacks process production system' concerns the use of simulation to measure the performance of a conveyor system in a continuous operation producing food items. When a breakdown occurred in the original manual system, flexibility was demonstrated in the manual downstream packing area to deal with the spike in demand when the breakdown was fixed. When implementing an automated packing facility, much of this flexibility was lost. The simulation was able to test policies for ensuring flexibility of operation of the automated system in response to conveyor breakdown events.

The case study 'A simulation of a proposed textile plant' concerns the design of a proposed textile production facility, which supplies garment manufacturers with rolls of material suitable for clothing manufacture. The simulation will assess the performance of the production system for two scenarios of production capacity. The case provides an example of the use of simulation for design purposes of a system that did not exist.

The case study 'A simulation of a rail vehicle bogie production facility' provides an analysis of a line layout production facility and employs simulation to predict the effect of changes on the line cycle time and thus output. This case is used to explore how the value of simulation could be maximised in an organisational setting.

Service Systems

The productivity of service sector systems has not increased at the rate of manufacturing systems, and as the service sector has increased, the potential increase in productivity from improving services has been recognised. Simulation is now being used to help analyse many service processes to improve customer service and reduce cost. For example, the emphasis on performance measures in government services such as healthcare has led to the increased use of simulation to analyse systems and provide measures of performance under different configurations. Design decision areas include customer queuing time estimation, layout planning and service capacity planning. Management decision areas include staff scheduling, customer service priorities and emergency planning.

The case study 'A simulation of a police call centre' concerns the use of simulation to measure the performance of a UK police emergency call centre. The simulation is used to identify the staffing cost of the current operation. Simulation is then used to test designs for a revised staffing rota that enables the necessary speed of call response to be maintained while reducing staffing costs.

The case study 'A simulation of a police arrest process' concerns the use of simulation to identify the costs of operating a police custody suite that processes arrested people for interview, detention or release. The simulation uses historical data in a descriptive model to identify the costs of the operation from a process, resource and activity perspective. Simulation is used in a predictive model to estimate the resource and thus cost implications of a change in the law, which leads to an increase in arrested persons.

The case study 'A simulation of a rail carriage maintenance depot' concerns the use of the simulation technique to ensure that a service delivery system can undertake a number of service tasks to specified service levels. In this case, the requirement was to operate a rail carriage maintenance depot on existing infrastructure meant that capacity would be constrained by the number of existing stabling and refurbishment lines. Management needed to assess if sufficient capacity was available in order to carry out the refurbishment tasks in the time period between delivery to the depot and request for the next service.

The case study 'A simulation of advanced service provision' provides an analysis of three variants of service offering for a computer numerical controlled (CNC) machine manufacturer. The simulation reports on revenue and cost estimates and thus provides an estimate of profit for the three variants under base conditions. One variant is also analysed under two further scenarios involving changes to revenue payments and a decrease in equipment failure rate. This case shows the use of simulation to estimate revenue and cost for future service provision under conditions of uncertainty. The information provided by the simulation can reduce risk when tendering advanced service offerings to clients.

Supply Chain Management Systems

Supply chain systems are a network of activities that entities flow through from raw materials supply to production, distribution and then retail to the customers. The supply chain should aim to minimise costs while maintaining service levels. Supply chains will incorporate transportation systems such as rail and airline services as well as internal systems such as automated guided vehicles (AGVs), which can be analysed using simulation. Many simulation software packages have special facilities to model track-based and conveyor-type systems, and simulation is ideally suited to analyse the complex interactions and knock-on effects that can occur in these systems. Design decision areas include supply chain structure, process redesign, supplier selection, facilities and capacity planning, supply chain integration, the bullwhip effect, reverse logistics, replenishment control policies, supply chain optimisation, cost reduction, system performance, inventory planning and management and customer service levels.

The case study 'A simulation of a "last mile" logistics system' concerns the use of simulation to measure the performance of a logistics service provider. Simulation is used to investigate if delivery time windows can be met when moving from a policy of separate delivery runs for retail and non-retail customers to a mixed delivery policy for both retail and non-retail customers.

The case study 'A simulation of a food retail distribution system' concerns the use of simulation to model a food distribution network in order to assess its performance in terms of empty vehicle running. The model is then developed to encompass an extension to the distribution network that offers a pickup from tier 2 suppliers and a drop-off service to tier 1 suppliers as part of the return to depot route of the main distribution network design.

The case study 'A simulation of an end-of-life reverse supply chain for electric vehicle batteries' investigates the operation of an integrated end-of-life (EOL) supply chain network in which authorised treatment facilities (ATFs), remanufacturers and recyclers offer to electric vehicle (EV) manufacturers the EOL management of batteries within the UK. Although the current demand for the management of the EOL for the batteries is low, there is a prediction of a rapid increase in demand as EV sales increase and the EV batteries within these vehicles reach their EOL. It is intended that the simulation will provide an indication of the potential capacity requirements through the supply chain that are required to deal with this future demand. See Venegas Vallejos et al. (2021) for more details.

Information Systems

Simulation is used to predict the performance of the computerisation of processes. This analysis can include both the process performance and the technical performance of the computer network itself, often using specialist network simulation software. Design decision areas include the effects of automation by IS systems on customer service levels, estimating IS capacity requirements to meet customer transaction volumes and designing client-server systems.

The case study 'A simulation of an enterprise resource planning system' concerns the use of simulation to measure customer service performance when introducing an enterprise resource planning (ERP) system into a customer order processing activity. Simulation is used to measure the performance of three scenarios – the original manual operation, the ERP operation and combined operations of an ERP and ESS (enterprise social system). Customer service quality is considered in terms of the trade-off between the flexibility provided in meeting individual customer needs and the cost of serving individual customers.

The case study 'A simulation of a road traffic accident process' concerns predicting the cost savings made on front-line road traffic officer staff when changes are made to the road traffic accident reporting process. The changes were based on the use of mobile devices to record and map the location of traffic accidents at the location of the incident. Observation of performance measures provided by the simulation model helped to secure an acceptance of the need for change by demonstrating the increased performance of the proposed system. This case provides an example of how simulation can support public sector organisations in quantifying outcomes to support business cases for action.

Benefits and Limitations of DES

In summary, the benefits and limitations of DES are now outlined.

Benefits of DES

- Provides capability for descriptive analytics

  - Often, an outcome of undertaking a simulation study is that the structured approach to problem-solving can lead to a better understanding of system behaviour. This can come from activities such as bringing together data collected from various disparate sources within the organisation and building a process map to provide an overview of the relationships between process elements. The understanding gained at the conceptual modelling stage may negate the need for model development. If a model is developed, it may be to increase understanding of a current system without necessarily predicting future performance. An example of this is the use of simulation to provide information regarding process costs.

- Provides capability for predictive analytics

  - Simulation helps to minimise the risk involved when predicting future behaviour. It does this by dealing with the uncertainty inherent in the behaviour of business systems. Rather than provide a single prediction of future behaviour, simulation allows for comparison between different future scenarios to provide an indication of the level of risk and sensitivity of the predictions.

- Provides capability for prescriptive analytics

  - By completing multiple-scenario analysis, either manually or automatically using optimisation software, simulation allows a best course of action to be recommended. The parameters that define the scenarios can take into account contextual factors that constrain design choices so that only feasible solutions are provided.

- Simulation can address issues at the design stage before the new system exists so that problems that might have appeared later (with greater time and cost) are dealt with.
- Simulation can help convert strategic aims into reality by providing specific workable implementations of change at an operational level. Simulation can help specify how work should be done to successfully operate a system and specify what tasks and what resources are needed. Addressing the operational issue of how work will be done enables specific, workable implementations to be designed.
- A simulation model is an explanatory model that is explainable and can extrapolate to new situations not contained in the data it uses.

Limitations of DES

- Surveys have indicated that a lack of skills for simulation development and statistical analysis is a major reason against the use of simulation (Greasley, 2008; Kirchhof and Meseth, 2012).
- Establishing a capability in simulation can be expensive in terms of items such as the initial costs of simulation software and staff training (see chapter 11).
- It may be difficult to verify and validate the simulation model, and consequently, there may be a lack of credibility in the simulation results.
- The cost of a simulation project may not be warranted by the decision. If a cost-benefit approach is used, the payback from a better-informed decision using simulation must substantially outweigh the costs of the simulation study. However, the non-financial

benefits of better decisions (such as generating customer demand through better-designed services) are often overlooked.

- A simulation project may take too long to be useful for a decision. Consultancy organisations can be used to provide a faster team approach to simulation development at a higher cost.

- Simulation analysis often ignores the human element in system performance. However, the increased interest in behavioural factors in operations management and operations research has increased interest in incorporating human behaviour in models.

- The benefits of simulation are not maximised, leading to its underuse. The perception of simulation as a one-off method, a lack of skills transfer and a lack of communication in the organisation can limit the benefits of the simulation approach (see chapter 11).

- Simulation may be relatively slow to execute compared to machine learning algorithms (see chapter 13).

- Simulations, like analytic techniques, are algorithms executed as computer programs that map input data to output data and, as such, cannot actually create new knowledge. What they can do is provide us with new information or information presented in a new way that may lead us to the new knowledge we need to solve a problem.

- When used for prediction, simulation is about the reduction of risk; actual prediction of the future in terms of business processes is impossible due to uncertainty!

Simulation for Descriptive Analytics

Simulation can be used in a descriptive mode to develop understanding. Here, the emphasis is not necessarily on developing accurate predictive models but on using the simulation model to help develop theories regarding how an organisational system works. In this role, simulation is used as an experimental methodology where we can explore the effect of different parameters by running the simulation under many different conditions. What we do is start with a deductive method in which we have a set of assumptions and test these assumptions and their consequences. We then use an experimental method to generate data which can be analysed in an inductive manner to develop theories by the generalisation of observations. In fact, the simulation analyst can alternate between a deductive and inductive approach as the model is developed.

Summary

This chapter introduces simulation modelling in the context of a systems view of the organisation. The three approaches of SD, DES and ABS are described. The main features of DES are explanatory modelling of the process structure, descriptive modelling of the process elements and the ability to move the model over time. We also cover the use of DES to model the variability and interdependence inherent in organisational systems and present some benefits and limitations of the use of DES.

Exercises

- Past proceedings of the Winter Simulation Conference can be found at https://informs-sim.org. Browse the web and find case studies of the use of simulation in various types of organisations. Draw up a table indicating the number of applications by industry sector. Categorise each application by the categories of simulation use outlined in the 'Application Areas for DES' section in chapter 1.

- Describe how variability and interdependence affect the operation of a railway system.
- Evaluate static and dynamic mathematical model types.
- Discuss the advantages and disadvantages of using simulation for problem-solving.
- Compare and contrast the three main types of simulation software.
- Describe the differences between discrete and continuous simulation.
- Read the article by A.J. Collins, F.S.A. Pour and C.A. Jordan (2021), 'Past challenges and the future of discrete-event simulation', in the *Journal of Defense Modeling and Simulation: Applications, Methodology, Technology*, and summarise the main historical developments and future challenges for DES.

References

Collins, A.J., Pour, F.S.A. and Jordan, C.A. (2021) Past challenges and the future of discrete event simulation, *Journal of Defense Modeling and Simulation: Applications, Methodology, Technology*, 1–19.

García-García, J.A., Enríquez, J.G., Ruiz, M., Arévalo, C. and Jiménez-Ramírez, A. (2020) Software process simulation modeling: Systematic literature review, *Computer Standards and Interfaces*, 70.

Goldsman, D., Nance, E. and Wilson, J.R. (2010) A brief history of simulation revisited, *Proceedings of the 2010 Winter Simulation Conference*, 567–574.

Greasley, A. (2019) *Simulating Business Processes for Descriptive, Predictive and Prescriptive Analytics*, deGruyter Press.

Greasley, A. (2008) *Enabling a Simulation Capability in the Organisation*, Springer-Verlag.

Greasley, A. (1998) An example of a discrete-event simulation on a spreadsheet, *SIMULATION*, 70(3), 148–166.

Kirchhof, P. and Meseth, N. (2012) A survey of the use of simulation in German healthcare, *Proceedings of the 2012 Winter Simulation Conference*, 1082–1091.

Law, A.M. (2015) *Simulation Modeling and Analysis*, 5th edition, McGraw-Hill Education.

Ören, T., Mittal, S. and Durak, U. (2018) A shift from model-based to simulation-based paradigm: Timeliness and usefulness for many disciplines, *International Journal of Computer Software Engineering*, 3, 126.

Pidd, M. (2004) *Computer Simulation in Management Science*, 5th edition, John Wiley & Sons Ltd.

Railsback, S.F. and Grimm, V. (2019) *Agent-Based and Individual-Based Modelling*, 2nd edition, Princeton University Press.

Siebers, P.O., Macal, C.M., Garnett, J. Buxton, D. and Pidd, M. (2010) Discrete-event simulation is dead, long live agent-based simulation! *Journal of Simulation*, 4, 204–210.

Suri, R. (2010) *It's About Time: The Competitive Advantage of Quick Response Manufacturing*, CRC Press.

Tolk, A. (2018) Simulation and modelling as the essence of computational science, *Proceedings of the SummerSim Conference*, Society for Modeling and Simulation (SCS) International, 106–117.

Venegas Vallejos, M., Greasley, A. and Matopoulos, A. (2021) A simulation of an end-of-life reverse supply chain for electric vehicle batteries, *33rd European Modeling and Simulation Symposium*, 315–319.

Zeigler, B.P., Muzy, A. and Kofman, E. (2019) *Theory of Modeling and Simulation: Discrete Event & Iterative System Computational Foundations*, Academic Press.

2 Overview of the Steps in a Simulation Modelling Study

Introduction

This chapter provides an overview of the structure of this book which follows the steps needed to undertake a simulation modelling study.

Steps in a Simulation Study

The main steps in undertaking a simulation modelling study with the chapter numbers indicated are shown in figure 2.1. We can consider modelling as the abstraction of a real-world system and simulation as experimentation with that model to obtain knowledge about that system. This means modelling is covered in the material in chapters 1–8, and simulation is covered in the material in chapters 9 and 10.

The study begins with a problem in the real world that we wish to investigate. We move from the real world to the model world through the activity of conceptual modelling. The conceptual model provides a specification for the computer-based simulation model that will be developed. Conceptual modelling is treated in this book as four elements.

1   The conceptual model will be based on our understanding and assumptions of the problem situation and the definition of the study objectives. This will allow a definition of the model inputs (factors) and outputs (responses). The conceptual model contents will be determined by the use of simplifications to define the scope and level of detail (chapter 3).
2   Explanatory modelling will be used to define the structure of the conceptual model. A process map can be used to provide a link between the conceptual model definition and the structure of the computer model implemented (chapter 4).
3   Descriptive modelling, termed input modelling in simulation, is used to model variability in terms of process durations, resource availability, decision points, demand patterns and other areas (chapter 5).
4   The conceptual model should include a specification for the data requirements for the model (chapter 6).

The next step after conceptual modelling involves the collection of any data required (chapter 6) and then the implementation of the conceptual model specification on a computer using a selected simulation software package (chapter 7).

Before the model can be used for analysis, it must be verified and validated. Verification involves ensuring that the computer model is a correct representation of the conceptual model

DOI: 10.4324/9781003124092-2

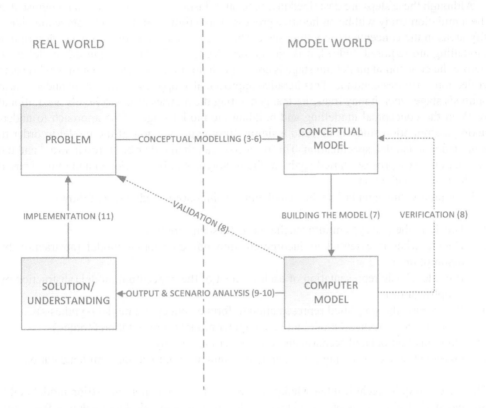

Figure 2.1 Steps in a simulation study

developed (chapter 8). Validation concerns ensuring that the simplifications and assumptions made about the real-world system are acceptable in the context of the simulation study objectives (chapter 8).

The next step involves the use of the model to provide information for decision-making by studying the effect that changes in the model have on performance measures defined in the model. For each scenario, the statistical analysis required should be defined, and the use of a terminating or steady-state analysis should be stated (chapter 9). Comparing performance between different versions of the model is termed scenario analysis (chapter 10).

The results of the simulation study should be presented in report form and include full model documentation, study results and recommendations for further studies. An implementation plan may also be specified (chapter 11).

Not all of these steps may be followed in a simulation study, and it is not unusual for the understanding gained at the conceptual modelling stage to remove the need to implement the computer model. This should not be surprising, as the need for a simulation model was likely driven by a problem that was not well understood. This emphasises that the reason for the study is to address a problem that a client has in the real world. If that client perceives the problem is solved, then the simulation study should be halted. More details on the different forms of output from a simulation study are covered in chapter 11.

Although these steps are described in a sequential fashion, it is important to recognise that the simulation study will be an iterative process. The building of the model stage may identify areas in the conceptual modelling stage where additional data collection and descriptive modelling are required. Indeed, it is normal practice to begin the building the model stage before the conceptual modelling stage is complete to minimise development time while data collection activities continue. This iterative approach also applies to the output and scenario analysis stage when it may transpire that generating the metrics required involves additional work in the conceptual modelling and building the model stages. One approach to undertaking a simulation study is to build a simple 'prototype' version of the model in order to help define a detailed specification. This prototype can then either be 'thrown away' and the simulation study process started again, or the prototype can be developed and refined based on the new specification.

In summary, the main tasks when conducting a simulation study are as follows:

1   Break up the real system into smaller parts (systems analysis).
2   Decide what is essential to incorporate into our conceptual model (abstraction by assumptions).
3   Provide a basic representation of each element of the conceptual model (abstraction by simplification).
4   Recombine the simplified representation to form a conceptual model (synthesis).
5   Convert the conceptual model into a computer model representation (coding).
6   Undertake output and scenario analysis (experimentation).
7   Oversee the understanding provided by the simulation into action (implementation).

These steps require technical knowledge in areas such as computer simulation model building and statistical analysis but also human judgement and domain knowledge to frame relevant objectives, access appropriate data sources, provide a suitable abstraction in the form of the conceptual model and interpret the model results in terms of their implications for decision-making.

Summary

The steps in a simulation study are outlined, which provides the structure for this text.

3   Conceptual Modelling (Abstraction)

Introduction

The conceptual modelling process involves deciding what is relevant and should be included in the model to meet the aims of the current investigation. Robinson (2008) defines a conceptual model as 'a non-software specific description of the computer simulation model (that will be, is or has been developed), describing the objectives, inputs, outputs, content, assumptions and simplifications of the model'. Thus, the conceptual model defines what is to be represented and how it is to be represented in the computer simulation model and this is the approach taken in this text. This means a key aspect of a simulation study is that the modeller understands the context of the problem so that they are able to identify what elements of the real system will be relevant to the conceptual model and also the relationship between these elements. Conceptual modelling is sometimes referred to as the art of simulation as contrasted with the scientific aspects involving model coding and statistical analysis. Robinson (2020) indicates the relatively limited amount of attention that has been paid to this creative side of modelling compared to the scientific aspects. One exception is the classic text by Robert E. Shannon (1975).

The term 'abstraction' is used to express that in our conceptual model, we will represent the essential aspects of the real-world system but not necessarily in the same form or depth of analysis (termed level of detail). The art of simulation is about how we make choices around these activities, as even for relatively simple models it becomes apparent that there are many different conceptual models that can be developed to solve a particular task. In instances such as this, the analyst might consider how we determine which of these models is best for the task at hand.

Robinson in van der Zee et al. (2018) states that an overarching principle of model simplification is to build the simplest model to achieve the modelling objectives, and beyond this, it is useful to observe the following set of general principles:

- Focus on the decision, not the system.
- Abstract – do not model all you know about the world.
- The model should drive the data requirements and not the available data drive the model.
- Start small and add.

Brooks and Tobias (2000) state that starting with a simple model still requires us to define a number of simplifications to define that simple model, even if most of them are just done in the modeller's mind. An alternative approach to abstraction is to start by building a complex model and then try to simplify it. This can be particularly relevant when a complex model

DOI: 10.4324/9781003124092-3

already exists – perhaps from a previous simulation study. This approach does have the advantage that we can observe the complex model's behaviour and use this information to guide us in the simplification process.

The Stages of Conceptual Modelling

The following activities for the first stages of conceptual modelling are shown in figure 3.1.

The first activity of defining the problem situation provides the context for the further development of the conceptual model. This involves making assumptions about the real world, and the outcome of this stage is a system description. We then undertake a further abstraction process to define the study objectives, model inputs and outputs and model content. The outcome of this stage is the conceptual model specification. Further stages in the conceptual modelling process are described in chapter 4 (explanatory modelling) and chapter 5 (descriptive modelling). Data collection issues relevant to conceptual modelling are covered in chapter 6 (data collection). The computer model developed in chapter 7, derived from the conceptual model, then provides information for decision-making that can be used to make predictions of real-world system behaviour. We will now explore the steps in the conceptual modelling abstraction process in more detail.

Define the Problem Situation

This step involves the modeller understanding the context of the problem so that they are able to identify what elements of the real system will be relevant for incorporation in the system description. Usually, the problem situation will differ for each simulation project and will require knowledge of the process being modelled, whether it is a just-in-time (JIT) system in a manufacturing context or a customer call centre in the service industry. This will most likely require the collection of contextual data (see chapter 7) through discussions with personnel involved in the process and the use of existing documentation. It may be necessary to seek this information from a number of people in order to obtain a full understanding, as in a complex problem situation, people may well have different views about the problem. Thus, we need to understand the context of the problem situation to ask the right questions and acquire the relevant data meaning.

Assumptions are made when there are gaps in our knowledge about the real system. These are made when converting elements of the real system to a description of the system we are to model. Simplifications are when the real system is understood but we choose to simplify it in order to reduce model complexity and modelling time. Explaining the assumptions and simplifications made is very important in order that decision-makers can understand how the model has made its prediction.

One way of understanding a problem situation is to construct a process flow diagram (chapter 4) outlining the serial and parallel relationships of the transformation processes

Figure 3.1 The conceptual modelling abstraction process

(see chapter 1) involved within the problem situation. This provides a description of the elements of the real world that are relevant to the problem. We should also provide a list of any assumptions we have made regarding the real system that have been made when forming our system description. We should then obtain agreement with the client on the model assumptions and our overall understanding of the problem situation, which is termed establishing the model credibility.

In general, discrete-event simulation is suited to well-structured problems and tends to leave the human aspect of systems aside. For example, the different values, beliefs and interests of people involved in the problem lead to what are called different world views of the problem situation. Also, different model builders may well have a different definition of what the real system is (i.e. exhibit bias). Thus, a modeller will produce a model that will differ from another person modelling the same system based on their different knowledge and interpretation of reality. For certain types of problems, the need to take into consideration the human aspects of systems and provide a holistic view of issues has led to the use of approaches such as soft systems methodology (Checkland, 2001; Lehaney and Paul, 1996; Kotiadis, 2007), systems thinking (Senge, 1993), cognitive mapping (Eden and Ackermann, 2001) and causal loop diagrams (Sterman, 2000). The case study 'Using System Dynamics in a Discrete-Event Simulation Study of a Manufacturing Plant' shows how the undertaking of a DES study led to a reassessment of the problem situation using a systems thinking approach.

Case Study: Using System Dynamics in a Discrete-Event Simulation Study of a Manufacturing Plant

The Case Study

The case study company manufacture a range of aluminium gas cylinders for a global market. The cylinders are used in applications such as beverage machines and fire extinguishers. Although a DES was able to investigate the operational issues of the manufacturing process itself, a different approach was taken to tackle the wider problem of production planning disruption due to the order scheduling process. This would normally be treated as the 'environment' around which the DES is based. Systems thinking, termed the 'fifth discipline' by Senge (1993), is an approach to seeing the structures that underlie complex situations and thus identifying what causes patterns of behaviour. In an organisational setting, it is postulated that there are four levels of the systems view operating events, patterns of behaviour, underlying structures and mental models simultaneously (Maani and Cavana, 2000). Events are reports that only touch the surface of what has happened and offer just a snapshot of the situation. Patterns of behaviour look at how behaviour has changed over time. Underlying structures describe the interplay of the different factors that bring about the outcomes that we observe, and mental models represent the beliefs, values and assumptions held by individuals and organisations that underlie the reasons for doing things the way we do them. This framework is now used to analyse the case study scenario.

Events

A recurring event was that of missing customer order dates. This was leading to dissatisfied customers and an increasing reliance on a few 'strategic' customers who were using their buying power to negotiate price reductions and so reduce profitability.

Patterns of Behaviour

Orders are made to customer demand (i.e. not supplied from stock) and are placed on to the capacity plan over a number of months before the actual order is manufactured. The position of an order in the plan is a result of negotiations between the customer, the sales manager who liaises with the customer and a capacity planner. A senior manager is also involved in strategic orders, which are deemed to be of particular importance to the company. There is no fixed definition of what makes an order strategic. The production plan for an order is only fixed when the order enters the manufacturing process, approximately seven weeks before delivery to the customer. Because of the wide variety of products offered, the extended amount of time an order is on the capacity plan and the changing capacity situation led to a great deal of uncertainty in the capacity planning process. In particular, the process of expediting *strategic* orders has led the company to be labelled by many *non-strategic* customers as unreliable in terms of delivery performance. This behaviour has increasingly led to some customers over-ordering or ordering in advance to ensure on-time delivery leading to a capacity plan which overstates the actual capacity requirements. Also, due to poor delivery performance, some customers have chosen to move to alternative suppliers, which has also led to an increasing proportion of the output being dedicated to strategic customers. This has meant even greater use of expediting as the strategic customers become an ever-increasing proportion of the company's output.

Underlying Structures

One of the tools of systems thinking is system archetypes which are certain dynamics that recur in many different situations. An archetype consists of various combinations of balancing and reinforcing loops. The 'fixes that fail' archetype (Kim, 1992) describes a situation in which a solution is quickly implemented that alleviates the symptom of the problem, but the unintended consequences of the 'fix' exacerbate the problem. Over time the problem symptom returns to its previous level or becomes worse. An example of the 'fixes that fail' archetype is that of 'expediting customer orders' (figure 3.2).

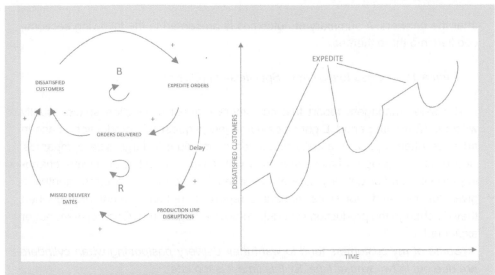

Figure 3.2 'Expediting customer orders' systems archetype (source: Kim [1992])

Figure 3.2 shows how in an effort to ensure on-time delivery, an order is expedited, resulting in a satisfied customer. However, the disruption caused by this policy has led to the need to expedite further orders, and a feedback loop is established where more expediting leads to disruptions, leading to missed delivery dates leading to dissatisfied customers and more expediting. The reason this situation occurs is that the pain of not doing something right away is often more real and immediate than the delayed negative effects. The situation is exacerbated by the fact that the reinforcing nature of unintended consequences ensures that tomorrow's problems will multiply faster than today's solutions. In other words, solving one problem today will not create another one tomorrow but will create multiple problems. Breaking the archetype requires the acknowledgement that the fix is merely alleviating a symptom and making a commitment to solving the real problem now. In this case, the idea of strategic orders is creating a self-fulfilling prophecy in which eventually all orders will be strategic. In this situation, the company will supply to fewer and fewer customers, who, if they realise their market power, can exert substantial pressure on prices and profit margins.

Mental Models

This concerns the most 'hidden' level of systems thinking and concerns assumptions, beliefs and values that people hold about the system. In order to investigate these issues, a questionnaire was administered to ten sales managers who provide the interface between the customer and the capacity plan. The questionnaire consists of a number of closed questions with space for open-ended comments after the answers. A summary of outcomes is presented in the following sections, codified into three themes.

Theme 1: Changes to the Order Specification (Questions 1–4)

The sales managers report that customers request production space usually within a 12-month period. Eight sales managers request this production space in advance often. Space is usually requested by medium to large size companies. Seven sales managers have experience with customers often or always changing the size and/or delivery date of the order. A notice of up to three months is given for this, and four sales managers report disruption to other orders when they do change the production schedule to accommodate this. One sales manager explained,

'Some of my customers tend to want their delivery postponing when cylinders are due out in two weeks' time. By this time it is too late'.

The reason for making these changes is clear in that eight sales managers report they gain orders from accommodating these changes, while only two claim orders are lost. One reason customers may do this is that they have a misunderstanding about the production process; according to one sales manager,

'Some customers still believe cylinders to be "off the shelf"'.

Theme 2: Capacity Planning Rules (Questions 5–9)

Nine sales managers always consult the capacity planner before quoting a delivery date, and nine sales managers never or rarely are refused space by the capacity planner for the order. Only six sales managers understand the current capacity planning rules, and only five sales managers actually work to these rules. The following quotes underline the current misunderstanding of the capacity planning rules:

'Don't know if any hard fast rules exist'.

'Rules changed three times since we started forecasting. Sometimes there is a lot of confusion about what is requested'.

'Don't know of any rules. The larger customers tend to plan their requirements for the whole year'.

Of the four sales managers who don't understand the rules, all agree it would help them in their task if they did.

Theme 3: Priority Customers (Questions 10–11)

All ten sales managers have priority customers, and nine sales managers often or always have priority orders scheduled. The need to satisfy strategic customers is underlined by the comment from one sales manager:

'Companies X, Y and Z more or less always get what they want'.

In summary, from a customer perspective, the late changing of orders is accepted as if it was part of the normal trading practices with the company. Poor delivery performance has labelled the company as unreliable. Consequently, the customers regard themselves as being in a strong bargaining position. Customers prefer to book provisional orders in advance as the lead time is long. Some customers believe the company makes to stock, which in reality has never happened. A feeling of confusion exists over the capacity planning rules. The effect of this is that rules are made up to suit the needs of the individual with the consequence that order quantities are overbooked, enquires and reservations are booked as 'provisions' for their customers. Non-standard practices are accepted as normal as this enables some element of control over a system that is poorly understood. Finally, a priority system operates in order to ensure what the sales managers consider are the most important customers receive on-time deliveries.

Senge (1993) states that most people assume cause and effect are close in time and space. Thus, a fixation on short term events will fail to uncover the longer-term pattern of behaviour caused by their actions – in this case, the longer-term effect on scheduling stability of short-term expediting decisions. In order to break the cycle, both beliefs and assumptions about the planning process had to be addressed, and an even greater understanding of the systemic structures was needed in order to understand the relationship between short-term fixes and a longer-term drop in performance. In order to achieve this, meetings were held with the sales managers and use was made of the archetype diagrams and the results of the questionnaire to discuss the effect of the current planning rules. As a result of these meetings, the following policies were agreed upon:

- Quotes for delivery times to strategic customers would not disrupt the current production plan.
- Delivery times would be maintained and not brought forward if they caused disruption to the current production plan.
- Sales would liaise closely with manufacturing to gauge realistic delivery performance.
- Manufacturing would liaise closely with sales regarding up-to-date production schedule information.

Discussion

As the project progressed, it became clear that although the DES would solve the objectives of the study in a technical sense, the organisational problem of delivery performance would not be solved by the DES study alone. After a request by the author, a wider brief of the project was agreed upon involving an assessment of the order scheduling process undertaken by the sales managers. DES can incorporate more qualitative analysis than at first might be realised. The process-mapping stage incorporates qualitative input and does this without the need for a deeper level of detail needed to construct the discrete-event model itself. The output of a DES study can generate data that facilitates qualitative output in the form of discussions between participants. What the systems thinking approach does provide is a framework for understanding why things are happening in the way they are by identifying the structure behind the behaviour. The DES approach generally replicates the structure and identifies behaviour under a number of scenarios. Thus, a system thinking approach, which involves identifying an archetype which describes the systemic structure of the system and assessing the underlying beliefs and assumptions of the participants, can be a useful addition to the toolkit of the DES practitioner.

Extract from Greasley, A. (2005)

What is termed classic or hard Operational Research (OR) takes an ontological point of view that there are systems out there that we can make models of (parts of) the real world, show that they are valid models and use them to find improvements that can be implemented in the real-world system. Soft OR takes an epistemological point of view in which system models can be useful to help thinking about the world, and a wide range of models can be built to help a debate on understanding the real system. Thus, the soft OR approach takes into account that any problem situation involving people will, at some level, entail differences in worldviews, judgements and interpretations. Within the framework of the soft OR approach, any or all of the hard OR frameworks can be adopted. However, the reverse strategy of moving from a hard to soft strategy entails abandoning the ontological stance of hard OR – hence what is termed an asymmetric complementarity between hard OR and soft OR (Checkland and Holwell, 2004). See Robinson (2001) for more on the relationship between soft OR and hard OR in simulation.

Define the Study Objectives

Once an overall understanding of the problem situation has been achieved, an outline of the decisions that the simulation model will address can be made. In an organisational context for operations systems, these decisions can be categorised as design decisions and management decisions.

Design Decisions

Design decisions in operations include the design of the process, the layout, the supply network, the use of process technology, the design of the product or service and the design of the job and work. More detail on these can be found in operations management textbooks (for example, Greasley, 2013). When using simulation to assess design decisions, there are many ways in which a process can be redesigned to meet particular objectives, and so it may be necessary to generate a range of innovative solutions (scenarios) for evaluation. Peppard and Rowland (1995) provide a number of areas for the potential redesign of processes of eliminating, simplifying, integrating and automating (ESIA) (table 3.1).

Table 3.1 ESIA Areas for Potential Redesign (Peppard and Rowland, 1995)

Eliminate	*Simplify*	*Integrate*	*Automate*
Over-production	Forms	Jobs	Dirty
Waiting time	Procedures	Teams	Difficult
Transport	Communication	Customers	Dangerous
Processing	Technology	Suppliers	Boring
Inventory	Problem areas		Data capture
Defects/failures	Flows		Data transfer
Duplication	Processes		Data analysis
Reformatting			
Inspection			
Reconciling			

Generating a new design offers the greatest scope for radical improvements to the process design but represents a risk in the implementation of a totally new approach. A deep understanding of the process is required so that the design will be feasible and so simulation can be useful in this situation to reduce risk. Modifying an existing design is less risky than generating a new design but may mean that the opportunity for a radical improvement in process design is missed. Even so, simulation can be employed to ensure that the modified design does actually provide better performance with no unintended effects. A further approach, often termed benchmarking, applies the idea of identifying the best-in-class performer for the particular process in question and adopting that design.

It may be necessary to prioritise or reduce the number of design alternatives generated, and this can be achieved by a rating scheme that scores each design solution against key performance dimensions, such as response time and cost of operation. The outcome of this analysis will be a reduced number of design solutions, which can then be subjected to a more detailed analysis using simulation.

Using the Balanced Scorecard to Prioritise Processes for Improvement

The following presents a measurement system consisting of a two-dimensional marking guide based on the impact of a process on critical success factors (CSF) determined in a balanced scorecard review and an assessment of the scope for innovation (the amount of improvement possible) to the current process design. Processes which are strategically important and offer the largest scope for improvement are prioritised under this model. The marking guide marks each process on a scale of 0 to 5 against two measures: *impact*, the extent to which the achievement of the CSF depends on the process, and *innovation*, the extent of the change required for the process in order to meet the CSF. The marking guides for each measure are shown in figure 3.3 and figure 3.4.

In terms of the balanced scorecard, the impact measure relates to the achievement of the CSF from the stakeholder/customer and financial (external) perspectives of the balanced scorecard. The innovation measure relates to the amount of change required

Mark   Impact (external perspective) marking guide
0   This individual process has minimal or no effect on the individual CSF
1   This individual process is dependent on another process, in order for it have an effect on this CSF
2   This individual process has a marked influence on this CSF
3   The individual process has substantial impact on whether another process can maximise its beneficial effects on this CSF
4   The individual process has substantial influence on this CSF
5   The individual process is a critical part of being able to achieve the individual CSF

Figure 3.3 Impact (external perspective) marking guide

Mark   Innovation (internal perspective) marking guide
0   This process cannot be improved for this CSF
1   This process achieves its objective but could be improved even further.
2   This process achieves its objective but could be improved by review of both automation and process improvement.
3   This process does not effectively achieve all its objectives and could be improved by review of both automation and process improvement.
4   The process exists and functions but needs substantial alteration to meet its objectives.
5   The process either does not exist or only partially exists and fails to meet any objectives.

Figure 3.4 Innovation (internal perspective) marking guide

from the innovation and learning and business process (internal) perspectives. Each process element is scored (0–5) against each CSF for the impact and innovation measures. The score for each measure is multiplied to provide a composite score (0–25) for each CSF. An overall composite score for each process is calculated by adding the composite score for each CSF. The processes with the highest overall composite score should be prioritised for improvement.

Extract from Greasley, A. (2004)

Management Decisions

Management decisions relate to the day-to-day management of the operation that has been previously designed and implemented in the organisation. Management decisions include capacity management, inventory management, lean operations, enterprise resource planning, supply chain management, project management and the management of quality. More detail on these can be found in operations management textbooks (for example, Greasley, 2013).

Because DES provides a dynamic capability, it is ideal to report on the performance of an operation over time. Most operations do not operate in a closed environment, and even though the major elements of the process are in place and resources have been allocated, there will need to be decisions taken in response to external events such as changes in demand for products or services. Simulation can thus be used to help devise policies for future operating conditions.

Defining Objectives

Once we have decided on the decision areas we wish to investigate, we can define specific objectives for our simulation study. Here, are some example objectives for design and management decisions in manufacturing and service application areas.

Service (Design)

- To determine how long customers wait for service.
- To determine the number of customers that can be served.
- To establish an efficient flow of customers through the operation.
- To compare current performance to that of an automated system.
- To determine the best layout of the customer service facility.

Service (Management)

- To determine the optimum sequence to service customers.
- To determine the best appointment schedule for customers.
- To determine an optimum staff schedule.
- To determine a maintenance schedule for equipment.

Manufacturing (Design)

- To determine the best layout of the factory machinery.
- To compare current performance to that of an automated system.
- To determine the effect of a reduction in setup time on production.
- To establish the location of production bottlenecks.
- To determine the production capability of a given system.

Manufacturing (Management)

- To determine the shift pattern required to meet production requirements.
- To determine the optimum production batch size.
- To determine the optimum job sequence.
- To assess the effect of a proposed preventative maintenance policy.

Define Model Inputs and Outputs

We can think of our simulation study as an experiment which involves subjecting the model to input variables at various values and interpreting their effects on output variables. Thus, our study objectives should be complemented by a definition of what should be achieved by the analysis. This can be represented as output variables termed responses and input variables termed factors (figure 3.5). Responses can be defined as flow times, flow rate, inventory or other measures defined in our model. If we have a certain level of performance of our response variable we wish to measure against, we can define a response target. We will also

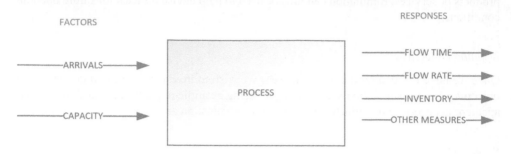

Figure 3.5 Responses and factors for a simulation experiment

wish to know under what conditions we will be measuring the performance of our system, and these are defined as input variables termed factors. Factors are either concerning the nature of entity arrivals (for example, customer demand and breakdown events) in our model or the form of the resource capacity (for example, staff and equipment) available to process these arrivals. The different values we give to the factors in our simulation experiments are termed levels.

Defining Responses (Output Variables)

Simulation is mostly associated with the measurement of processes at the operational level, and a number of these measures are found in the reports provided by simulation software. These include the following.

Flow Time Measures

- Flow/lead time. The time taken to undertake the steps in a process. This can be an internal measure, such as the lead time for a production line or an external measure related to the speed of delivery of goods and services to customers. Flow time is important as a short flow time enables a quick response to customer demand.
- Waiting/queue time. The time taken between being ready to be processed and the resource undertaking the processing to become available and processing to commence. In a manufacturing process, the aim is to minimise the proportion of flow lead time that is waiting time (the flow time for a process is the process time + waiting time). In a service operation, we need to minimise the queue time to ensure customer service quality.

Flow Rate Measures

- Flow/throughput rate. Throughput is the average number of units that flow out of a process per unit of time. Process capacity can be defined as the maximum sustainable throughput. Flow rate is important as the higher the throughput of a process, the higher the output and thus the scale of the operation.
- Cycle time. The time between each unit of output. This is the reciprocal of the throughput time and is also referred to as the takt time.

- Resource utilisation. The time that a resource is in operation as a proportion of the total time. If resource utilisation is too high and depending on the level of arrival variability, then queuing will occur. The relationship between utilisation and variability is covered in chapter 1.

Inventory Measures

- Inventory. The amount of units in the system. This is termed work-in-progress (WIP) when referring to the units being processed in a service or manufacturing system. Using Little's law, in a stable process, average inventory (I) = throughput (R) × average flow time (T). Thus, any two of these measures determine the performance of the third measure, and so controlling inventory allows us to indirectly control throughput and average flow time. Inventory also directly affects cost.
- Queue length. If space is constrained, then the measurement of interest may be the number of people in the queue rather than the waiting time.

Other Measures
Event-Based Measures

- Other measures may include any events that occur during the simulation run. For example, the number of facility and equipment breakdown events may be recorded. If the time to repair is known, then an estimate can be made of equipment downtime over a simulated period of time. Baulking and reneging of customers in service systems and targets such as the number of on-time deliveries in a logistics system can also be recorded.

Cost Measures

- Cost is traditionally calculated by estimating in terms of staff, facilities and materials, the resources that are required for the input and transformation processes in an operation. However, the way these costs are allocated to products and services is often arbitrary. For example, the actual costs of producing a product in a factory where hundreds of other products are also being made are dependent on an accurate allocation of direct costs (staff, equipment and material costs directly connected to the product) and indirect costs (for example, overhead such as factory space, energy, administration and central staffing costs). The aim of performance measurement is to identify where cost is being incurred within an operation, so improvement efforts can be focused on the correct areas. As an alternative to the usual overhead-based costing methods, activity-based costing provides a way of allocating costs to manufacturing and service activities in order that a company can determine how much it costs to make a certain product or deliver a service. In activity-based costing (ABC), there are three main drivers of cost: the cost driver, the resource driver and the activity driver.

  - The cost driver relates to the number of resources needed to perform an activity and can be reduced – for example, by redesigning the process.
  - The resource driver relates to the type of resources needed for an activity and can be reduced – for example, by using different personnel, information technology or equipment.

- The activity driver relates to the number of times the process occurs and can be reduced – for example, by training to improve the reliability of a process.

The cost assignment view of ABC allocates costs to activities by identifying resource drivers, which determine the cost of resources, and activity drivers, which determine the use of these resources. The process view of ABC provides information about the effort needed for the activity (called the cost driver) and provides performance measures of the outcome of the activities. The cost assignment view can be used to reduce the activity cost by either reconfiguring the resources needed for an activity (resource driver) or reducing the number of resources required (activity driver). The process view provides a link between the inputs needed to perform an activity (cost driver) and the outputs required by the internal or external customer of that activity (performance measure). Thus, an investigation of a combination of resource drivers, activity drivers and cost drivers for an activity can improve the performance of the process by identifying why the cost has been incurred.

Productivity Measures

- Productivity (output/input) is used at both the organisational and national levels as a comparative measure of performance. Productivity can be increased by either increasing the output without a proportionate increase in the input or by decreasing the input without a proportionate decrease in the output. Although productivity provides an indication of the level of utilisation of resources, it can be difficult to find appropriate input and output parameters for the calculation, and the measure also fails to consider performance from a wider viewpoint encompassing customer and other stakeholder needs. Efficiency (actual output/effective capacity) is defined as a measure of the use of capacity remaining after the loss of output due to planned factors such as maintenance and training. In other words, efficiency relates to the use of a resource in terms of availability. However, a high level of efficiency does not necessarily imply that resources are being used effectively in improving the overall performance. Effectiveness can be defined as the extent to which the output of a process meets the requirements of its customers. This is more difficult to measure quantitatively than productivity or efficiency. In service operations, effectiveness is often measured by surveys of customer satisfaction. However, customer satisfaction will be dependent on the perceptions and expectations of individual customers. Other indicators of effectiveness could be sales volume and sales margin figures for products and services.

Balanced Scorecard Measures

- The balanced scorecard approach is an attempt to incorporate the interests of a broader range of stakeholders through performance measures across four perspectives of finance, customer, business process and learning/growth. The idea of the scorecard is to provide managers with multiple perspectives on the goals that need to be met for organisational success. Although designed for performance measurement at a strategic level, its relevance to operations is that it provides a direction for the organisation that will impact on and be impacted by operations. The balanced scorecard also provides a way of translating strategy into action. It does this by deriving operational performance measures from strategic objectives.

Deriving Operational Measures from Strategic Objectives

For an organisation's sickness and absence process, the process is related to the CSF identified in the balanced scorecard initiative of increasing individual performance. At a strategic level, the measure of staff productivity was chosen with a target to increase the availability of police officers by 5%. In order to meet this strategic target, measures and targets are needed at an operational level. These are derived both from the strategic measure and an understanding of the relevant business process. The measure chosen for the sickness and absence process was the average days lost per year. The target for this measure is 11.9 days lost per year per employee for sickness and absence. This benchmark was derived from the national average performance. The current performance was at 14.1 days lost per year per employee. Simulation can be now used to measure the effect of changes to the process at an operational level and thus gauge their impact on meeting strategic targets.

Extract from Greasley, A. (2004)

Performance Objective Measures

- From the area of operations management comes the five operations performance measures of quality, speed, dependability, flexibility and cost, which relate to different aspects of performance (table 3.2).

  Two methodologies that use these measures to identify where performance should be improved are as follows.

- The Hill methodology (Hill and Hill, 2012) is based on market requirements. The concepts of 'order winning' and 'qualifying factors' are used to distinguish between those factors that directly contribute to winning business and those that are necessary to qualify for the customer's consideration between a range of products/services. While it may be necessary to raise performance on some qualifying factors to a certain level in order to be considered by the customer, a further rise in the level of performance may not achieve an increase in competitiveness. Instead, competitiveness will depend on raising the level of performance of different 'order-winning' factors. Because these factors are critical to winning customers, they are translated into the five performance measures mentioned earlier.

Table 3.2 Performance Objective Example Measures

Performance Objective	Description
Speed	Can we do it fast?
Cost	Can we meet our target for cost?
Quality	Can we meet the specification?
Dependability	Can we deliver to a time slot every time?
Flexibility (service)	Can we introduce a new service design?
Flexibility (product)	Can we introduce a new product design?
Flexibility (volume)	Can we adjust our output level?
Flexibility (mix)	Can we change our mix of products/services?
Flexibility (delivery)	Can we change our delivery dates?

- The Slack methodology (Slack, 1991) uses a combination of market and competitive factors and two dimensions – importance and performance – to help prioritise performance measures. The relative importance of a competitive factor is assessed in terms of its importance to internal or external customers using a nine-point scale. The degrees of 'order winning', 'order qualifying' and 'less important customer viewed' competitive factors are measured on this scale. The next step ranks the relative performance of a competitive factor against competitor achievement. A nine-point performance scale (rating from 'consistently better than the nearest competitor' to 'consistently worse than most competitors') is used for each performance measure.

  Once key performance areas have been identified using the previously mentioned methods, the performance measures can provide both an indication of the performance that can be derived from customer requirements and can be used to align the physical resources and management systems of the company's operations. Thus, the pursuit of a subset of these measures provides a way of connecting the strategic direction of the company with its operational decisions. For example, if key metrics are identified as speed and cost, then investments in resources such as customer-processing technology should improve these aspects of performance.

  An additional aspect regarding the five performance measures is that there is both an external benefit in improving performance within a performance area and an internal benefit in terms of reducing cost in that area. For example, improving quality performance not only means higher customer satisfaction but also reduces internal costs through a reduction in the need to rectify mistakes. This shows the potential of replacing strategies that rely on immediate cost-cutting, which might achieve short-term savings by lowering the costs of inputs such as staff and equipment into the process, but risks lowering the capability of the process to meet customer needs.

  Simulation can be used to measure performance across all five of the performance measures of speed, cost, quality, dependability and flexibility.

Response Targets

For each response, we can also define a target to determine when we have achieved our objective. Either we can record our measurement, such as flow time, and compare it to a target value or we can use the simulation to record if the target has been reached, such as by defining a missed service event variable. Targets can be defined in terms of service quality – for example, the maximum waiting time for any customer should not exceed ten minutes. Capacity constraints can also be reflected in targets – for example, the number of customers queuing should not exceed ten customers (due to limited floor space in our customer service area).

Benchmarking

In order to identify where performance improvement should take place, it may be necessary to compare current performance against a performance standard. This standard can be internal to the organisation, such as comparing against previous performance or against targets for future performance. Internal targets are often based on a comparison between past financial and sales performance and targets for future performance. The advantage of these measures is that they are widely used and comparable across organisations and use data that are readily available. However, they may be of limited value in identifying why performance is above or below a target value. External targets include the comparison to competitor performance, best-practice or best-in-class performance and market requirements. External performance targets have the advantage of providing a comparison of performance against competitors operating in similar competitive markets. This approach is often termed benchmarking.

Defining Experimental Factors (Input Variables)

In order to achieve the performance required in terms of the defined responses, we need to define the experimental factors that we would like to change. There will usually be a number of ways in which the required (output) response may be achieved, and so the choice of (input) factors will be dependent on discussion with the client and what is deemed to be appropriate and feasible. If we wish to limit the number of factors to investigate, it may be that we use a simplified version of our model to determine those factors that have the most significant impact on our responses.

In terms of an analysis of the process design, the two key drivers of process performance are the utilisation of capacity and the amount of stochastic variability in our system. These are determined by the mean and variability of interarrival times (arrivals) and the mean and variability of processing times (capacity). A number of strategies for changes to arrivals and capacity in a process design are now shown with example experimental factors indicated in brackets. Many projects will study a combination of experimental factors, but it is important to study each area in turn to establish potential subjects for investigation at the project proposal stage.

Arrivals/Demand

- Decrease arrival rate (breakdown events reduced by preventative maintenance).
- Increase arrival rate (marketing campaign).
- Decrease variability in customer interarrival times (customer appointment system).
- Decrease variability in product interarrival times (suppliers with narrower delivery time windows).
- Schedule of orders (predicted orders for the next six months).

Capacity

- Decrease processing times (automation or staff training).
- Increase units of capacity (investment appraisal of more staff or equipment).
- Decrease units of capacity (less staff to reduce costs).
- Synchronise capacity to interarrival times (staff shift patterns, dynamic allocation of staff).
- Decrease variability in processing times (standardise process).

- Pool units of capacity across customers (single-queue system for customers).
- Segregate units of capacity to different customer types (multiple-queue system for different customer services).

Factor Levels

As well as the factors, we need to determine the levels or range of values that we wish to set the factors too. For example, for an investment appraisal of increasing capacity, we may wish to assess the responses when we have between three and five tills operating in a supermarket. We may also simply wish to assess between capacity options such as manual and automated till service.

We can specify our objectives, factors and responses using the following template.

Project Title Objective:

Factors	Levels	Responses	Target

Here are some examples of study objectives with defined factors, levels, responses and targets that relate to previous studies the author has conducted. Each study is related to an individual experimental factor with the analysis indicated for arrivals or capacity. In addition, the proposed factor levels are indicated. The responses are related to operations performance objectives. A target is provided for each response. More details of these studies are contained in the work of Greasley (2019).

Police Call Centre
Objective: To reduce direct staffing costs while maintaining the call response time target

Factors	Levels	Responses	Target
Staff schedule (capacity)	8-hour shift pattern 9-hour shift pattern	Flow time (speed) Direct staffing cost (cost)	<10 seconds for 90% of emergency calls −10% (£)

'Last Mile' Logistics Distribution
Objective: To compare the delivery performance of separated and mixed retail and non-retail 'last mile' delivery runs

Factors	Levels	Responses	Target
Delivery schedule (capacity)	Separate retail/non-retail Mixed retail/non-retail	Flow time (speed) Missed timed deliveries (dependability)	Minimise (mins) Zero

---

Enterprise Resource Planning (ERP) System
Objective: To compare manual, ERP and ERP combined with an ESS-based customer service processes

Factors	Levels	Responses	Target
Service automation (capacity)	Manual, ERP, ERP/ESS	Flow time (speed) Direct staff cost (cost)	Minimise (mins) Minimise (£)

Rail Carriage Maintenance Depot
Objective: To determine the train depot capacity required to ensure no loss in service due to train breakdown events.

Factors	Levels	Responses	Target
Train breakdown rate/day (arrivals)	0, 1, 2, 3	Missed service events (dependability)	Zero
Spare trains on depot (capacity)	0, 1, 2		

Textile Manufacturing Plant
Objective: To determine the WIP storage area required for two production scenarios

Factors	Levels	Responses	Target
Production output (capacity)	60 tons/week 100 tons/week	Inventory storage area (quality)	None (m²)

The issue of how we use the simulation to assess the responses for the different levels of factors is covered in experimental design in chapters 9 and 10. Once we have defined a system description and the study objectives, we may wish to supplement our documentation of the real-world problem with the use of diagramming methods such as process maps and, for service systems, service blueprints (see chapter 4). It is at this stage that we may be submitting a proposal to undertake the simulation study in full to the simulation client. More information on the requirements for putting forward a simulation proposal is contained in chapter 11 in the section 'Simulation Project Management'.

Define the Model Content

Here the abstraction process takes place using the methods of scoping and simplification. This stage of the conceptual modelling process can be approached by breaking up the system into smaller parts, deciding for each part the form and level of detail to incorporate into our model and recombining each part with a suitable representation of the interaction between them.

Defining What to Model

Scoping or the task of defining what to model can be summarised as decisions regarding what should be left out (or included in the model). The model scope is the definition of the boundary between what is to be included in the model and what is considered external to the specification. The scope will need to encompass the study objectives and aspects of the system that connect the defined factors (e.g. customer arrivals) with our responses (e.g. customer flow time). The main components of the conceptual model can be considered to be entities with their associated attributes, processes with their associated resources, queues and decision logic elements (figure 3.6).

Entities

Entities flow through a network of modules that describe their logical behaviour and can represent people, materials or information flows in the system being modelled. Entities must be created and enter the model and are disposed of when they leave. Entities are distinguished

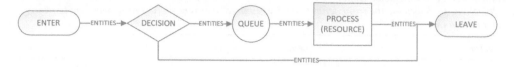

Figure 3.6 Main components of the conceptual model

by their attributes, which can refer to the characteristics of the people, parts or any other information regarding the entity that can be expressed in numerical form. Attributes are useful as their value stays with the entity as it moves through the model, and their value can be used at any time by the model. Values that are not associated with an individual entity are defined as variables. Not all entities or entity types in the real system will usually need to be modelled in the simulation. We will often model product types as different entity types if they have different process routes, for example, but some product types may be aggregated if they are processed in a similar fashion. Customers may also be grouped into different types if they require directing to resources based on conditional decisions. Customers arriving in groups that are processed as a group may be treated as a single entity within the model. Alternatively, the model software can generate group arrivals by specifying both the interarrival time and batch size of the arrival.

Processes

Processes represent an activity that takes place over a period of time. When an entity arrives at a process, it will try to obtain (seize) the resource necessary to undertake that process. If no resource is required for the activity, then the process is modelled as a delay. If a resource is not available, the entity waits in a queue associated with the process. When the resource is available, the length of time in which the entity uses the resource is the process duration. The entity releases the resource when processing is complete. The resource is then available to process further entities if necessary. Real processes are often merged or grouped into a single modelled process if that provides the detail necessary. Processes that do not consume a resource (such as storage time when the storage resource is not modelled) are represented by a delay. Processes that do consume a resource must request the resources required from a resource pool. Multiple resources may be needed to undertake a process (such as two members of the staff for an interview). The process cannot commence until suitable resources are available. Different processes can be assigned priorities over other processes for the use of resources.

Resources

Resources include staff and equipment and facilitate the operation of a process. Resources have a capacity (number of identical units of this resource) and can have a schedule of availability (how many resources are available when). Resources that enable processes can be modelled with either a capacity that varies with a fixed capacity or a capacity that varies with time (termed a schedule). A fixed capacity resource can simply represent a fixed number of staff members who are available to serve any process in the model that requires them. A schedule will alter staff availability in time buckets (for example, every 60 minutes) to represent a staff rotation. Resource availability can also be affected by planned maintenance and equipment failures, both of which can be modelled by changing the capacity of a resource at the appropriate time. Consumable resources, such as energy use, may be modelled using variables.

Queues

Queues of entities occur when they arrive at a process which has insufficient available resources to process those entities. Entities can be ordered in the queue according to different rules, such as first in, first out (FIFO).

Decisions

Decisions control the flow of individual entities and can use either probabilities or conditional rules to direct flow. Probability rules are represented as a percentage or fraction, while conditional rules are represented as an if-then-else rule. If conditional rules are understood, then decisions can be modelled in this way. Conditional rules may take any form and be quite complex, such as the rules around scheduling parts in a factory may incorporate many variables. Some of the most used conditional rules include checking the smallest queue for customer service operations, checking resources in turn and choosing the first resource that is available or simply choosing a flow path at random. If conditional rules are not used, then a probabilistic approach is taken based on historical data. Decisions are also required when entities are held in queues. For example, customers assigned as priority customers can jump the queue.

For our main components which make up our model, we can provide a specification of scoping decisions by the use of a table. The example in table 3.3 is for the 'Police Call Centre' study objectives defined earlier.

Defining the Level of Detail (How to Model)

Once the model scope has been defined, the next stage is to specify the level of detail of the modelling of components within the scope of our model. Simplification is a fundamental part of modelling and simulation, and projects often fail because too much detail is included in the model (Brooks and Tobias, 2000). We have many choices in how we model a system, so in determining the level of detail, the aim is to minimise model complexity while providing a model capable of achieving the project objectives. The reason to minimise complexity is that one of the aims of simulation is to not only report the results of experiments but to understand how the results are generated (i.e. it is not a black box). The less complex the model, the easier it is likely to be to understand and lead to insights into the problem. On a practical level, a simple model should lead to easier and faster model build, verification and validation and experimentation. Model complexity can be considered in terms of the number of components within the model (combinatorial complexity) and the nature of the interaction between the activities (dynamic complexity) (see chapter 1 for a description of combinatorial complexity and dynamic complexity). One reason we wish to minimise complexity is that verification and validation become more difficult as the complexity of the model increases. However, if we leave too much out of the model, there is a greater conceptual leap between the conclusions drawn from the model and interpretation in relation to the system. Thus, a model that meets the objectives of the study with the least amount of complexity required would be the ideal solution.

Table 3.3 Model Scope: Police Call Centre Example

Component Type	Component	In Scope (✓)/ Out of Scope (✗)	Comments
Entities	Callers	✓	Flow through the system
Processes	Respond to calls	✓	Determine system response
	Deploy police to attend	✗	Police deployment not modelled
Resources	Call handlers	✓	Respond to emergency calls and non-emergency calls not handled by the switchboard
	Switchboard operators	✓	Respond to non-emergency calls
	Police controllers	✗	Police deployment not modelled
Queues	Switchboard	✓	
	Call centre	✓	
	Controllers	✗	Police deployment not modelled
Decisions	999 emergency call?	✓	Route emergency calls direct to call handlers
	Switchboard resolved query?	✓	Resolved queries not directed to call handlers
	Require police to attend?	✗	Police deployment not modelled

Strategies for reducing model complexity by reducing the level of detail of how we model system components are termed simplifications. Mechanisms for simplification can be classified into omission, aggregation and replacement.

- Omission: omitting aspects of the system from the model. For example, the model may omit staff breaks for meals and presume staff are continuously available. Infrequent events, such as machine breakdowns, may also be omitted if the objective is to analyse the operation of the system under normal working conditions. Often machine-based processes are modelled without reference to the human operator they employ.
- Aggregation: merging individual processes into a single process. For example, processes or the work of whole departments may be aggregated if their internal working is not the focus of the simulation study. The model may only consider a customer service process as a whole rather than modelling individual transactions within that process. A single entity can also be used to represent a group of customers or products. Entities can be grouped by attributes such as customer type.
- Replacement: replacing complex processes. For example, human processes are often substituted by a 'resource' element in a simulation model. This simplifies a human process as a machine-type process removing many of the complicating factors of human behaviour. Decisions made based on complex rules may be replaced by a simple rule set that covers most situations.

From a modelling perspective, simplification strategies are useful in reducing model complexity and may be necessary to produce a model within the time and cost constraints of the development, often imposed by the model client. In addition to these strategies, we can treat the system component at various levels of abstraction. The three approaches of scenario, impact and individual used to model people's behaviour can be related in general to treating model components as an experimental factor (scenario), as a global variable (impact) or at the entity attribute level (individual) (see 'Defining the Level of Detail When Modelling People's Behaviour' in chapter 6).

This stage of the simulation study requires the skill and experience of the modeller to decide on the level of model detail required. Practical considerations, such as data availability, will also need to be taken into account, but the main decisions should be based on the objectives of the simulation study, reflecting that the model is not universally valid but is designed for a specific purpose. As a guide, it is usually the case that greater detail is required for models that are for predictive and prescriptive analysis than for descriptive purposes.

Finally, it should be remembered that the model will normally be used in conjunction with the model user (client) in order to achieve understanding and make predictions. If this is the case, then the level of detail in the model should take into consideration that some aspects of the system understanding can be derived from the user's knowledge, and the model can be seen as a tool to support the user's decision-making.

For our main components which make up our model content, we can provide a specification of the level of detail decisions by the use of a table. The example in table 3.4 is for the 'Police Call Centre' study objectives defined earlier.

Table 3.4 Model Level of Detail: Police Call Centre Example

Component Type	Component	Include (✓)/ Exclude (✗)	Level of Detail	Comments
Entities	Callers	✓	Individual callers	
		✓	Hourly schedule of arrivals by call type	
		✓	Abandoned calls	
Processes	Respond to calls		Individual calls	Experimental response
Resources	Call handlers	✓	Answer each call	Modelled as distribution by call type
		✓	Work shift pattern	Experimental factor defined by schedule
		✓	Absenteeism	Factored into availability
	Switchboard	✓	Answer each call	Modelled as distribution
		✗	Absenteeism	100% availability assumed
Queues	Switchboard	✓	Individual calls	
	Call centre	✓	Individual calls	
Decisions	999 emergency call?	✓	Route emergency calls direct to call handlers	
	Switchboard resolved query?	✓	If switchboard has not dealt with the call, route to call handler.	

Summary

This chapter covers the process of abstraction from the real-world system to the conceptual model. The conceptual model will represent what we consider to be the essential elements of the system to be modelled to meet the study objectives. When defining the problem situation, we will make a number of assumptions about how the real-world system works. The outcome of this understanding of the context of the problem is the system description. From this, we define the model objectives, the model inputs and outputs and the model content. When we define the model content, we will make simplifications of the system description depending on the level of detail we decide is appropriate for the study. It is important that all aspects of the abstraction process are documented, including the assumptions and simplifications, in order to establish credibility with the model client.

Exercises

- What is the relationship between flow time and flow rate with process capacity?
- The objective of a simulation of a supermarket is to find if an additional till will ensure average customer till queuing time is less than five minutes. Define the factors, levels, responses and targets for this objective.
- Identify the possible entities, processes, resources, queues and decisions for the following systems:

  - Supermarket
  - Fast-food restaurant
  - Estate agency
  - Bank
  - Car production line

References

Brooks, R.J. and Tobias, A.M. (2000) Simplification in the simulation of manufacturing systems, *International Journal of Production Research*, 38(5), 1009–1027.

Checkland, P.B. (2001) Soft Systems methodology, in J. Rosenhead and J Mingers (eds.) *Rational Analysis for a Problematic World Revisited*, Wiley.

Checkland, P.B. and Holwell, S. (2004) "Classic" OR and "soft" OR – an asymmetric complementarity, in M. Pidd (ed.) *Systems Modelling Theory and Practice*. Wiley, 45–60.

Eden, C. and Ackermann, F. (2001) SODA – The principles, Chapter 2 and Journey making and mapping in practice, Chapter 3 in J Rosenhead and J Mingers (eds.) *Rational Analysis for a Problematic World Revisited*, Wiley.

Greasley, A. (2019) *Simulating Business Processes for Descriptive, Predictive and Prescriptive Analytics*, DeGruyter Press.

Greasley, A. (2013) *Operations Management*, 3rd edition, John Wiley and Sons Ltd.

Greasley, A. (2005) Using system dynamics in a discrete-event simulation study of a manufacturing plant, *International Journal of Operations and Production Management*, 25(5/6), 534–548.

Greasley, A. (2004) Process improvement within a HR division at a UK police force, *International Journal of Operations and Production Management*, 24(2/3), 230–240.

Hill, A. and Hill, T. (2012) *Operations Management*, 3rd edition, Palgrave Macmillan.

Kim, D.H. (1992) *Systems Archetypes: Diagnosing Systemic Issues and Designing High-Leverage Interventions*, Toolbox Reprint Series: Systems Archetypes, Pegasus Communications, 3–26.

Kotiadis, K. (2007) Using soft systems methodology to determine the simulation study objectives, *Journal of Simulation*, 1, 215–222.

Lehaney, B. and Paul, R.J. (1996) The use of soft systems methodology in the development of a simulation of out-patients services at Watford general hospital, *Journal of the Operational Research Society*, 47, 864–870.

Maani, K.E. and Cavana, R.Y. (2000) *Systems Thinking and Modelling: Understanding Change and Complexity*, Pearson Education.

Peppard, J. and Rowland, P. (1995) *The Essence of Business process Re-Engineering*, Prentice Hall.

Robinson, S. (2020) Conceptual modelling for simulation: Progress and grand challenges, *Journal of Simulation*, 14(1), 1–20.

Robinson, S. (2008) Conceptual modelling for simulation part I: Definition and requirements, *Journal of the Operational Research Society*, 59(3), 278–290.

Robinson, S. (2001) Soft with a hard Centre: Discrete-event simulation in facilitation, *Journal of the Operational Research Society*, 52, 905–915.

Senge, P.M. (1993) *The Fifth Discipline: The Art and Practice of the Learning Organization*, Random House.

Shannon, R.E. (1975) *Systems Simulation: The Art and the Science*, Prentice-Hall.

Slack, N. (1991) *Manufacturing Advantage: Achieving Competitive Manufacturing Operations, Mercury*.

Sterman, J.D. (2000) *Business Dynamics Systems: Thinking and Modeling for a Complex World*, McGraw-Hill.

Van der Zee, D.J., Tako, A., Robinson, S., Fishwick, P. and Rose, O. (2018) Panel: Education on simulation model simplification – beyond the rules of thumb, *Proceedings of the 2018 Winter Simulation Conference*, IEEE.

4   Conceptual Modelling (Explanatory Model)

Introduction

As stated in chapter 1, DES takes a systems approach to create an explanatory model consisting of individual processes and their interdependencies. The explanatory model will provide a structural representation of the system. This structure enables a variety of future behaviours and provides a representative that helps explain the simulation model results. In general, pure explanatory models are seldom found, and in a DES model, we usually depend on descriptive sub-models (chapter 5) to describe individual relationships and variability. For conceptual modelling, in regard to the explanatory model, the emphasis should be on representing those processes which are decisive for system behaviour. This requires an understanding of the problem situation and making suitable abstraction decisions (chapter 3).

In some instances, we may have a choice of the use of an explanatory modelling approach or a descriptive modelling approach. For example, we could model the cause of customers leaving a queue as a decision rule based on queue length (explanatory model), or we could use a probability distribution to model the proportion of customers leaving the queue (descriptive model). We need to make these choices of approach during the conceptual modelling stage. For instance, it may be that we can understand the behaviour of the process well enough by a discussion with people involved in the process to codify the decision rule. If the explanatory structure is not apparent, then we could represent its behaviour by the use of the descriptive modelling methods described in chapter 5. Alternatively, if there is insufficient knowledge for either of these approaches, then we may need to make assumptions or simplifications at the conceptual modelling stage that negate the need to model that element of the real world.

It is useful to express the explanatory model in diagrammatic form, so we will now consider the main simulation worldviews before describing the graphical notations that are associated with each view.

Simulation Worldviews and Graphical Notation

Part of the conceptual modelling process is to produce a diagram or chart showing the process flow of the real system. This diagram may be used as the basis for the computer model design for the model-building stage (chapter 7). There are a number of process diagramming methods available, including process flowcharts, process maps, workflow diagrams and activity diagrams. These terms are often used in an interchangeable fashion. There are also a number of formalised graphical notations aimed at particular application areas, including Business Process Modelling Notation (BPMN) for business process management initiatives, Unified Modelling Language (UML) diagrams for object-oriented applications and

DOI: 10.4324/9781003124092-4

Table 4.1 Simulation Worldviews and Graphical Notations

Worldview	Graphical Notation	DES Software
Process-based	Process/entity flow diagram	Arena, Simio, Simul8
Activity-based	Activity cycle diagram	ECSL
Event-based	Event graph	SIGMA
State-based	State charts	Anylogic

event-driven process chain (EPC) diagrams for enterprise resource planning (ERP) applications. This chapter outlines the main graphical notation methods that are associated with DES.

Although some DES software tools implement the simulation model in code (for example, Java in AnyLogic), most modern specialist DES software packages, such as Arena and Simio, specify the logic of the simulation model by employing interactive graphics facilities to drag and drop predefined sub-models which are then parameterised by the user (model building is covered in chapter 7). For simple models in particular, users may specify the model logic directly in terms of the simulation software package implementation. However, it is useful to formulate the conceptual model logic using a graphical notation before translation into the simulation software implementation. A graphical diagram is a useful method for representing the conceptual model that can be used as a basis for the model build stage and provides a communication tool between model developer and client when gathering data to understand the current and proposed process designs. Process maps can also be useful in identifying and prioritising potential process improvement areas for subsequent analysis by the simulation (chapter 3).

A DES can be defined in terms of its physical components, its entities and resources and its logical components, and its activities, events and states. There are various approaches to representing these different components in graphical form, and table 4.1 outlines the corresponding main simulation worldviews and their associated graphical notation. Example software implementations are shown that relate to each worldview, although software such as Arena and Simio are not associated with a particular graphical notation approach.

Of the three worldviews in table 4.1, the process-based view provides a full context for the life cycle of an entity and thus is considered to provide an easy to understand and concise description of the conceptual model. This text will mainly focus on these diagrams as they align most closely with the DES software implementations of Arena, Simio and Simul8 covered in this text. However, activity cycle diagrams are also widely used and are covered along with event graphs which provide a useful event-based perspective of the DES method and state charts. The four graphical notations will now be considered.

Process/Entity Flow Diagrams

Process or entity flow diagrams (also termed logic flow diagrams) follow the life cycle of an entity (e.g. customer, product) through a system comprising a number of activities with queuing at each process (e.g. waiting for service, equipment). A process-oriented approach to modelling considers a process as a series of time-ordered events that entities flow through. Thus, the term 'process flow diagram' is used particularly in the context of developing a conceptual model when using software such as Arena, which uses a process-based worldview. Figure 4.1 shows the main symbols that are employed in a process flow diagram. Here,

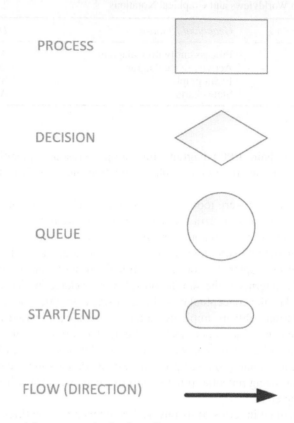

PROCESS

DECISION

QUEUE

START/END

FLOW (DIRECTION)

Figure 4.1 Symbols used for a process/entity flow diagram

the flow of entities is described as they move through a series of processes with associated queues and the branching of the entity flow is represented by a decision symbol. A process is subdivided into a number of activities represented by a rectangle and the flow of materials, information and customers between activities is represented by a directed line which may be labelled with the content of the flow. Sometimes the information flows may be distinguished by the use of a dashed line. Decisions in which the process flow is split into multiple routes are represented by a diamond shape. The decision rule, which can be a conditional rule (for example, IF (x==1) THEN BRANCH1 ELSE BRANCH2) or probabilistic (for example, WITH 20% BRANCH1 ELSE BRANCH2), can be indicated within the diamond or for more complex rules may be noted separately from the diagram. The flow lines from a decision can be labelled to indicate how they relate to the outcome of the decision rule. Normally the flow from a decision will take one route only, but in some cases, duplication of flows may take place. Flows may be labelled to improve the clarity of the diagram.

The process-mapping stage provides a link between the conceptual model definition and the structure of the model implemented in the DES software in the model build stage covered in chapter 7. Most specialist DES software tools such as Arena and Simio implement models that are based on drag and drop modules that relate to the graphical notation of the associated simulation worldview. Figure 4.2 shows an example of a process flow diagram. Process flow

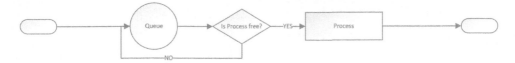

Figure 4.2 Process flow diagram

Figure 4.3 Process map

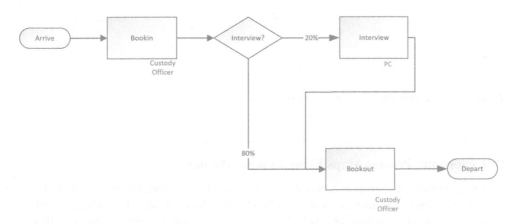

Figure 4.4 Process map for a simplified interview process for an arrested person

diagrams generally include the logic flow associated with entity queuing and checking for process availability.

Most software implementation will incorporate the queuing behaviour of entities waiting for processes internally, and so it may not be necessary to include this level of detail of flow logic in the conceptual model. Figure 4.3 shows the flow diagram without internal queuing behaviour, which is termed a process map in this text.

Figure 4.4 shows a process map for a simplified interview process for an arrested person. Here, the allocation of resources is defined by a label against each activity. Resources can also be shown by partitioning the process map into horizontal bands, one for each resource.

When designing a process map, the aim should be to have a 'balanced' map, which avoids too much detail in some areas and not enough detail in others. The process map should also not be too 'busy' and thus be difficult to read. To avoid these issues, and particularly when dealing with larger processes, it may be necessary to represent a given sub-process at several levels of detail. Thus, a single process may be shown as a series of sub-processes on a separate diagram. The use of this representation is termed cascading (figure 4.5).

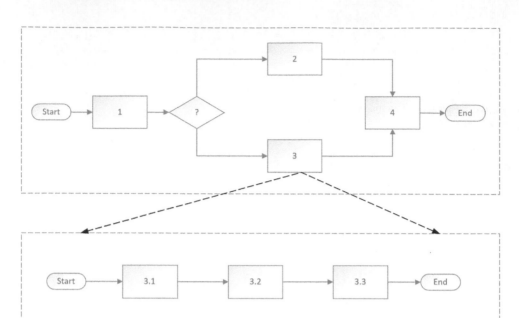

Figure 4.5 Cascading process 3 into sub-processes

Generating Process Maps Using Process Mining

The analytics software of process mining can be used to generate a process map design from raw data that can then be used to build a simulation model. For example, calls to an emergency call service can be logged on arrival, and through the process, they flow through. Process mining offers the promise of fast construction of representations of complex processes incorporating activities that may not be captured by traditional manual development of the simulation process map. However, process mining does not generally generate a usable process map directly from the event logs but uses a variety of analytic techniques, such as inductive mining for abstraction, dealing with issues such as noisy and incomplete data. These approaches abstract events in an automated way that may not capture the required detail to meet the simulation project objectives. Thus, process maps derived using process mining should be cross-checked and validated prior to their use for developing simulation models.

Service Blueprinting

A variation on the process map notation is the service blueprint diagram. Let's consider a case where a service consists of a number of sub-processes that are not linked and the service 'output' is a number of customer-employee interactions. In this case, the process design may first focus on the design of the customer-employee interactions and then identify external performance measures such as customer satisfaction. To assist in the analysis of customer-employee interactions, the process maps can be extended to show how a business interacts with customers. One system is a flow chart (termed a service blueprint) that structures the process activities on either side of a customer's 'line of visibility' (figure 4.6). The activities above the line are visible to the customer, and those below the line are operations that the customer does not see. Activities above the line of visibility are subdivided into two fields separated by the 'line of interaction'; this divides activities undertaken by the customer and the service provider. In the case of below the line of visibility, a line of internal interaction separates the activities of front-line personnel who carry out setting-up actions prior to service provision (not in view of the customer) and support personnel who contribute materials or services required for the provision of the service. Finally, the 'line of implementation' separates support activities from management activities such as planning, controlling and decision-making. Figure 4.6 shows an example of a service blueprint for a restaurant.

The objective of the service blueprint is that it not only charts the service process flow (from left to right) as does a process map but also shows the structure of the service organisation on the vertical axis, showing relationships between, for example, internal customers, support staff and front-line providers. In particular, the diagram aims to highlight the interactions between the customer and the process where customer services can be affected. The diagrams can also be used as a design tool to determine staffing levels, job descriptions and selection of equipment and as a control tool to identify gaps in service provision through the analysis of fail points. Fail points are potential service system shortfalls between what the service delivers and what the targeted customers have been led to expect.

Activity Cycle Diagrams

Activity cycle diagrams (ACDs) consist of activity cycles for each entity type and each resource. An entity or an active resource is either in a passive state called a queue or in an active state called an activity. The symbols of an ACD are shown in figure 4.7 with activities represented by rectangles and queues by circles, resources represented by ellipses, and there is a feeder symbol to represent entity generation and a disposer symbol to represent entity disposal. There is a resource activity cycle for each resource shown by dashed lines and one entity activity cycle shown by solid lines. Queue nodes and activity nodes are connected by arcs which indicate the direction of the flow of entities.

Figure 4.8 provides an example of an ACD for a simplified interview process for an arrested person.

Event Graphs

While processes and activities occur over a period of time, an event is simply a change of state in the system at a point in time. Figure 4.9 shows the relationship between activities and events. A create activity leads to an arrive event at a point in time. An activity (process) event leads to a start event and an end event. The depart activity leads to a depart event.

Simulation models are developed to understand processes, but events may be important if we are interested in the timing of occurrences. A characteristic of a DES is that changes to elements can be associated with events that occur at particular instances in time. Chapter 1 covers the underlying mechanism of a DES which consists of a simulation clock and a future events list than contains information about future events and their time of execution. Event graphs are a way of representing the future event list logic for a DES. Event graphs use nodes (vertices) to represent the events, and directed arcs (edges) are used to represent

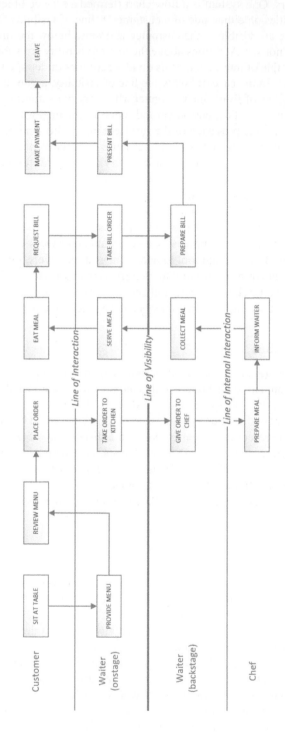

Figure 4.6 Service blueprint for a restaurant

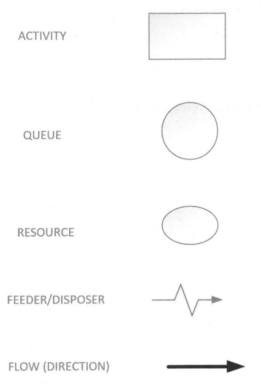

ACTIVITY

QUEUE

RESOURCE

FEEDER/DISPOSER

FLOW (DIRECTION)

Figure 4.7 Symbols used in activity cycle diagrams

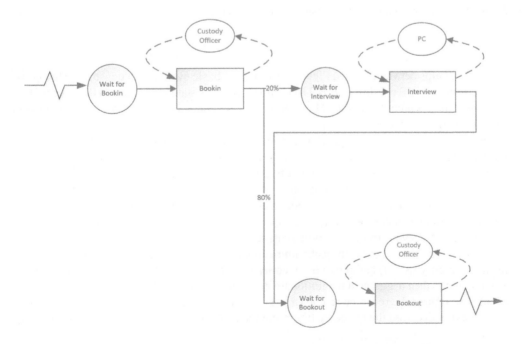

Figure 4.8 Activity cycle diagram for a simplified interview process for an arrested person

Figure 4.9 Arrive events and associated activities

Figure 4.10 An event graph

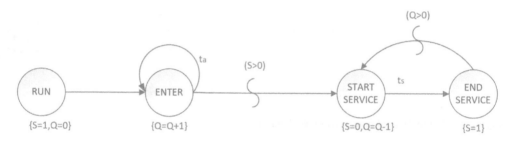

Figure 4.11 An event graph model of a single-server queue

the relationships between events. Figure 4.10 shows a basic event graph construct which can be interpreted as 'IF condition (*i*) is TRUE after event A's state transition, THEN event B is scheduled after a time delay of *t*'. The condition *i* may contain constants, variables and logical and relational operators.

Figure 4.11 shows an event graph model of a single-server queue system. The variable S represents the status of the resource (0 = busy, 1 = idle), and Q is the number of entities in the queue. t_a represents the time between entity arrivals, and t_s represents the time required for service. The RUN event is processed once at the beginning of the simulation and initialises the resource to idle (S = 1) and the queue to empty (Q = 0). The run event triggers the first ENTER event, which adds an entity to the queue (Q = Q + 1) and unconditionally schedules the next ENTER event to occur t_a time units later. If the resource is idle (S > 0), a START SERVICE event is triggered to occur immediately. The START SERVICE event sets the resource to busy (S = 0) and removes an entity from the queue (Q = Q − 1). An END SERVICE event is then triggered unconditionally to occur t_s time units later. The END SERVICE event then returns the resource to idle (S = 1) and, if possible (Q > 0), initiates the removal of the next entity from the queue by triggering the START SERVICE event to occur without delay.

SIGMA (simulation graphical modelling and analysis) is a graphical environment for building, testing and experimenting with DES models. Although event graphs offer a precise view of a simulation's dynamic transitions, they lack an intuitive view of the process to be modelled and so are generally not used in practical simulation applications. For more information on event graphs in general, see Law (2015).

State Charts

State charts provide a hierarchical structure in which to construct large-scale simulation models. They provide an indirect description of events as internal and external transitions. Figure 4.12 shows a simple model of a laptop running on a battery. When the laptop is on and the user is working (i.e. pressing the keyboard keys and moving the mouse), the laptop stays in the On state. However, after five minutes of user inactivity, the laptop turns off the screen to save power. This fragment of the laptop behaviour is modelled by two transitions exiting the On state: a timeout transition Time5min and a loop transition triggered by KeyOrMouse. State charts are arguably less intuitive than activity-based and process flow-based methods when modelling organisational processes.

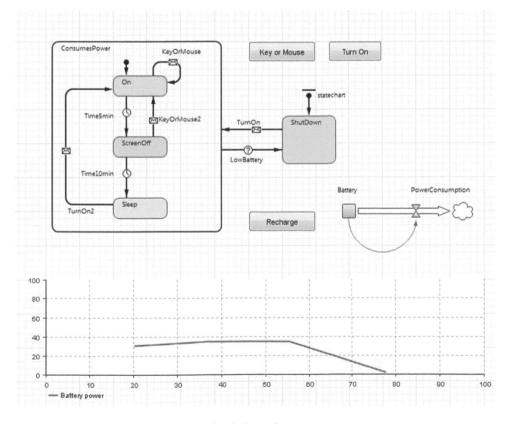

Figure 4.12 State chart in the AnyLogic simulation software

Summary

This chapter provides an overview of diagramming techniques that can be used to provide a structural representation of the system. The main methods used in DES are process flow diagrams, process maps and ACDs. Event graphs and state charts are also covered in this chapter for reference.

Exercises

- Draw a process map for an estate agency.
- Sheets of metal enter a machine shop and can go on either of two cutting machines. The cutter with the smallest queue has a preference. The metal can now go through one of three process routes, with type 1 metal through 'lathe, drill and inspect', type 2 metal through 'drill and inspect' and type 3 metal through 'lathe and inspect'. Draw a process map of the process.

Reference

Law, A.M. (2015) *Simulation Modeling and Analysis*, 5th edition, McGraw-Hill Education.

5 Conceptual Modelling (Descriptive Model)

Introduction

In chapter 4, we covered the use of diagramming techniques to represent the explanatory model that provides a structural representation of the system. In general, pure explanatory models are seldom found, and in a DES model, we usually depend on descriptive sub-models. For conceptual modelling, when employing a descriptive model, the emphasis is on the collection and analysis of quantitative data from observations of system behaviour. There are a number of descriptive modelling (also termed input modelling in simulation studies) methods, but we may be constrained in our choice by the availability and time required for data collection. Greasley and Owen (2016) show examples from the literature of where descriptive approaches to modelling people's behaviour have been applied to model different aspects of model content such as resource availability, process durations and decisions.

The following eight input modelling methods are presented:

1   Estimation
2   Theoretical distribution
3   Empirical distribution
4   Bootstrapping
5   Mathematical equation
6   Cognitive architectures
7   Machine learning
8   Trace

1. Estimation

When little or no data exists because the system does not currently exist or there is no time for data collection, then an estimate must be made. This option may also be used in the simulation model development phase before further data collection is undertaken when time permits. One approach is to simply use a fixed value representing an estimate of the mean time of the process, but this does not represent the stochastic variability in the process duration. However, this treatment of what appears to be probabilistic behaviour as deterministic may be acceptable if it attains the level of detail required by the conceptual model.

DOI: 10.4324/9781003124092-5

2. Theoretical Distribution

Deriving a theoretical distribution is the most common descriptive modelling method in simulation and may be feasible when over around 25 sample data points are available. This method can 'smooth out' certain irregularities in the data to show the underlying distribution and is not restricted to generating values within the data sample used. Another important reason to employ a theoretical distribution is that it allows us to easily change the parameters of our distribution for scenario analysis. For example, if we are using the exponential distribution for the interarrival rate, we can simply change the mean parameter of the exponential distribution to represent either slower or faster arrival rate scenarios.

There are two options for choosing an appropriate theoretical distribution. The choice can be made based on known properties of the variability of the modelling area being represented. For example, times between arrivals (interarrival times) are often modelled using an exponential distribution. The overview of the main theoretical distributions given in this chapter includes common applications of these distributions to different modelling areas. Some examples of common usage are shown in table 5.1

The second approach and standard procedure is to match a sample distribution to a theoretical distribution by constructing a histogram of the data and comparing the shape of the histogram with a range of theoretical distributions. A histogram is a bar chart that shows the frequency distribution of the sample data. It should be noted that the histogram summarises the frequency distribution and does not show how it varies over time.

Further examples of choosing a theoretical distribution are provided here:

- A sample size of below 25 to 30 is probably too small to fit a theoretical distribution with any statistical confidence, although it may be appropriate to construct a histogram to assist in finding a representative distribution.
- Statistical theory suggests that if we assume arrivals are one at a time, the number of arrivals in a time interval is independent of the number of arrivals in the earlier time interval, and the arrival rate is independent of time (over short time periods this may be true), then arrival times can be represented by a Poisson process, and thus, interarrival times can be represented using the exponential distribution.
- The triangular distribution is often used when there is a lack of data. Here, the parameters of the distribution can be estimated by consulting personnel with knowledge of the process or planned process. For the triangular distribution, it will be necessary to estimate the range parameters (minimum value and maximum value) and the most likely parameter.
- Process durations can be represented using a uniform or triangular distribution with the minimum and maximum values at a percentage variability from the mean. For example, a mean of 100 with a variability of ±20% would give values for a triangular distribution of 80 for minimum, 100 for most likely and 120 for maximum.

Table 5.1 Example Distribution Type by Modelling Area

Modelling Area	Distribution
Interarrival times	Exponential
Process/activity duration	Gamma, Weibull, log-normal, triangle
Other elements: failure time	Exponential, Weibull

- The normal distribution may be used when an unbounded (i.e. the lower and upper levels are not specified) shape is required. The normal distribution requires mean and standard deviation parameters.
- When only the minimum and maximum values are known and behaviour between those values is not known, a uniform distribution generates all values with an equal likelihood.
- The probability values at a decision point can be derived from sample data by simply calculating the number of occurrences within the sample for each decision choice. So a choice for a decision made 24 times out of a sample of 100 observation provides a probability of 0.24.

Once a potential distribution candidate is found, it is necessary to estimate the parameters of the distribution which provides the closest fit to the data. The relative goodness of fit can be determined by using an appropriate statistical method. Examples of 'goodness of fit' tests include the chi-square test, the Kolmogorov-Smirnov test and the Anderson-Darling test. See Law (2015) for more details on these tests and the procedure. Figure 5.1 shows an example of a histogram of sample data – in this case, machine breakdown events in a factory. A Poisson distribution has been fitted to the data using a chi-square test.

Although in this case a spreadsheet has been used for the analysis (see Greasley, 2004), most simulation practitioners use a statistical software package to undertake the matching

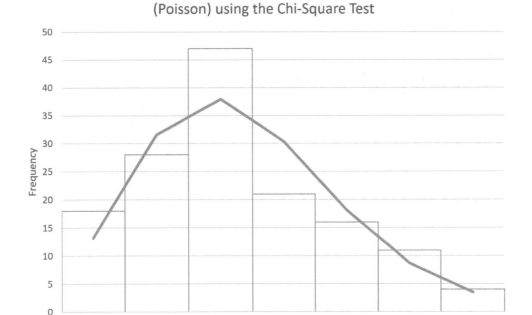

Figure 5.1 Histogram of breakdowns and fitted Poisson distribution using the chi-square test

process, such as the Input Analyzer for Arena (see chapter 5A) and Stat:Fit for Simio (see chapter 5B) and Simul8 (see chapter 5C). It should be noted that if a statistical software package is employed, then the software will simply find the best mathematical fit of the data to a distribution. Because the software can check against a wide range of theoretical distributions, then in some instances, it may make sense to choose a distribution which offers a very close fit rather than the closest fit. This is in order to employ a distribution that is suggested by statistical theory. For example, this may mean choosing an exponential distribution for interarrivals even if it is not the closest fit. This decision will need to be made based on the experience and intuition of the simulation practitioner.

The following provides details of some of the potential continuous and discrete theoretical distributions that could be used to represent variability. These represent a subset of the distributions available in simulation software packages, such as Arena, Simio and Simul8. A wider selection of distributions is covered in Law (2015).

Continuous Distributions

Continuous distributions can return any real value quantity and are often used to model interarrival times, timing and duration of breakdown events, and process durations. For a continuous random variable, the mapping from real numbers to probability values is governed by a probability density function *F(x)*. A number of continuous distributions are now shown. Please note that these are examples and the distribution shape will change depending on the parameter values chosen. The shape of the distribution is described by its skewness (the asymmetry of the distribution about its mean) and its kurtosis (the degree of peakedness of the distribution).

Beta

The beta distribution is used in project management networks for process duration. It is most often used when there is limited data available from which to derive a distribution. It can also be used to model proportions such as defective items as the distribution can only go between 0 and 1. The parameters beta and alpha provide a wide range of possible distribution shapes (figure 5.2).

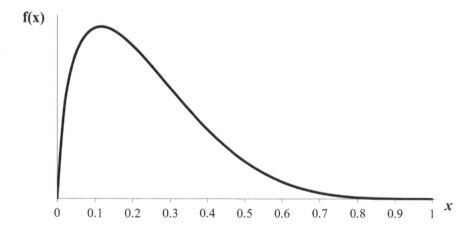

Figure 5.2 Beta (beta, alpha) distribution

Exponential

The exponential distribution (which may also be referred to as the negative exponential) is used for independent interarrival events or time between process failures. As such, it is often used to represent the interarrival time between customers or orders, where the majority of arrivals occur quite close together with occasional long gaps between arrivals. When used to represent process failures, the exponential should only be used when the history of the process is not relevant to future failure times (so if past tool wear is a factor in equipment breakdown, the exponential should not be used). This is because the exponential distribution has 'no memory' of previous events (figure 5.3).

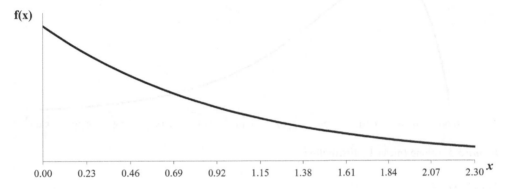

Figure 5.3 Exponential (mean) distribution

Gamma

The gamma distribution has parameters alpha (shape) and beta (scale), which determine a wide range of distribution shapes. The gamma distribution is used to measure process duration. When the shape parameter is close to 1, exponential-like distributions may be a close fit, and when the shape parameter is close to 2, Weibull-like distributions may be a close fit (figure 5.4).

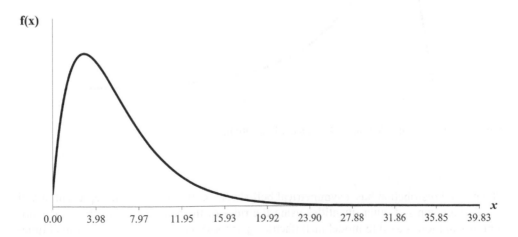

Figure 5.4 Gamma (beta, alpha) distribution

Erlang

The distribution is Erlang when the shape (skew) parameter k is an integer (typically, values between 2 and 5 are used). The Erlang distribution is used to model several sequential and independent service phases within one distribution when the parameter k is used to represent the number of service phases (figure 5.5).

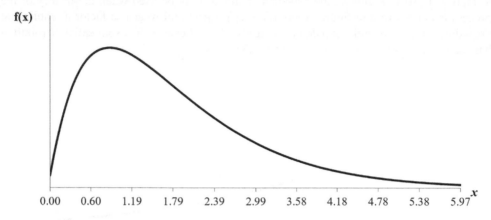

Figure 5.5 Erlang (mean, k) distribution

Log-Normal

The log-normal distribution is used to model the product of a large number of random quantities. Its shape is similar to the gamma distribution, and it can also be used to represent process durations, in particular those that have a relatively low amount of variability (figure 5.6).

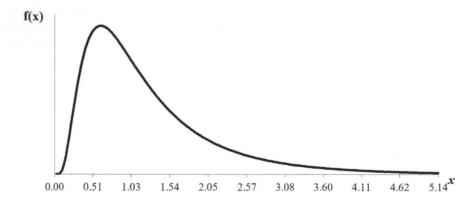

Figure 5.6 Log-normal (log mean, log standard deviation) distribution

Normal

The normal distribution has a symmetrical bell-shaped curve. It is used to represent quantities that are sums of other quantities using the rules of the central limit theorem. The normal distribution is used to model manufacturing and service process times and travel times. Because the theoretical range covers negative values, the distribution should be used with care for positive quantities such as process durations. A truncated normal distribution may be used to eliminate negative values, or the log-normal distribution may be an appropriate alternative (figure 5.7).

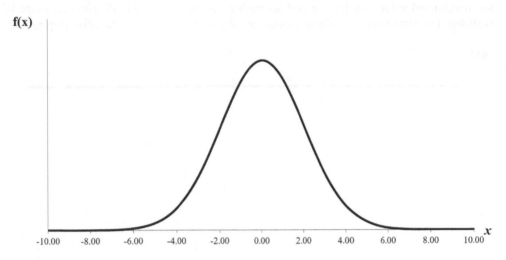

Figure 5.7 Normal (mean, standard deviation) distribution

Triangular

The triangular distribution is difficult to match with any physical process but is useful for an approximate match when few data points are available, and the minimum, mode (most likely) and maximum values can be estimated. Thus, the triangular distribution might be used when requesting an estimate of minimum, maximum and most likely times from the process owner. What can be a useful property of the triangular distribution is that the values it generates are bounded by the minimum and maximum value parameters. The mean value is calculated by (minimum + mode + maximum)/3 (figure 5.8).

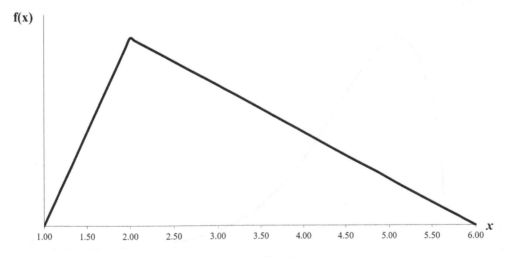

Figure 5.8 Triangular (minimum, mode, maximum) distribution

Uniform

This distribution has a rectangular shape and specifies that every value between a minimum and maximum value is equally likely. It is sometimes used when only the range (minimum and maximum) values are known and no further information on the distribution shape is available, but a triangular distribution would usually provide a better alternative (figure 5.9).

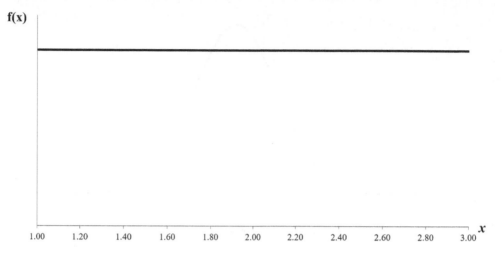

Figure 5.9 Uniform (minimum, maximum) distribution

Weibull

The Weibull distribution can be used to measure reliability in a system made up of a number of parts. The assumptions are that the parts fail independently and a single part failure will cause a system failure. If a failure is more likely to occur as the activity ages, then an alpha (shape) value of more than one should be used. The distribution can also be used to model process duration (figure 5.10).

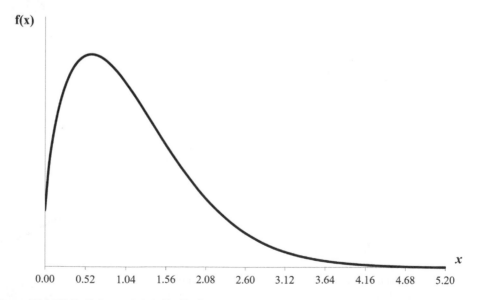

Figure 5.10 Weibull (beta, alpha) distribution

Discrete Distributions

Discrete distributions return only whole-number or integer values and are used to model whole-number values, such as decision choices, batch sizes and customer numbers. For a discrete random variable, the mapping from discrete numbers to probability values is governed by the probability mass function *P(x)*. The binomial and Poisson discrete distributions are now shown.

Binomial

The binomial distribution is used to model repeated independent trials such as the number of defective items in a batch, the number of people in a group or the probability of error (figure 5.11).

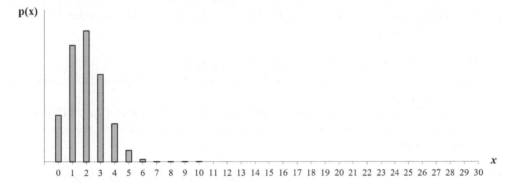

Figure 5.11 Binomial (probability, trials) distribution

Poisson

The Poisson distribution can model-independent events separated by an interval of time. If the time interval is exponentially distributed, then the number of events that occur in the interval has a Poisson distribution. It can also be used to model random variation in batch sizes (figure 5.12)

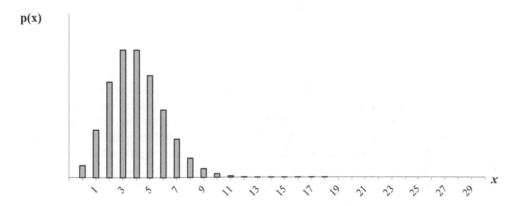

Figure 5.12 Poisson (mean) distribution

Dependent and Non-stationary Processes

When using the previously mentioned distribution fitting procedures, it is important to recognise that they are based on the assumption of independent and identically distributed data. However, this may not always be the case; for example, weekly demand amounts may be partly based on inventory held, which is based on previous order amounts. This example requires a time-series model in which the correlations between the observations in the series, termed autocorrelation, are taken into account.

Another issue is when input processes change over time, they are termed non-stationary processes. For example, many arrival patterns, such as customer arrivals in service systems, vary greatly with time due to outside factors such as lunch breaks and customer behaviour and are thus modelled as non-stationary Poisson processes. In order to model this behaviour, periods of time when the arrival rate remains constant must be identified (e.g. for each hour of the day) and an arrival rate calculated for each time period per unit of time. It should be noted that simply changing the parameter (e.g. mean) value of the distribution for each time period will generally cause incorrect results, and the following method should be used.

1   Determine the maximum arrival rate for all time periods.
2   Generate arrivals using a stationary Poisson process (i.e. exponential distribution between arrivals).
3   'Thin out' the arrivals by only allowing them to enter the system with a probability of the arrival rate for the current time period divided by the maximum arrival rate determined in the first step.

Details are provided on how to model non-stationary processes in Arena (chapter 7A) and Simio (chapter 7B).

3. Empirical Distribution

An empirical or user-defined distribution is a distribution that has been obtained directly from raw data. This could take the form of a summary of event log data as used by process mining software. An empirical distribution is usually chosen if a reasonable fit cannot be made with the data and a theoretical distribution. A disadvantage is that it lacks the capability of a theoretical distribution to be easily scaled (by adjusting its parameters) for simulation scenario analysis. Most simulation practitioners use a statistical software package to define an empirical distribution, such as the Input Analyzer for Arena (see chapter 7A) and Stat:Fit for Simio (see chapter 7B) and Simul8 (see chapter 7C).

4. Bootstrapping

This approach involves sampling randomly from raw data, which may be held in a table or spreadsheet. This creates a discrete distribution with values drawn from a data set and with their probabilities being generated by the number of times they appear in the data set. This method does not involve the traditional methods of fitting the data to a theoretical or empirical distribution and thus may be relevant when these traditional methods do not produce a distribution that appears to fit the data acceptably. This approach will only generate data values that occur within the sampled data set, and so the method benefits from large data sets to ensure that the full range of values that might be generated are present in the data set. For example, occasionally, large service times may have an important effect on waiting time metrics, and so the data set should be large enough to ensure these are represented.

5. Mathematical Equation

Examples of this approach in DES include the following use of mathematical equations to compute:

- The choice of customers using self-service or face-to-face hotel check-in facilities.
- The shortest path to determine customer movements in a retail store.
- Worker performance in terms of job accuracy and job speed.
- The selection of tasks from a queue dependent on workload and task importance.
- The choice of service provider depending on variables, including queue length for service, distance to the service provider and service process duration.
- The effect of operator fatigue on task duration.

The most common use of mathematical equations is the use of learning curve equations which predict the improvement in productivity that can occur as experience of a process is gained. If an estimate can be made of the rate at which a process time will decrease due to increased competence over time, then more accurate model predictions can be made. Mathematically, the learning curve is represented by the function

$$Y = ax^b$$

where
y represents the process time of the xth process activation,
a is the initial process time,
x is the number of process activations and
b equals ln p/ln 2.
Here, $\ln = \log_{10}$ and p is the learning rate (e.g. 80% = 0.8).
Thus, for an 80% learning curve,
$b = \ln 0.8 / \ln 2 = -0.322$.

To implement the learning curve effect in the simulation, a matrix can be used, which holds the current process time for the combination of each process and each person undertaking this process. When a process is activated in the simulation, the process time is updated, taking into account the learning undertaken by the individual operator on that particular process. The use of the learning curve equation addresses the assumption that all operators within a system are equally competent at each process at a point in time. The log-linear learning curve is the most popular and simplest learning curve equation and takes into account only the initial process time and the workers learning rate. Other learning curve equations can be used, which take into account other factors such as the fraction of machine time that is used to undertake the process. Examples of constructing a mathematical equation for a DES, such as a learning curve equation, are contained in Nembhard (2014), Dode et al. (2016) and Malachowski and Korytkowski (2016).

6. Cognitive Architectures

When attempting to model human behaviour in a simulation model, the use of cognitive models can be employed. An example is the use of the Psi theory, which is a theory about how cognition, motivation and emotion control human behaviour. Here, task performance can be modelled over time, showing how competence oscillates based on experienced success and failure at a new task. This approach provides an alternative to the traditional learning curve effect, which implies a continuous improvement over time without any setbacks in performance due to failures. Another cognitive model that has been used is the theory of planned behaviour, which takes empirical data on demographic variables and personality traits and transforms these into attitudes toward behaviour, subject norms and perceived behavioural control. Cognitive architectures used to represent the cognitive process include the physical, emotional, cognitive and social (PECS) architecture (Schmidt, 2000) and the theory of planned behaviour (TPB) (Ajzen, 1991). Examples of their use in the context of DES are in the works of Riedel et al. (2009) and Brailsford et al. (2012).

7. Machine Learning

Machine learning (ML) techniques are increasingly being used in simulation projects. While simulation is based on a model of a system, ML generates a model of behaviour from the relationship between input data and output data. The combined use of simulation and ML falls under a hybrid modelling approach (see chapter 13).

A decision tree is an example of a representation of an ML algorithm that is not 'black box', and thus it is possible to trace the path by which an outcome is reached. This makes them ideal for modelling as they can be translated into if-then-else statements for use in the simulation model. Figure 5.13 provides a simple example of a credit application decision tree.

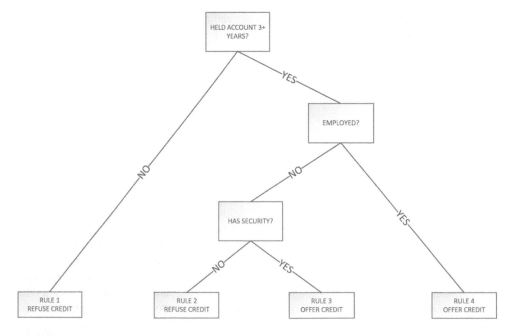

Figure 5.13 Decision tree for credit application

The decision tree can then be directly converted to program code, as shown in the following section. The rules derived are indicated by the comments to the right of the code. This program code can then be used in the simulation model, for example, in a conditional decision at a decision point.

```
IF Held Account 3+ Years THEN
IF Employed THEN
Offer Credit        {Rule 4}
ELSE
IF Has Security THEN
Offer Credit        {Rule 3}
ELSE
Refuse Credit       {Rule 2}
ENDIF
ENDIF
ELSE
Refuse Credit       {Rule 1}
ENDIF
```

8. Trace

Trace-driven simulations use historical process data or real-time information directly. An example would be a simulation of a historical demand pattern (for example, actual customer or order arrival times) in order to compare the current process design with a proposed process design. The advantage of a trace or data-driven simulation is that validation can be achieved by a direct comparison of model performance metrics to real system performance over a historical time period. In addition, model credibility is enhanced as the client can observe model behaviour replicating real-life events. The disadvantages are the need for suitable data availability and the possible restriction in scope derived from a single trace that may not reflect the full variability of the process behaviour. Trace simulation is normally used for understanding process behaviour (descriptive analytics) and for checking conformance to the 'official' process design and cannot be used for predictive analytics such as scenario analysis as it only contains historical data. Trace simulation is similar to process mining which uses historical event logs, although process mining can check conformance of the process map in addition to operational process performance. A summary of the trace can be used to form an empirical distribution.

Summary of Modelling Methods

Table 5.2 provides guidance on the various descriptive modelling methods:

Table 5.2 Descriptive Modelling Methods

	Disadvantages	*Advantages*	*Comments*
Estimation	Lack of accuracy.	May be the only option.	May be used in the model development phase before further data collection is undertaken.

(*Continued*)

Table 5.2 (Continued)

	Disadvantages	Advantages	Comments
Theoretical distribution	No available theoretical distributions may fit data. Generates values outside of the data range which may not be appropriate.	Can 'smooth' data to the underlying distribution. Generates values outside of data sampled. For example, rare events at the tail of the distribution which may be missing from a small data sample collected. Compact method of representing data values. Distribution is easy to scale for scenario analysis.	Best choice if a reasonable data fit can be made.
Empirical distribution	Cannot usually generate values outside the range of data (therefore may miss 'extreme' values). Difficult to scale for scenario analysis.	Provides distribution when no theoretical distribution provides an adequate fit to data.	An option if no theoretical distribution can be fit.
Bootstrapping	Distributions are derived only from values held in the data set.	Avoids an issue of poorly fitted distributions.	Likely to require large data set to ensure coverage of a full range of data values.
Equation	May require extensive data collection.	Shows relationships that are a consequence of simulated time, such as learning effects.	Can be useful for expressing relationships between variables.
Cognitive	Difficult to validate cognitive models.	Attempts to model factors leading to individual human behaviour.	Limited use due to demanding data collection and validation needs.
Machine learning	Using some ML techniques, the logic implemented may not be inspected.	Can employ complex logic processes.	Need for modeller to have analytic skillset. May require interface between simulation and ML software.
Trace	Only uses values held in the data set.	Replicates reality to check for conformance.	Not suitable for prediction.

What Variability Are We Modelling?

When modelling variability, we need to consider both the granularity of our modelling and the need to distinguish the 'normal' variability we wish to model and variability caused by a change in the process.

In terms of granularity, we need to ensure that we model variability at a sufficient level of detail to ensure that it can be represented correctly. For example, if data is collected of the checkout process at a supermarket, this will entail placing goods onto a conveyor, scanning the items by the checkout operative and then paying for the items. To collect data on the overall process ignores that the conveyor and scanning process times are dependent on the number of items being bought while the payment process is not. Thus, if we are using the method of fitting to a theoretical distribution, the overall process should not be fitted to a single distribution but broken down for analysis. As well as sequential processes, care should also be taken with parallel processes in which different options may require fitting to separate distributions. For example, mutually exclusive payment types (cash, card, touch payment) will have different distributions.

In addition, we need to note that the theoretical distribution represents the normal variability, which is inevitable and what we would expect of a process design operating in a given environment. We can only remove this variability by improving the design of the process. If the variability is normal (i.e. the variability is due to random causes only), then the process is in a stable state of statistical equilibrium, and for example, if we are modelling using a probability distribution, then the parameters of its probability distribution are unchanging. Conversely, if the performance variability is abnormal (i.e. due to a change in process procedures or environment, for example), then the abnormal variability disturbs the state of the statistical equilibrium of the process leading to a change in the parameters of the distribution.

Summary

Eight input modelling methods are presented in this chapter: estimation, theoretical distribution, empirical distribution, bootstrapping, mathematical equation, cognitive architectures, machine learning and trace. The most common approach employed in DES is the theoretical distribution method, which provides a compact method of representing data values, with the distribution easy to scale for scenario analysis.

Exercises

- Compare and contrast theoretical and empirical distribution input modelling methods.
- Evaluate the trace input modelling method for a simulation study.
- Evaluate the use of machine learning as an input modelling method.
- Compare the process of deriving a theoretical and empirical distribution.
- A number of observations have been made of arrivals to a supermarket (see table 5.3). The frequency of arrivals in a ten-minute period is as follows. Using a chi-square 'goodness of fit' test, find if the arrivals can be described by a Poisson distribution with a mean of 1 at a significance level of 0.1.

Table 5.3 Supermarket Arrivals

Number of Arrivals	Frequency
0	70
1	80
2	34
3	12
4	4
Total	200

Table 5.4 Customer Serve Time

Serve Time (minutes)	Observed Relative Cumulative Frequency
Less than 1	0.02
Less than 2	0.29
Less than 3	0.54
Less than 4	0.59
Less than 5	0.90
Less than 6	0.95
Less than 7	1.00

Table 5.5 Arrival Times

4.9	4.4	3.8	5.9	4.6
2.9	3.9	3.8	6.8	5.3
3.5	1.3	3.1	4.3	3.5
6.5	5.3	4.6	5.1	3.5
5.4	4.3	4.7	3.7	3.8
5.5	2.6	6.2	4.5	8.8
3.3	6.5	7.2	2.8	6.2
5.0	6.9	3.9	7.6	5.3
2.7	1.9	2.0	5.2	4.6
5.1	4.3	2.4	4.6	7.9

- A number of observations have been taken of customers being served at a cafeteria (see table 5.4). Analysis has revealed a mean of 2 minutes and a standard deviation of 0.5 minutes for the data. Investigate using a Kolmogorov-Smirnov test that the observations are normally distributed at a significance level of 0.1.
- The following data has been collected on arrival times (see table 5.5). Find the parameters of an empirical distribution that fits the data.

References

Ajzen, A. (1991) The theory of planned behaviour, *Organizational Behaviour and Decision Processes*, 50(2), 179–211.

Brailsford, S.C., Harper, P.R. and Sykes, J. (2012) Incorporating human behaviour in simulation models of screening for breast cancer, *European Journal of Operational Research*, 219(3), 491–507.

Dode, P., Greig, M., Zolfaghari, S. and Neumann, W.P. (2016) Integrating human factors into discrete event simulation: A proactive approach to simultaneously design for system performance and employees' well-being, *International Journal of Production Research*, 54(10), 3105–3117.

Greasley, A. (2004) *Simulation Modelling for Business*, Ashgate Limited.

Greasley, A. and Owen, C. (2016) Behavior in models: A framework for representing human behavior, in M. Kunc, J. Malpass, and L. White (eds.) *Behavioral Operational Research: Theory, Methodology and Practice*, Palgrave Macmillan.

Law, A.M. (2015) *Simulation Modeling and Analysis*, 5th edition, McGraw-Hill Education.

Malachowski, B. and Korytkowski, P. (2016) Competence-based performance model of multi-skilled workers, *Computers and Industrial Engineering*, 91, 165–177.

Nembhard, D.A. (2014) Cross training efficiency and flexibility with process change, *International Journal of Operations and Production Management*, 34(11), 1417–1439.

Riedel, R., Mueller, E., Von Der Weth, R. and Pflugradt, N. (2009) Integrating human behaviour into factory simulation – A feasibility study, *IEEM 2009 – IEEE International Conference on Industrial Engineering and Engineering Management*, 2089–2093.

Schmidt, B. (2000) *The Modelling of Human Behaviour*, SCS Publications.

5A: Deriving Theoretical and Empirical Distributions Using Arena

Introduction

The Arena software incorporates an Input Analyzer software tool (on the Arena Tools menu), which provides facilities to derive theoretical and empirical distributions. The Input Analyzer is a separate application to Arena, so it may be necessary to run it from Windows (use Windows Search for Input Analyzer to find the application). This chapter also covers how to generate non-stationary arrivals in Arena.

Deriving Theoretical Distributions Using the Arena Input Analyzer Tool

The following steps are required to save data in the required format for the Input Analyzer and then undertake the analysis.

1   Enter your sample data in a numeric format in an Excel spreadsheet in column A only and save it as a text file (use the CSV (MS-DOS) option on the Excel Save As pull-down menu). For arrival data, you will need the interarrival times in column A. This means that you may need to subtract the consecutive times of the arrival data from one another to obtain the time-between-arrival (i.e. interarrival) values that are placed in column A. For process times, you may need to subtract 'start of process' times from 'end of process' times to obtain the process duration values that are placed in column A.
2   Run the Input Analyzer application from the Arena tools menu or from Windows.
3   Select File/New, then File/Data File/Use Existing.
4   Select the file you have saved from your spreadsheet. A histogram of the data will be displayed. Select the Fit/Fit All option.
5   Select Window/Fit All Summary for a ranked (best-to-worst) list of the fit for all the distributions. This list should be used as a guide only as often a number of distributions will show a similar result on this test, and the best-fit distribution should not automatically be chosen. Usually, the distribution fit tests can be used in an advisory role to provide evidence against a choice of distribution made based on the knowledge the modeller has of the real process.
6   To fit to a particular distribution, use the Fit option and pick the distribution from the list. Arena will display the nearest fit to the data (measured by the square error) for that distribution type. Figure 5A.1 shows a plot of the theoretical distribution superimposed on the sample data histogram. Note that the apparent level of fit shown by the graphical display will be dependent on the width of the histogram cells, so it may be useful to

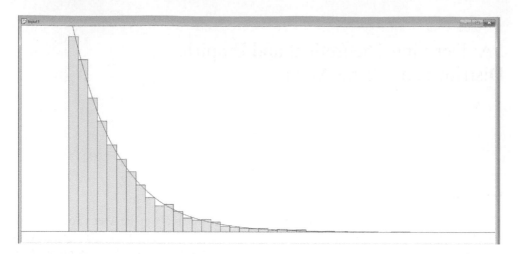

Figure 5A.1 Arena Input Analyzer histogram

alter the number of cell divisions to provide a fuller perspective on the fit. A distribution summary report below the histogram provides information on the specification of the theoretical distribution and the goodness of fit with the sample data (figure 5A.2). Arena calculates the parameters for the chosen distribution type. In this case, the mean parameter for the exponential distribution is given as 4.97, giving an Arena expression of EXPO (4.97). The 'goodness of fit' information is given with a chi-square analysis providing a p-value of 0.432. For these tests, a higher p-value indicates a better fit between the collected data and the theoretical distribution formed. A p-value of less than around 0.05 indicates a not-very-good fit, while if the p-value is greater than 0.1, then we would have a fair degree of confidence that the theoretical distribution represents the data, assuming that the sample size is sufficient for the test.

7   Copy and paste the chosen distribution expression – in this case, EXPO (4.97) – into your block in your ARENA model. This may be a CREATE block for a time between arrivals or a PROCESS block for a process duration.

Deriving Empirical Distributions Using the Arena Input Analyzer Tool

The Arena Input Analyzer allows both discrete and continuous empirical distributions to be formed using the Fit/Empirical option. In Arena, select the Input Analyzer using the Tools/ Input Analyzer option. Select File/New and then select File/Data File/Use Existing. Select the file containing the data, and a histogram of the data will be generated. Select the Fit/ Empirical option, and Arena will display the empirical distribution as in figure 5A.3.

The distribution is given a list of probabilities and values to return a real-valued quantity (figure 5A.4). The values given by the Input Analyzer should be used in conjunction with the Arena CONTINUOUS expression. The values are interpreted as follows: 0.184, 1.05 provides a 18.4% chance that the number generated will be between 0 and 0.345, 2.1

```
Distribution Summary

Distribution:   Exponential
Expression:     EXPO(4.97)
Square Error:   0.000169

Chi Square Test
  Number of intervals   = 25
  Degrees of freedom    = 23
  Test Statistic        = 23.6
  Corresponding p-value = 0.432

Kolmogorov-Smirnov Test
  Test Statistic        = 0.00995
  Corresponding p-value > 0.15

          Data Summary

Number of Data Points   = 5000
Min Data Value          = 0.000131
Max Data Value          = 41.6
Sample Mean             = 4.97
Sample Std Dev          = 4.97

         Histogram Summary

Histogram Range         = 0 to 42
Number of Intervals     = 40
```

Figure 5A.2 Arena Input Analyzer theoretical distribution statistical summary

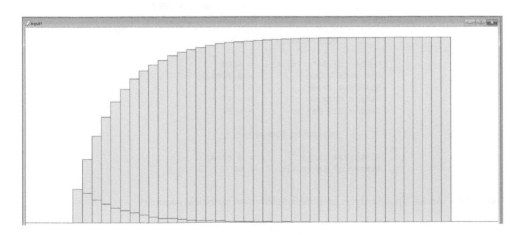

Figure 5A.3 Arena Input Analyzer empirical distribution

```
                 Distribution Summary

Distribution:   Empirical
Expression:     CONT or DISC (0.000,  0.000,
                              0.184,  1.050,
                              0.345,  2.100,
                              0.470,  3.150,
                              0.574,  4.200,
                              0.655,  5.250,
                              0.722,  6.300,
                              0.778,  7.350,
                              0.821,  8.400,
                              0.853,  9.450,
                              0.877, 10.500,
                              0.903, 11.550,
                              0.922, 12.600,
                              0.935, 13.650,
                              0.946, 14.700,
                              0.958, 15.750,
                              0.967, 16.800,
                              0.972, 17.850,
                              0.977, 18.900,
                              0.980, 19.950,
                              0.983, 21.000,
                              0.987, 22.050,
                              0.989, 23.100,
                              0.991, 24.150,
                              0.993, 25.200,
                              0.995, 26.250,
                              0.996, 27.300,
                              0.997, 28.350,
                              0.998, 29.400,
                              0.998, 30.450,
                              0.998, 31.500,
                              0.998, 32.550,
                              0.999, 33.600,
                              0.999, 34.650,
                              0.999, 35.700,
                              0.999, 36.750,
                              1.000, 37.800,
                              1.000, 38.850,
                              1.000, 39.900,
                              1.000, 40.950,
                              1.000, 42.000)


                 Data Summary

Number of Data Points    = 5000
Min Data Value           = 0.000131
Max Data Value           = 41.6
Sample Mean              = 4.97
Sample Std Dev           = 4.97

               Histogram Summary

Histogram Range          = 0 to 42
Number of Intervals      = 40
```

Figure 5A.4 Arena Input Analyzer empirical distribution statistical summary

provides a 16.1% (0.345–0.184) chance that the number generated will be between 1.05 and 2.1, and so on.

Generating Non-stationary Arrivals in Arena

The ability to generate non-stationary arrivals is important because many manufacturing and service systems experience arrival rates that vary dramatically over time. For example, a food retailer may experience an increase in demand during lunch hours. A probabilistic model for this, the non-stationary Poisson process, can be used to reflect time-varying arrival patterns in an accurate manner. To deal with time-varying patterns, we can identify periods over which the arrival rate is fairly flat (say, 30-minute slots, but each slot period can vary) and then count the number of arrivals in each of these slots. From that, a rate of arrival for each slot can be calculated. In Arena, we can then use the Create and Schedule modules to implement non-stationary arrivals. Note that you may also need to model non-stationary (time-varying) processes in your model. For example, when resource availability that is required to execute the processes varies over time.

Arena has the ability to generate non-stationary Poisson arrivals in the Create module. To enter non-stationary arrivals, do the following. In the Create module, choose the 'Time Between Arrivals' Type option as Schedule. This creates an arrival schedule, which in this case is named Schedule 1 (figure 5A.5).

In the data definition template, select the Schedule module. In the spreadsheet view, the schedule 'Schedule 1' will appear. Select the type 'Arrival' and time units as 'Hours'. Click on the duration, and a table can be created specifying the arrival rate for each defined time period or slot (figure 5A.6). Note the arrival rate value must be per hour, whatever units

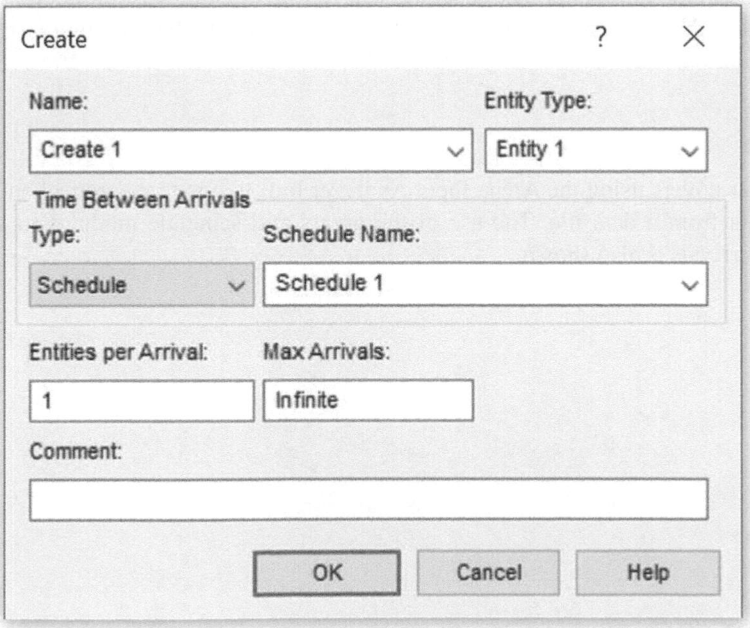

Figure 5A.5 Choosing the schedule arrival option in Arena

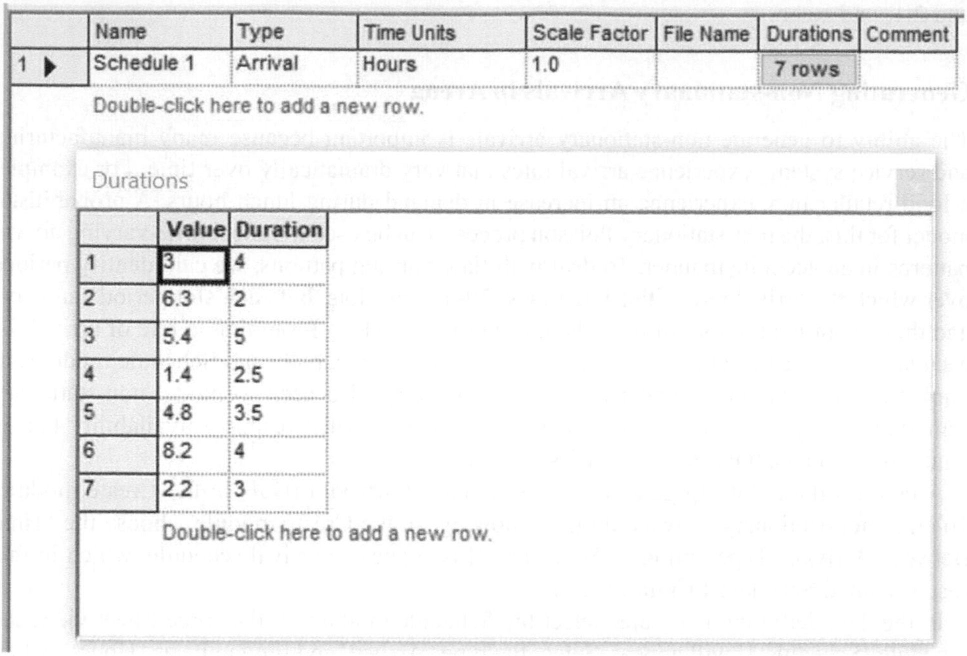

	Name	Type	Time Units	Scale Factor	File Name	Durations	Comment
1 ▶	Schedule 1	Arrival	Hours	1.0		7 rows	

Double-click here to add a new row.

Durations

	Value	Duration
1	3	4
2	6.3	2
3	5.4	5
4	1.4	2.5
5	4.8	3.5
6	8.2	4
7	2.2	3

Double-click here to add a new row.

Figure 5A.6 Entering non-stationary arrival rates in the Arena schedule module

are specified in the time units. The schedule will repeat when the last duration has occurred unless the last duration is specified as Infinite. In that case, the duration will last for the rest of the simulation run.

Summary

This chapter covers using the Arena Input Analyzer tool to create theoretical and empirical distributions from a data file. The use of the create and schedule modules to create non-stationary arrivals is also shown.

5B: Deriving Theoretical and Empirical Distributions Using Simio

Introduction

The Simio simulation software does not provide distribution fitting capabilities, and it is suggested to use third-party packages such as StatFit (www.geerms.com), @RISK (www.palisade.com), ExpertFit (www.averill-law.com) and Easyfit (www.mathwave.com). This chapter demonstrates the use of the StatFit package. This chapter also covers how to generate non-stationary arrivals in Simio.

Deriving Theoretical Distributions Using the StatFit Package

1   Enter your sample data in a numeric format in an Excel spreadsheet and copy it to the clipboard. For arrival data, you will need the interarrival times. This means that you may need to subtract the consecutive 'time of arrival' data samples from one another to obtain the 'time between arrival' (i.e. interarrival) values. For process times, you may need to subtract 'start of process' times from 'end of process' times to obtain the process duration values.
2   Run the StatFit application from Windows.
3   Right-click on the data table window and paste your data into the window (figure 5B.1).

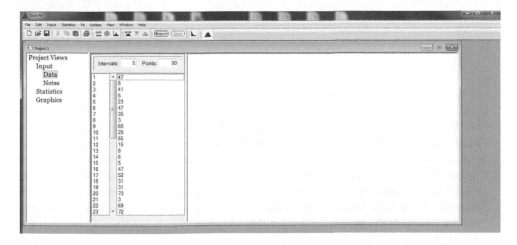

Figure 5B.1 Data pasted into the StatFit Data window

4   Click on the Setup icon on the menu and click on Select All. Click OK.

5   Click on the Auto-Fit icon and select the continuous distribution and unbounded options. Click on OK, and the distribution list should appear (figure 5B.2). StatFit calculates the parameters for the chosen distribution type. In this case, the parameters for the normal distribution are given as 31.4 and 23.7. The aforementioned tells you that you can fit the arrival data to the top three distributions, and the other (uniform) distribution tested is not appropriate. StatFit calculates a rank value for each distribution fitted that indicates the relative goodness of fit of that distribution to the input data compared to the other distributions used. While a good rank usually indicates that the fitted distribution is a good representation of the input data, it should not be used blindly. You should always also consider such issues as the type of input process involved (this example is an arrival process), the detailed results of the 'goodness of fit' tests and the graphical fit to the data (double-click on the distribution names to see the fit), as well as any issues with the quality of the data.

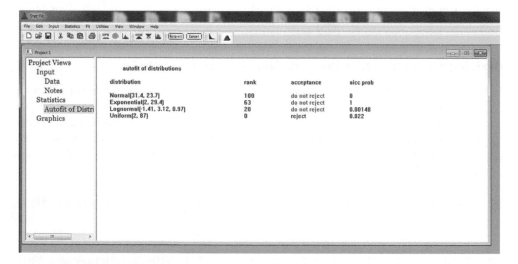

Figure 5B.2 Autofit of distributions

6   Double-click on the distribution names to see the fit histogram (figure 5B.3).

7   Click on the Fit icon on the menu to run the 'goodness of fit' test. Figure 5B.4 shows the test for the exponential distribution, but the tests for the other fitted distributions are also available by scrolling down the screen. The null hypothesis is that the selected distribution fits the input data. This means when the distribution is at the level of significance specified, 'Do Not Reject' will be displayed. Alternatively, the p-value can be used for these tests. A higher p-value indicates a better fit between the collected data and the theoretical distribution formed. A p-value of less than around 0.05 indicates a not-very-good fit, while if the p-value is greater than 0.1, then we would have a fair degree of confidence that the theoretical distribution represents the data, assuming that the sample size is sufficient for the test.

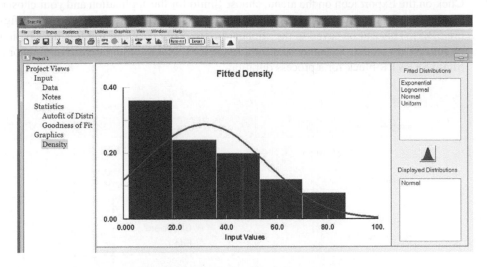

Figure 5B.3 Fitted density for normal distribution

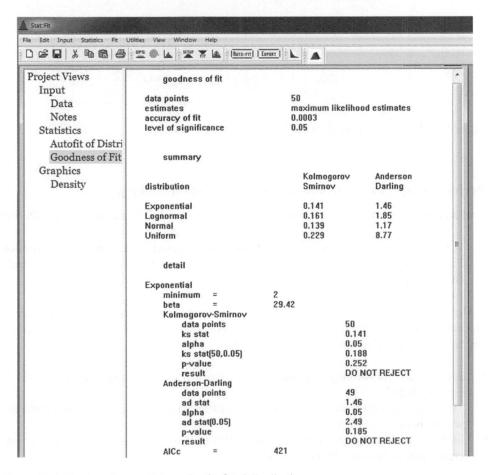

Figure 5B.4 The 'goodness of fit' test for the fitted distributions

8   Click on the Export icon on the menu, choose Simio for the application and your chosen distribution for the fitted distribution. Your Simio distribution should be displayed (figure 5B.5). This can be saved to the clipboard or to a file. You can use this distribution in your Simio model. This may be a Simio SOURCE block for an interarrival time or a Simio SERVER block for a process duration.

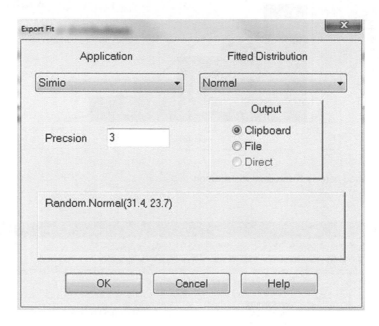

Figure 5B.5 Fitted distribution shown in Simio format

Deriving Empirical Distributions Using the StatFit Package

StatFit allows continuous empirical distributions to be formed. For an empirical distribution:

1   Select the Export option from the File menu and then select the Export Empirical option.
2   From the menu, select either a continuous or discrete distribution and select the cumulative option (figure 5B.6).

The distribution is given a list of probabilities and values to return a real-valued quantity. The values given by StatFit should be used in conjunction with the Simio Random.Continuous function. The values are interpreted as follows:

- 2 (value), 0 (probability) provides a 0% chance that the number generated will be between 0 and 2.
- 19 (value), 0.36 (probability) provides a 36% (0.36–0) chance that the number generated will be between 2 and 19.
- 36 (value) and 0.6 (probability) provides a 24% (0.6–0.36) chance that the number generated will be between 19 and 36, and so on.

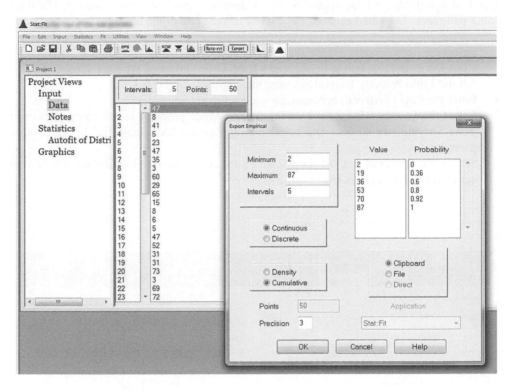

Figure 5B.6 StatFit Export Empirical distribution

The Simio function will be Random.Continuous(2,0,19,0.36,36,0.6,53,0.8,70,0.92,87,1.0). For an empirical discrete distribution the Simio function Random.Discrete can be used.

Generating Non-stationary Processes in Simio

Generating non-stationary arrivals is important because many manufacturing and service systems experience arrival rates that vary dramatically over time. For example, a food retailer may experience an increase in demand during lunch hours. A probabilistic model for this, the non-stationary Poisson process, can be used to reflect time-varying arrival patterns in an accurate manner. To deal with time-varying patterns, we can identify periods over which the arrival rate is fairly flat (say, 30-minute slots, but each slot period can vary) and then count the number of arrivals in each of these slots. From that, a rate of arrival for each slot can be calculated. In Simio, we can then use Rate Tables to implement non-stationary arrivals. Note that you may also need to model non-stationary (time-varying) processes in your model. For example, when resource availability that is required to execute the processes varies over time.

In Simio, to create a non-stationary Poisson process from a Source object, we use a Simio Rate Table. The Rate Table consists of a set of equal duration time intervals and, for each interval, the specification of the mean arrival rate. The rate of arrivals for each interval is specified in arrivals per hour, regardless of the duration specified for the interval. The Rate Table will repeat from the beginning once it reaches the end of the last time interval.

1   Select the Data window and the Rate Tables panel.
2   Click the Rate Table button to add a new Rate Table and name the Rate Table.
3   Set the Table Property Interval Size and the Number of Intervals.
4   Enter the Rate of Arrivals per Hour for each Interval (figure 5B.7).
5   Select the Facility window and set the Arrival Mode property in the Source object to Time Varying Arrival Rate and select the appropriate Rate Table for the Rate Table property.
6   Within the Source object, the Rate Scale Factor can be used to increase the arrival rate across all of the intervals (figure 5B.8).

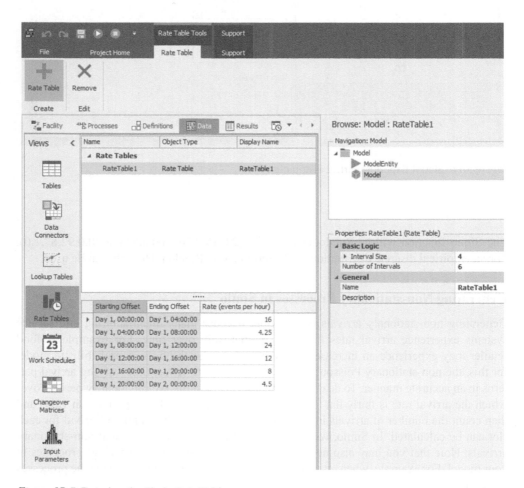

Figure 5B.7 Entering the Simio Rate Table

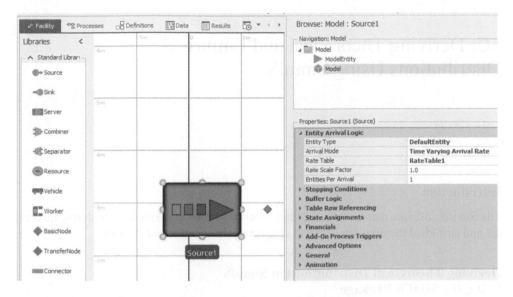

Figure 5B.8 Set the Simio source object Arrival Rate to a Rate Table

Summary

This chapter covers using Simio to create theoretical and empirical distributions from a data file. The use of the Rate Table and Source object to create non-stationary arrivals is also shown.

5C: Deriving Theoretical and Empirical Distributions Using Simul8

Introduction

The Simul8 software incorporates the StatFit (www.geerms.com) package to derive theoretical and empirical distributions. We will also create time-dependent arrivals.

Deriving Theoretical Distributions in Simul8
Using the StatFit Package

1 Enter your sample data in a numeric format in an Excel spreadsheet and copy it to the clipboard. For arrival data, you will need the interarrival times. This means that you may need to subtract consecutive 'time of arrival' data samples from one another to obtain the 'time between arrival' (interarrival) values. For process times, you may need to subtract 'start of process' times from 'end of process' times to obtain the process duration values.
2 Run the StatFit application from either the Advanced Menu in Simul8 or as a separately installed program in Windows.
3 Right-click on the data table window and paste your data into the window (figure 5C.1).
4 Click on the Setup icon on the menu and click on Select All. Click OK.

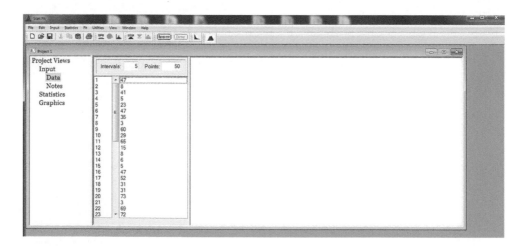

Figure 5C.1 Data pasted into the Data window

5   Click on the Auto-Fit icon and select the continuous distribution and unbounded options. Click on OK, and the distribution list should appear (figure 5C.2). StatFit calculates the parameters for the chosen distribution type. In this case, the parameters for the normal distribution are given as 31.4 and 23.7. The aforementioned tells you that you can fit the arrival data to the top three distributions, and the other distribution tested is not appropriate. StatFit calculates a rank value for each distribution fitted that indicates the relative goodness of fit of that distribution to the input data compared to the other distributions used. While a good rank usually indicates that the fitted distribution is a good representation of the input data, it should not be used blindly. You should always also consider such issues as the type of input process involved (this example is an arrival process), the detailed results of the 'goodness of fit' tests and the graphical fit to the data (double-click on the distribution names to see the fit), as well as any issues with the quality of the data.

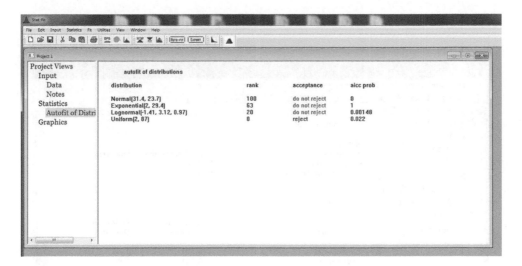

Figure 5C.2 Autofit of distributions

6   Double-click on the distribution names to see the fit histogram (figure 5C.3).
7   Click on the Fit icon on the menu to run the 'goodness of fit' test. Figure 5C.4 shows the test for the exponential distribution, but the tests for the other fitted distributions are also available by scrolling down the screen. The null hypothesis is that the selected distribution fits the input data. This means when the distribution is at the level of significance specified, 'Do Not Reject' will be displayed. Alternatively, the p-value can be used for these tests. A higher p-value indicates a better fit between the collected data and the theoretical distribution formed. A p-value of less than around 0.05 indicates a not-very-good fit, while if the p-value is greater than 0.1, then we would have a fair degree of confidence that the theoretical distribution represents the data, assuming that the sample size is sufficient for the test.

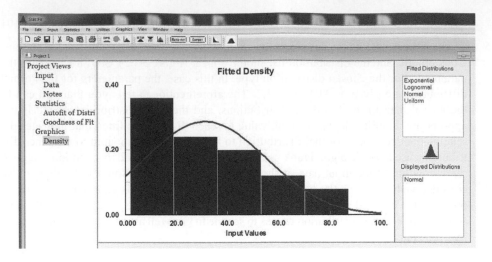

Figure 5C.3 Fitted density for normal distribution

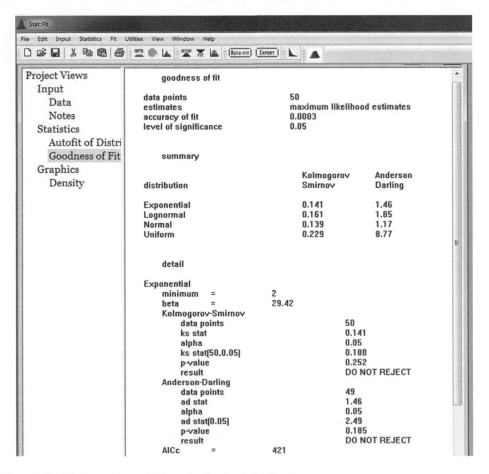

Figure 5C.4 The 'goodness of fit' test for the fitted distributions

8   Click on the Export icon on the menu and the Simul8 for the application and your chosen distribution for the fitted distribution. Your Simul8 distribution should be displayed.
This can be saved to the clipboard or to a file. You can use this distribution in your
Simul8 model. This may be a Start Point block for an interarrival time or an Activity
block for a process duration.

Deriving Empirical Distributions Using the StatFit Package

StatFit allows both discrete and continuous empirical distributions to be formed. For an
empirical distribution:

1   Select the Export option from the File menu and then select the Export Empirical option.
2   From the menu, select either a continuous or discrete distribution and select the cumulative option (figure 5C.5).

The distribution is given a list of probabilities and values to return a real-valued quantity.
The values given by StatFit should be interpreted as follows:

•   2 (value), 0 (probability) provides a 0% chance that the number generated will be
between 0 and 2.
•   19 (value), 0.36 (probability) provides a 36% (0.36–0) chance that the number generated
will be between 2 and 19.

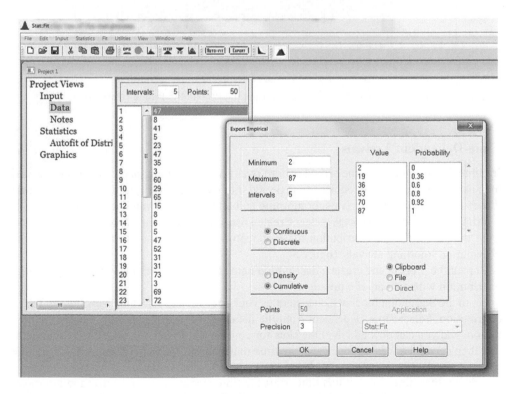

Figure 5C.5 StatFit Export Empirical distribution

- 36 (value) and 0.6 (probability) provides a 24% (0.6–0.36) chance that the number generated will be between 19 and 36, and so on.

These values can be used to construct an empirical distribution using the Create Distribution menu option on the Data and Rules tab. Select the Probability Profile option from the main menu. Choose between a discrete or continuous empirical distribution. Click on the bars in the graphical display and enter the relative frequency of each bar as a percentage. Right-click for options to add and delete bars. The named distribution can now be used in your model (see figure 5C.6).

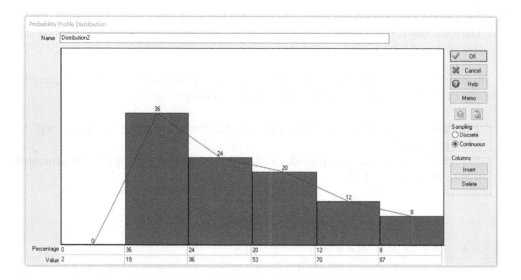

Figure 5C.6 Entering the empirical distribution using the Probability Profile Distribution

Time-Dependent Arrivals

In Simul8, we can change the arrival pattern over time by defining named distributions and then assigning them to the required time period. For example, if we wish to have a different distribution for customer arrivals for morning and afternoon, we would do the following.

From the Data and Tables tab, select Create Distributions and choose Named Distribution from the menu. Enter a distribution for exponential with a mean of 10 minutes. Name the distribution 'morning arrivals' (figure 5C.7).

Repeat the process and create a distribution named afternoon arrivals with an exponential distribution with a mean of 5 minutes.

Go to the Start Point block which generates your arrivals, and select the New button for the distribution. Select Time Dependent from the list of types of distribution. Click on the next button, and you can now add the time slots for your arrivals. Name the slot 'Arrival Pattern' and then select the Add button. Enter the time that your arrival pattern commences and the name of the distribution (figure 5C.8).

Add another time slot, but this time, start the time slot at 12:00 and select the afternoon arrivals distribution. The Arrival Pattern should look as in figure 5C.9.

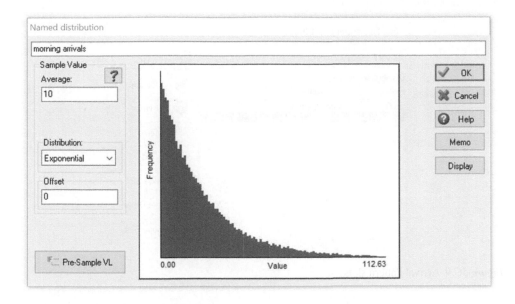

Figure 5C.7 Creating a named distribution

Figure 5C.8 Adding the time slot for the time-dependent arrivals

Figure 5C.9 Arrival Pattern slots

Figure 5C.10 Start Point using the Arrival Pattern time-dependent distribution

The Start Point will now use the Arrival Pattern distribution and so follow the 'morning arrivals' distribution from 8 to 12 and the 'afternoon arrivals' distribution for the remainder of the day (figure 5C.10). You can define additional slots; for example, you could define a different distribution for each hour in the day. You can also assign time-dependent distributions to other blocks in the model, such as activity times. Note you can also use the Day Planner to define time dependent arrivals from the Start Point block.

Summary

This chapter covers using Simul8 to create theoretical and empirical distributions from a data file. The use of time-dependent arrivals is also shown.

6 Data Collection

Introduction

Data plays an important part in the construction and use of a simulation model, and table 6.1 summarises the main types of data required (Pidd, 2009) at different stages of the simulation study.

To understand the problem situation, we use what is termed contextual data. Along with assumptions we make about the real world, this provides us with an understanding of the real system known as the system description. We then undertake an abstraction process which makes simplifications of the real system to reduce model complexity. This includes defining the scope and level of detail of the model content, along with an explanatory model (process map) and a descriptive model (input modelling). The outcome of the conceptual modelling is termed realisation data, which we use to build our computer model. We will also use data for the verification and validation process covered in chapter 8. Figure 6.1 shows the relationship between the simulation study and the data collection needs. The figure also indicates the chapter numbers relating to the transformation between the simulation study stages.

Data Requirements

We now describe the data requirements for each data type in more detail. This activity can be considered as part of the conceptual modelling stage.

Contextual Data Requirements

In terms of contextual data required for the system description, we would normally expect to collect this from discussions and interviews with personnel involved in the real system (domain experts), observations and walkthroughs of the system (a walkthrough of a factory, for example) and documentation, such as schematics of the layout of the manufacturing or service system. This will require the simulation analyst to work with a number of personnel, and aspects of these relationships are covered in the project management section of chapter 11.

Realisation Data Requirements

In terms of the realisation data for the scope and level of detail of the model, we determine what to model (scope) and how to model (level of detail) by reference to the study objectives and the system description defined earlier. At this stage, we need to know what data we can

DOI: 10.4324/9781003124092-6

Table 6.1 Main Data Types for a Simulation Study

Simulation Study Stage	Data Type	Outcome	Chapter
Conceptual modelling (problem situation)	Contextual	System description	3
Conceptual modelling	Realisation	Conceptual model	3, 4, 5
Verification and validation	Validation	Validated model	8

acquire and collect in a timely manner. For example, the decision to undertake simplification may be based on data availability issues as well as study objectives.

Figure 6.2 shows the modelling areas within the process defined by an explanatory modelling approach and the system defined using a descriptive modelling approach. Note, however, that we often have a choice on whether to model a particular aspect of the real system using the explanatory approach of chapter 4 or the descriptive approach of chapter 5.

In the explanatory modelling approach, our data requirement is limited to mostly qualitative information about the system structure (process flow) and decision points. Thus, for model realisation, we need to define the process logic data, which makes the explanatory model that is required to represent the processes. This provides us with an outline of what is being performed and defines the design of the process (chapter 4). The process definition model consists of the following.

Process Flow

This has all possible routes through the process. The process flow can be of people, materials or information. Data collection may be from observation or discussion with people familiar with the process design. Process mining can be used to derive the process routing.

Decision Points

These are the logic defining each decision point within the process routing. These are needed to represent the branching and merging of the process flow. Decisions can be modelled by conditional (if . . . then x, else y) rules. Conditional decisions occur when certain defined conditions are satisfied and thus are unpredictable and cannot be known in advance. It may be difficult to codify conditional decisions, and so they may be represented by a probability. This represents substituting a cause-and-effect relationship (explanatory approach) by a distribution based on historical behaviour (descriptive approach). For a probabilistic decision, a sample value is drawn from a continuous, uniform distribution that generates a value between 0 and 1. This means any value is equally likely to occur. For a decision of (0.1, x; 0.5, y; else z), a value generated of 0.76 would lead to a flow following the route defined by the z option. Data collection for probability values may be by sampling methods, while conditional decision rules may be determined by data collection from interviews with personnel involved in decision-making. Decision points may also be modelled as other mechanisms such as triggers that activate on an event (e.g. reorder of inventory when levels drop below a defined point).

In a descriptive modelling approach, the emphasis requires the collection of a relatively large amount of quantitative data from observations of system behaviour. We may use a descriptive modelling approach to represent aspects of the system such as the time taken

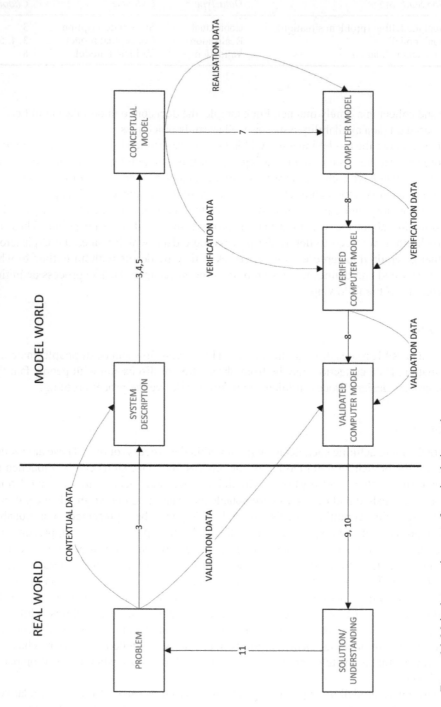

Figure 6.1 Main data requirements for a simulation study

to understand the basic processes of the system. Secondly, it should ensure that these processes remain in sync and consistent with the real-world process. Finally, the process diagram clarifies the core constructs.

Area Overview

There are constructs for an area of the system that act as outlet points. These points are briefly integrated within or outside the system area to represent the modelling area. A construct can either sit within an area or extend from it. In this way a construct that is part of the system area will integrate within the area.

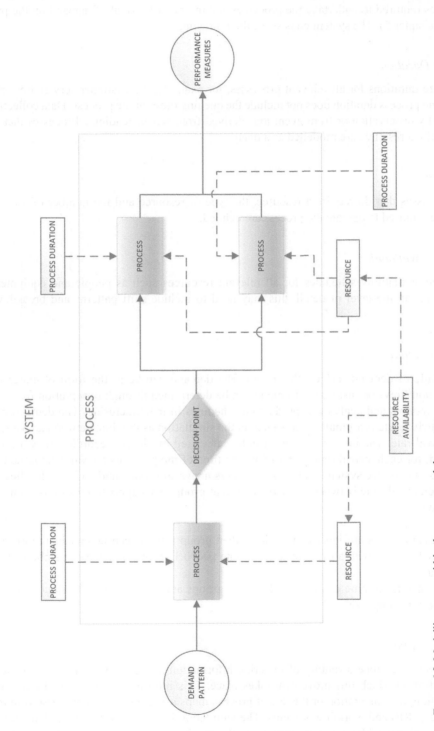

Figure 6.2 Modelling areas within the process and the system

to undertake the processes (process durations), the resources and the availability of those resources required to undertake the processes and the rate of arrival of demand on the processes (chapter 5). The system consists of the following.

Process Duration

These are durations for all relevant processes, for example, the customer service time at a bank. The process duration does not include the queuing time for the process. Data collection may be by observation or from event logs derived from sensor readings. Processes that do not require a resource are modelled as a delay.

Resource

For processes that do require a resource, the type of resource and the number of units of resource required to operate the process are defined.

Resource Availability

Resource availability schedules for all relevant resources such as people and equipment. Depending on the level of detail, this may need to include shift patterns and breakdown events.

Demand Pattern

A schedule of demand 'drives' the model. The demand can be in the form of materials, information flows or customers. Demand can be determined through observation for some service systems and analysis of production schedules in manufacturing. The demand pattern or arrival rate is normally represented in the simulation as the time between arrivals, or interarrival rate. The interarrival time can be calculated by simply recording arrival times and then, for each arrival time, subtracting the time of the previous arrival. One issue that may arise in service systems is when customers arrive in groups and so have, in effect, a zero interarrival time between individuals in that group. Two approaches to this issue are as follows:

- If most arrivals are individual entities, then group arrivals can be considered as individual arrivals with a small interarrival rate (say 0.1 seconds) between members of the group.
- An interarrival time can be calculated for groups and a probability distribution calculated for group size.

Process Layout

This covers the process routing of material, information and customers and the layout of the location in which this movement takes place. This information can be gathered from observation, documentation or the use of process maps associated with enterprise resource planning (ERP) and workflow systems. The simulation background display and animation can be developed with the use of simulation software draw facilities and the import of graphics files.

Other Elements

Note other fixed or random variables that may need modelling, including quantities or levels, such as batch sizes, worker absences, the group size of customer arrivals and characteristics of components in the model, such as staff skill levels, component sizes and customer types.

Validation Data Requirements

To ensure that a conceptually valid model is produced, the model builder should discuss and obtain information from people familiar with the real-world system, including operating personnel, industrial engineers, management, vendors and documentation. Operational validity entails observing system behaviour over time and comparing it with model behaviour and communicating with project sponsors throughout the model build. Believability can be obtained by regular meetings of interested parties, using the simulation animation display to provide a discussion forum.

Data Acquisition

The data collection phase may be a daunting and time-consuming task depending on the complexity of the model and the availability of the data required. A well-defined conceptual model specification is vital in providing a realistic assessment of data needs. One of the issues with data collection is the reliance of the simulation analyst on company personnel to collect or provide access to the required data in a timely manner. This will require a clear specification of the data requirements and effective communication with the data providers and, if required, company management to ensure prioritisation is given to this task.

A number of factors will impact how the data collection process is undertaken, including the time and cost constraints within which the project must be conducted. Compromises will have to be made on the scale of the data collection activity, and so it is important to focus effort on areas where accuracy is important for simulation results and to make clear assumptions and simplifications made when reporting those results.

As with other stages of a simulation project, data collection is an iterative process, with further data collection usually required as the project progresses. In the early stages of the simulation project, data collection will be concentrated on input variables (factors) that drive the system. Statistical tests during the modelling of input data may suggest a need to collect further data in order to improve the accuracy of results. Later output data (responses) from the real system, such as customer waiting times and WIP values, may be needed for validation purposes. The validation process may also expose inaccuracies in the model, which require further data collection activities. Thus, it should be expected that data collection activities will be ongoing throughout the project as the model is refined. Data acquisition can be classified into three categories (table 6.2).

Table 6.2 Classification of Data Acquisition (Based on Robinson and Bhatia, 1995)

Category	Acquisition
A	Can acquire directly (Available)
B	Can acquire through data collection (not available but collectable)
C	Cannot acquire (not available and not collectable)

Category A Data

For data that can be acquired directly, the main issue here is to ensure that the data is accurate and has been collected in an appropriate way. Checks should be made for issues such as appropriate sample size and the time period when data collection has occurred. If a theoretical distribution has been derived for a previous simulation project, we would need to check the method used to fit a distribution to the data. If we are not sure of the accuracy of category A data, then it may necessitate treating the data as category B and undertaking a new collection procedure.

Category B Data

When undertaking data collection for category B data, then data quality and efficient data collection are two of the challenging issues in many simulation projects. Inefficient data collection has been identified as one of the serious barriers to developing and deploying useful models within an appropriate timeframe and within budget (Onggo and Hill, 2014). Many companies lack IT systems that provide fully automated data collection, with Volovoi (2016) reporting that DES is mainly an offline activity where the collection and processing of input data creates a major bottleneck in the modelling process. This is becoming increasingly important in DES projects for two reasons:

- The use of big data requires an increased need for data collection and data cleaning activities to ensure data quality.
- Real-time DES applications imply the need for interoperability between simulation software and software applications to provide automated data collection.

One way of providing efficient data collection is through the use of sensors, such as RFID-enabled devices. However, in terms of data quality, data generated from sensors may also require a cleaning or pre-processing stage. In terms of real-time DES applications, standards such as CMSD (Core Manufacturing Simulation Data) can be implemented for data exchange between simulation and other software applications. See chapter 13 for more on these issues.

Category C Data

If no data exist or there is insufficient time to collect data (essentially moving category B data into category C), then a number of options are available. One approach is to use estimates from third parties. For example, equipment vendors or manuals may quote production rates for equipment that might be used instead of sample data of actual performance. This information might also be obtained by discussions with process stakeholders. Another option is to use transaction data instead of actual demand data. This approach does not take into account 'lost' demand when, for example, customers baulk at service due to excessive queue times.

Generally, if it has not been possible to collect detailed data in certain areas of the process, it is not sensible to then model in detail that area. Thus, there is a close relationship between simulation objectives, model detail (abstraction) and data collection needs. If the impact of the level of data collection on results is not clear, then it is possible to use sensitivity analysis (i.e. trying different data values) to ascertain how much model results are affected by the data accuracy. It may be then necessary to either undertake further data collection or quote results over a wide range. This strategy can be extended by treating the data value as an experimental variable rather than a fixed parameter within the model. We can then run the model with various estimates of our data value and observe the effect on the simulation results as part of the experimentation stage. The boxed text 'Defining the Level of Detail When Modelling People's Behaviour' outlines the modelling approaches of 'scenario', 'impact' and 'individual', where each simplification approach is related to the level of abstraction and data requirements when modelling people's behaviour. These strategies can be extended to the modelling of any data values within the simulation model. If these approaches are not feasible, we may need to change the conceptual model specification such as to limit the scope of the modelling exercise. In some cases, if the lack of data means we are not able to produce a credible model for the client, then we may need to abandon the simulation project.

Data Acquisition for Descriptive and Explanatory Modelling

When discussing data collection and acquisition in simulation, we normally do not distinguish between data required to develop the explanatory model (chapter 4) and data required for our descriptive (sub)models (chapter 5). If we consider these separately and consider the explanatory model of the system as a structural representation of the system based on our theory of how the system works, then we have our theory (explanatory model) of the system where our data acquisition needs to follow the classification of category A, B or C as described in the previous section (table 6.3). If, however, we have no model or theory regarding how the system works, but we can acquire data to develop a descriptive model that imitates observed behaviour, we can employ methods for prediction such as machine learning (table 6.3).

Table 6.3 Prediction Methods by Model and Data

	Model	*No Model*
Data	Simulation (Category A, B)	Machine Learning
No Data	Simulation (Category C)	

Defining the Level of Detail When Modelling People's Behaviour

When considering what to model for our DES, we would normally focus our analysis at the process context level (see chapter 12) in terms of identifying activities that are relevant to our study by referring to our factors and responses. We may, however, wish to extend our scope to an analysis of the people at the organisational context level that enables our processes. When modelling people, as in any model, the level of detail (how to model them) in the model should be based on the study objectives. This can be considered in terms of 'does the human behaviour affect the goals (output variables) to a sufficient degree that they require consideration in the model?' It may be that when dealing with larger models with complex SD, it is difficult to predict whether the inclusion of people's behaviour will have a significant effect on overall performance or not. However, as well as the study objectives, there is also a need to consider the effort required to incorporate the modelling of people in the simulation in relation to the gains obtained from doing so. If we consider the modelling of human behaviour as a question of data collection, then this effort may be minimised by the use of sensors and tracking devices which can collect far more data on individual behaviour than was possible in the past. In any case, there should be an evaluation of the modelling impact in terms of cost and workload to introduce these aspects. One approach is to use a highly simplified representation of the tasks undertaken by people but determine that the level of abstraction is appropriate for the aims of the study. This trade-off between meeting simulation study objectives against the cost and effort of doing so may be resolved by adjusting the conceptual model specification. However, it is apparent that there are a number of modelling strategies for achieving the required trade-off. Figure 6.3 outlines the modelling approaches of 'scenario', 'impact' and 'individual', where each simplification approach is related to the level of abstraction and data requirements when modelling people's behaviour.

The scenario approach considers the effect of people 'outside' of the model by observing model results under a range of scenarios. Using this approach, people's behaviour is codified into a model input variable. For example, worker capacity is set to 'normal' or 'low', and a scenario is run for each value of the variable. The approach is related to studies when data is not available for collection and is treated as an experimental factor rather than a fixed parameter. The remaining approaches to modelling people are termed impact and individual and are implemented 'inside' the model (figure 6.4). The effect of people's behaviour on system performance can be modelled with the use of impact variables that relate to the task that the person is undertaking or to organisational variables that impinge on a person's performance. Using the 'individual' approach, the characteristics of people are used to distinguish the differences in behaviour between different people (termed 'across' differences) or differences in behaviour of an individual over time (termed 'within' differences). An example of an 'across' difference is competence level at an operation which will differ across people. A 'within' difference would be an increase in operating performance of an individual over time due to learning.

Extract from Greasley, A. and Owen, C. (2018)

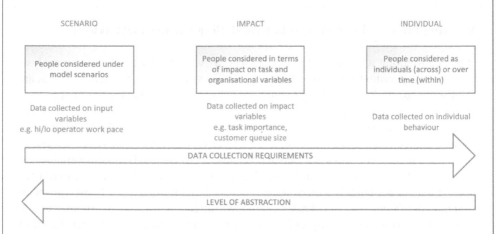

Figure 6.3 Approaches to modelling people's behaviour using discrete-event simulation

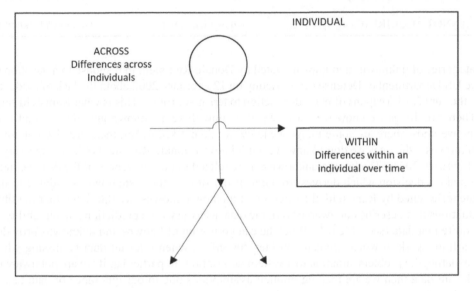

Figure 6.4 Modelling people's behaviour 'inside' the model by impact and individual approaches

Aleatory Uncertainty and Epistemic Uncertainty

When using DES, we consider that we are using simulation to attempt to make predictions under conditions of uncertainty. Uncertainty is defined as we are aware of the potential outcome of our prediction, but we do not know the probability of it occurring. This is distinguished from risk, which is when we are aware of the potential outcome of our prediction and can estimate the probability of it occurring. Thus, simulation is a way of dealing with the randomness in the world, known as aleatory uncertainty. Aleatory uncertainty may be characterised in a simulation by a probability distribution that represents the frequency of occurrence of an event of interest. However, there is another type of uncertainty caused by a lack of knowledge termed epistemic uncertainty. This happens when we lack sufficient knowledge (theory) to develop predictions from our data set or when we lack sufficient data necessary for developing our knowledge (theory) to provide a prediction.

Data Awareness and Data Acquisition

When considering data acquisition, we should be aware that there may be additional data or knowledge out there in the world which we have not considered. This issue of the ability to be aware and the ability to acquire data for prediction can be viewed using the famous

Table 6.4 Known and Unknowns for Data Awareness and Data Acquisition

DATA	AWARE	NOT AWARE
CAN ACQUIRE (Category A, B)	Known Knowns	Unknown Knowns
CANNOT ACQUIRE (Category C)	Known Unknowns	Unknown Unknowns

categories of unknowns and knowns stated by Donald Rumsfeld in response to a question at the US Department of Defense news briefing on 12 February 2002 about the lack of evidence of the supply of weapons of mass destruction to terrorist groups. This is what Rumsfeld said: 'There are things we know we know. We also know there are known unknowns – that is to say, we know there are some things we know we do not know. But there are also unknown unknowns – the ones we don't know we don't know' (Donald Rumsfeld obituary, the *Times*, 1 February 2021). The known/unknown can be related to our awareness of the data we need to make a decision which derives from our theory of how the system works. Adding to the categories cited by Rumsfeld, the category of unknown knowns, we thus have four possible situations that describe our awareness of the data necessary for a prediction and our ability to acquire that data (see table 6.4). What the categorisation of knowns and unknowns provides is a framework in which we can consider the pitfalls when relevant data is missing when translating the problem situation to a system description. In particular, if we are not aware of relevant data then we are making implicit assumptions due to our ignorance of data that is out there (unknown knowns).

Known Knowns

This is when we think we know everything we need to know and employ simulation to make a prediction. This implies we assume we have knowledge of any data items that may affect our prediction. We are also confident that we can acquire the data we require to make a prediction. In fact, simulation may not be necessary to make a prediction in some cases of low or no uncertainty if, in fact, a theory has been defined and all relevant data has been acquired. However, in most organisational situations, this is unlikely to be the case. We need to be careful that our perspective on the data is only a narrow viewpoint, and we are not eliminating data from our analysis that is relevant. This may be difficult to judge as we know that our model is a simplification of the real world and we cannot use all the data in the real world to make our predictions.

Known Unknowns

This is when we are aware of knowing that we do not have all the data we need to make a prediction, but we are unable to acquire the data that we know we need. In other words, we know there is stuff we don't know about affecting our prediction. Known unknowns occur when we are trying to make predictions based on too little data, such as rare events like earthquakes or new designs like the operation of a proposed factory. This requires an investigation to uncover the data we need and turn the unknowns into knowns and thus turn category C data into category B data (table 6.4). Methods for doing this are covered in the earlier section on category C data.

Unknown Knowns

This is when we are able to acquire the data we need to make a prediction, but we are unaware of the need for this data. Unknown knowns occur because although we are using data to inform our decisions in terms of predictions, the data we are using is in itself an outcome of decisions made in the real world. Thus, an association that appears strong can be the result of some unknown decisions generating the data. If those decisions change, then the data generated will make any subsequent prediction unreliable. This requires an investigation to make sure that we consider if additional data is required to make robust predictions. Further work is thus needed in terms of considering how might improve our data awareness. Potential approaches to moving an unknown known to a known known (table 6.4) could include:

- Using problem structuring ideas (Pidd, 2009) to provide a greater understanding of the context of the simulation study and thus data needs.
- Consult a wide range of stakeholders.
- Check for signals (Taleb, 2007) that might indicate unknown processes that are data sources.
- Consider carefully the timescale over which the sample data has been collected to ensure sufficiently representative model behaviour.
- Use methods such as machine learning that may uncover relationships between data whilst not requiring an understanding of (unknown) processes.

An example of an unknown known is the Fukushima nuclear accident, which occurred in 2011. This accident arose due to an earthquake releasing seismic energy, which in turn caused a tsunami that reached the northeast part of Japan with a height of 14 m. The Fukushima Daiichi nuclear reactors were designed for a maximum wave height of only 5.7 m, and so flooding of the generators occurred, leading to a serious incident. The design height of 5.7 m was based on an estimate that the probability that a tsunami in the Fukushima area could be more than 6 m high was less than 0.01 in the next 50 years. However, data was available detailing previous earthquakes, such as the Sanriku earthquake of 869 of magnitude 8.1, which is estimated to have caused a tsunami up to 20 m high (Paté-Cornell, 2012). What makes this an unknown known is that it seems that events occurring more than 1,000 years ago were ignored and considered outside the scope of the data set used for the risk prediction. Thus, even though data could have been acquired to inform a prediction, there was a lack of awareness of the need for this data.

Unknown Unknowns

This is when we are not aware of knowing what data we need, and we are unable to acquire this data even if we did know it was needed! Unknown unknowns are also termed the unknowable. Unknown unknowns may not be imagined *a priori*, but signals that occur suddenly or even gradually over time may be observed. These observations require interpretation and integration in the analysis to move an unknown to a known.

Unknown unknowns caused by epistemic uncertainty are sometimes classified as black swan events (Taleb, 2007). At one time, it was assumed in Europe that all swans in the world were white – until black swans were discovered by Dutch sailors in Australia in the 17th century. There was no awareness of the possibility of black swans and no way of acquiring this knowledge. The black swan event points to how predictions based on an assessment of aleatory uncertainty (randomness) using statistics may be flawed due to a lack of consideration of rare events that are not part of the data set (unknowns). Could it have been considered that until swans were observed on a global scale, our prediction of only white swans was potentially faulty?

The 9/11 attacks are an example of an unknown unknown, but the prior flight training of terrorists could have been interpreted as a signal for what was then an unimagined event. In terms of all the options of known and unknowns, it should be noted that events over time can change what have been unknowns into knowns. For example, the 9/11 attack represented a new scale and type of terrorism that was not considered feasible before that event (an unknown), but precautions are now taken, such as locked flight deck cabins to prevent any further occurrences.

Data Sources

In order to amass the data required, it is necessary to use a variety of data sources shown in table 6.5. Empirical data may be collected from historical records and observation of the system if it exists. If no direct empirical data is available, then subjective evaluation through the use of interviews with stakeholders may be appropriate. Data may also be gathered from IT systems and the internet of things either for input modelling purposes or to be used in raw data form for trace simulations or for real-time simulation applications such as digital twins.

Historical Records

A mass of data may be available within the organisation regarding the system to be modelled in the form of schematic diagrams, production schedules, shift patterns and so on. This data may be in a variety of formats, including paper and electronic. However, this data may not be in the right format, be incomplete or not relevant for the study in progress. The statistical validity of the data may also be in doubt.

Table 6.5 Sources of Data

Data Source	Example
Historical records	Diagrams, schematics, schedules
Observations	Time studies, walkthroughs
Interviews	Discussion of process steps, Process time estimates for equipment
IT systems and the internet of things (IoT)	Timings of events from RFID sensors. Data streamed for scheduling maintenance activities.

Observations

In terms of observations, a walkthrough of the process by the analyst is an excellent way of gaining an understanding of the process flow. Time studies can also be used to estimate process parameters when current data is not available.

Interviews

An interview with the process owner can assist in the analysis of system behaviour, which may not always be documented. Interviews are particularly useful when building an understanding of cause-and-effect relationships in the model. This could be regarding aspects such as the interdependencies between processes or codifying conditional decisions. Process owner and vendor estimates are used most often when the system to be modelled does not exist and, thus, no historical data or observation is possible. This approach has the disadvantage of relying on the ability of the process owner (e.g. machine operator, clerk) to remember past performance. If possible, a questionnaire can be used to gather estimates from a number of process owners and the data statistically analysed. Vendor information may also be based on unrealistic assumptions of ideal conditions for equipment operation. If no estimates can be made, then the objectives relating to those aspects may need to be changed to remove that aspect of the analysis from the project. The small sample size of interview data means that it is often used to set the parameters of the triangular distribution. The Delphi procedure may be used to elicit the collective judgement of a panel of individuals rather than that of a single person (see Shannon, 1975).

IT Systems and the Internet of Things (IoT)

Many simulation projects involve manual data collection, where the collection and processing of input data can create a major bottleneck in the modelling process. An alternative approach is the automated generation and collection of data using devices such as RFID and other sensors. Because of the automated nature of the collection, large data sets can be quickly amassed, often referred to as big data. Technically big data is considered as a data set of at least 1 TB but is often used to refer to any large data set. Preparation in terms of IT infrastructure and data compatibility may be required to utilise big data generated by these devices.

Real-time simulation applications imply the need for interoperability between simulation software and software applications to provide automated data collection. A standard originating from the area of DES is Core Manufacturing Simulation Data (CMSD), which is the most implemented standard for data exchange between simulation and other software applications. The standard is incorporated into simulation software such as Arena and ProModel. In terms of data quality, data generated from sensors may also require a cleaning or pre-processing stage. Procedures for cleaning data may need to undertake tasks such as removing typos, such as misspelt or joined-up words; removing outliers, such as out-of-range numeric values; and replacing missing values with approximations. Applications of automated data collection in respect of simulation include the generation of event log files for process mining software to generate process maps and data collection for machine learning algorithms that can be used for input modelling, implementing adaptable runtime models, and experimentation and analysis.

Trace or data-driven simulations use historical process data or real-time information directly. The advantage of a trace simulation is that validation can be achieved by a direct comparison of model performance metrics to real system performance over a historical time period. In addition, model credibility is enhanced as the client can observe model behaviour replicating real-life events. The disadvantages are the need for suitable data availability and the possible restriction in scope derived from a single trace that may not reflect the full variability of the process behaviour. Trace simulation is normally used for understanding process behaviour (descriptive analytics) and for checking conformance to the 'official' process design and cannot be used for predictive analytics, such as scenario analysis, as it only contains historical data. Trace simulation is similar to process mining which uses historical event logs, although process mining can check conformance of the process map in addition to operational process performance.

The IoT can refer to the use of the internet as a network to enable the connection and communication between objects with embedded sensors. The wired and wireless networks that connect the IoT often use the same Internet Protocol (IP) that connects the internet. These very large networks create huge volumes of data for analysis and are a key generator of big data used for analytics. Much of the data gathered through the IoT is from people who are unaware of its capture, such as through location data transmitted from a mobile phone to search terms entered into Google. A primary driver of the IoT is the broad deployment of sensors that are smaller, cheaper and more powerful than in the past. There are many applications of the IoT:

- Manufacturing: Sensors can be used for real-time monitoring of production processes to allow early correction of errors and increased efficiency.
- Transportation: Data streamed from trucks in use can be used to schedule maintenance activities outside of operating hours.
- Retail: Customer-tracking devices can be used to present targeted promotions to customers as they move through a store.

One issue with these applications may be the volume and velocity of data generated from sensors and the ability to monitor this in real time. This has led to the move to computing to the 'edge', often termed edge computing, where data-driven processes are undertaken by the devices closest to the action or the event. However, this can be difficult due to the limited processing capability of devices such as smartphones. A key issue with the IoT is the data management issues involved in storing and generating insights from the large volume of data generated.

The term 'big data' refers to the large data sets that are enabled by IT systems which support, capture and disseminate this data. The limitations of big data are important to consider, and despite claims that the sheer volume of big data will permit prediction by causation without the need for analysis by models, the complexity of dynamic systems, such as human-based systems, means that it is unlikely that even big data will have captured sufficient historical data for prediction of system behaviours under all possible future scenarios defined by input parameters. In other words, the real value of big data is not the sheer volume of data but our ability to analyse these vast data sets using analytic tools. This analysis has been enabled by innovations, such as improved computer network speeds and storage on cloud computing platforms. A particular emphasis of the analysis of big data is the use of unstructured data, such as email exchanges, social media posts, and video and voice recordings. This has found applications, such as in retail, where companies are seeking to collect as much information about their customers' lives as possible so as target them and meet their needs more effectively.

In general terms, we can classify the different types of data as follows:

- Structured data: This is what might be considered the traditional data that is processed by IT systems and includes financial and customer data that can be defined in a field within a database file. Customer data fields might include name and address details, held in relational databases and queried using the Structured Query Language (SQL) as described earlier in this chapter.
- Unstructured data: This represents the majority of business-related data and includes videos, graphic images, websites, emails and social media posts.
- Semi-structured data: This represents data that has elements of structure but also contains arbitrary aspects. An example is a customer list which is missing certain entries for some customer details, such as a postal address, and will contain unformatted entries for notes on customer preferences, such as a safe location for delivery items. Emails also represent semi-structured data in that the sender name and timestamp are provided but the content of the email is unstructured.

Big data is associated with an increase in the use of unstructured data, but it is also the source of these data streams that is evolving. In particular, the extensive use of websites and social media sites has allowed the monitoring of people's browser history, online shopping habits and conversations through email and social media, such as Twitter and Facebook. In addition, there are vast amounts of photo and video content uploaded to sites such as Flickr, Instagram and YouTube. Two sources of data particularly associated with big data are sensors and the IoT.

Although the term big data relates to the sheer size of the data sets, this is just one aspect of the nature of the data. The four Vs of big data describes the concept from the following aspects:

- Volume: This relates to the huge amounts of data generated every second by IT systems.
- Velocity: This relates to the speed of transmission of data across the globe.
- Variety: This relates to the many types of data that are being generated, such as numeric (e.g. financial data), text (e.g. social media feeds) and video.
- Veracity: This relates to the messiness of the data being generated, such as speech patterns, Twitter posts with hashtags, and abbreviations and typos.

Ethics in Data Collection

The simulationist should be aware of ethical considerations when collecting data, particularly when this relates to human performance and behaviour. Fair and ethical data use and the right of individuals to privacy are part of an ongoing debate. Authors such as Zuboff (2015) have discussed the pervasive nature of surveillance enabled by the collection and analysis of personal data. O'Neil (2016) discusses how decisions based on data collection introduce the potential for biases and decisions made on incomplete or incorrect knowledge. Oliff et al. (2020) propose an approach to avoid the dependency on direct monitoring, or stored data sets, that a small volume of data on individual human performance may provide enough information to build useful profiles to enable appropriate variability within simulation and modelling.

Summary

In terms of data requirements, this chapter covers the main data types used in a simulation study of contextual data, realisation data and validation data. Then in terms of data acquisition, category A data is defined as data that can be acquired directly, category B data is that data which requires data collection activities, and category C data is data that cannot be currently acquired. This means we have data that can be acquired (category A or category B) and data that cannot be acquired (category C). We also need to consider our awareness that we need to acquire this data so we can be aware or unaware of a theory that defines a data requirement. Finally, a variety of data sources are discussed that can be utilised for a simulation study, including the increased use of sensors through the IoT.

Exercises

- Explain the difference between contextual data, realisation data and validation data in a simulation study.
- Explain the three categories of data acquisition in a simulation study.
- List the data requirements for a simulation of a supermarket. Suggest a possible data source for each data requirement.
- Explain when the scenario, impact and individual approaches to modelling human behaviour are appropriate.
- What are the main issues when using data from an IT system for a simulation study?
- What is the Core Manufacturing Simulation Data (CMSD) standard?

References

Greasley, A. and Owen, C. (2018) Modelling people's behaviour using discrete-event simulation: A review, *International Journal of Operations and Production Management*, 38(5), 1228–1244.

Oliff, H., Liu, Y., Kumar, M. and Williams, M. (2020) The ethical use of human data for smart manufacturing: An analysis and discussion, *Procedia CIRP*, 93, 1364–1369.

O'Neil, C. (2016) *Weapons of Math Destruction: How Big Data Increases Inequality and Threatens Democracy*, Allen Lane.

Onggo, B.S.S. and Hill, J. (2014) Data identification and data collection methods in simulation: A case study at ORH Ltd., *Journal of Simulation*, 8, 195–205.

Paté-Cornell, E. (2012) On "black swans" and "perfect storms": Risk analysis and management when statistics are not enough, *Risk Analysis*, 32(11), 1823–1833.

Pidd, M. (2009) *Tools for Thinking: Modelling in Management Science*, 3rd edition, John Wiley and Sons Ltd.

Robinson, S. and Bhatia, V. (1995) Secrets of successful simulation projects, *Proceedings of the Winter Simulation Conference*, IEEE, 61–67.

Shannon, R.E. (1975) *Systems Simulation: The Art and the Science*, Prentice-Hall.

Taleb, N.N. (2007) *The Black Swan: The Impact of the Highly Improbable*, Random House.

Volovoi, V. (2016) Simulation of maintenance processes in the big data era, *Proceedings of the 2016 Winter Simulation Conference*, IEEE, 1872–1883.

Zuboff, S. (2015) Big other: Surveillance capitalism and the prospects of an information civilization, *Journal of Information Technology*, 30(1), 75–89.

7 Building the Simulation Model

Introduction

This text features three DES software packages (Arena, Simul8 and Simio) that are used to build the computer simulation model. All three packages incorporate a graphical interface for building the model, which uses a process-based approach (with no requirement for program code to be entered) and also provides an animated display. The combination of a process flow approach and a graphical interface provides a clear and powerful way to build DES models and is widely adopted in many of the DES software packages currently in use.

The model-building process involves using computer software to translate the conceptual model into a computer simulation model that can be run over time. There are checks made to ensure that the computer model has been translated correctly (verification) and that the computer model is, in fact, a suitable representation of the real system for the purposes of our study (validation). Verification and validation are covered in chapter 8.

Many former simulation software packages, such as SIMAN/CINEMA, required coding of the simulation model in a programming language. In the case of SIMAN/CINEMA, this requires coding of the model in SIMAN and coding of file processing routines using the general-purpose language FORTRAN. These packages have been largely replaced by software systems such as Arena, Simio and Simul8, which are covered in this text and are referred to as visual interactive modelling systems (VIMS) (Pidd, 2004). VIMS provide an interactive environment in which the model can be built using drag and drop icons and menus and run using animated graphics. There are, however, some modern simulation software packages, such as AnyLogic, that require coding (in this case in Java) within a menu and graphics environment.

In terms of an approach to building the model, there are three main options based on software development frameworks (Bocij et al., 2019):

- A 'waterfall' approach is to go through the whole model build process before obtaining feedback from the client.
- A 'spiral' approach is to build sub-models to a high level of detail and obtain feedback from the client on the operation of these sub-models.
- A 'prototype' approach is to build a model to a certain level of detail and obtain feedback from the client on this model before further refinement takes place.

With the use of visual interactive modelling systems (VIMS) such as Arena, Simio and Simul8, then the prototype approach is most often used. This is enabled by the use of the

DOI: 10.4324/9781003124092-7

visual animation facilities of these software packages provide a useful platform for communication between the model builder and client, allowing further refinements to the model to be discussed as the model is developed.

The first stage of building the computer model is to undertake the explanatory modelling, which will entail entering the structure of the model based on one of the diagramming methods described in chapter 4. This is achieved using VIMS by dragging and dropping icons representing the structural elements of the process from a menu onto a main model screen.

The second stage of building the computer model is to undertake the descriptive modelling (chapter 5), which will entail setting the parameters for the modelling components. This is achieved using VIMS by selecting the icons previous placed on the main screen and entering parameters using dialog boxes. The main parameters will be the arrival time for entities, process durations, resource capacities and decision logic conditional rules or probabilities.

The simulation model should be documented to enable understanding by future model users and developers, and there are facilities within the software packages to enable documentation of model elements. Documentation of the model and documentation of how to use the model should form part of the project report, which is delivered at the end of the simulation study (see chapter 11).

Depending on how the model is intended to be used, we may need to consider other aspects during the model build. For example, depending on the level of interaction, we may need to incorporate a menu system to enable easy entering of simulation model parameters. Depending on the level of integration, we may need to consider the nature of the interface between the model and the data source. This may range from incorporating the data in data arrays within the software to the use of external spreadsheet data to interfacing with a company database. More details of the different requirements of the simulation model, depending on its usage are covered in chapter 11.

In terms of the design of simulation output reports, we will need to produce a report that will provide us with an initial gauge of system performance. The statistics that are collected when we do this are termed within-replication statistics as they are collected during a single replication of the simulation. A replication is defined as a single execution or run of the simulation model over time.

There are two main types of statistics that are collected and reported by the simulation:

- Observational data involves each observation being treated as an individual occurrence and being equally weighted (i.e. the time over which this occurrence happens is not taken into consideration). So to calculate the average customer time in the system would entail summing the observations for time in the system and dividing by the number of observations.
- Time-weighted or time-persistent data is when the time over which the occurrence happened is taken into account. To do this, the simulation records the current value of the variable and the last point in time that the variable changed value. When the variable value changes, again the variable value is multiplied by the time it was at the value and then added to the cumulated value for this statistic. If the value of the variable was plotted over time, this calculation would represent the area under the plotline. So to calculate the number of customers in a queue would entail recording the time period for each number in queue value and summing these values.

In addition to the within-replication simulation output presented in chapters 7A for Arena, 7B for Simio and 7C for Simul8, the following performance measures are covered here:

Chapters 9, 9A, 9B, 9C: Here, statistics are presented to measure a single simulation output performance over multiple replications.

Chapters 10, 10A, 10B, 10C: Here, statistics are presented for measures of the comparative performance of different simulation model designs or scenarios.

The implementation of the computer model components for Arena will be covered in chapter 7A; for Simio, in chapter 7B; and for Simul8, in chapter 7C.

Summary

This chapter describes approaches to the model-building process and defines the main types of statistics that are reported by the simulation.

Exercises

Using a simulation system, simulate the following. Two types of customers arrive at a system for processing. Type 1 customers arrive according to an exponential interarrival distribution with a mean of 10 minutes. These customers wait in a dedicated queue (for type 1 customers) until an operator is ready to process them. The processing time is a triangular distribution with parameters of 5, 6 and 8 minutes. Type 2 customers arrive according to an exponential distribution with a mean of 15 minutes. These customers wait in a dedicated queue (for type 2 customers) until an operator is ready to process them. The processing time is a triangular distribution with parameters of 3, 7 and 8 minutes. All customers then go through a further operation with a processing time distribution that is triangular with parameters of 4, 6 and 8 minutes. Customers then leave the system. Assume transfer times between operations are negligible. Determine the average time in the system for each customer type and the average queue size for each operation.

Using a simulation system, simulate the following. Parts arrive at a single machine according to an exponential interarrival distribution with a mean of 15 minutes. The processing time is a triangular distribution with parameters of 10, 14 and 17 minutes. Each part has then a 10% chance of being inspected for quality. The inspection time is given by a normal distribution with a mean of 100 minutes and a standard deviation of 10 minutes. About 15% of the inspected parts fail the quality test and are scrapped. The remaining parts join the non-inspected parts and are transferred out of the system. Run the simulation for 10,000 minutes to determine the number of inspected parts, the number of scrap parts and the total number of parts that leave the system.

A harbour consists of 4 docks for unloading and loading ships. Ships arrive at the harbour with an interarrival time of 5 hours with an exponential distribution. Ships unload at the first available dock with a normal distribution with a mean duration of 6 hours and a standard deviation of 24 hours. Ships then load immediately (with a normal distribution with a mean of 8 hours and a standard deviation of 3 hours) and immediately leave the harbour. Build a simulation model to estimate the utilisation of the 4 harbour docks and the maximum time a ship is required to wait for an available dock.

A university car park has a staff car park holding 100 vehicles and a student car park holding 50 vehicles. Staff arrive during the day with an interarrival rate given by an exponential distribution with a mean of 10 minutes. Staff stay on campus for an average of 4 hours and then leave. Students' interarrival rate is described by an exponential distribution with a mean of 15 minutes. Students stay on campus for an average of 3 hours. Run the simulation for 5 days, and note the length of time wither car park is full during this time. Discuss changes to the model to make it a more realistic representation of a typical car park system.

Reference

Bocij, P., Greasley, A. and Hickie, S. (2019) *Business Information Systems: Technology, Development and Management for the Modern Business*, 6th edition, Pearson Education Ltd.

7A: Building the Simulation in Arena

Introduction

In order to undertake the exercises in this chapter requires the installation of the Arena simulation software system. This is available as a free download with full functionality but with a limited model size at www.arenasimulation.com/simulation-software-download.

This chapter uses version 16.1 of Arena. A selection of modules from the main templates in Arena is described. These provide the building blocks for the models presented in this chapter, but there are numerous additional modules available in Arena if required. The following templates are described:

*   Discrete processing
*   Decisions
*   Grouping
*   Input output
*   Data definition

The following tutorials are presented in order to demonstrate the basic functionality of the Arena software:

*   The single-queue bank clerk simulation.
*   The double-queue bank clerk simulation.
*   The double-queue bank clerk simulation with animation.
*   The loan application simulation.
*   The petrol station simulation.

Getting Started in Arena

When the Arena system is run, the screen display shown in figure 7A.1 should be displayed.

The project bar (to the left of the screen display) contains a number of templates such as 'Discrete Processing', 'Decisions' and 'Data Definition'. More templates are available depending on which version of Arena you are using. The current selected template is 'Discrete Processing', and the modules within this template are displayed. These modules are used to build your simulation model by dragging them onto the 'model window flowchart view'. To connect the modules together to create the simulation, the module connector tool should be selected from the toolbar at the top of the screen display. Data can be entered into

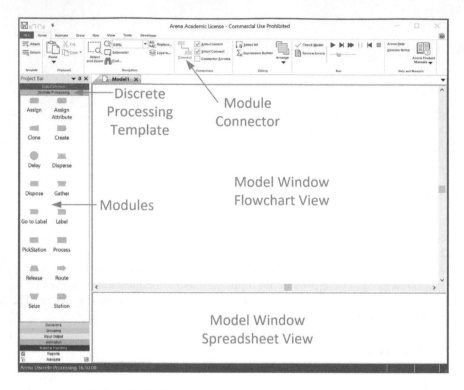

Figure 7A.1 Arena 16.1 model display

each module by either double-clicking each module to obtain a dialog box or by using the 'model window spreadsheet view' at the bottom of the screen.

A selection of Arena modules is now described. There are many more Arena modules in the Arena templates, and more information is provided with the Arena software help system and support files.

Discrete Processing Template

The Discrete Processing panel is used for general model building and consists of 16 flow-chart modules. A selection of these is now described.

Create

This module generates entities that move through the simulation. It defines the time delay between entity arrivals (i.e. interarrival time) and the number of entities that arrive together.

Dispose

This module removes entities when they have finished moving through the system.

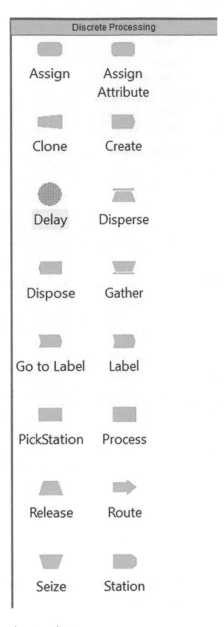

Figure 7A.2 Discrete Processing template

Assign

This module can be used to assign a value to an entity attribute. An entity attribute is a type of local variable that is associated with an entity as it flows through the model. The Assign module can also be used to assign a value to a variable. A variable is a type of global variable that is not associated with an individual entity.

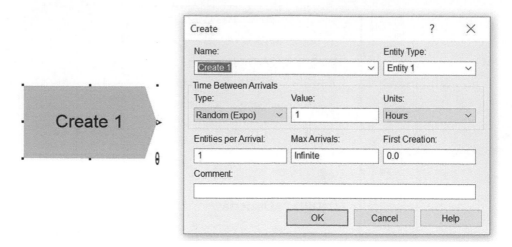

Figure 7A.3 Arena Create module

Figure 7A.4 Arena Dispose module

Process (Delay)

If in the Process module the Logic Action parameter is defined as Delay, then it can be used to model a delay or wait in the process flow.

Process (Seize Delay Release)

If in the Process module the Logic Action parameter is defined as Seize Delay Release, it can be used to model the use of a resource to undertake a process.

Process (Add Resource)

To define the resources used by the process, the Add Resource option can be used. Each resource can be named. The Units to Seize/Release defines the number of resource units

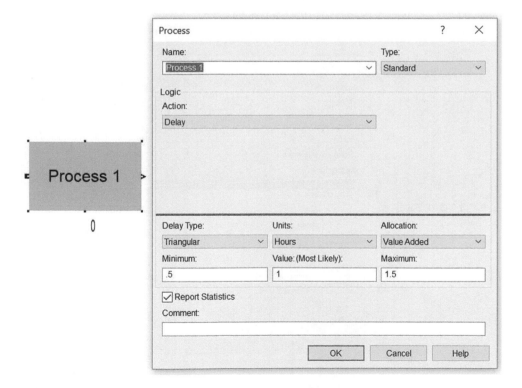

Figure 7A.5 Arena Assign module

Figure 7A.6 Arena Process (Delay) module

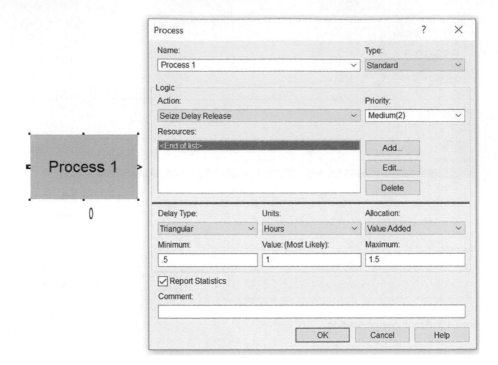

Figure 7A.7 Arena Process (Seize Delay Release) module

Figure 7A.8 Arena Process (Add Resource) module

needed to undertake this process (this is not the capacity of the resource which is defined in the Resources module in the data definition template). A number of different resources can be allocated to a process by using the Add Resource option.

Decisions Template

This template controls the flow of entities through the model and consists of six modules. A selection of these is now described.

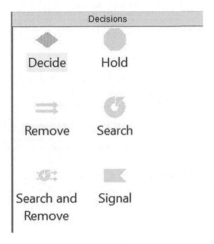

Figure 7A.9 Decide template

Decide (Chance)

When the Type parameter is set to Chance, this module defines the percentage of the entities that take each flow route out of the decision module.

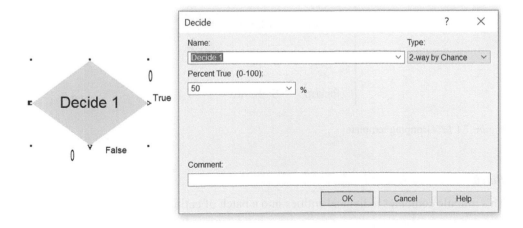

Figure 7A.10 Arena Chance Decide module

Decide (Conditional)

When the Type parameter is set to Condition, this module defines conditional (such as if-then-else rules) for entities that take each flow route out of the decision module.

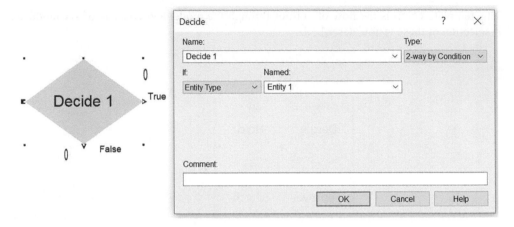

Figure 7A.11 Arena Conditional Decide module

Grouping Template

This template controls the flow of entities that are grouped (batched).

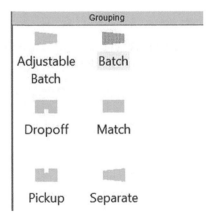

Figure 7A.12 Grouping template

Batch

This module combines individual entities into a batch of entities.

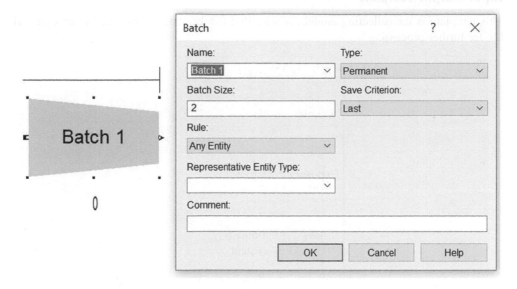

Figure 7A.13 Arena Batch module

Separate

This module splits individual entities from a batch.

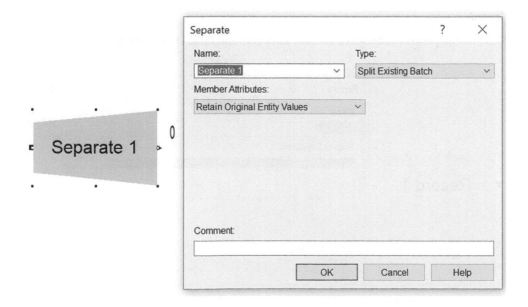

Figure 7A.14 Arena Separate module

Input Output Template

This template is for collecting model statistics that can be reported or saved to an external file for further processing.

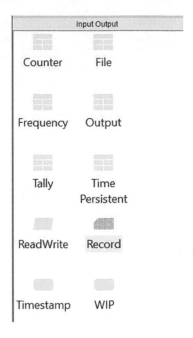

Figure 7A.15 Input Output template

Record

This module permits statistical data such as counts and tallies to be reported.

Figure 7A.16 Arena Record module

Data Definition Template

This module defines data elements within the model.

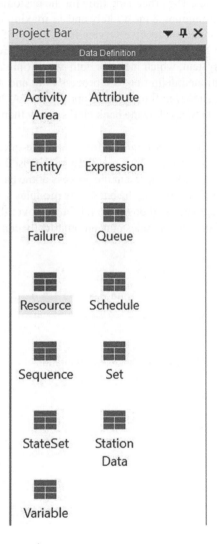

Figure 7A.17 Data Definition template

Resource

This module defines the capacity in units of each resource. This is shown in the spreadsheet data module window.

	Name	Type	Capacity	Busy / Hour	Idle / Hour	Per Use	StateSet Name	Failures	Report Statistics	Comment
1 ▶	Resource 1 ⌄	Fixed Capacity	1	0.0	0.0	0.0		0 rows	☑	

Double-click here to add a new row.

Figure 7A.18 Arena Resource module

The Single-Queue Bank Clerk Simulation

Customers arrive at a bank with the time between arrivals estimated as exponentially distributed with a mean of 5 minutes. The processing time for the customers is a triangular distribution with parameters of 5 minimum, 8 most likely and 11 maximum minutes. In this system, customers form a single queue and receive service from either of the two members of staff when they reach the front of the queue. Performance statistics are required on the average time a customer is in the system, which includes both queue time and service time.

Based on the aforementioned definition, the process map and ACD for the single-queue bank clerk simulation are shown in figure 7A.19 and figure 7A.20. Customers arrive from outside the system and are processed by the bank clerks. They then leave the system after the process has been completed.

Figure 7A.21 shows the modules required for the single-queue bank clerk simulation placed on the flowchart view screen. The Create module is used to generate the bank customers. A Process module is used to represent the process at the bank tills. A Dispose module is used to simulate the customers leaving the bank. The modules are added to the model window flowchart view by dragging (hold down the left button over the module) them from the Discrete Processing template. The modules may automatically connect together to define the

Figure 7A.19 Process map for single-queue bank clerk simulation

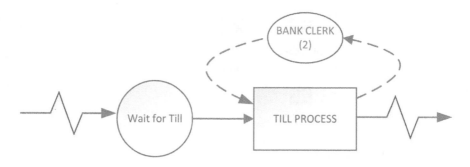

Figure 7A.20 Activity cycle diagram for single-queue bank clerk simulation

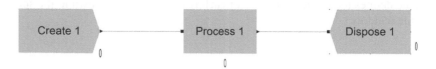

Figure 7A.21 Arena modules on the flowchart view screen

relationship between the modules if they are entered on the screen in order from left to right. If the modules are not connected by the connecting lines, they can be connected manually using the module connect button on the home toolbar. Click on the module connector, and the cursor will change to a crosshair. Then click on the exit point (▶) of the first module and click on the entry point (■) of the module you wish to connect to. The connection will then be made. To remove a connection, click on the connection line to highlight it and press the Delete key on your keyboard.

Double-click on the 'create 1' module, and the dialog box will appear as in figure 7A.22. For the name parameter, enter 'customer arrivals'. For the Entity Type parameter, enter 'customer'. For the type parameter, select Random(Expo), and for the value parameter, enter 5. For units, select the 'minutes' option. The module will then create customer arrivals that are exponentially distributed, with a mean of 5 minutes. Press OK to enter the data. Note that the data is also shown in the spreadsheet data module window, which provides an alternative way to enter and update the module data.

The Process module can be used to represent the process at the bank till. To undertake this process, a resource is required – in this case, a bank clerk. Double-click on the Process module to observe the dialog box as shown in 7A.23. Enter 'Till 1 and Till 2' for the name parameter. The process is currently set as a delay. As we wish to allocate (seize) a resource to undertake the process, set the Seize Delay Release option from the pull-down action menu. Click on the Add button and enter 'bank clerk' for the resource name. The Units to Seize/ Release value is the number of resource units needed to undertake the process. In this case, we only require one bank clerk to undertake the process, so this should be left as 1. Select the

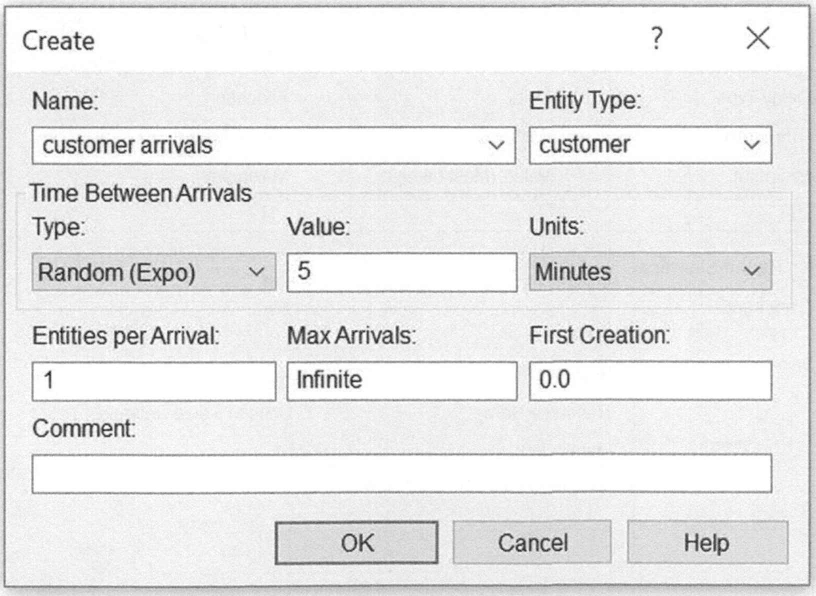

Figure 7A.22 Enter the Create module parameters

Triangular option for the delay type. Select the units as minutes and enter 5 for the minimum value, 8 for the most likely value and 11 for the maximum value (figure 7A.23).

Move to the data definition template and click on the resource module. A spreadsheet view of the currently defined resources should appear in the model window spreadsheet view (figure 7A.24). A bank clerk resource was automatically created when this was entered in the Process module. Change the capacity entry from 1 to 2 to fix a maximum capacity level of two bank clerks.

Select the Run tab on the menu, then select the Setup option. Then select the Replication Parameters option from the menu bar. The dialog box shown in figure 7A.25 should appear. Set the replication length to 40320 minutes and all unit entries as minutes.

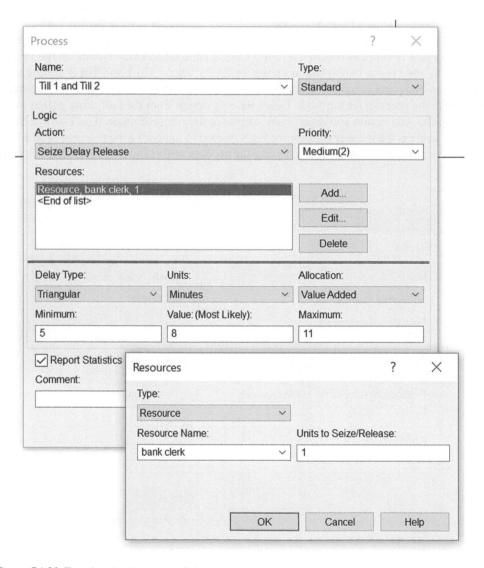

Figure 7A.23 Entering the Process module parameters

		Name	Type	Capacity	Busy / Hour	Idle / Hour	Per Use	StateSet Name	Failures	Report Statistics	Comment
1	▶	bank clerk	Fixed Capacity	2	0.0	0.0	0.0		0 rows	☑	

Double-click here to add a new row.

Figure 7A.24 Setting the bank clerk capacity

Run Setup   ×

Run Speed
Run Control   Establish replication-related options for the current model. Settings include the number of simulation replications to be run, the length of the
                   replication, the start date and time of the simulation, warm-up time length, time units, and the type of initialization to be performed between
Reports   replications.

Project Parameters

Replication Parameters

Replication Param...

Array Sizes   Number of Replications: 1

Arena Visual Desig...   Start Date and Time: ☐ 07 September 2021 10:18:59   ▦▾

                   Warm-up Period: 0.0   Minutes   ∨

                   Replication Length: 40320   Minutes   ∨

                   Hours Per Day: 24

                   Terminating Condition: _____

                   Base Time Units: Minutes   ∨

Parallel Replications

                   ☐ Run Replications in Parallel

                   Number of Parallel Processes: 8

                   Parallel Replication Input Data Files:

                   Data File   Add

                                                            OK   Cancel   Apply   Help

Figure 7A.25 Setting the simulation run length

A variety of reports are available in Arena. In order to provide information on the customer time in the system, select the Reports option (figure 7A.26). Select the Always button and then select the default report as SIMAN Summary Report (.out file) from the pull-down menu.

Move to the Home tab on the menu and run the model by clicking on the run icon (▶). If there are any errors in your model, a message will appear on the screen, indicating the source of the problem. When you have a working model, you will see the entities moving through the system as the model runs through time. You can control the speed of the display using the < and > keys. The run can be paused by pressing the Esc key or using the run control toolbar. You can fast-forward to the end of the run (without animation) using the fast-forward icon (⏭). The simulation can be stopped at any time using the stop icon (■) on the run control toolbar. When the simulation has completed its run, the output report (figure 7A.27) should appear.

The top of figure 7A.27 reports the replication or runtime of the simulation. In this case, this also defines the time over which the output statistics below cover, but the statistics collection period may be defined as less than the runtime if required. Figure 7A.27 shows the

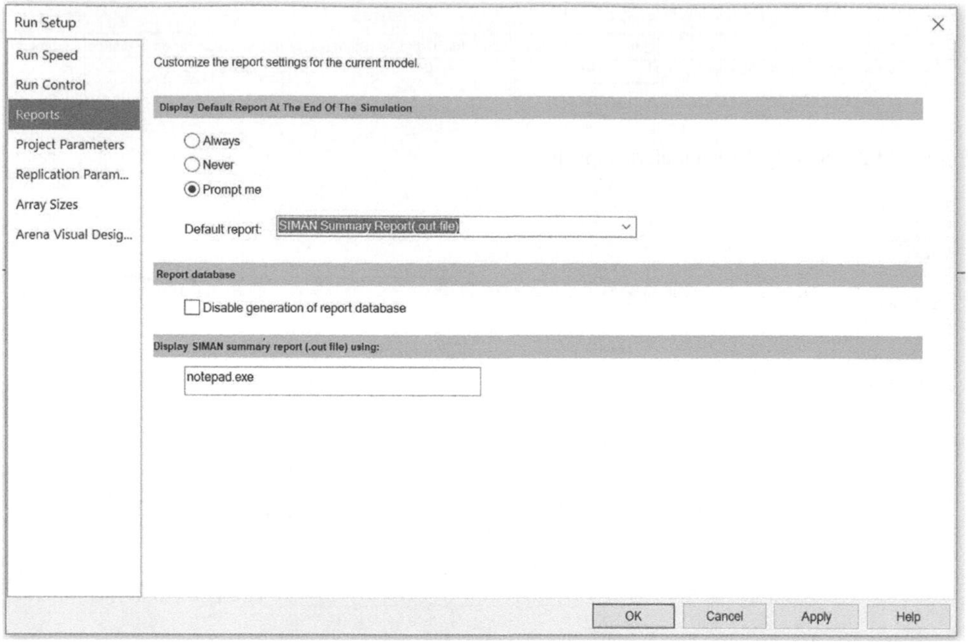

Figure 7A.26 Setting the output report format

average number of customers in the system (WIP) (customer.WIP) is 3.06 customers. The average time in the system for the customer (customer.TotalTime) is given as 15.5 minutes, with a maximum time of 66 minutes. The maximum customer waiting time (Till 1 and Till 2.Queue.WaitingTime) is given as 58.64 minutes. The maximum number of customers in a queue (Till 1 and Till 2.Queue.NumberInQueue) is given as 15. The bank clerk utilisation or percentage of busy time (bank clerk.utilisation) is given as 0.79 or 79% utilisation for each bank clerk. The maximum number of customers in the bank at any one time (customer. WIP) is given as 17 customers, and the number of customers (observations) who have passed through the bank in the 28 days of runtime is 7,955. Thus, this very simple model provides us with a variety of performance measures for our bank clerk system. Note that the models incorporate probability distributions, and so the results you get may differ slightly from those in the text due to random variation. This is to be expected, and you can see that the results from the same model run on different simulation software will also vary.

Note that our replication length is 28 days, each of 24 hours (28 × 24 × 60 = 40,320 minutes). Thus, we are assuming here that the bank operation is running continuously 24 hours a day. In reality, a physical bank branch facility would be open for around 8 hours a day, beginning empty of customers at the start of the day and returning to an empty state at the end of the day. This is termed a terminating system in simulation, and the procedure for analysis of results of a terminating simulation in Arena is covered in chapter 9A.

Arena Variables Guide

There are many variable definitions in Arena; here is a small selection.

NQ(Queue Name) – number in queue

```
                        ARENA Simulation Results
                      IT Services - License: STUDENT

                      Summary for Replication 1 of 1

Project: Unnamed Project                          Run execution date : 9/ 6/2021
Analyst: IT Services                              Model revision date: 9/ 6/2021

Replication ended at time      : 40320.0 Minutes
Base Time Units: Minutes

                             TALLY VARIABLES

Identifier                   Average  Half Width Minimum   Maximum  Observations

customer.VATime               7.9977    (Corr)    5.0585   10.952      7955
customer.NVATime              .00000    .00000    .00000   .00000      7955
customer.WaitTime             7.5053   1.3452     .00000   58.641      7955
customer.TranTime             .00000    .00000    .00000   .00000      7955
customer.OtherTime            .00000    .00000    .00000   .00000      7955
customer.TotalTime           15.503    1.3509    5.0879    66.039      7955
Till 1 and Till 2.Queue.WaitingTime  7.5034  1.3454  .00000  58.641    7957

                         DISCRETE-CHANGE VARIABLES

Identifier                   Average  Half Width Minimum   Maximum  Final Value

customer.WIP                  3.0589    .33479    .00000   17.000    2.0000
bank clerk.NumberBusy         1.5781    .03897    .00000    2.0000   2.0000
bank clerk.NumberScheduled    2.0000    (Insuf)   2.0000    2.0000   2.0000
bank clerk.Utilization        .78908    .01949    .00000    1.0000   1.0000
Till 1 and Till 2.Queue.NumberInQueue  1.4807  .30786  .00000  15.000  .00000

                               OUTPUTS

Identifier                   Value

customer.NumberIn            7957.0
customer.NumberOut           7955.0
bank clerk.NumberSeized      7957.0
bank clerk.ScheduledUtilization  .78908
System.NumberOut             7955.0


Simulation run time: 0.13 minutes.
Simulation run complete.
```

Figure 7A.27 The Arena output summary report

   MR(Resource Name) – resource capacity (defined in Data Definitions, Resources)
   NR(Resource Name) – number of busy resources
   TNOW – current simulation time
   NC(Counter Name) – count value

   Logical Operators
   .EQ.   equal to
   .NE.   not equal to
   .LT.   less than
   .GT.   greater than
   .LE.   less than or equal to
   .AND.   and
   .OR.   or

Arena Simulation Statistics

The statistics that Arena generates and reports are explained here in more detail. In this model, the entities are the bank customers. Firstly, what Arena terms Tally Variables are more generally known as observational data. Here, each observation is treated as an individual occurrence and is equally weighted (i.e. the time over which this occurrence happens is not taken into consideration). So for figure 7A.27, to calculate the average entity time in the system (labelled as customer.TotalTime) would entail summing the 7,955 observations for time in the system and dividing by the number of observations. Table 7A.1 presents the following observational data by default for the bank clerk simulation.

Discrete-change variables, discussed in the next section, are more generally known as time-weighted or time-persistent data. Here, the time over which the occurrence happened is taken into account. To do this, the simulation records the current value of the variable and the last point in time that the variable changed value. When the variable value changes, again the variable value is multiplied by the time it was at the value and then added to the cumulated value for this statistic. If the value of the variable was plotted over time, this calculation would represent the area under the plotline. So for figure 7A.27 to calculate the Till 1 and Till 2.Queue.NumberInQueue value would entail recording the time period for each number in queue value and summing these values. Table 7A.2 presents the following time-weighted data values by default for the bank clerk simulation.

Outputs reports, discussed in the final section, are various additional measures by default, such as the number of entities entering and leaving the system and measures regarding the bank clerk resource (table 7A.3). This section is mostly used for the analysis of multiple replications.

Table 7A.1 Arena Report Tally Variables

Identifier	Description
customer.VATime	Value-added time that the entity-type customer spends in the system. In this model, this represents processing (i.e. non-queuing time).
customer.NVATime	Non-value-added time. Not defined in this model
customer.WaitTime	Wait or queuing time
customer.Other Time	Other categories of time. Not defined in this model
customer.TotalTime	The summation of all time categories. Also termed flow time
Till 1 and Till 2.Queue.WaitingTime	The time each entity spends in the queue for the bank tills

Table 7A.2 Arena Report Discrete-Change Variables

Identifier	Description
customer.WIP	The WIP or number of entity-type customers that are in the system
Bank.clerk.NumberBusy	The utilisation as a proportion of the total number of bank clerks (2)
Bank.clerk.numberscheduled	The number of bank clerks (2)
Bank.clerk.utilisation	The utilisation of each individual bank clerk
Till 1 and Till 2.Queue.NumberInQueue	The number of entities in the queue for the bank tills

Table 7A.3 Arena Report Outputs

Identifier	Description
customer.NumberIn	The number of entity-type customers created
customer.NumberOut	The number of entity-type customers disposed
Bank clerk.numberseized	The number of times the bank clerk resource is seized
Bank clerk.scheduledutilisation	The utilisation of the bank clerk resource
System.numberout	The number of all entity types disposed

Table 7A.4 Statistics for Arena Tally and Discrete-Change Variables

Statistic	Description	Tally	Discrete-Change
Average	The average value (time weighted for time-weighted measures)	TAVG	DAVG
Half-Width	The half-width of the confidence interval at 95%. A value of Insuf (Insufficient) or Correlated means that the simulation run is not long enough to provide a valid half-width estimation.	THALF	DHALF
Minimum	The minimum value recorded during the simulation run.	TMIN	DMIN
Maximum	The maximum value recorded during the simulation run.	TMAX	DMAX

For each identifier the following statistics are defined for tally (observational) and discrete-change (time-weighted) output measures (table 7A.4). Arena uses the terms as shown for the tally variables. For example, TMAX(Till 1 and Till 2.Queue.WaitingTime) collects the maximum value over a simulation run for the waiting time in the queue named Till 1 and Till 2 and DAVG(customer.WIP) collects the average value over a simulation run for the WIP or number in the system of entity-type customer.

Note that the Identifier names for entity types, processes and resources are set in the model. If multiple entity types, processes, queues and resources are defined in the model, then these will automatically be reported on in the simulation output report. Any other elements or variables that require reporting can be included in the summary report. Note also that any variables can be plotted during runtime using the animation facilities of the software.

The Double-Queue Bank Clerk Simulation

An alternative double-queue system is proposed. Here, customers make a choice of which of two queues to join when they enter the bank. Customers make this decision based on a rule depending on which of the two till queues holds the minimum number of customers. Once customers have joined a queue, they are not permitted to leave the queue they have joined. The scenario can be represented with a process map and ACD as follows (figure 7A.28 and figure 7A.29).

To implement the double-queue system, add a decision module and a further process. Delete any connecting lines you need to by clicking on the lines and pressing the Delete key on the keyboard. Then click on the connect button on the toolbar and connect and name the additional modules, as shown in figure 7A.30.

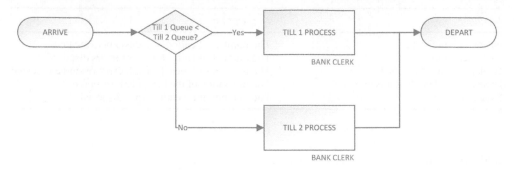

Figure 7A.28 Process map for double-queue bank clerk simulation

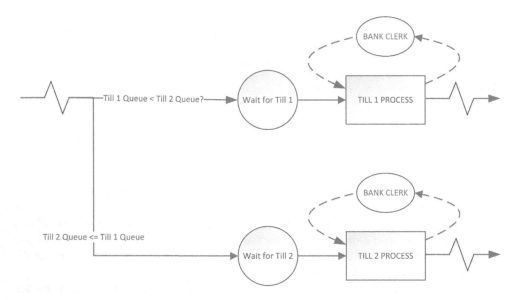

Figure 7A.29 Activity cycle diagram for double-queue bank clerk simulation

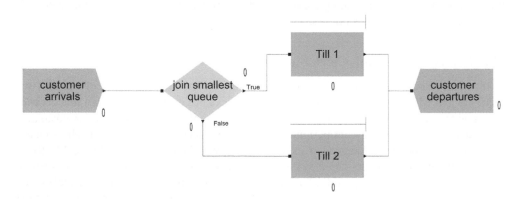

Figure 7A.30 Double-queue Arena model

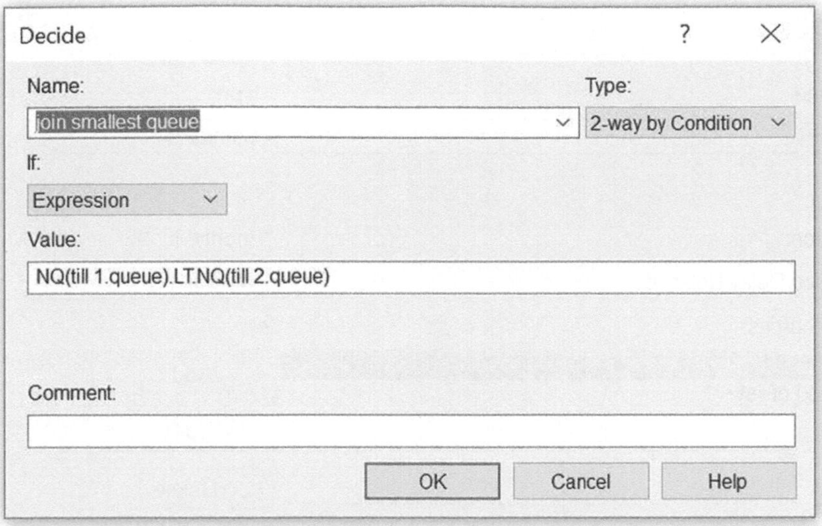

Figure 7A.31 Entering the Decide module parameters

The next step is to define the parameters of the two new modules placed on the screen. Arena decisions can be represented by either an if-then-else conditional formula ('by Conditional' option) or a probability formula ('by Chance' option). Double-click on the Decide module and select two-way 'by Condition' as the type parameter (figure 7A.31). For the If parameter, select Expression. For the value parameter, enter the following expression:

NQ(till 1.Queue).LT.NQ(till 2.Queue)

This expression demonstrates the use of a conditional logic statement in Arena. The statement NQ(till 1.Queue) means the number in queue of the queue named till 1.Queue. The logical operator. LT. provides a 'less than' comparison. Further logical operators are as follows:. GT. provides a greater than comparison,. L.E. provides a less than or equal to comparison and. EQ. checks for equality. In this case, the formula compares the number of customers in the queue for till 1, and if this is less than the number in the till 2 queue, the condition is TRUE, and the entity/customer leaves the Decide module on the TRUE route. Otherwise, the entity/customer leaves on the FALSE route. In this case, the TRUE route should connect to till 1 process, and the FALSE route will connect to till 2 process.

Double-click on the till 2 module, select the Seize Delay Release option for action and add the resource name 'bank clerk2' with a quantity of 1. Select the Triangular option for the delay type. Select the units as minutes and enter 5 for the minimum value, 8 for the most likely value and 11 for the maximum value (figure 7A.32). Double-click on the till 1 process and using the Edit button change the resource name from 'bank clerk' to 'bank clerk1'.

After entering the new bank clerk1 and bank clerk2 resources in the till 1 and till 2 processes, they should appear in the Resources module (found in the Data Definition panel). The original bank clerk resource can be removed (right-click and select Delete) to leave these two resources as in figure 7A.33.

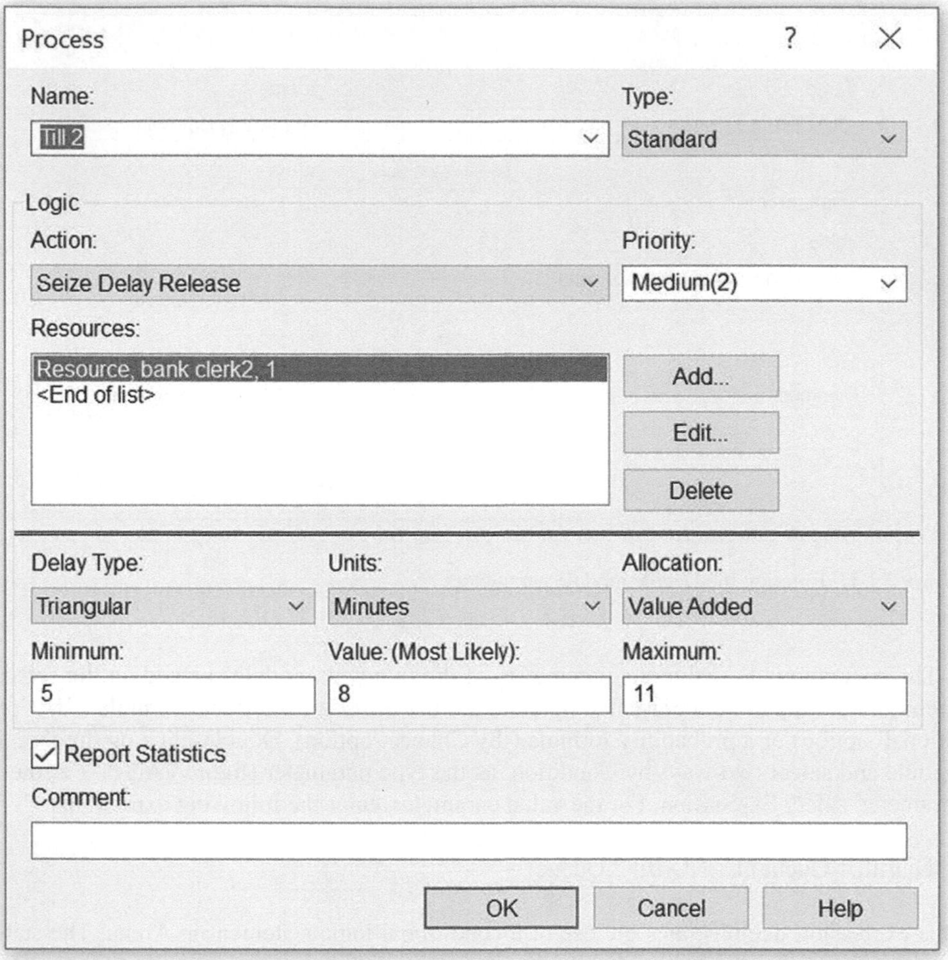

Figure 7A.32 Entering the till 2 parameters

	Name	Type	Capacity	Busy / Hour	Idle / Hour	Per Use	StateSet Name	Failures	Report Statistics	Comment
1 ▸	bank clerk1	Fixed Capacity	1	0.0	0.0	0.0		0 rows	☑	
2	bank clerk2	Fixed Capacity	1	0.0	0.0	0.0		0 rows	☑	

Double-click here to add a new row.

Figure 7A.33 The Resource model for the double-queue model

Run the simulation by clicking on the run (▶) button on the toolbar. When the simulation is completed, the results screen will be displayed as in figure 7A.34. This shows the average number of customers in the system (WIP) (customer.WIP) is 3.57 customers. The average time in the system for the customer (customer.TotalTime) is given as 17.9 minutes, with a maximum time of 81.78 minutes. The maximum customer waiting time for

```
                        ARENA Simulation Results
                    IT Services - License: STUDENT

                     Summary for Replication 1 of 1

Project: Unnamed Project                     Run execution date : 9/ 6/2021
Analyst: IT Services                         Model revision date: 9/ 6/2021

Replication ended at time      : 40320.0 Minutes
Base Time Units: Minutes
                             TALLY VARIABLES

Identifier                   Average  Half Width  Minimum   Maximum  Observations


customer.VATime               8.0202    .02748    5.0166    10.952      8051
customer.NVATime              .00000    .00000     .00000    .00000     8051
customer.WaitTime             9.8775    1.3501     .00000   71.794      8051
customer.TranTime             .00000    .00000     .00000    .00000     8051
customer.OtherTime            .00000    .00000     .00000    .00000     8051
customer.TotalTime           17.897    1.3593    5.1411    81.782      8051
Till 2.Queue.WaitingTime     10.314    1.2446     .00000   71.794      4655
Till 1.Queue.WaitingTime      9.2789    1.4326     .00000   67.895      3396

                        DISCRETE-CHANGE VARIABLES

Identifier                   Average  Half Width  Minimum   Maximum  Final Value


customer.WIP                  3.5738    .29987     .00000   21.000      .00000
bank clerk.NumberBusy         .00000   (Insuf)     .00000    .00000     .00000
bank clerk.NumberScheduled   2.0000   (Insuf)    2.0000    2.0000     2.0000
bank clerk.Utilization        .00000   (Insuf)     .00000    .00000     .00000
bank clerk2.NumberBusy        .92671    .00928     .00000   1.0000      .00000
bank clerk2.NumberScheduled  1.0000   (Insuf)    1.0000    1.0000     1.0000
bank clerk2.Utilization       .92671    .00928     .00000   1.0000      .00000
bank clerk1.NumberBusy        .67475    .02473     .00000   1.0000      .00000
bank clerk1.NumberScheduled  1.0000   (Insuf)    1.0000    1.0000     1.0000
bank clerk1.Utilization       .67475    .02473     .00000   1.0000      .00000
Till 2.Queue.NumberInQueue   1.1908    .14147     .00000   10.000      .00000
Till 1.Queue.NumberInQueue    .78153    .13589     .00000   9.0000      .00000

                                OUTPUTS

Identifier                   Value


customer.NumberIn            8051.0
customer.NumberOut           8051.0
bank clerk.NumberSeized       .00000
```

Figure 7A.34 Results screen for Arena double-queue model

till 1 (Till 1.Queue.WaitingTime) is given as 67.9 minutes. The maximum waiting time for till 2 (Till 2.Queue.WaitingTime) is 71.79 minutes. The maximum number of customers in the queue for till 1 (Till 1.Queue.NumberInQueue) is given as 9. The maximum number of customers in the queue for till 2 is given as 10. The bank clerk1 utilisation or percentage of busy time (bank clerk1.Utilization) is given as 0.675 or 67.5% utilisation. The bank clerk2 utilisation is given as 0.927 or 92.7% utilisation. The maximum number of customers in the bank at any one time (customer.WIP) is given as 21 customers, and the number of customers (observations) who have passed through the bank in the 28 days of runtime is 8,051; 3,396 customers have been processed at till 1 and 4,655 at till 2.

Comparing the Single-Queue and Double-Queue Bank Clerk Models

It can be seen from the results of the simulation that with no other changes, the single-queue system has a lower average WIP of 3.06 customers compared to the double-queue simulation average WIP of 3.57 customers. Thus, the results indicate when we have variability in customer arrival and customer process times, the single-queue arrangement provides better performance than double or parallel servers. A further advantage of a single-queue system is that it ensures that customers are processed in the order that they arrive. However, the single queue may not be practical when there is limited space for an extended single queue. The maximum queue size is reported by the simulation for single queue as 17 customers and double queue as 9 customers for till 1 and 10 customers for till 2. One option is to implement a hybrid queue design where a single queue feeds smaller queues of 1 or 2 customers for each till.

The Double-Queue Bank Clerk Simulation with Animation

We now provide animation facilities to the double-queue bank clerk simulation. Although we do not need to add animation features to the simulation to generate the results and undertake simulation experimentation, animation provides a useful validation tool to check model behaviour and also provides a user-friendly demonstration tool for decision-makers.

In order to animate entities (e.g. people, materials) in a model, Arena uses the concepts of stations and routes. Stations define the start points and endpoints on the screen for movement, and the routes define the path taken on the screen by entities when moving from one station to the next. Stations and routes are modules found in the Discrete Processing template. Now we need to specify the stations that entities move through as they pass through the Arena model. To do this, delete the connector line between the Create module block and the decision block. Do the same for the connectors between the decision module and the till processes. Drag three station modules between modules just disconnected. Drag two route modules onto the screen also. Connect the modules as shown in figure 7A.35. Double-click on the Station 1 module and define the station type as 'station' and name it Station 1. Do the same for Station 2 and Station 3. Double-click on the Route 1 module and enter a route time of 5, units as 'minutes', the destination type as 'station name', and station as Station 2. Do the same for the Route 2 module but make the destination station Station 3. The simulation should look as in figure 7A.35.

The next stage is to define the entity and resource pictures you will use in your animation. Select the Edit Entity Pictures option from the Animate menu on the toolbar. The pictures available to you for animation are shown on the left-hand scroll-down bar. You can select

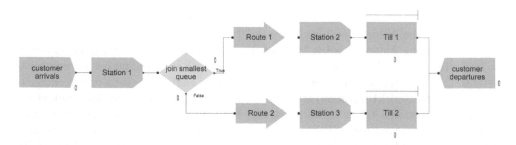

Figure 7A.35 Simulation with station and route modules added

any of these and create your own versions of these pictures, or you can also load in pictures from picture libraries (file extension. plb). In this case, click on the Picture.Person icon in the left-hand list and enter a size factor of 2 (see figure 7A.36). If you wish, you could now double-click on the picture to enter the picture drawing facility to change the picture. In this case select the OK button to proceed. Move to the Entity module in the Data Definition

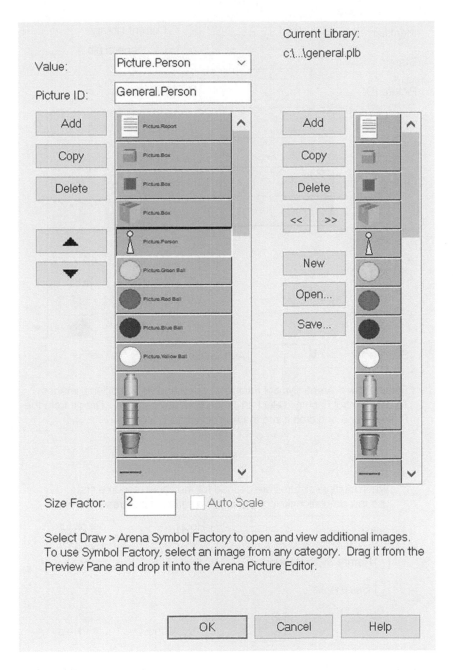

Figure 7A.36 Adding an entity picture

template, and in the data spreadsheet window, alter the initial picture name to Picture.Person. (Pictures of entities can be changed at any time in the module by changing the name of the Entity Picture type attribute.)

Next, click on the resource button on the animate toolbar. Click on the idle icon and select the name 'bank clerk1' in the identifier box (figure 7A.37).

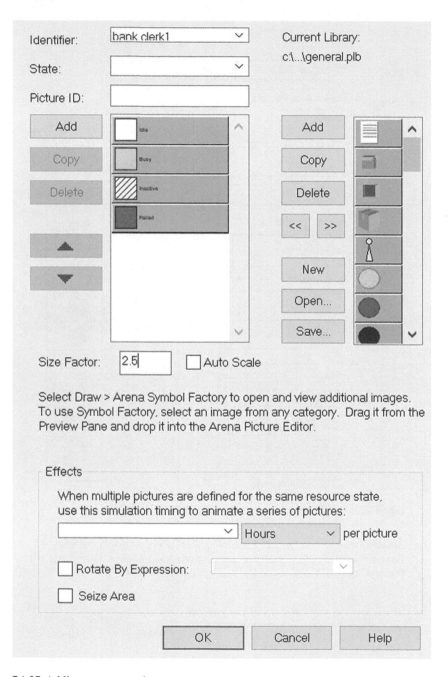

Figure 7A.37 Adding a resource picture

Set the size factor to 2.5 and tick the Seize Area checkbox. Click on OK, and you will have a crosshair cursor on the simulation screen. Click the left button to place your resource on the view screen. Move the seize area to position the entity that is seizing your resource (i.e. the customer who is being served). Repeat the operation to create another resource, but this time, enter the name 'bank clerk2' in the identifier box and place this resource on the screen.

You can now design your animation display. Move to somewhere away from the current Arena model on your screen and drag your bank clerk 1 and bank clerk 2 resource pictures to an appropriate location. You will now define the movement of the entities to the bank clerks. Select the station option from the animate menu toolbar. Select identifier as station 1. Place the station at the entry point for customers. Select the station option again and place station 2 next to your bank clerk 1 resource picture. Repeat for station 3 next to bank clerk 2. Select the route icon from the animate toolbar and click on station 1, then click as required to define the path, finally clicking on station 2. Repeat for the route from station 1 to station 3. This defines all possible routes that entities could take in the current simulation. The animation screen should look something like as shown in figure 7A.38.

Now you can add other elements to the animation, such as queues and counters. The queue displays will be on your flow version of your model above the till 1 and till 2 process modules. If they are, then drag each queue symbol adjacent to its resource (i.e. process 1 queue should be in front of bank clerk 1 resource). If you have no queues displayed at present, you can add queues using the queue option on the animate toolbar. You can add counters using the variables option on the animate toolbar. To display the queue size next to each queue (the queue size may be too large to be displayed using the animation), select the variables option from the animate toolbar and enter the expression NQ(Till 1.queue). Any other variables can be displayed using the variables option. You can display the simulation runtime using the clock option on the animate toolbar. Choose the digital display option. Finally, you can add background graphics (which are not animated) using the Draw toolbar, which lets you draw lines, boxes, shapes and text. You can add the background before the animated elements if you wish. Run the simulation, and you should get something like an image as in figure 7A.39.

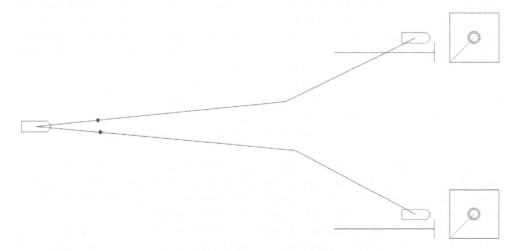

Figure 7A.38 Animation display showing stations, routes, resources and queues

Bank Clerk Simulation Model

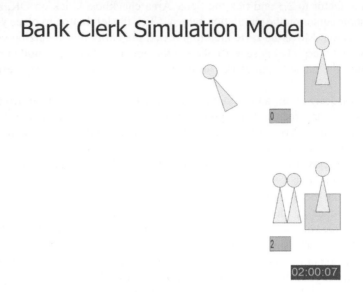

Figure 7A.39 Running the animated bank clerk simulation

Figure 7A.39 is obviously a (very!) basic example of the kind of animation that is possible in Arena. The example does show how Arena separates the model flow version of the simulation (which is all that is needed to report results) from the animation display.

The Loan Application Simulation

This simulation will introduce the concept of resource pooling, entity attribute values and entity statistics collection.

Loan applications arrive at a loan application centre and are assessed by a member of staff. The application is then checked again by a supervisor who makes a decision to approve, reject or request a modification to the application. Approved and rejected applications leave the system. For modified applications, a member of staff specifies changes to the application, and when agreed, the application returns the assessment process. The process map and ACD for the system are shown in figure 7A.40 and figure 7A.41.

Figure 7A.42 shows the loan application model in Arena. In addition to the modules required by the process map, additional modules have been added to count and report on the number of times each loan application has been processed.

To construct the loan application model, the following Arena modules should be placed on the flowchart screen (table 7A.5).

For the loan application Create module, enter the parameter time between arrivals as EXPO(60) minutes and the entity-type parameter as Application. For the Staff Assess Application Process, enter the delay as TRIANGULAR(30,40,50) minutes. The process should have a seize-delay-release action and be allocated a Staff Resource type.

In order to provide an account of the number of times each application is processed, an attribute value is incremented each time the application has completed the Staff Assess Application process. This is achieved using the Arena Assign module and assigning the value

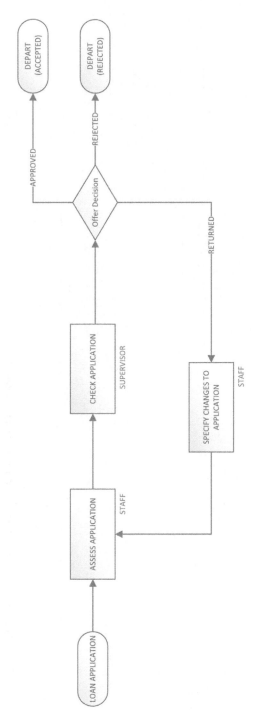

Figure 7A.40 Process map for the loan application simulation

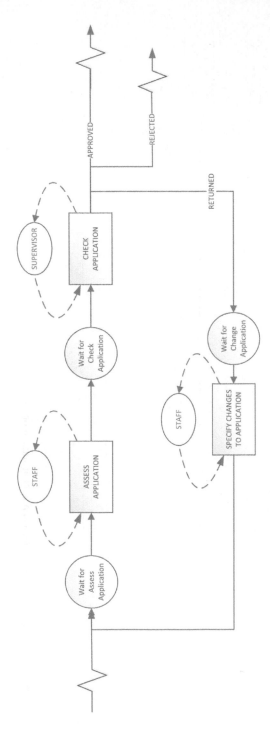

Figure 7A.41 Activity cycle diagram for the loan application simulation

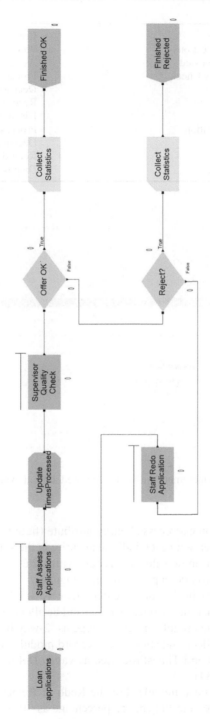

Figure 7A.42 Loan application Arena model

Table 7A.5 Arena Modules for the Loan Application Model

Module Name	Arena Module Type
Loan Applications	Create
Staff Assess Applications	Process
Update TimesProcessed	Assign
Supervisor Quality Check	Process
Offer OK?	Decision
Collect Statistics	Record
Finished OK	Dispose
Staff Redo Application	Process
Reject?	Decision
Collect Statistics	Record
Finished Rejected	Dispose

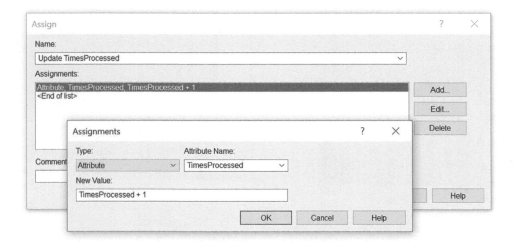

Figure 7A.43 Assign module to increment the TimesProcessed attribute value

TimesProcessed + 1 to the TimesProcessed entity attribute (figure 7A.43). Please note that the attribute value is associated with each individual entity in the simulation. This is distinct from a variable value that is a single value that is held within the model; this type of variable may be defined as a global variable in programming language.

For the Supervisor Quality Check Process, enter the delay as UNIFORM(20,40) minutes. The process should have a seize-delay-release action and be allocated a Supervisor Resource type. For the Offer OK Decide module, define the type as '2-way by chance' and the chance percentage as 60. For the Collect Statistics, add a Record module and add a Statistic definition with Type as expression and TimesProcessed as value. Define the tally name as Tally Times Processed (figure 7A.44)

Add the Finished OK Dispose module. For the Redo or Reject Decide module, define the type as '2-way by chance' and the chance percentage as 30. For the Collect Statistics, add a second Record module and add a Statistic definition with Type as expression and TimesProcessed as value. Define the tally name as Tally Times Processed (figure 7A.44).

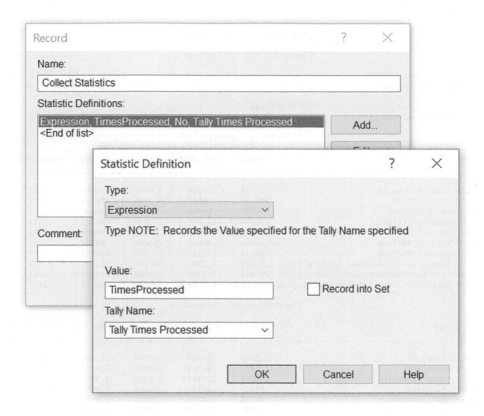

Figure 7A.44 Adding the Record Arena module

	Name	Type	Capacity	Busy / Hour	Idle / Hour	Per Use	StateSet Name	Failures	Report Statistics	Comment
1 ▶	Staff	Fixed Capacity	2	0.0	0.0	0.0		0 rows ☑	☑	
2	Supervisor	Fixed Capacity	1	0.0	0.0	0.0		0 rows ☑	☑	

Double-click here to add a new row.

Figure 7A.45 Resources module

Add the Finished Rejected Dispose module. For the Specify Changes to Application Process, enter the delay as TRIANGULAR(20,40,60) minutes. The process should have a seize-delay-release action and be allocated a Staff Resource type. The staff resource should be defined with a capacity of 2 and the supervisor resource with a capacity of 1 in the Resources module (figure 7A.45).

Connect the modules using the connector tool as shown in figure 7A.1. Select the Run Setup option from the toolbar and select the Replication Parameters tab. Set the replication length as 72000 minutes and all units as minutes. On the Reports tab select the SIMAN Summary reports option from the pull-down menu. Run the simulation and the results should be as in figure 7A.45.

The report in figure 7A.46 includes the following information. The Tally Times Processed variable indicates that loan applications are processed on average 1.3 times, they are all

```
                         ARENA Simulation Results
                       IT Services - License: STUDENT

                       Summary for Replication 1 of 1

Project: Unnamed Project                        Run execution date : 9/ 6/2021
Analyst: IT Services                            Model revision date: 9/ 6/2021

Replication ended at time   : 72000.0 Minutes
Base Time Units: Minutes

                              TALLY VARIABLES

     Identifier                    Average  Half Width  Minimum  Maximum  Observations


     Tally Times Processed          1.3528    .04020    1.0000    7.0000      1213
     application.VATime            108.50     4.4907    52.963   705.85       1213
     application.NVATime            .00000    .00000    .00000    .00000      1213
     application.WaitTime          57.590    13.047     .00000   688.06       1213
     application.TranTime           .00000    .00000    .00000    .00000      1213
     application.OtherTime          .00000    .00000    .00000    .00000      1213
     application.TotalTime         166.10    15.514    55.034   1305.7        1213
     Staff Redo Application.Queue.WaitingTime  14.247   4.2181   .00000  152.49    429
     Supervisor Quality Check.Queue.WaitingTime 26.803  7.1469   .00000  178.36   1643
     Staff Assess Applications.Queue.WaitingTim 12.117  3.4080   .00000  124.38   1645

                        DISCRETE-CHANGE VARIABLES

     Identifier                    Average  Half Width  Minimum  Maximum  Final Value


     application.WIP                2.8076    .38563    .00000   12.000     3.0000
     Staff.NumberBusy               1.1499    .08368    .00000    2.0000     .00000
     Staff.NumberScheduled          2.0000   (Insuf)    2.0000    2.0000    2.0000
     Staff.Utilization              .57499    .04184    .00000    1.0000     .00000
     Supervisor.NumberBusy          .68158    .04299    .00000    1.0000    1.0000
     Supervisor.NumberScheduled    1.0000    (Insuf)    1.0000    1.0000    1.0000
     Supervisor.Utilization         .68158    .04299    .00000    1.0000    1.0000
     Staff Redo Application.Queue.NumberInQueue  .08489  .02996  .00000  3.0000   .00000
     Supervisor Quality Check.Queue.NumberInQue  .61437  .18786  .00000  7.0000  2.0000
     Staff Assess Applications.Queue.NumberInQu  .27686  .08007  .00000  6.0000   .00000

                                 OUTPUTS

     Identifier                    Value


     application.NumberIn           1216.0
     application.NumberOut          1213.0
     Staff.NumberSeized             2074.0
     Staff.ScheduledUtilization      .57499
     Supervisor.NumberSeized        1643.0
     Supervisor.ScheduledUtilization .68158
     System.NumberOut               1213.0


     Simulation run time: 0.05 minutes.
     Simulation run complete.
```

Figure 7A.46 Loan application model results screen

processed at least 1 time and the maximum times processed is 7 (1 original and 6 times the application process is redone). The number of items processed during the runtime (72,000 minutes) is 1,213. The average time taken to process an application is 166.1 minutes, with the maximum application process time being 1,305.7 minutes. The average number of applications in the system at any one time is 2.8 applications; the average number of staff busy is

1.15 (for 2 staff), giving an individual staff utilisation of 57.5%. The supervisor utilisation is given as 68.15%.

The Petrol Station Simulation Model

The petrol station model will introduce the concepts of baulking at resources and calculation of income and cost metrics.

Customers arrive at the petrol station, and 25% of customers head for the manual pumps (with payment at a separate till service). If no manual pumps are available, they drive away; otherwise, they refill their vehicle with petrol and then proceed to the payment till and continue with the payment process. About 75% of customers head for the pay at pumps. If no pay at pumps is available, they drive away; otherwise, they refill their vehicle with petrol and pay at the pump.

These current simulation parameters apply:

- The customer arrival rate is an exponential distribution with a mean of 3 minutes.
- The manual pump service time is a triangular distribution with a minimum of 4 minutes, mode of 6 minutes and maximum of 10 minutes.
- The pay at pump service time is a triangular distribution with a minimum of 6 minutes, mode of 8 minutes and maximum of 12 minutes.
- The payment at till service is a triangular distribution with a minimum of 8 minutes, mode of 10 minutes and maximum of 12 minutes.
- Currently there are 2 manual petrol pumps, 2 pay at pumps and 1 payment till.
- The total cost per day of renting and operating the station is £50 per manual pump installed, £100 per pay pump installed and £200 per payment till. There is an estimated income of £50 per customer served at the petrol station.

The management wish to assess their operating profit on a typical day's operation.

The petrol station process map (figure 7A.47) and the ACD (figure 7A.48) are as follows.

Figure 7A.49 shows the petrol station model in Arena. In addition to the modules required by the process map, additional modules have been added to count 'driveaways' – customers that find either the manual pumps or the pay at pumps unavailable and leave the petrol station. There is also an assignment to calculate the daily profit from the operation of the petrol station.

To construct the model, the following Arena modules should be placed on the flowchart screen (table 7A.6).

Enter the interarrival time for the customer arrivals module and the processing times for the three Process modules from the model description. Add the resources manual pump, pay pump and payment till to the appropriate processes. Enter the initial capacity for the three resources in the resource element. In the TotalCostPerDay Assign module, enter the following state assignment before exiting:

TotalCostPerDay = MR(manual pump)*50+MR(pay pump)*100+MR(till service)*200

For the 'manual pumps?' decision enter a '2-way by chance' decision and enter 25 for the percentage. For the 'No Manual Pumps available?' decision, enter the '2-way by condition' statement:

NR(manual pump).EQ.MR(manual pump)

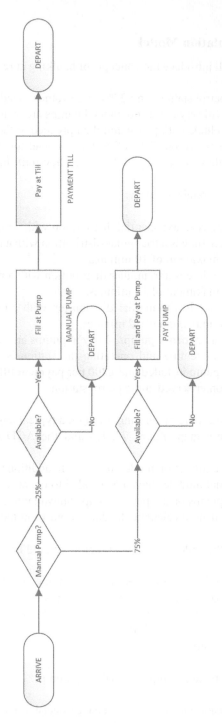

Figure 7A.47 Petrol station process map

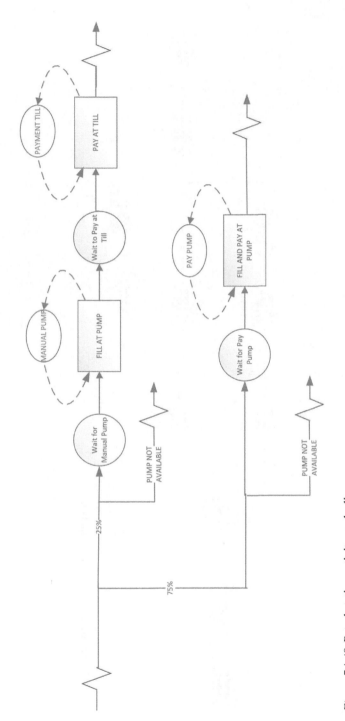

Figure 7A.48 Petrol station activity cycle diagram

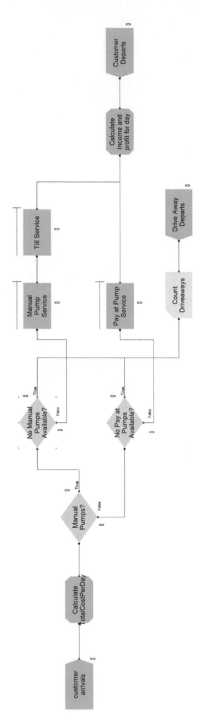

Figure 7A.49 Arena petrol station simulation

Table 7A.6 Arena Modules for Petrol Station Model

Module Name	Arena Module Type
Customer arrivals	Create
Calculate TotalCostPerDay	Assign
Manual Pumps?	Decision
No Manual Pumps Available?	Decision
No Pay at Pumps Available?	Decision
Manual Pump Service	Process
Till Service	Process
Pay at Pump Service	Process
Count Driveaways	Record
Driveaway Departs	Dispose
Calculate Income and Profit for day	Assign
Customer Departs	Dispose

```
Replication ended at time     : 480.0 Minutes
Base Time Units: Minutes
```

```
                          TALLY VARIABLES

Identifier                      Average  Half Width  Minimum   Maximum   Observations


Entity 1.VATime                 7.7174   (Insuf)     .00000    20.616    152
Entity 1.NVATime                .00000   (Insuf)     .00000    .00000    152
Entity 1.WaitTime               1.6763   (Insuf)     .00000    25.932    152
Entity 1.TranTime               .00000   (Insuf)     .00000    .00000    152
Entity 1.OtherTime              .00000   (Insuf)     .00000    .00000    152
Entity 1.TotalTime              9.3937   (Insuf)     .00000    43.373    152
Pay at Pump Service.Queue.WaitingTime   .00000   (Insuf)  .00000  .00000  68
Manual Pump Service.Queue.WaitingTime   .00000   (Insuf)  .00000  .00000  35
Till Service.Queue.WaitingTime  7.4055   (Insuf)     .00000    25.932    35

                     DISCRETE-CHANGE VARIABLES

Identifier                      Average  Half Width  Minimum   Maximum   Final Value


profit Value                    1926.3   (Insuf)     -450.000  4600.0    4600.0
Entity 1.WIP                    3.0039   (Insuf)     .00000    8.0000    1.0000
payment till.NumberBusy         .72588   (Insuf)     .00000    1.0000    1.0000
payment till.NumberScheduled    1.0000   (Insuf)     1.0000    1.0000    1.0000
payment till.Utilization        .72588   (Insuf)     .00000    1.0000    1.0000
manual pump.NumberBusy          .49275   (Insuf)     .00000    2.0000    .00000
manual pump.NumberScheduled     2.0000   (Insuf)     2.0000    2.0000    2.0000
manual pump.Utilization         .24637   (Insuf)     .00000    1.0000    .00000
pay pump.NumberBusy             1.2453   (Insuf)     .00000    2.0000    .00000
pay pump.NumberScheduled        2.0000   (Insuf)     2.0000    2.0000    2.0000
pay pump.Utilization            .62265   (Insuf)     .00000    1.0000    .00000
Pay at Pump Service.Queue.NumberInQueue  .00000  (Insuf)  .00000  .00000  .00000
Manual Pump Service.Queue.NumberInQueue  .00000  (Insuf)  .00000  .00000  .00000
Till Service.Queue.NumberInQueue  .53998  (Insuf)   .00000    3.0000    .00000

                          COUNTERS

Identifier                      Count    Limit


driveaways                      50       Infinite
```

Figure 7A.50 Petrol station model results screen

Enter the equivalent statement for the 'no pay at pumps available?' decision.

For the Count Driveaways record, enter the type as Count, the value as 1 and the counter name as driveaways. For the Calculate Income and profit for day assign, enter:

Income = Income + 50
Profit = Income − TotalCostPerDay

Go to the variable module in the data definition template and tick the report statistics box to enable reporting of the profit variable. On the Run setup, set the runtime as 480 minutes and run the model. The results should look similar to figure 7A.50.

For this single run, the following results are shown:

Average customer time in the system = 9.4 minutes
Number of customers entering the system = 152
Number of driveaways = 50
Queuing times – no queuing at the pumps, average time of 7.4 minutes at the till.
Profit = £4,600

Summary

A selection of Arena modules are introduced, and their use is demonstrated using the bank clerk, loan application and petrol station simulation models.

7B: Building the Simulation in Simio

Introduction

Undertaking the exercises in this chapter requires the installation of the Simio Personal Edition simulation software system. This is available as a free download with full functionality but with a limited model size at www.simio.com/evaluate.php.

This chapter uses version 14.2 of Simio. A selection of objects from the object library in Simio is described. These provide the building blocks for the models presented in this chapter, but there are numerous additional objects available in Simio if required. The following objects are described:

- Source
- Sink
- Server
- Combiner
- Separator
- Resource
- BasicNode
- Connector
- Path

The following tutorials are presented in order to demonstrate the basic functionality of the Simio software:

- The single-queue bank clerk simulation.
- The double-queue bank clerk simulation.
- The double-queue bank clerk simulation with animation.
- The loan application simulation.
- The petrol station simulation.

Getting Started in Simio

When the Simio system is run, the screen display shown in figure 7B.1 should be displayed.

The ribbon across the top of the screen has a number of screen tabs that collect together commands into logical groups. Screen tabs are included for run commands and view options. Below the ribbon, there is a further series of tabs called the Project Model Tabs that are used to select options regarding the active model. If the Facility tab is selected as in figure 7B.1,

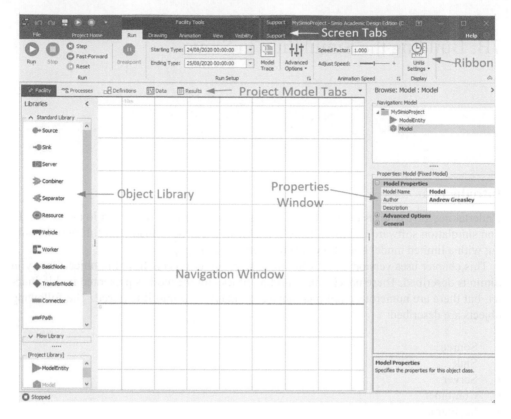

Figure 7B.1 Simio 14.2 model display

then to the left of the screen the object library is displayed. By default, the screen will display the Standard Library and, at the bottom of the screen, the Project Library. The Properties Window is on the right-hand side of the screen and shows the characteristics of any object or item currently selected. The main area of the screen (with grid) is named the Navigation Window. Objects are placed from an Object Library onto the Navigation Window and are defined/edited from the Navigation Window in the Properties Window. To move around the Navigation Window, hold down the left mouse button and move the mouse. To zoom in and out of the Navigation Window, hold down the right mouse button and move the mouse.

A selection of Simio objects is now described; they are used in the exercises in this text. There are many more Simio objects in the Simio object libraries, and more information is provided with the Simio software help system and support files.

Simio Objects

Source

This object generates entities that move through the simulation. It defines the time delay between entity arrivals (interarrival time). Also, the number of entities that arrive together (entities per arrival).

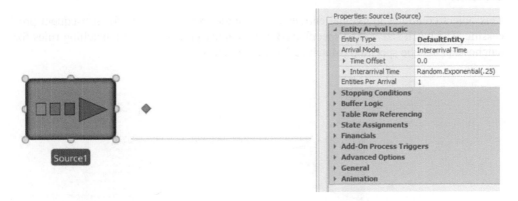

Figure 7B.2 Simio Source object

Sink

This object removes entities when they have finished moving through the system.

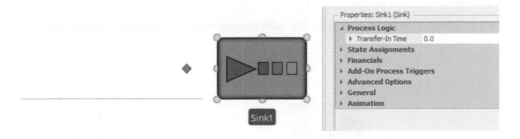

Figure 7B.3 Simio Sink object

Server

This object defines a process and associated resource capacity. The capacity of the server is set by the Initial Capacity parameter, and the process duration is set by the Processing Time parameter.

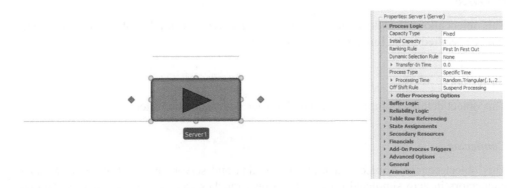

Figure 7B.4 Simio Server object

Combiner

This object combines individual entities into a single (batched) entity for subsequent processing. The batch size can be specified (Batch Quantity parameter), and matching rules for batches can also be specified (Matching Rule parameter).

Figure 7B.5 Simio Combiner object

Separator

This object splits batches of entities into individual entities for subsequent processing.

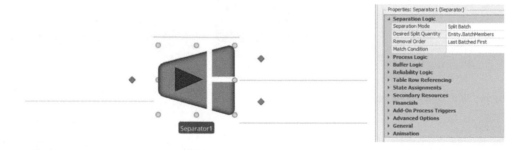

Figure 7B.6 Simio Separator object

Resource

This object allows the allocation of a resource to a server. The number of resources available can be specified in the Initial Capacity parameter.

BasicNode

This object defines a simple intersection between paths and connectors.

Connector

This object connects objects such as source, sink and server objects. Entities flow along connectors in zero simulated time. Entity flow branches can be implemented by defining multiple connectors from a node and setting the Selection Weight parameter for each branch.

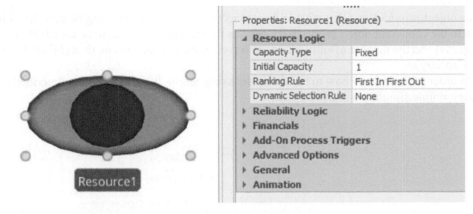

Figure 7B.7 Simio Resource object

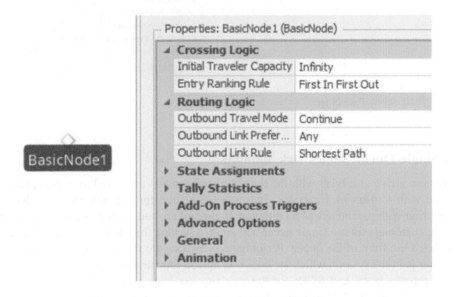

Figure 7B.8 Simio BasicNode object

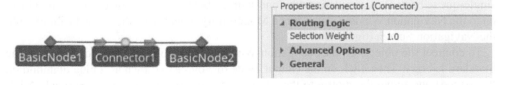

Figure 7B.9 Simio Connector object

Path

This object provides an alternative to the connector object for connecting objects. In addition to the connector object properties, it permits the direction of travel to be specified (Type property) and the number of entities that can travel on the path at any one time (Initial Traveler Capacity).

In order to understand how to build a model using Simio, the steps are now described for a very simple simulation of a bank clerk.

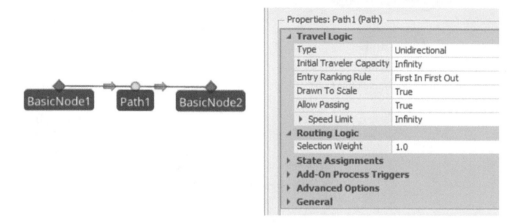

Figure 7B.10 Simio Path object

The Single-Queue Bank Clerk Simulation

Customers arrive at a bank with the time between arrivals estimated as exponentially distributed with a mean of 5 minutes. The processing time for the customers is a triangular distribution with parameters of 5 minimum, 8 most likely and 11 maximum minutes. In this system, customers form a single queue and receive service from two members of staff when they reach the front of the queue. Performance statistics are required on the average time a customer is in the system, which includes both queue time and service time.

The process maps and ACDs for the single-queue bank clerk simulation are shown in figure 7B.11 and 7B.12. Customers arrive from outside the system and are processed by the bank clerks. They then leave the system once the process has been completed.

To add the objects to the Navigation Window, make sure the Facility Tab is selected in the Project Model Tabs. The objects are added to the model window flowchart view by dragging (hold down the left button over the module) them from the Object Library. To begin the single-queue bank clerk simulation drag one source object, a server object and a sink object on to the Navigation Window. Also, drag a ModelEntity object from the Project Library onto the Navigation Screen (figure 7B.13).

To connect the objects on the Navigation Window, click on the Connector Object in the Standard Library. Then click on the Output Node of Source1 (shown as a blue diamond on the screen) and move the mouse to the input node (grey diamond) for the Server1. A left mouse click will define the connection. Repeat the operation to connect Server1 to the sink

Figure 7B.11 Process map for single-queue bank clerk simulation

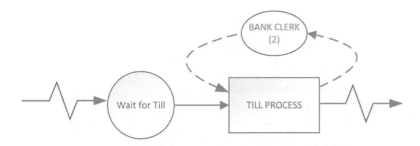

Figure 7B.12 Activity cycle diagram for single-queue bank clerk simulation

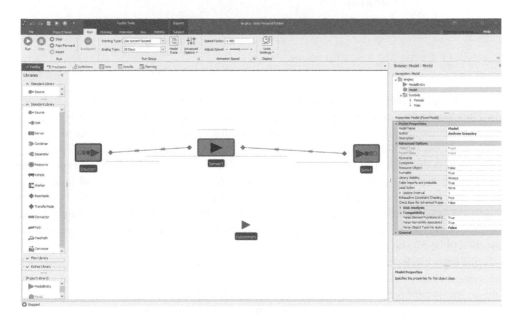

Figure 7B.13 Simio objects on the Navigation Window

(figure 7B.13). To remove a connection, click on the connection line to highlight it and press the Delete key on your keyboard.

Now double-click on the Source1 object and enter Random.Exponential(5) for the interarrival time in the Source1 Object Properties Window as shown in figure 7B.14. Make sure the Units entry immediately below the Interarrival Time entry is set to minutes.

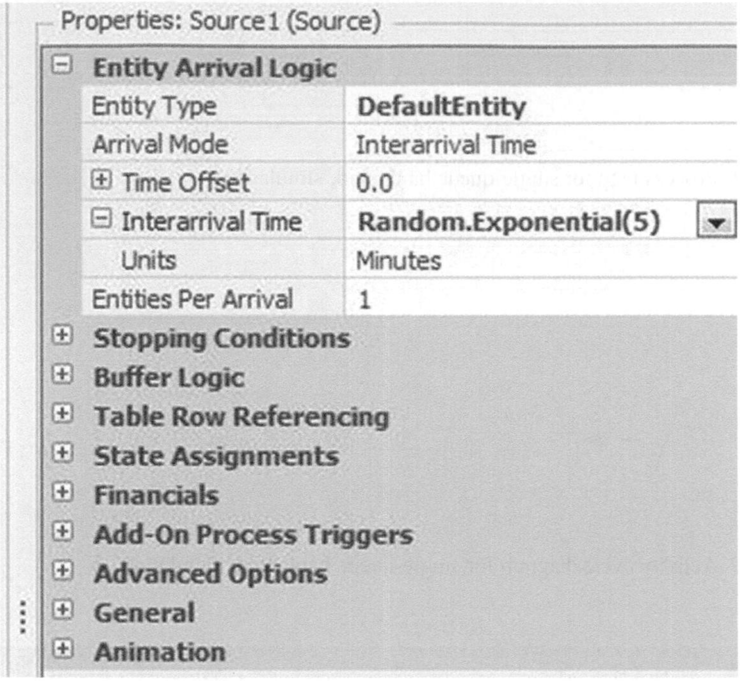

Figure 7B.14 Entering the Source1 properties

Move to the Server1 in the Navigation Window. In the Properties Window for the Processing Time parameter, enter Random.Triangular(5,8,11). Make sure the Units entry is set to minutes. Set the Initial Capacity entry in the Properties Window to 2 (figure 7B.15).

We can now run the model. Click on the Run Tab in the Facility ribbon and select the Unit Settings tab. Select Minutes for Time Units. On the Run Tab for Ending Type, select Run Length from the pull-down menu and enter 28 days for the simulation end time. Click on the Run button to the left of the tab. The simulation should now run through 28 days of simulated time. To run through time at a faster pace, click on the fast-forward button. When the simulation run has finished, click on the Reports tab in the Project Model ribbon, and the results will be displayed (figure 7B.16).

In the bank clerk simulation, referring to figure 7B.16, the average number of customers in the system (WIP) (ModelEntity.NumberInSystem.Average) is 2.79 customers. The average time in the system for the customer (ModelEntity.TimeInSystem.Average) is given as 14.27 minutes, with a maximum time of 57.12 minutes. The maximum customer waiting time (Server1.InputBuffer.TimeInStation.Maximum) is given as 49.14 minutes. The maximum number of customers in a queue (Server1.InputBuffer.NumberInStation) is given as 14. The bank clerk utilisation or percentage of busy time (Server1.UnitsUtilized) is given as 1.57 for the 2 bank clerks or 0.785% utilisation for each bank clerk. The maximum number of customers in the bank at any one time (ModelEntity.NumberInSystem.Maximum) is given as 16 customers, and the number of customers (observations) who have passed through the bank (ModelEntity.NumberDestroyed) in the 28 days of runtime is 7,887. Thus, this very simple model provides us with a variety of performance measures for our bank clerk system.

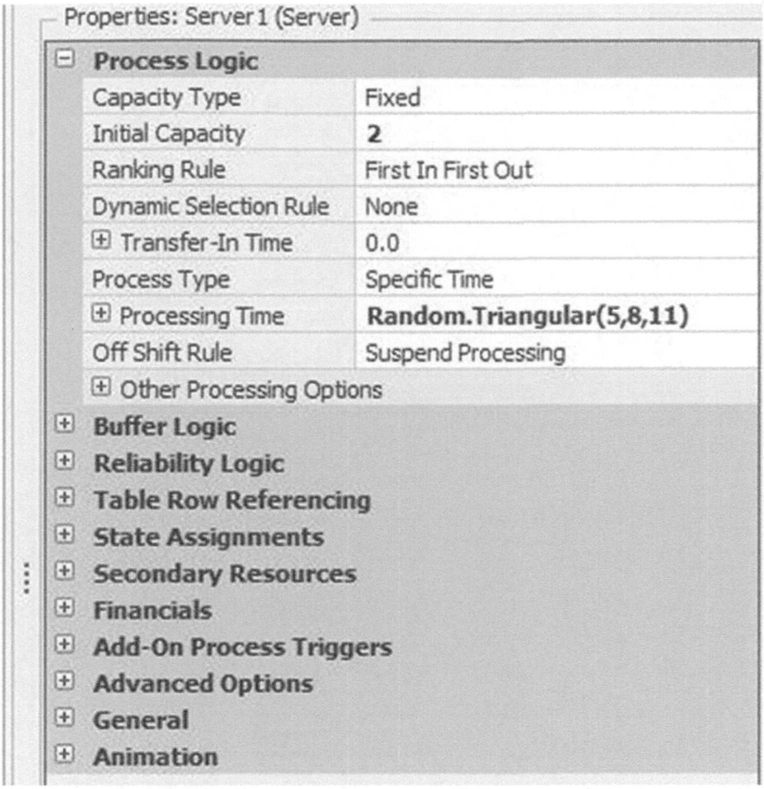

Figure 7B.15 Entering the Server1 properties

Note that the models built in this chapter incorporate probability distributions, and so the results you get may differ slightly from those in the text due to random variation. This is to be expected, and you can see that the results from the same model run on different simulation software will also vary.

Note that our replication length is 28 days, each of 24 hours ($28 \times 24 \times 60 = 40{,}320$ minutes). Thus, we are assuming here that the bank operation is running continuously 24 hours a day. In reality, a physical bank branch facility would be open for around 8 hours a day, beginning empty of customers at the start of the day and returning to an empty state at the end of the day. This is termed a terminating system in simulation, and the procedure for analysis of results of a terminating simulation in Simio is covered in chapter 9B.

Simio Simulation Statistics

Although the report shown in figure 7B.16 is particular to the Simio software, most simulation software will present simulation output data in these categories. For observational data, each observation is treated as an individual occurrence and is equally weighted (the time over which this occurrence happens is not taken into consideration). So for figure 7B.16, to calculate the average ModelEntity.TimeInSystem would entail summing the 7,887 observations

Object Type	Object Name	Data Source	Category	Data Item	Statistic	Average Total
ModelEntity	customers	[Population]	Content	NumberInSystem	Maximum	16.0000
					Average	2.7921
			FlowTime	TimeInSystem	Maximum (Minutes)	57.1153
					Average (Minutes)	14.2698
			Throughput	NumberCreated	Total	7,890.0000
				NumberDestroyed	Total	7,887.0000
Server	Server1	[Resource]	Capacity	UnitsAllocated	Total	7,889.0000
				UnitsScheduled	Maximum	2.0000
					Average	2.0000
				UnitsUtilized	Maximum	2.0000
					Average	1.5668
			ResourceState	TimeProcessing	Total (Minutes)	35,869.6642
					Average (Minutes)	38.6527
				TimeStarved	Total (Minutes)	4,450.3358
					Average (Minutes)	4.8008
		InputBuffer	Content	NumberInStation	Maximum	14.0000
					Average	1.2253
			HoldingTime	TimeInStation	Maximum (Minutes)	49.1384
					Average (Minutes)	6.2621
			Throughput	NumberEntered	Total	7,890.0000
				NumberExited	Total	7,889.0000
		OutputBuffer	Throughput	NumberEntered	Total	7,887.0000
				NumberExited	Total	7,887.0000
		Processing	Content	NumberInStation	Maximum	2.0000
					Average	1.5668
			HoldingTime	TimeInStation	Maximum (Minutes)	10.9613
					Average (Minutes)	8.0079
			Throughput	NumberEntered	Total	7,889.0000
				NumberExited	Total	7,887.0000
Sink	Sink1	[DestroyedEntities]	FlowTime	TimeInSystem	Maximum (Minutes)	57.1153
					Average (Minutes)	14.2698
		InputBuffer	Throughput	NumberEntered	Total	7,887.0000
				NumberExited	Total	7,887.0000
Source	Source1	OutputBuffer	Throughput	NumberEntered	Total	7,890.0000
				NumberExited	Total	7,890.0000
		Processing	Throughput	NumberEntered	Total	7,890.0000
				NumberExited	Total	7,890.0000

Figure 7B.16 Simio single-queue bank clerk simulation results

Table 7B.1 Simio Report Observational Data

Identifier	*Description*
Server1.InputBuffer.TimeInStation	Customer wait or queuing time at Server1
Server1.Processing.TimeInStation	Customer processing time at Server1
ModelEntity.TimeInSystem	Total customer time in the system. Also termed flow time.

for the time in the system and dividing by the number of observations. Table 7B.1 presents the following observational data by default for the bank clerk simulation.

The next section covers time-weighted or time-persistent data. Here, the time over which the occurrence happened is taken into account. So for figure 7B.16, to calculate the Server1. NumberInStation value would entail recording the time period for each number in queue value and summing these values. Table 7B.2 presents the following time-persistent data values by default for the bank clerk simulation.

The report also provides information on various additional measures such as the number of customers entering and leaving the system (table 7B.3).

For each identifier the following statistics are defined for observational and time-persistent output measures (table 7B.4).

Table 7B.2 Simio Report Time-Persistent Data

Identifier	Description
ModelEntity.NumberInSystem	The WIP or number of customers in the system
Server1.UnitsUtilized	The utilisation as a proportion of the number of bank clerks
Server1.Units Scheduled	The number of bank clerks
Server1.ScheduledUtilization	The utilisation of each individual bank clerk
Server1.InputBuffer.NumberInStation	The number of customers in the server queue

Table 7B.3 Simio Report Outputs

Identifier	Description
ModelEntity.NumberCreated	The number of customers created
ModelEntity.NumberDestroyed	The number of customers disposed

Table 7B.4 Statistics for Simio Observational and Time-Persistent Data

Statistic	Description
Average	The average value (time weighted for time-weighted measures)
Minimum	The minimum value recorded during the simulation run
Maximum	The maximum value recorded during the simulation run

The Double-Queue Bank Clerk Simulation

An alternative double-queue system is proposed. Here, customers make a choice of which of two queues to join when they enter the bank. Customers make this decision based on a rule depending on which of the two till queues holds the minimum number of customers. Once customers have joined a queue they are not permitted to leave the queue they have joined. The scenario can be represented with a process map and ACD as follows (figure 7B.17 and figure 7B.18).

For the double-queue bank clerk model, drag an additional server object to the Navigation Window of the single-queue bank clerk model. Add connector objects; Source1 should be connected to both Server1 and Server2. Both servers should be connected to the sink. The model is shown in figure 7B.19.

Move to the Server1 in the Navigation Window. Set the Initial Capacity entry in the Properties Window to 1. Move to the Server2 in the Navigation Window. In the Properties Window for the Processing Time parameter, enter Random.Triangular(5,8,11). Make sure the Units entry is set to 'minutes'. Set the Initial Capacity entry in the Properties Window to 1.

We can now direct customers to the server with the smallest queue size for our double-queue model. We need to set up a list of destinations from which we can choose our destination. To do this, select the Definitions tab and select the List option. Click on the Node option in the ribbon at the top of the screen. Give the node the name Servers in the Properties Window. Click on the Node grid and select from the pull-down menu the Input@Server1 option. Click on the Node grid again and select the Input@Server2 option. If further destinations are possible, they can be easily added here. For the two server bank clerks, the screen is as shown in figure 7B.20.

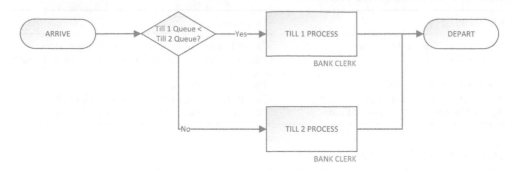

Figure 7B.17 Process map for double-queue bank clerk simulation

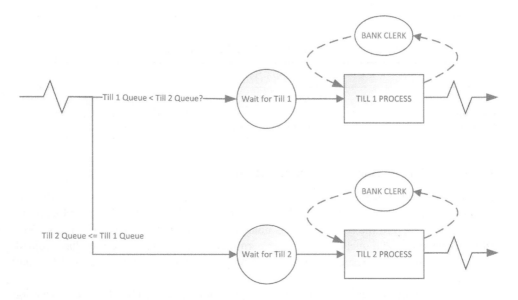

Figure 7B.18 Activity cycle diagram for double-queue bank clerk simulation

Return to the Facility window and click on the output node for Source1 (named Output@ Source1). In the Properties Window, select Entity Destination Type and select the Select from List option. Select Node List Name and select the Servers option, which should appear on the pulld-own menu if it has been defined previously. For Selection Goal, select Smallest Value. For Selection expression, enter Candidate.Node.AssociatedStation.Contents.NumberWaiting. The Properties Window should look as shown in figure 7B.21.

Run the model and the customers should be directed to the server with the smallest queue. At the end of the run, select the Results tab for the results (figure 7B.22). In this case, the average number of customers in the system (WIP) (ModelEntity.NumberInSystem.Average) is 3.17 customers. The average time in the system for the customer (ModelEntity.TimeInSystem.Average) is given as 16.22 minutes. The maximum customer waiting time at Server1 (Server1.InputBuffer.TimeInStation.Maximum) is given as 52.9 minutes. The maximum

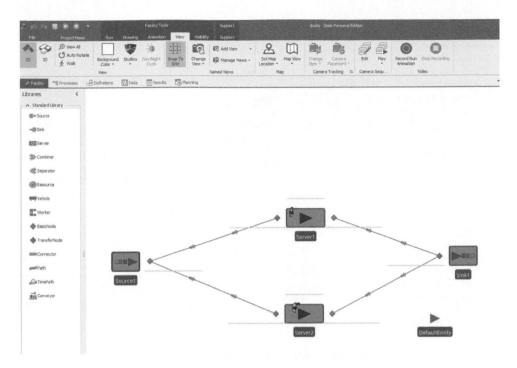

Figure 7B.19 Connecting the bank clerk objects with paths

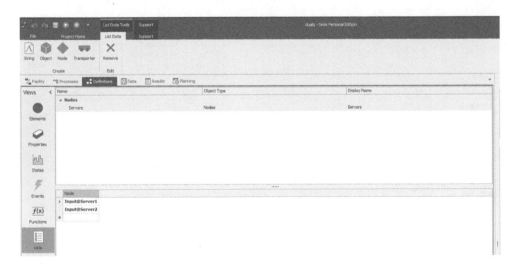

Figure 7B.20 Defining the server list

number of customers in a queue (Server1.InputBuffer.NumberInStation) is given as 7. The Server1 bank clerk utilisation or percentage of busy time (Server1.UnitsUtilized) is given as 0.92 or 92% utilisation, and the Server2 bank clerk utilisation or percentage of busy time (Server2.ScheduledUtilization) is given as 0.64 or 64%. The maximum number of customers

Properties: Output@Source1 (TransferNode)

⊟ **Crossing Logic**	
Initial Traveler Capacity	Infinity
Entry Ranking Rule	First In First Out
⊟ **Routing Logic**	
Outbound Travel Mode	Continue
Outbound Link Preference	Any
Outbound Link Rule	Shortest Path
⊟ Entity Destination Type	**Select From List**
Node List Name	**Servers**
⊟ Selection Goal	**Smallest Value**
Selection Expression	**Candidate.Node.AssociatedStation.Contents.NumberWaiting**
Selection Condition	
Blocked Destination Rule	Select Available Only
⊞ Other Routing Out Options	
⊟ **Transport Logic**	
Ride On Transporter	False
⊞ **State Assignments**	
⊞ **Tally Statistics**	
⊞ **Add-On Process Triggers**	
⊞ **Advanced Options**	
⊞ **General**	
⊞ **Animation**	

Figure 7B.21 Entering the customer destination decision rule

Object Type	Object Name	Data Source	Category	Data Item	Statistic	Average Total
ModelEntity	DefaultEntity	[Population]	Content	NumberInSystem	Maximum	16.0000
					Average	3.1660
			FlowTime	TimeInSystem	Observations	7,870.0000
					Maximum (Minutes)	61.6207
					Average (Minutes)	16.2196
Server	Server1	[Resource]	Capacity	UnitsAllocated	Total	4,652.0000
				UnitsScheduled	Maximum	1.0000
					Average	1.0000
				UnitsUtilized	Maximum	1.0000
					Average	0.9230
		InputBuffer	Content	NumberInStation	Maximum	7.0000
					Average	0.9787
			HoldingTime	TimeInStation	Maximum (Minutes)	52.8953
					Average (Minutes)	8.4829
		Processing	Content	NumberInStation	Maximum	1.0000
					Average	0.9230
			HoldingTime	TimeInStation	Maximum (Minutes)	10.9048
					Average (Minutes)	8.0011
	Server2	[Resource]	Capacity	UnitsAllocated	Total	3,219.0000
				UnitsScheduled	Maximum	1.0000
					Average	1.0000
				UnitsUtilized	Maximum	1.0000
					Average	0.6411
		InputBuffer	Content	NumberInStation	Maximum	7.0000
					Average	0.5924
			HoldingTime	TimeInStation	Maximum (Minutes)	51.0871
					Average (Minutes)	7.4206
		Processing	Content	NumberInStation	Maximum	1.0000
					Average	0.6411
			HoldingTime	TimeInStation	Maximum (Minutes)	10.9613
					Average (Minutes)	8.0302
Sink	Sink1	[DestroyedEntities]	FlowTime	TimeInSystem	Observations	7,870.0000
					Maximum (Minutes)	61.6207
					Average (Minutes)	16.2196

Figure 7B.22 Simio double-queue bank clerk simulation results

in the bank at any one time (ModelEntity.NumberInSystem.Maximum) is given as 16 customers, and the number of customers (observations) who have passed through the bank (ModelEntity.NumberDestroyed) in the 28 days of runtime is 7,870.

Comparing the Single-Queue and Double-Queue Bank Clerk Models

It can be seen from the results of the simulation that with no other changes, the single-queue system has a lower average WIP of 2.79 customers compared to the double-queue simulation average WIP of 3.17 customers. Thus, the results indicate when we have variability in customer arrival and customer process times, the single-queue arrangement provides better performance than double or parallel servers. A further advantage of a single-queue system is that it ensures that customers are processed in the order that they arrive. However, the single queue may not be practical when there is limited space for an extended single. The maximum queue size is reported by the simulation for single queue as 14 customers and double queue as 7 customers for each queue. One option is to implement a hybrid queue design where a single queue feeds smaller queues of 1 or 2 customers for each till.

The Double-Queue Bank Clerk Simulation with Animation

Simio provides facilities that allow 3D representations of a model to be developed quickly. For the bank clerk simulation with the Facility tab selected and the model visible, select the View Tab on the top ribbon and select the 3D option. The model will be redrawn in a 3D view. Hold down the right mouse button and move up and down to zoom, and move left and right to rotate the image on the screen. Hold down the left button and move to move around the model landscape.

We can make changes to the image so that it more closely represents the system we are modelling. To replace the entity image from green triangles to people select the Default-Entity icon, select the Symbols tab on the top ribbon and select the Apply Symbols option. A pull-down menu provides a selection of images to choose from. Select the people option in the Type selection box, and the people images will be displayed. Scroll down and pick one of the images from the Library/People/Animated/Female category. Now click on Server1, and select an image from the same category for Server1 and from the Library/People/Animated/ Male category for Server2. You can change the image display when the servers are activated (move from idle to busy) by selecting the server image and selecting the Active Symbol option. Select the Processing option from the list and then apply a different symbol using the Apply Symbol option. When the simulation is run, the symbol image will change when the server is activated (figure 7B.23).

The Loan Application Simulation

This simulation will introduce the concept of resource pooling, entity attribute values and entity statistics collection.

Loan applications arrive at a loan application centre and are assessed by a member of staff. The application is then checked again by a supervisor who makes a decision to approve, reject or request a modification to the application. Approved and rejected applications leave the system. For modified applications, a member of staff specifies changes to the application, and when agreed, the application returns the assessment process. The process map and ACD for the system are shown in figure 7B.24 and figure 7B.25.

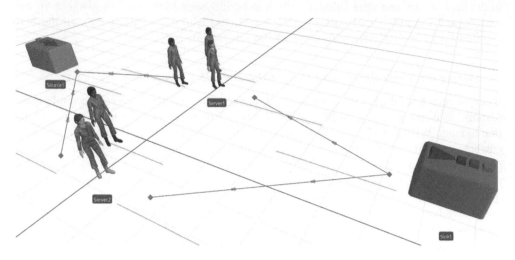

Figure 7B.23 Simio 3D animation of bank clerk simulation

Figure 7B.26 shows the loan application model in Simio. In addition to the objects required by the process map, additional coding has been added to count and report the number of times each loan application has been processed.

To construct the applications model, the following Simio objects should be placed on the Navigation screen (table 7B.5). Then connect the modules using the connector tool as shown in figure 7B.26.

For the source object, enter the parameter Interarrival Time as Random.Exponential(60). For the Staff Assess Application server, first enter the Initial Capacity as Infinite. Here, the capacity for this process will be allocated from the Secondary Resource object named Staff. Enter the Processing Time as Random.Triangular(30,40,50) (figure 7B.27).

In order to provide an account of the number of times, each application is processed a state value is incremented each time the application has completed the Staff Assess Application process. This is achieved by defining a state variable named TimesProcessed. Select the DefaultEntity object in the Navigation Model Properties Window. Select the Definitions tab on the Project Model Tabs. Select States on the views window and then select the States tab on the Screen tab. Select the Integer type to add an integer state variable to the state variables list. Change the name of the state variable to TimesProcessed by setting the Name field in the Properties window (figure 7B.28). Please note that the state value is associated with each individual ModelEntity object in the simulation. This is distinct from a variable that is held within the Model object, this type of variable may be defined as a state variable but within the Model definition rather than the ModelEntity definition.

The state variable can now be incremented when the Staff_Assess_Application server has been executed. Click on the Model object in the Navigation Model Window and select the Facility tab in the Project Model Tabs to return to the model. Click on the Staff_Assess_ Application server. Click on the Before Exiting in the State Assignments Property. Define the state variable name as ModelEntity.TimesProcessed and the New Value as ModelEntity. TimesProcessed + 1 (figure 7B.29). Close the Property editor.

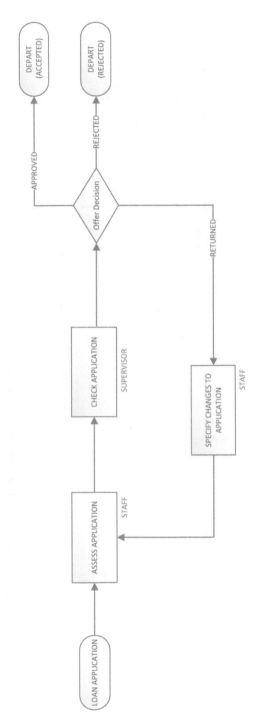

Figure 7B.24 Process map for the loan application simulation

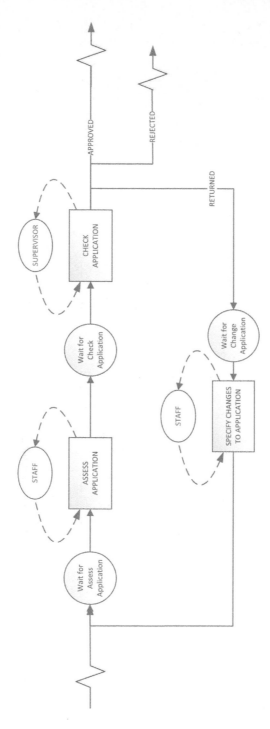

Figure 7B.25 Activity cycle diagram for the loan application simulation

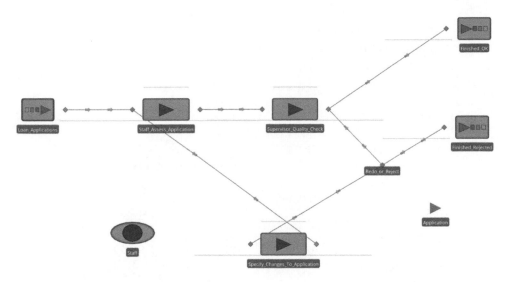

Figure 7B.26 Loan application Simio model

Table 7B.5 Simio Objects for the Loan Application Model

Module Name	Simio Object Type
Loan Application	SOURCE
Staff Assess Application	SERVER
Supervisor Quality Check	SERVER
Finished OK	SINK
Specify Changes to Application	SERVER
Redo or Reject	BASIC NODE
Finished Rejected	SINK
Staff	RESOURCE
Application	ENTITY

Now we can allocate the pooled staff resource to the server. Select the resource and in the general menu change the name to Staff. Click on the Secondary Resources Seizes Property and then the Other Resources Seizes property. Select the Before Processing property. Select the object name as Staff. Repeat this, adding the object name Staff for the After Processing property of the Other Resources Releases Property (figure 7B.30).

For the Supervisor Check Application servers, enter the Processing Time as Random.Uniform(20,40). For the Output Node on the Supervisor Check Application server, enter the Outbound Link Rule as By Link Weight (figure 7B.31).

Click on the Connector between the Supervisor Check Application server and the Finished_OK sink. Enter the Selection Weight as 0.6. Click on the Connector between the Supervisor Check Application server and the Redo or Reject Basic Node. Enter the Selection Weight as 0.4. Click on the Connector between the Redo or Reject Basic Node and the Finished_Rejected sink. Enter the Selection Weight as 0.3. Click on the Connector between

Properties: Staff_Assess_Application (Server)

Process Logic	
Capacity Type	Fixed
Initial Capacity	**Infinity**
Ranking Rule	First In First Out
Dynamic Selection Rule	None
▸ Transfer-In Time	0.0
Process Type	Specific Time
▸ Processing Time	**Random.Triangular(30,40,50)**
Off Shift Rule	Suspend Processing
▸ **Other Processing Options**	
▸ **Buffer Logic**	
▸ **Reliability Logic**	
▸ **Table Row Referencing**	
State Assignments	
On Entering	0 Rows
Before Processing	0 Rows
After Processing	0 Rows
Before Exiting	**1 Row**
On Balking	0 Rows
On Reneging	0 Rows
Secondary Resources	
For Processing	
Repeat Group	True
Resources For Processing	0 Rows
Off Shift Rule	Suspend Processing
▸ **Required Quantity & Constraints**	
▸ **Advanced Options**	
Other Resource Seizes	
▸ On Entering	0 Rows
▸ Before Processing	**1 Row**
▸ After Processing	0 Rows
Other Resource Releases	
▸ On Entering	0 Rows
▸ Before Processing	0 Rows
▸ After Processing	**1 Row**
▸ **Financials**	
▸ **Add-On Process Triggers**	
▸ **Advanced Options**	
▸ **General**	
▸ **Animation**	

Figure 7B.27 Properties Window for Staff_Assess_Application

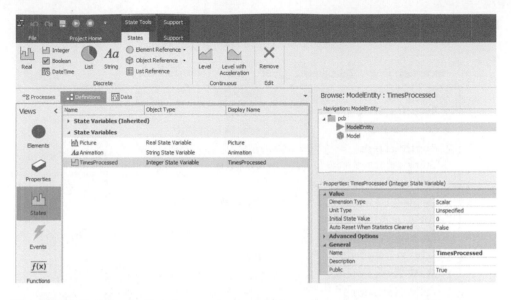

Figure 7B.28 Defining the TimesProcessed state variable

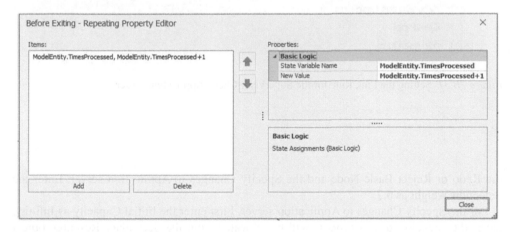

Figure 7B.29 Incrementing the TimeProcessed state variable

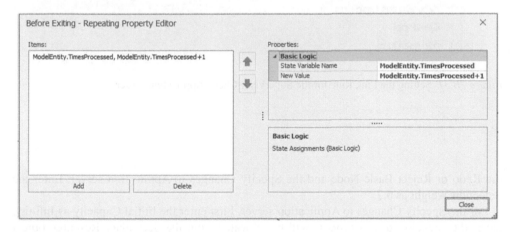

Figure 7B.30 Allocating the resource staff to the Staff_Assess_Application server

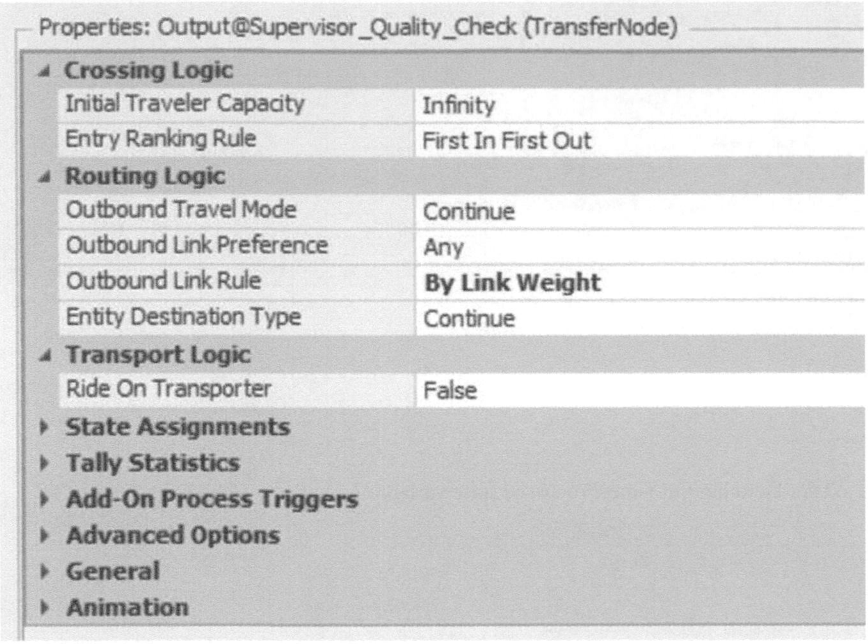

Figure 7B.31 Setting the Link Rule for the Supervisor Check Application server

the Redo or Reject Basic Node and the Specify Changes to Application server. Enter the Selection Weight as 0.7.

For the Specify Changes to Application server. First enter the Initial Capacity as Infinity. Here, the capacity for this process will be allocated from the Secondary Resource object named Staff. Enter the Processing Time as Random.Triangular(20,40,60). Click on the Secondary Resources Seizes Property and then the Other Resources Seizes property. Select the Before Processing property. Bring up the Repeating Property Editor for this tab. Select the object name as Staff and close the Properties Window. Repeat this, adding the object name Staff for the After Processing property of the Other Resources Releases Property.

The staff resource should be defined with a capacity of 2 in the property window of the Staff Resource object (figure 7B.32).

Go to the Run tab on the ribbon and enter 72000 minutes for the RunLength. Run the simulation, and the results should be as in figure 7B.33.

The report in figure 7B.33 includes the following information. The NumTimesProcessed variable indicates that loan applications are processed on average 1.3 times, and the maximum times processed is 8 (1 original and 7 times the application process is redone). The number of items processed during the runtime (72,000 minutes) is 1,226. The average time taken to process an application is 163.4 minutes, with the maximum application process time being 1,305.9 minutes. The average number of applications in the system at any one time is 2.8 applications; the average number of staff busy is 1.15 (for 2 staff).

Figure 7B.32 Staff Resource object

Object Type	Object Name	Data Source	Category	Data Item	Statistic	Average Total
Model	Model	NumTimesProcessed	UserSpecified	TallyValue	Average	1.3483
					Maximum	8.0000
					Observations	2,254.0000
ModelEntity	Application	[Population]	FlowTime	TimeInSystem	Average (Minutes)	163.4343
					Maximum (Minutes)	1,305.8684
					Observations	1,226.0000
			Content	NumberInSystem	Average	2.7852
					Maximum	17.0000
Resource	Staff	[Resource]	Capacity	UnitsScheduled	Average	2.0000
					Maximum	2.0000
				UnitsUtilized	Average	1.1530
					Maximum	2.0000
Server	Specify_Changes_T...	InputBuffer	HoldingTime	TimeInStation	Average (Minutes)	14.7904
					Maximum (Minutes)	217.6909
			Content	NumberInStation	Average	0.0877
					Maximum	3.0000
		[Resource]	Capacity	UnitsScheduled	Average	Infinity
					Maximum	Infinity
				UnitsUtilized	Average	0.3195
					Maximum	4.0000
	Staff_Assess_Applic...	InputBuffer	HoldingTime	TimeInStation	Average (Minutes)	12.8147
					Maximum (Minutes)	199.1798
			Content	NumberInStation	Average	0.2946
					Maximum	8.0000
		[Resource]	Capacity	UnitsScheduled	Average	Infinity
					Maximum	Infinity
				UnitsUtilized	Average	1.2158
					Maximum	10.0000
	Supervisor_Quality_...	InputBuffer	HoldingTime	TimeInStation	Average (Minutes)	24.5418
					Maximum (Minutes)	199.5962
			Content	NumberInStation	Average	0.5639
					Maximum	7.0000
		[Resource]	Capacity	UnitsScheduled	Average	1.0000
					Maximum	1.0000
				UnitsUtilized	Average	0.6860
					Maximum	1.0000
Sink	Finished_OK	[DestroyedEntities]	FlowTime	TimeInSystem	Average (Minutes)	162.9502
					Maximum (Minutes)	1,305.8684
					Observations	1,028.0000
	Finished_Rejected	[DestroyedEntities]	FlowTime	TimeInSystem	Average (Minutes)	165.9479
					Maximum (Minutes)	1,234.0049
					Observations	198.0000

Figure 7B.33 Loan application model results screen

The Petrol Station Simulation Model

The petrol station model will introduce the concepts of routing by link weight and defining tally statistics.

Customers arrive at the petrol station, and 25% of customers head for the manual pumps (with payment at a separate till service). If no manual pumps are available, they drive away; otherwise, they refill their vehicle with petrol and then proceed to the payment till and continue with the payment process. About 75% of customers head for the pay at pumps. If no pay at pumps is available, they drive away; otherwise, they refill their vehicle with petrol and pay at the pump.

These current simulation parameters apply:

- The customer arrival rate is an exponential distribution with a mean of 3 minutes.
- The manual pump service time is a triangular distribution with a minimum of 4 minutes, mode of 6 minutes and maximum of 10 minutes.
- The pay at pump service time is a triangular distribution with a minimum of 6 minutes, mode of 8 minutes and maximum of 12 minutes.
- The payment at till service is a triangular distribution with a minimum of 8 minutes, mode of 10 minutes and maximum of 12 minutes.
- Currently there are 2 manual petrol pumps, 2 pay at pumps and 1 payment till.
- The total cost per day of renting and operating the station is £50 per manual pump installed, £100 per pay pump installed and £200 per payment till. There is an estimated income of £50 per customer served at the petrol station.

The management wish to assess their operating profit on a typical day's operation.

The petrol station process map (figure 7B.34) and the ACD (figure 7B.35) are as follows.

Figure 7B.36 shows the petrol station model in Simio. In addition to the objects required by the process map, additional objects have been added to count 'driveaways' – customers that find either the manual pumps or the pay at pumps unavailable and leave the petrol station. There is also an assignment to calculate the daily profit from the operation of the petrol station.

To construct the model, the following Simio objects modules should be placed on the flowchart screen (table 7B.6).

The following state variables should be defined in the Definitions Tab under States:

    TotalCostPerDay (Real)
    Income (Real)
    Driveaways (Integer)

The following statistic elements should be defined in the definitions tab under Elements. Driveaway_Tally is defined as a state statistic with the state variables name as Driveaways. Profit_Tally is defined as a tally statistic (see figure 7B.37).

Enter the interarrival time for the customer arrivals object and the processing times for the three server objects from the model description. Enter the initial capacity for the three servers. In the customer arrivals object, enter the following state assignment before exiting:

    TotalCostPerDay = Manual_Pump_Service.InitialCapacity*50+Pay_at_Pump_Service.
      InitialCapacity*100+Till_Service.InitialCapacity*200

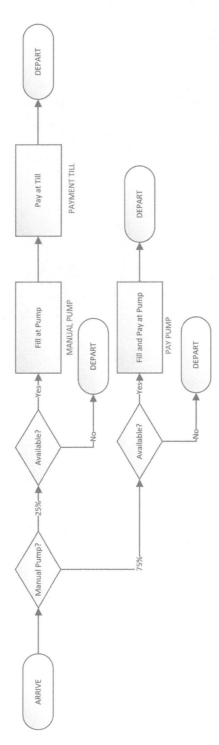

Figure 7B.34 Petrol station process map

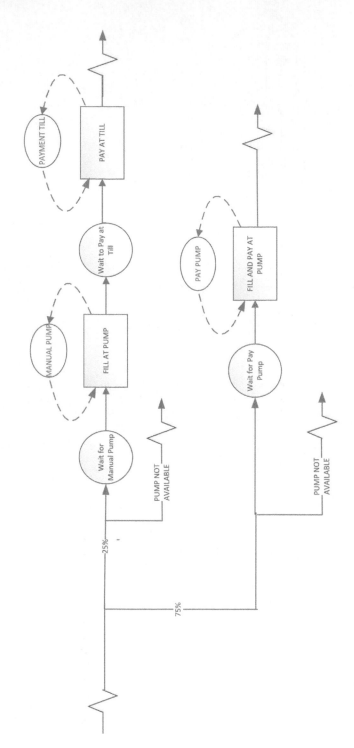

Figure 7B.35 Petrol station activity cycle diagram

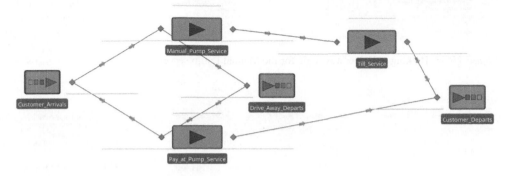

Figure 7B.36 Simio petrol station simulation

Table 7B.6 Simio Objects for Petrol Station Model

Module Name	Simio Object Type
Customer Arrivals	SOURCE
Manual_Pump_Service	SERVER
Pay_at_Pump_Service	SERVER
Drive_Away_Departs	SINK
Till_Service	SERVER
Customer_Departs	SINK

Figure 7B.37 Defining the statistic elements

Connect the customer arrivals object to the manual pump and pay at pump servers using connectors. Click on the connector connecting the customer arrivals and manual pump objects and enter a selection weight of 0.25. Click on the connector connecting the customer arrivals and pay at pump objects and enter a selection weight of 0.75. Add connectors for the pumps to the driveaway sink and the manual pump to the till service server. Finally, connect the till service server and the pay at pump servers to the customer departs sink.

For the manual pump server, for the baulking and reneging options for the input buffer, add the baulking details see figure 7B.38. This ensures drivers drive away from the petrol station if all the petrol pumps are busy.

Repeat the Balking logic for the Pay at Pump server.

At the Input@Customer_Departs node for the State Assignments On Entering, add the following:

Income = Income + 50

▲ Buffer Logic
　▲ Input Buffer
　　Capacity — Infinity
　　▲ Balking & Reneging Options
　　　Balk Decision Type — Conditional
　　　Balk Condition Or Probability — Manual_Pump_Service.Capacity.Allocated==Manual_Pump_Service_InitialCapacity
　　　Balk Node Name — Input@Drive_Away_Departs
　　　Renege Triggers — 0 Rows

Figure 7B.38 Balking to Driveaway logic for the Manual Pump server

Object Type ▲	Object Name ▲	Data Source ▲	Category ▼ ▼	Data Item ▲	Statistic ▲ ▼	Average Total
Model	Model	Driveaway_Tally	UserSpecified	StateValue	Average	16.0838
					FinalValue	35.0000
					Maximum	35.0000
		Profit_Tally	UserSpecified	TallyValue	Average (USD)	2,075.0000
					Maximum (USD)	4,600.0000
					Observations	102.0000
ModelEntity	DefaultEntity	[Population]	FlowTime	TimeInSystem	Average (Min...	9.8763
					Maximum (Min...	35.2030
					Observations	137.0000
			Content	NumberInSystem	Average	2.9150
					Maximum	7.0000
Server	Manual_Pump_Service	[Resource]	Capacity	ScheduledUtilization	Percent	28.8402
				UnitsAllocated	Total	40.0000
				UnitsScheduled	Average	2.0000
					Maximum	2.0000
				UnitsUtilized	Average	0.5768
					Maximum	2.0000
		Processing	HoldingTime	TimeInStation	Average (Min...	6.9993
					Maximum (Min...	9.7503
			Content	NumberInStation	Average	0.5768
					Maximum	2.0000
	Pay_at_Pump_Service	[Resource]	Capacity	ScheduledUtilization	Percent	59.4689
				UnitsAllocated	Total	66.0000
				UnitsScheduled	Average	2.0000
					Maximum	2.0000
				UnitsUtilized	Average	1.1894
					Maximum	2.0000
		Processing	HoldingTime	TimeInStation	Average (Min...	8.7329
					Maximum (Min...	11.4636
			Content	NumberInStation	Average	1.1894
					Maximum	2.0000
	Till_Service	[Resource]	Capacity	ScheduledUtilization	Percent	76.3511
				UnitsAllocated	Total	38.0000
				UnitsScheduled	Average	1.0000
					Maximum	1.0000
				UnitsUtilized	Average	0.7635
					Maximum	1.0000
		InputBuffer	HoldingTime	TimeInStation	Average (Min...	4.5514
					Maximum (Min...	17.5906
			Content	NumberInStation	Average	0.3853
					Maximum	2.0000
		Processing	HoldingTime	TimeInStation	Average (Min...	9.8402
					Maximum (Min...	11.6798
			Content	NumberInStation	Average	0.7635
					Maximum	1.0000
Sink	Customer_Departs	[DestroyedEntities]	FlowTime	TimeInSystem	Average (Min...	13.2652
					Maximum (Min...	35.2030
					Observations	102.0000
	Drive_Away_Departs	[DestroyedEntities]	FlowTime	TimeInSystem	Average (Min...	0.0000
					Maximum (Min...	0.0000
					Observations	35.0000

Figure 7B.39 Petrol station model results screen

For the Tally Statistics On Exited enter:
Profit_Tally = Income − TotalCostPerDay

From the Animation tab, add a Status Label and enter the expression Driveaways. Move the label next to the Drive_Away_Departs sink. On the Run tab, set the ending type as 8 hours and run the model. The results should look similar to figure 7B.39. You may have to click on the Category pin and select the Holding Time box to display holding time information for the processes and the queues.

For this single run, the following results are shown in figure 7B.39:

Average Customer time in the system = 9.9 minutes
Number of customers entering the system = 137
Number of Driveaways = 35
Queueing times – no queuing at the pumps, average time of 4.5 minutes at the till.
Profit = £4,600

Summary

A selection of Simio objects are introduced, and their use is demonstrated using the bank clerk, loan application and petrol station simulation models.

7C: Building the Simulation in Simul8

Introduction

Undertaking the exercises in this chapter requires the installation of the Simul8 simulation software system. This chapter uses version 2020 of Simul8. The main building blocks of Simul8 are described:

- Start Point
- Queue
- Activity
- End
- Resource
- Edit Routing Arrows

The following tutorials are presented in order to demonstrate the basic functionality of the Simul8 software:

- The single-queue bank clerk simulation.
- The double-queue bank clerk simulation.
- The double-queue bank clerk simulation with animation.
- The loan application simulation.
- The petrol station simulation.

Getting Started in Simul8

When the Simul8 system is run, the screen display shown in figure 7C.1 should be displayed.

The building blocks bar (to the left of the screen display) contains a number of building blocks such as Queue and Activity. These blocks are used to build your simulation model by dragging them onto the main window (currently showing just the simulation clock). To connect the blocks together, click on the Edit Routing Arrows block and then click on the block on the main window you wish to connect from and then click on the block on the main window you wish to move to. Data can be entered into each block by double-clicking each block to obtain a dialog box.

The Simul8 building blocks are now described.

Start Point

The Start Point block allows the timing of arrival entities to be specified. The time between arrivals is entered in the Inter-arrival times parameter. The distribution type is entered in the Distribution parameter.

Figure 7C.1 Simul8 2020 model display

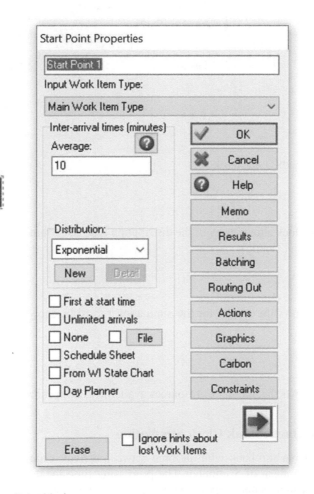

Figure 7C.2 Simul8 Start Point block

Queue

The Queue block allows entry of the capacity of the queue (maximum number of entities that can be in the queue at any one time).

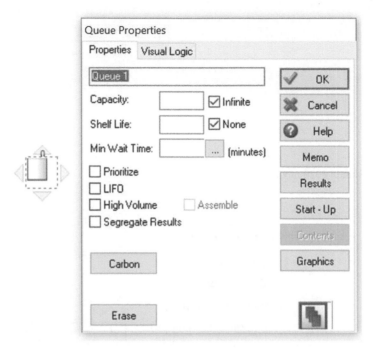

Figure 7C.3 Simul8 Queue block

Activity

The Activity block allows entry of the distribution type (Distribution) and the parameters for this distribution (Timing)

End

This block allows the results for the simulation run to be shown by selecting the Results button.

Resource

This block allows the number of resources available to be specified.

The Single-Queue Bank Clerk Simulation

Customers arrive at a bank with the time between arrivals estimated as exponentially distributed with a mean of 5 minutes. The processing time for the customers is a triangular distribution with parameters of 5 minimum, 8 most likely and 11 maximum minutes. In this

Figure 7C.4 Simul8 Activity block

system, customers form a single queue and receive service from two members of staff when they reach the front of the queue. Performance statistics are required on the average time a customer is in the system, which includes both queue time and service time.

Based on the aforementioned definition, the process map and ACD for the single-queue bank clerk simulation are shown in figure 7C.7 and figure 7C.8. Customers arrive from outside the system and are processed by the bank clerks. They then leave the system once the process has been completed.

Figure 7C.9 shows the blocks required for the single-queue bank clerk simulation placed on the main screen. The Start Point block is used to generate the bank customers. A Queue block is used to represent the customer queuing at the bank tills, and the Activity block is used to represent the service process at the bank tills. An End block is used to simulate the customers leaving the bank. The blocks are added to the model window view by dragging (hold down the left button over the block) them from the building blocks bar. The blocks will automatically connect together to define the relationship between the blocks if they are

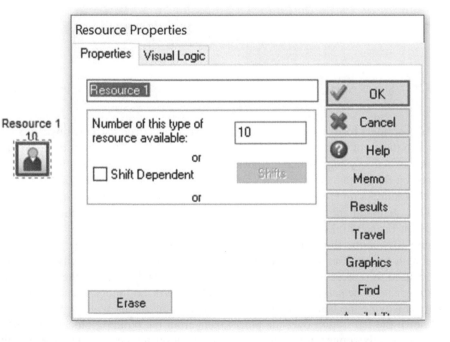

Figure 7C.5 Simul8 End block

Figure 7C.6 Simul8 Resource block

Figure 7C.7 Process map for single-queue bank clerk simulation

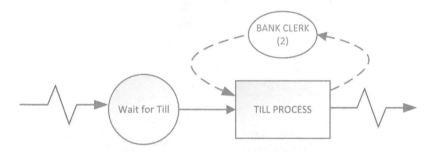

Figure 7C.8 Activity cycle diagram for single-queue bank clerk simulation

Figure 7C.9 Simul8 building blocks for single-queue bank clerk simulation

entered on the screen in order from left to right. If the blocks are not connected by the connecting lines, they can be connected manually using the Edit Routing Arrows block. Click on this connector, and the cursor will change to an arrow. Then click on the first block and then click on the block you wish to connect to. The connection will then be made. To remove a connection, click on the connection line to highlight it and press the Delete key on your keyboard.

Double-click on the starting point block, and the dialog box will appear as in figure 7C.10. For the distribution parameter, select Exponential, and for the Inter-arrival times parameter, enter 5. The block will then create customer arrivals that are exponentially distributed, with a mean of 5 minutes. Press OK to enter the data.

The Queue and Activity blocks can be used to represent the process at the bank till. For this model, we only need to enter the activity dialog box. The Replicate value is the capacity of work items that can be processed at this activity. Enter 2 for Replicate to represent that we have two bank clerks available to undertake the process. Select the Triangular option for the distribution. Enter 5 for the lower value, 8 for the mode and 11 for the upper value (figure 7C.11).

Select the Run For option on the home menu. Then select simulation time units (minutes) from the pull-down menu. Set the replication length to 40,320 minutes (figure 7c.12).

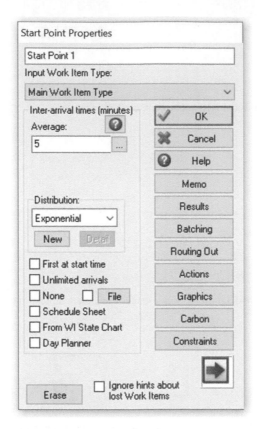

Figure 7C.10 Enter the Start Point block parameters

Move to the Home tab on the menu and run the model by clicking on the run icon. If there are any errors in your model, a message will appear on the screen, indicating the source of the problem. When you have a working model, you will see the entities moving through the system as the model runs through time.

Different results are available in Simul8 at the endpoints, activities and queues. When the simulation has completed its run, click on the End block and then click on the results button. The output report in figure 7C.13 should appear. Figure 7C.13 shows the average time in the system for the customer is given as 16.38 minutes, with a maximum time of 73.75 minutes. Twenty-six per cent of customers spend 10 minutes or less in the system. The number of customers (work completed) who have passed through the bank in the 28 days of runtime is 8,025. In the Activity Results report, we can see the average utilisation of the 2 bank clerks is 1.59 units. In the Queue Results, the average queuing time is given as 7.17 minutes. Seventy-three per cent of customers have a queuing time within 10 minutes. Thus, this very simple model provides us with a variety of performance measures for our bank clerk system. (Note that the models incorporate probability distributions, and so the results you get may differ slightly from those in the text due to random variation. This is to be expected, and you can see that the results from the same model run on different simulation software will also vary).

Figure 7C.11 Entering the process block parameters

Figure 7C.12 Setting the simulation run length

The Double-Queue Bank Clerk Simulation

An alternative double-queue system is proposed. Here, customers make a choice of which of two queues to join when they enter the bank. Customers make this decision based on a rule

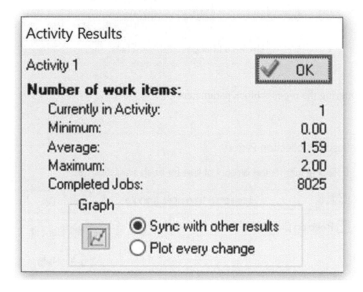

Figure 7C.13 The Simul8 End Results, Activity Results and Queue Results reports

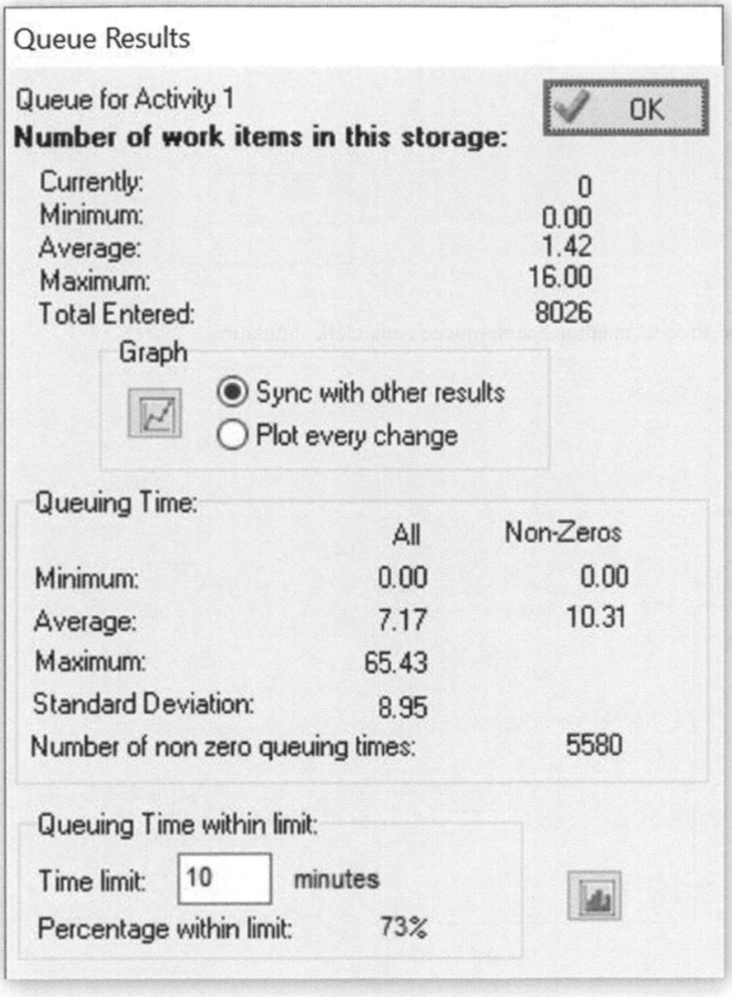

Queue Results

Queue for Activity 1

✓ OK

Number of work items in this storage:

Currently:	0
Minimum:	0.00
Average:	1.42
Maximum:	16.00
Total Entered:	8026

Graph

⦿ Sync with other results
◯ Plot every change

Queuing Time:

	All	Non-Zeros
Minimum:	0.00	0.00
Average:	7.17	10.31
Maximum:	65.43	
Standard Deviation:	8.95	
Number of non zero queuing times:		5580

Queuing Time within limit:

Time limit: 10 minutes

Percentage within limit: 73%

Figure 7C.13 (Continued)

depending on which of the two till queues holds the minimum number of customers. Once customers have joined a queue they are not permitted to leave the queue they have joined. The scenario can be represented with a process map (figure 7C.14) and ACD (figure 7C.15).

To implement the double-queue system, add a further Queue block and a further Activity block. Then click on Edit Routing Arrows and connect the additional blocks as shown in figure 7C.16.

To determine which of the two bank clerks each customer is routed to, select the Start Point block, and from the dialog box, select the Routing Out button. The Queue for Activity 1 and Queue for Activity 2 should appear in the dialog box if they have been connected. Select the Shortest Queue discipline, which will route customers (figure 7C.17).

Now double-click on the activity 2 block. Enter 1 for replicate to represent that we have one bank clerk available to undertake the process. Select the Triangular option for the

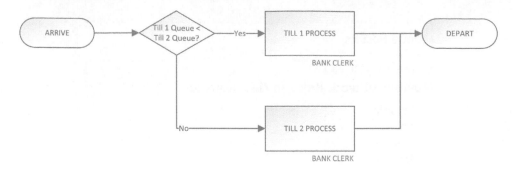

Figure 7C.14 Process map for double-queue bank clerk simulation

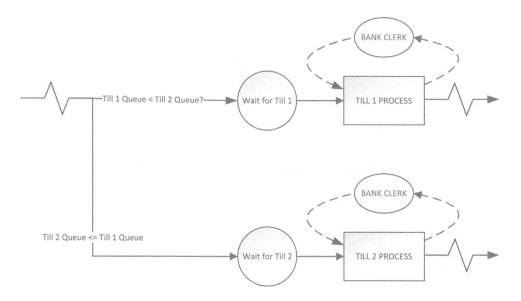

Figure 7C.15 Activity cycle diagram for double-queue bank clerk simulation

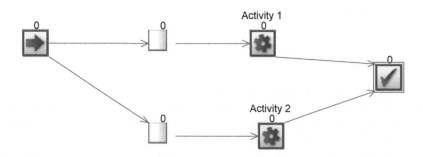

Figure 7C.16 Double-queue Simul8 model

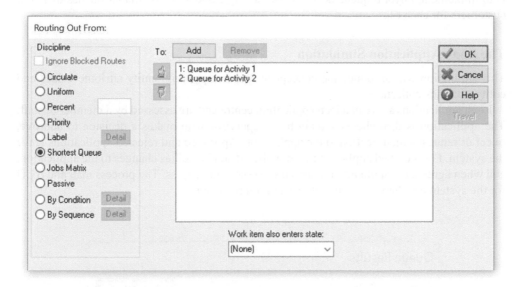

Figure 7C.17 Entering the Routing Out parameters

distribution. Enter 5 for the lower value, 8 for the mode and 11 for the upper value. Finally, double-click on the activity 1 block and change the replicate from 2 to 1. This creates a model with two separate bank clerk queues with customers choosing the queue to join by the shortest number of people in the queues.

Run the simulation by clicking on the run (▶) button. When the simulation has been completed, the results screen will be displayed as in figure 7C.18. In the bank clerk simulation, referring to figure 7C.18, the average time in the system for the customer is given as 17.9 minutes, with a maximum time of 73.9 minutes. The maximum customer waiting time for till 1 is given as 60.84 minutes. The maximum waiting time for till 2 is 63 minutes. The maximum number of customers in the queue for till 1 is given as 7. The maximum number of customers in the queue for till 2 is given as 8. The number of customers (observations) who have passed through the bank in the 28 days of runtime is 8,024; 4,056 customers have been processed at till 1 and 3,970 at till 2.

Comparing the Single-Queue and Double-Queue Bank Clerk Models

It can be seen from the results of the simulation that with no other changes, the single-queue system has an average time in the system of 16.38 minutes compared to the double-queue simulation average time in the system of 17.9 minutes. Thus, the results indicate when we have variability in customer arrival and customer process times, the single-queue arrangement provides better performance than double or parallel servers. A further advantage of a single-queue system is that it ensures that customers are processed in the order that they arrive. However, the single queue may not be practical when there is limited space for an extended single. The maximum queue size is reported by the simulation for single queue as 16 customers and double queue as 7 customers for till 1 and 8 customers for till 2. One option is to implement a hybrid queue design where a single queue feeds smaller queues of 1 or 2 customers for each till.

The Loan Application Simulation

This simulation will introduce the concept of resource pooling, entity attribute values and entity statistics collection.

Loan applications arrive at a loan application centre and are assessed by a member of staff. The application is then checked again by a supervisor who makes a decision to approve, reject or request a modification to the application. Approved and rejected applications leave the system. For modified applications, a member of staff specifies changes to the application, and when agreed, the application returns the assessment process. The process map and ACD for the system are shown in figure 7C.19 and figure 7C.20.

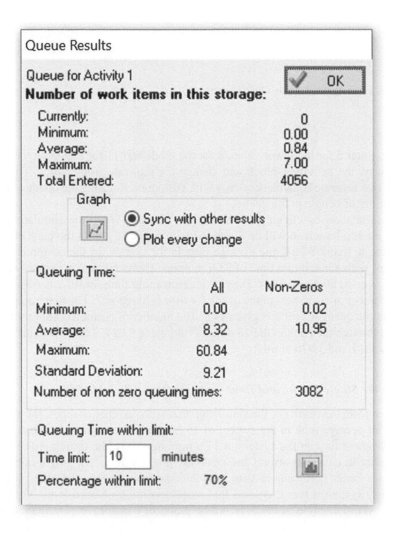

Figure 7C.18 Results screens for Simul8 double-queue model

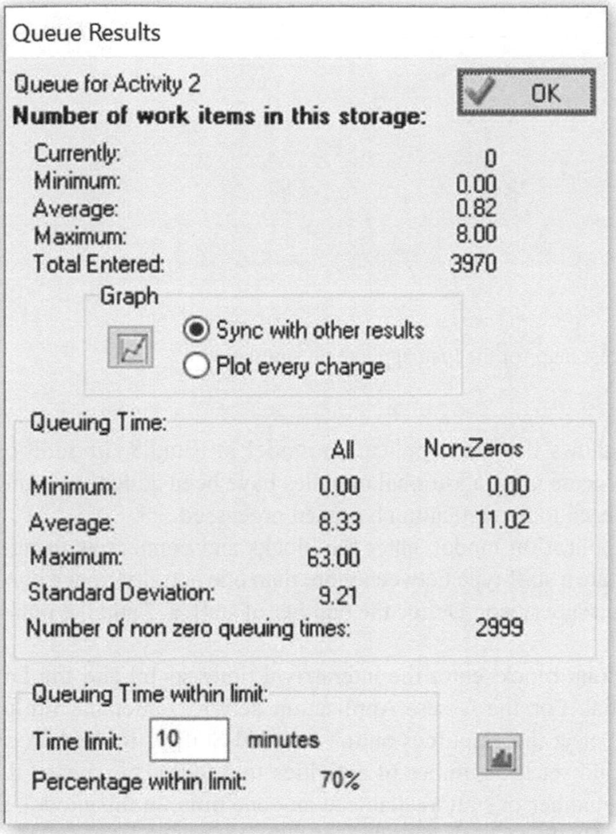

Queue Results

Queue for Activity 2
Number of work items in this storage:

Currently:	0
Minimum:	0.00
Average:	0.82
Maximum:	8.00
Total Entered:	3970

Graph

◉ Sync with other results
○ Plot every change

Queuing Time:

	All	Non-Zeros
Minimum:	0.00	0.00
Average:	8.33	11.02
Maximum:	63.00	
Standard Deviation:	9.21	
Number of non zero queuing times:		2999

Queuing Time within limit:

Time limit: 10 minutes
Percentage within limit: 70%

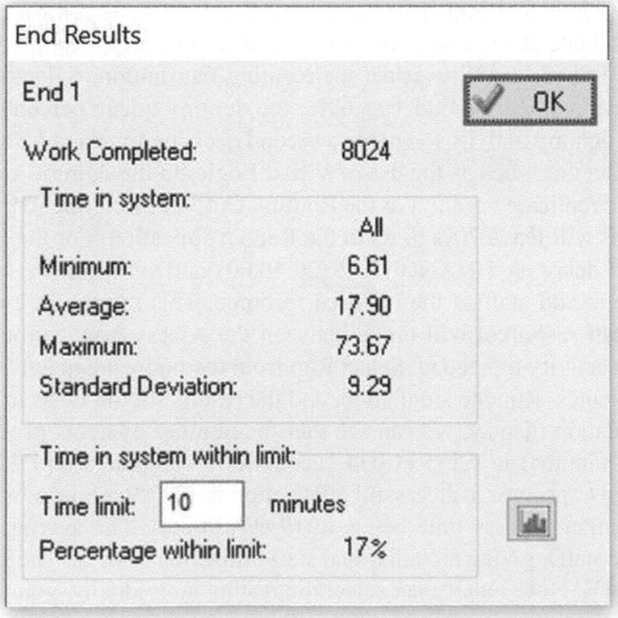

OK

End Results

End 1

Work Completed: 8024

Time in system:

	All
Minimum:	6.61
Average:	17.90
Maximum:	73.67
Standard Deviation:	9.29

Time in system within limit:

Time limit: 10 minutes
Percentage within limit: 17%

OK

Figure 7C.18 (Continued)

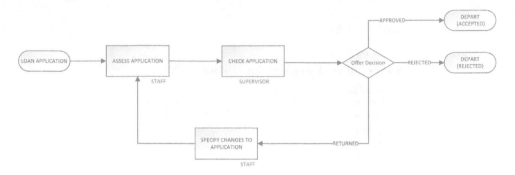

Figure 7C.19 Process map for the loan application simulation

Figure 7C.21 shows the loan application model in Simul8. In addition to the modules required by the process map, additional modules have been added to count and report on the number of times each loan application has been processed.

For the loan application model, enter the blocks and connect as in figure 7C.21. In this model, we will share a staff type between more than one activity, so we need to add Resource blocks for staff and supervisor. Define the number of staff as 2 and the number of supervisors as 1.

For the Start Point block, enter the interarrival times as 60 and the Distribution parameter as Exponential. For the Assess Application activity, enter the timing as TRIANGULAR(30,40,50). Select the resources button and add Staff as the required resource. Set the replicate button and set the number of activities to 1,000. This means that this activity is controlled by the number of staff available at any one time. In this model, this ranges from 0 to 2 staff. For the Quality Check activity, enter the timing as UNIFORM(20,40). Select the resources button and add Supervisor as the required resource. Set the replicate button and set the number of activities to 1,000. This means that this activity is controlled by the number of supervisors available at any one time. In this model, this ranges from 0 to 1 supervisor.

For the Quality Check activity, select the Routing Out button. Select Discipline as per cent. Define the percentage for End 1 as 60%; the dummy queue percentage will be 40%. We have added a dummy activity to enable a second decision to be made, although there are other ways of doing this, such as the use of Visual Logic. In the dummy activity, make sure the timing is 0 and replicate =1000. For the Routing Out, set discipline to percentage and set End2 to 30%. This will leave 70% to go to the Redo Application. For the Redo Application activity, enter the delay as TRIANGULAR(20,40,60) and set replicate =1000. Select the resource button and add staff as the required resource. This means the two staff available (defined in the staff resource) will move between the Assess Application activity and the Redo Application activity as needed. Select Run from the home menu and set the simulation time to 72,000 minutes. Run the simulation, and the results should be as in figure 7C.22.

From the simulation display, we can see that the number of items processed during the runtime (72,000 minutes) is 1,255 (1,034 successfully completed and 221 rejected). The average time taken to process a successful application is 191.89 minutes, with the maximum successful application process time being 1,917.69 minutes. The average number of staff busy is 1.29 (for 2 staff), giving an individual staff utilisation of 65%. The supervisor utilisation is given as 74%. Note rather than select the results individually, you can right-click on the results you wish to appear in the results manager reports.

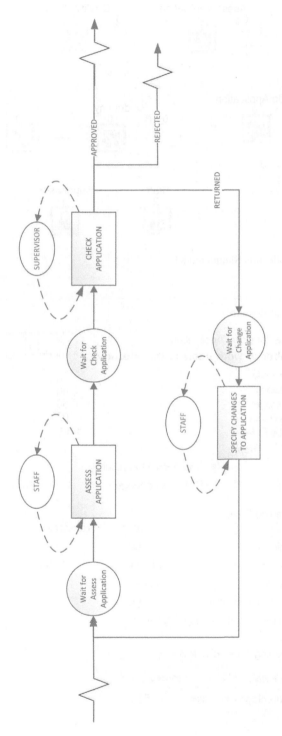

Figure 7C.20 Activity cycle diagram for the loan application simulation

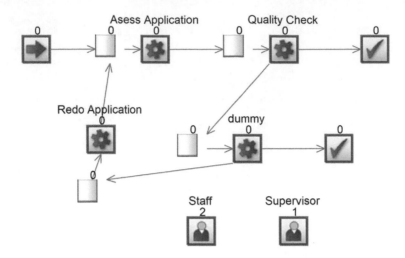

Figure 7C.21 Loan application Simul8 model

Queue Results

Queue for Asess Application
Number of work items in this storage:

Currently:	0
Minimum:	0.00
Average:	0.50
Maximum:	11.00
Total Entered:	1785

Graph
● Sync with other results
○ Plot every change

Queuing Time:

	All	Non-Zeros
Minimum:	0.00	0.00
Average:	**20.00**	42.59
Maximum:	304.93	
Standard Deviation:	37.58	
Number of non zero queuing times:		838

Queuing Time within limit:

Time limit: 10 minutes

Percentage within limit: 61%

OK

Figure 7C.22 A–F loan application model results screen

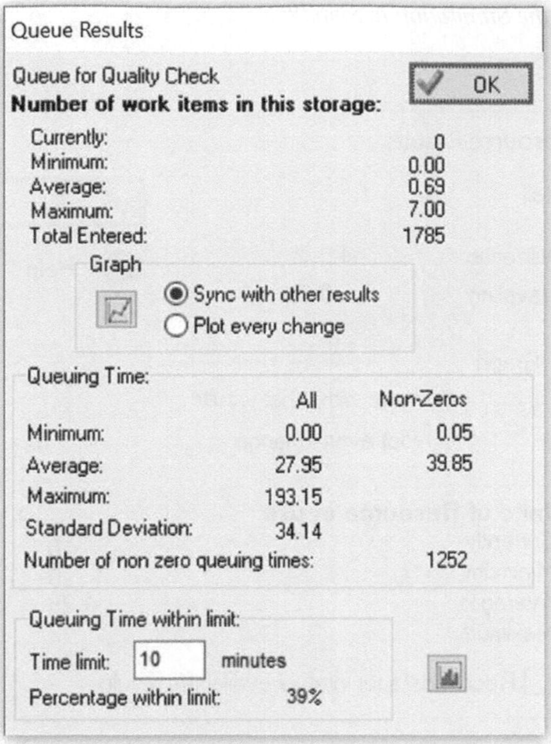

Queue Results

Queue for Quality Check   ✓ OK
Number of work items in this storage:

Currently:	0
Minimum:	0.00
Average:	0.69
Maximum:	7.00
Total Entered:	1785

Graph
☑   ● Sync with other results
     ○ Plot every change

Queuing Time:

	All	Non-Zeros
Minimum:	0.00	0.05
Average:	27.95	39.85
Maximum:	193.15	
Standard Deviation:	34.14	
Number of non zero queuing times:		1252

Queuing Time within limit:

Time limit: 10 minutes
Percentage within limit: 39%

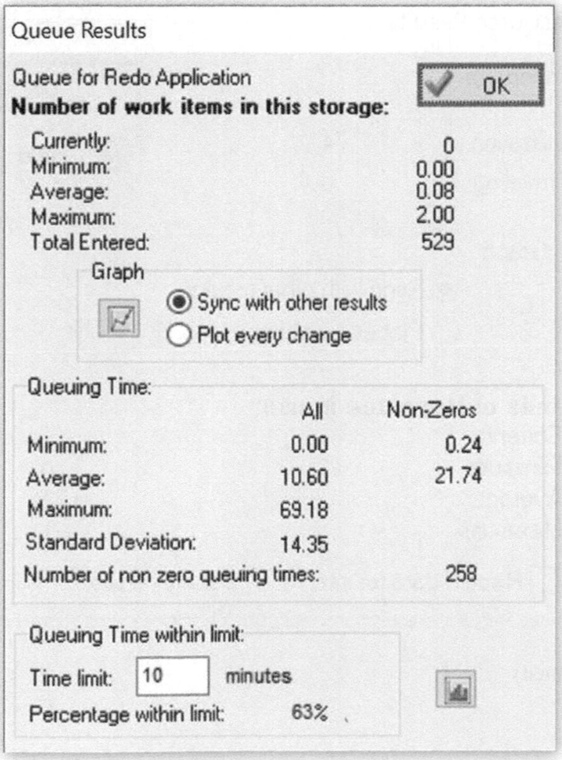

Queue Results

Queue for Redo Application   ✓ OK
Number of work items in this storage:

Currently:	0
Minimum:	0.00
Average:	0.08
Maximum:	2.00
Total Entered:	529

Graph
☑   ● Sync with other results
     ○ Plot every change

Queuing Time:

	All	Non-Zeros
Minimum:	0.00	0.24
Average:	10.60	21.74
Maximum:	69.18	
Standard Deviation:	14.35	
Number of non zero queuing times:		258

Queuing Time within limit:

Time limit: 10 minutes
Percentage within limit: 63%

Figure 7C.22 (Continued)

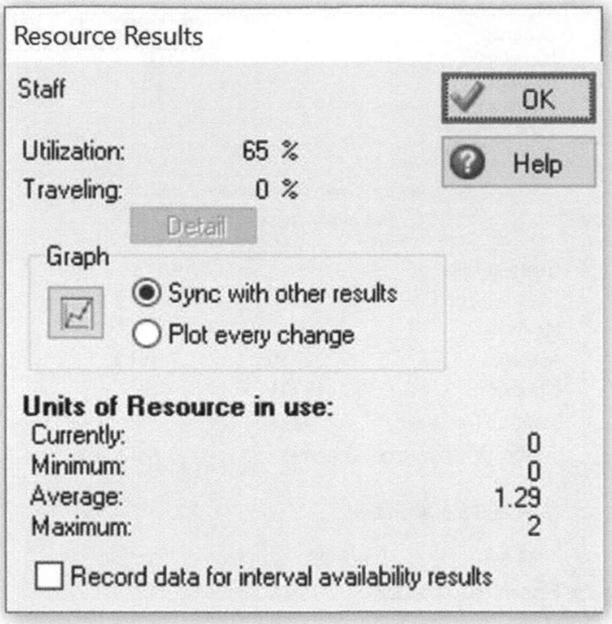

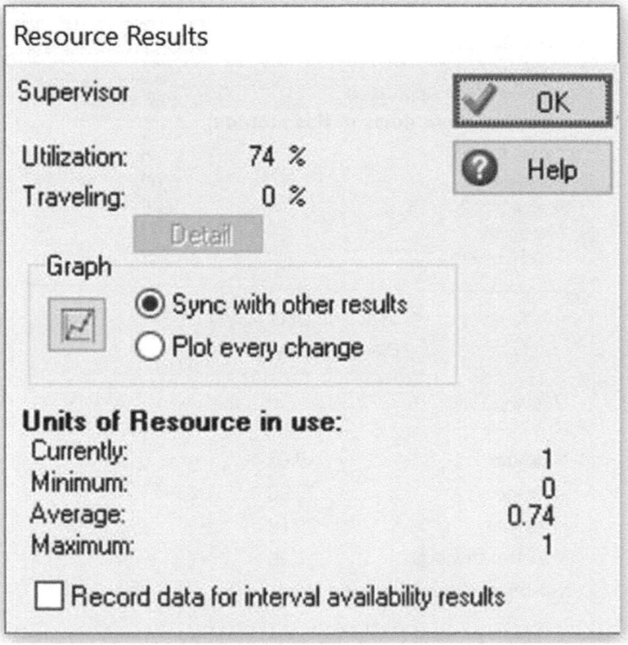

Resource Results

Staff
                                    ✓ OK

Utilization: 65 %   ❓ Help
Traveling: 0 %
           Detail
  Graph
   ☑   ● Sync with other results
        ○ Plot every change

Units of Resource in use:
Currently: 0
Minimum: 0
Average: 1.29
Maximum: 2
  ☐ Record data for interval availability results

Resource Results

Supervisor
                                    ✓ OK

Utilization: 74 %   ❓ Help
Traveling: 0 %
           Detail
  Graph
   ☑   ● Sync with other results
        ○ Plot every change

Units of Resource in use:
Currently: 1
Minimum: 0
Average: 0.74
Maximum: 1
  ☐ Record data for interval availability results

Figure 7C.22 (Continued)

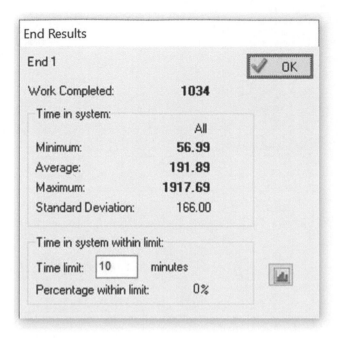

Figure 7C.22 (Continued)

The Petrol Station Simulation Model

The petrol station model will introduce the concepts of baulking at resources and calculation of income and cost metrics.

Customers arrive at the petrol station, and 25% of customers head for the manual pumps (with payment at a separate till service). If no manual pumps are available, they drive away; otherwise, they refill their vehicle with petrol and then proceed to the payment till and continue with the payment process. About 75% of customers head for the pay at pumps. If no pay at pumps is available, they drive away; otherwise, they refill their vehicle with petrol and pay at the pump.

These current simulation parameters apply:

- The customer arrival rate is an exponential distribution with a mean of 3 minutes.
- The manual pump service time is a triangular distribution with a minimum of 4 minutes, mode of 6 minutes and maximum of 10 minutes.
- The pay at pump service time is a triangular distribution with a minimum of 6 minutes, mode of 8 minutes and maximum of 12 minutes.
- The payment at till service is a triangular distribution with a minimum of 8 minutes, mode of 10 minutes and maximum of 12 minutes.
- Currently there are 2 manual petrol pumps, 2 pay at pumps and 1 payment till.
- The total cost per day of renting and operating the station is £500. There is an estimated income of £50 per customer served at the petrol station.

The management wish to assess their operating profit on a typical day's operation. The petrol station process map (figure 7C.23) and the ACD (figure 7C.24) are as follows.

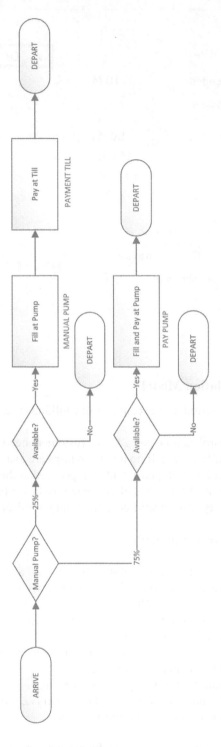

Figure 7C.23 Petrol station process map

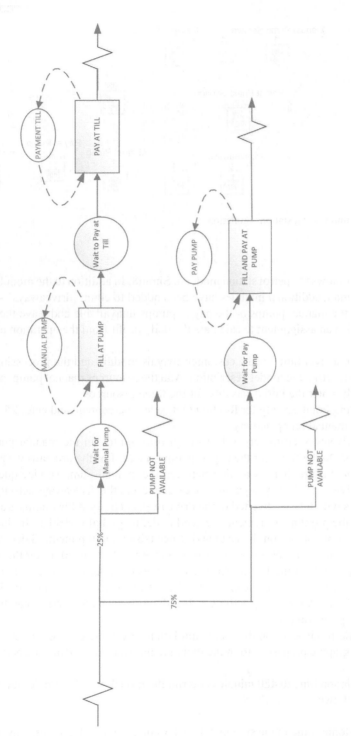

Figure 7C.24 Petrol station activity cycle diagram

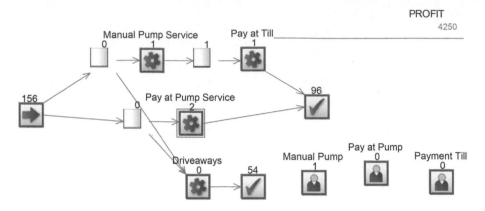

Figure 7C.25 Simul8 petrol station simulation

Figure 7C.25 shows the petrol station model in Simul8. In addition to the modules required by the process map, additional modules have been added to count 'driveaways' – customers that find either the manual pumps or the pay at pumps unavailable and leave the petrol station. There is also an assignment to calculate the daily profit from the operation of the petrol station.

Enter the interarrival time for the customer arrivals module and the processing times for the three activities from the model description. Add the resources manual pump, pay at pump and payment till. Enter the initial capacity for the three resources.

For the Starting Point activity for Routing Out, select percentage and enter 25 for the percentage for the manual pump activity.

To trigger driveaway customers, select the priority button in the manual pump service and enter 100%. Do the same for the pay at pump service. For the driveaway activity, enter a priority of 0%. Ensure there is routing between the manual pump service queue and the driveaways activity and the pay at pump service queue and the driveaways activity. This will mean customers will only be diverted to the driveaways activity if the pumps are busy.

To calculate the profit measurement, we need to define global variables. To do this, select the information store option on the Data and Rules tab on the top menu. Select the number from the pull-down list. Enter the name income and enter the value 0. Enter the name profit and enter the value 0. In the Pay at Till activity, select the Actions button. Select income to change and set the value to income + 50. Select Profit to change and set the value to income − 500. In the Pay at Pump activity, select the Actions button and repeat the setting of the income and profit values.

To display the profit level on the main simulation screen, select the Pay at Till activity. Select the data graphic properties from the main menu. Add a new item and set the data field to profit.

Set the simulation time to 480 minutes and run the model. For this single run, the following results are shown:

Average customer time in the system = 13.88 minutes (not including driveaways)
Number of customers entering the system = 156

Number of driveaways = 54
Queuing times – no queuing at the pumps, average time of 4.36 minutes at the till.
Profit = £4,250

Summary

A selection of Simul8 blocks is introduced, and their use is demonstrated using the bank clerk, loan application and petrol station simulation models.

8 Verification and Validation

Introduction

Before experimental analysis of the simulation model can begin, it is necessary to ensure that the model constructed provides a valid representation of the system we are studying. This process consists of verification and validation of the simulation model. Although verification and validation are critical in the development of a simulation model, unfortunately there is no set of specific tests that can easily be applied to determine the 'correctness' of a model (Sargent, 2013). This means the simulation developer will need to ensure that verification and validation methods are applied appropriately to each individual simulation study. Methods for verification and validation of DES models will now be discussed in more detail.

Verification

Verification means ensuring that the computer model built using the simulation software is a correct representation of the conceptual model of the system under investigation. The task of verification is likely to become greater with an increase in model size. This is because a large, complex program is more likely to contain errors, and these errors are less likely to be found. Due to this behaviour, most practitioners advise an approach of building a small, simple model, ensuring that this works correctly, and then gradually adding embellishments over time. This approach is intended to help limit the area of search for errors at any one time. It is also important to ensure that unnecessary complexity is not incorporated into the model design. The design should incorporate only enough detail to ensure the study objectives and not attempt to be an exact replica of the real-life system. It is also important to document all elements in the simulation to aid verification by other personnel or at a later date. Any simulation coding should have comments attached to each line of code. Each module or object within a model produced on a simulation system requires comments regarding its purpose and details of parameters and other elements.

As was stated earlier, verification is easiest with small, simple models. With larger and more complex models, it may be necessary to temporarily simplify model behaviour for verification purposes. This could be achieved by replacing distributions for arrival and process times with constant values or only routing one entity type through the model to check the entity path. If the model is not behaving in an appropriate manner, it is necessary to investigate the model design. This can be achieved through inspection of the model code and by analysing the event calendar using the debugging facilities. In testing both the model logic and performance, particular attention should be paid to any behaviour at variance from the real system (taking into consideration simplifications and assumptions made) or expected behaviour of a

DOI: 10.4324/9781003124092-8

system that does not yet exist. Verification is analogous to the practice of debugging a computer program in order to check that the program does what has been planned. Thus, many of the following techniques will be familiar to programmers of general-purpose computer languages. The following techniques for verification are described.

Structured Walkthrough

This enables the modeller to incorporate the perspective of someone outside the immediate task of model construction. The walkthrough procedure involves talking through the program modules or objects with another individual or team. The process may bring fresh insight from others, but the act of explaining the model can also help the person who has developed the model discover their own errors. In DES, the model elements are executed non-sequentially and simultaneously. This means that the walkthrough may best be conducted by following the 'life history' of an entity (for example, a customer or component) through the steps in the simulation model.

Animation Inspection

The animation facilities of simulation software packages provide a powerful tool in aiding the understanding of model behaviour. The animation enables the model developer to see many of the model components and their behaviour simultaneously. Most simulation software packages enable the flow of entities to be seen when the model is constructed. To aid understanding, model components can be animated, which may not appear in the final layout presented to a client. The usefulness of the animation technique will be maximised if the animation software facilities permit reliable and quick production of the animation effects. An animation inspection may be conducted by following the life history of an entity with the animation displayed at a slow speed. Errors can also be found by inspecting the measure of performance (e.g. machine utilisation, queue length) within the system and comparing them to estimated values made by using rough-cut calculations.

Trace Analysis

Due to the nature of DES, it may be difficult to locate the source of an error solely using a structured walkthrough or by inspection of the animation display. Most simulation packages incorporate an entity trace facility that is useful in providing a detailed record of the life history of a particular entity. The trace facility can show the events occurring for a particular entity or all events occurring during a particular timeframe. The trace analysis facility can produce a large amount of output, so it is most often used for detailed verification.

Test Runs

Test runs of a simulation model can be made during program development to check model behaviour. This is a useful approach as a defective model will usually report results (e.g. machine utilisation, customer wait times) that do not conform to expectations, either based on the real system performance or common-sense deductions. It may be necessary to add performance measures to the model (e.g. costs) for verification purposes, even though they may not be required for reporting purposes. One approach is to use historical (fixed) data, so model behaviour can be isolated from behaviour caused by the use of random variates in the model. It is also important to test model behaviour under a number of scenarios, particularly boundary conditions that are likely to uncover erratic behaviour. Boundary conditions could include minimum and maximum arrival rates, minimum and maximum service times and a minimum and maximum rate of infrequent events (e.g. machine breakdowns).

Validation

A verified model is a model which operates as intended by the modeller. However, this does not necessarily mean that it is a satisfactory representation of the real system for the purposes of the study. Validation is about ensuring that model behaviour is close enough to the real-world system for the purposes of the simulation study. In other words, validation concerns ensuring that the assumptions and simplifications made in the conceptual model about the real-world system are acceptable in the context of the simulation study objectives.

Unlike verification, the question of validation is one of judgement. Ideally, the model should provide enough accuracy for the measures required while limiting the amount of effort required to achieve this. Validation is difficult to do well, and insufficient time may be spent on this activity as there may be pressures to begin experimentation and analysis. There are a number of issues to consider, such as the sensitivity of model results to initial run conditions and ensuring a correct understanding of real-system behaviour to which the model can be compared. If the model fails the validation stage, then the conceptual modelling stage should be revisited and model revisions made. As a last resort, and if no solution can be found to achieve model validation, then the modelling project should be cancelled.

Simulation Modelling and Validation

Although we can validate our model to some extent by comparing our model behaviour to real-world observations, we cannot validate against real-world behaviour that we have not observed. This may lead us to question the usefulness of simulation, but we need to think of simulation as not just a mathematical process that provides us with what might be considered the truth in terms of how the real system will behave. Rather it aims to provide reliable results for particular simulation study objectives. Simulation results are not just data but visualised and used with other sources of knowledge, including observation, to provide an overall qualitative assessment for decision-making. Thus, in order to undertake validation, there is what might be termed the epistemological (relating to knowledge) challenge is to include all the important information correctly in our model. This may not occur due to errors in a number of the stages of the simulation study process, such as data collection, conceptual modelling and validation. It may be that elements of the real system that are unknown to us and, therefore, not included in our model make our simulation predictions faulty. In addition to what is included on the input side of the model, on the output side there is what might be termed the hermeneutical (relating to interpretation) challenge of ensuring we do not interpret something into a simulation result that is not part of the underlying model and basing our interpretation of simulation results along with other sources of knowledge we have about the real system.

Model Validation for Descriptive, Predictive and Prescriptive Analysis

Simulation models are, in essence, an attempt to quantify uncertainty in real-world processes. This text covers the use of simulation for descriptive (understanding), predictive (scenarios) and prescriptive (recommendations) analysis of real-world systems. Models are abstractions of these real systems, and the key concern of validation is how satisfactory this abstraction is. In one sense, because models are simplifications, they are by definition wrong or false in that they deliberately omit real-world processes – if they didn't, there wouldn't be much point in building the model! So models are never true, but we only need to make them useful for the purpose they were designed for. Validation may not be a major issue when the model is used as a tool for understanding and for generating interesting and testable hypotheses, but the issue of model validation and the 'truth' of the model becomes more acute when it is used as a tool for prediction and prescription.

For most systems of any complexity, validation can be achieved in a number of ways, and a key skill of the simulation developer is finding the most efficient way of achieving this goal. Pegden et al. (1995) outline three aspects of validation:

- Conceptual validity: Does the model adequately represent the real-world system?
- Operational validity: Are the model generated behavioural data characteristic of the real-world system behavioural data?
- Believability: Does the simulation model's ultimate user have confidence in the model's results?

These three aspects reflect that model validation can be seen as proving that the model is a suitable representation of the real system, but also validation can be seen as being concerned with the accuracy of the predictions of the model. When concerned simply with the predictive results of the model, the underlying assumptions and structure of the model are irrelevant, and this approach is often taken when validating data-driven analytics models. In reality, most simulation model developers will take both of these perspectives into account when conducting model validation. The model results can be tested for reasonableness (operational validity), and the model representation can be examined in terms of its representation of the real system (conceptual validity). Both the model developer and the model user (decision-maker) will need to be convinced that these tests have been passed (believability).

Conceptual Validity

Conceptual validation involves ensuring that the model structure and elements are correctly chosen and configured in order to adequately represent the real-world system. This is primarily concerned with ensuring that appropriate assumptions and simplifications have been made when building the conceptual model. Thus, as we know that the model is a simplification of the real world, then there is a need for a consensus around the form of the conceptual model between the model builder and the user. To ensure that a conceptually valid model is produced, the model builder should discuss and obtain information from people familiar with the real-world system, including operating personnel, industrial engineers, management, vendors and documentation.

Operational Validity

This involves ensuring that the results obtained from the model are consistent with the real-world performance. This entails observing system behaviour over time and comparing it with model behaviour.

Believability

Ensuring the implementation of actions recommended as a result of simulation experiments requires that the model output is seen as credible from the simulation user's point of view. This credibility will be enhanced by close cooperation between the model user and client throughout the simulation study. This involves agreeing on clear project objectives explaining the capabilities of the method to the client and agreeing on assumptions and simplifications made in the conceptual model. Regular meetings of interested parties, using the simulation animation display to provide a discussion forum, can increase confidence in model results. Believability emphasises how there is no one answer to achieving model validity, and the perspective of both users and developers needs to be satisfied that a model is valid. This aspect emphasises how simulation modelling is not just a technical exercise requiring model-building and statistical skills, but it also requires domain knowledge and social and political skills in order to interpret and ensure the use of the simulation results. Simulation credibility is not just from the theory of how the system works embedded in the model (content) but also from the credentials of the model-building techniques employed (process).

Simulation and Theory

The simulation model we build can be seen as our theory of describing the structure and inter-relationships of a system. We use our subjective beliefs in terms of our opinions and insights to gain knowledge about how the system works in order to build our model. Because this process is subjective, different people will develop different models given the same problem. The purpose of verification and validation is to make a largely objective assessment that the model is a suitable representation of the system we are studying.

The following techniques for validation are described.

Structured Walkthrough

This is similar to the walkthrough procedure described under verification, but rather than a walkthrough to check against the conceptual model, this involves asking a person with detailed knowledge of the real-world system to compare the model process map and data with what they understand of the real system.

Animation Inspection

This involves checking the performance of each element of the model by visual inspection to see if it behaves as expected. The animation can be stepped event by event and compared with the real system. For validation, the animation should be viewed by someone who has knowledge of the real system in order to get their opinion about any major dissimilarities.

Test Runs

One way to check model validity is to use actual historical data in the model rather than derived probability distributions. Data collected could be used for elements such as customer arrival times and service delays. By comparing output measures across identical time periods, it should be possible to validate the model. Thus, the structure or flow of the model could be validated and then probability distributions entered for random elements. Thus, any error in system performance could be identified as either a logic error or an inaccurate distribution. The disadvantage of this method is that for a model of any size, the amount of historical data needed will be substantial. It is also necessary to read this data, either from a file or an array, requiring additional coding effort.

Examples of the use of Test Runs are as follows:

- Set up conditions to force certain events to take place. For example, if you have a maximum queue size, set to 5 customers then force more than 5 customers in the queue to check that the condition is met.
- Create 'extreme' conditions to check that the model behaves as expected. For example, set a very high arrival rate to create queuing and observe if expected queue balking behaviour occurs. Also, check that the largest queues occur in the bottleneck areas you expected.
- Isolate areas of the model to reduce complexity and track down errors.

Sensitivity Analysis

Operational validity is primarily about ensuring that the amount and quality of the data used in the model are sufficient to represent the variability inherent in the real system. A common way of ensuring operational validity is to use the technique of sensitivity analysis to test the behaviour of the model under various scenarios and compare results with real-world behaviour. The technique of experimental design can be employed to conduct sensitivity analysis over two or more factors. Note that for validation purposes, these tests are comparing simulation performance with real-world performance, while in the context of experimentation, they are used to compare simulation behaviour under different scenarios. Sensitivity analysis can be used to validate a model, but it is particularly appropriate if a model has been built of a system that does not exist as the data has been estimated and cannot be validated against a real system. It should also be noted that an option may be to conduct sensitivity analysis on subsystems of the overall system being modelled which do exist. This emphasises the point that the model should be robust enough to provide a prediction of what would happen in the real system under a range of possible input data. The construction and validation of the model should be for a particular range of input values defined in the simulation project objectives. If the simulation is then used outside of this predefined range, the model must be revalidated to ensure that additional aspects of the real system are incorporated to ensure valid results.

Sensitivity analysis should be undertaken by observing the output measure of interest with data set to levels above and below the initial set level for the data. A graph may be used to show model results for a range of data values if detailed analysis is required (e.g. a non-linear relationship between a data value and output measure is apparent). If the model output does not show a significant change in value in response to the sensitivity analysis, then we can judge that the accuracy of the estimated value will not have a significant effect on the result. If the model output is sensitive to the data value, then preferably we would want to increase the accuracy of the data value estimate. This may be undertaken by further interviews or data collection. In any event, the simulation analysis will need to show the effect of model output on a range of data values. Thus, for an estimated value, we can observe the likely behaviour of the system over a range of data values within which the true value should be located. Further sensitivity analysis may be required on each of these values to separate changes in output values from random variation. When it is found that more than one data value has an effect on an output measure, then the effects of the individual and combined data values should be assessed. This will require 3^k replications to measure the minimum, initial and maximum values for k variables. The use of fractional factorial designs may be used to reduce the number of replications required.

Sensitivity Analysis

We conduct sensitivity analysis to determine if the model behaves in a way in which we expect and to ensure that both the input data and model representation are appropriate for our needs. We should view sensitivity analysis in a broad way not as just a technical exercise but as an opportunity to obtain a greater understanding of our abstraction of the real system and to indicate important processes and parameters that drive the cause-and-effect relationships we are interested in. This should be part of an iterative process, and we may need to conduct additional data collection to improve the accuracy of our model if our conceptualisation and/or understanding of the system is faulty. We should also not just look at sensitivity analysis in terms of input data, but as there are usually multiple ways in which a process can be represented in a model, it is important to evaluate how decisions about a model's representation affect its behaviour.

Input Model Uncertainty

Some researchers discuss the issue of uncertainty quantification along with model verification and validation procedures. One type of uncertainty is input uncertainty, which affects the model output. This is because our simulation output arises as a consequence of the input distributions used to drive the model, and these are often fitted using finite samples of real-world data. The finiteness of the samples introduces errors in the input distributions, affecting the output. Barton (2012) provides a tutorial which presents a discussion of input uncertainty issues and methodological approaches.

Also, note that while it may be possible to estimate the amount of error in an input distribution, the effect of missing or erroneous elements in the process map are more difficult to quantify. This implies the domain knowledge of the modelling team is crucial in understanding the relationship between the internal process logic of the model and the relationship between input and output parameters.

Summary

Verification means ensuring that the computer model built using the simulation software is a correct representation of the conceptual model of the system under investigation. Validation is about ensuring that model behaviour is close enough to the real-world system for the purposes of the simulation study. This chapter covers a range of approaches to ensure model verification and validation.

Exercises

- Distinguish between the techniques of verification and validation.
- Search for papers on the website https://informs-sim.org and discuss methods used by practitioners for verification and validation.
- How would you ensure conceptual validity, operational validity and believability?
- Discuss the role of sensitivity analysis in validation.

References

Barton, R.R. (2012) Tutorial: Input uncertainty in output analysis, *Proceedings of the 2012 Winter Simulation Conference*, IEEE, 67–78.

Pegden, C.D., Shannon, R.E. and Sadowski, R.P. (1995) *Introduction to Simulation using SIMAN*, 2nd edition, Mc-Graw-Hill.

Sargent, R.G. (2013) Verification and validation of simulation models, *Journal of Simulation*, 7, 12–14.

8A: Verification and Validation
with Arena

Introduction

Arena provides a number of facilities for model verification and validation which are covered briefly in this chapter.

Structured Walkthrough

A structured walkthrough can be achieved by reading through the computer model code to check that the correct data and logic have been entered. These should be checked against the conceptual model specification.

Arena is able to convert the model you have placed in the model window into the simulation language SIMAN. This consists of a model file containing the simulation logic modules and an experimental file containing the data modules. To view these files for a simulation, select the Run/SIMAN/View option. The SIMAN files for the single-queue bank clerk simulation are shown in figure 8A.1 and figure 8A.2.

These files are, of course, most useful if you are familiar with the SIMAN simulation language. Also, note also that the coding in the model listing (figure 8A.1) does not necessarily follow the sequence of modules in the order of the model logic. Unfortunately, the edited code cannot be converted back to an Arena program, so SIMAN code is restricted to an aid for verification. Also, debugging from a code listing is more difficult than that for a general-purpose language, such as C, as many parts of the model will be executing simultaneously because many entities are passing through the model at any one given time.

Animation Inspection

The animation facilities provide a powerful tool in aiding understanding of model behaviour and enable us to observe the flow of entities. To check the logic of the model, run the model slowly and watch how each element of the model behaves.

Trace Analysis

To enable a trace inspection of the actions of each entity, an event debugger is required. The debugging facilities are available in the Arena run controller, which provides a number of facilities for inspecting model behaviour. The run controller is activated on the Run menu by selecting the Command menu option. When activated, a window is opened and a prompt will appear. The SET TRACE command is used to provide a visual display of all the simulation

```
;
;
;    Model statements for module:  DiscreteProcessing.Create 1 (customer arrivals)
;

2$          CREATE,        1,MinutesToBaseTime(0.0),customer:MinutesToBaseTime(EXPO(5)):NEXT(3$);

3$          ASSIGN:        customer arrivals.NumberOut=customer arrivals.NumberOut + 1:NEXT(0$);


;
;
;    Model statements for module:  DiscreteProcessing.Process 1 (Till 1 and Till 2)
;
0$          ASSIGN:        Till 1 and Till 2.NumberIn=Till 1 and Till 2.NumberIn + 1:
                           Till 1 and Till 2.WIP=Till 1 and Till 2.WIP+1;
9$          QUEUE,         Till 1 and Till 2.Queue;
8$          SEIZE,         2,VA:
                           bank clerk,1:NEXT(7$);

7$          DELAY:         Triangular(5,8,11),,VA;
6$          RELEASE:       bank clerk,1;
54$         ASSIGN:        Till 1 and Till 2.NumberOut=Till 1 and Till 2.NumberOut + 1:
                           Till 1 and Till 2.WIP=Till 1 and Till 2.WIP-1:NEXT(1$);


;
;
;    Model statements for module:  DiscreteProcessing.Dispose 1 (Dispose 1)
;
1$          ASSIGN:        Dispose 1.NumberOut=Dispose 1.NumberOut + 1;
57$         DISPOSE:       Yes;
```

Figure 8A.1 Arena SIMAN model file code listing

```
PROJECT,    "Unnamed Project","IT Services",,,No,Yes,Yes,Yes,No,No,No,No,No,No;

VARIABLES:  Till 1 and Till 2.NumberIn,CLEAR(Statistics),CATEGORY("Exclude"):
            Till 1 and Till 2.NumberOut,CLEAR(Statistics),CATEGORY("Exclude"):
            customer arrivals.NumberOut,CLEAR(Statistics),CATEGORY("Exclude"):
            Dispose 1.NumberOut,CLEAR(Statistics),CATEGORY("Exclude"):
            Till 1 and Till 2.WIP,CLEAR(System),CATEGORY("Exclude-Exclude"),DATATYPE(Real);

QUEUES:     Till 1 and Till 2.Queue,FIFO,,AUTOSTATS(Yes,,);

PICTURES:   Picture.Person:
            Picture.Green Ball:
            Picture.Red Ball:
            Picture.Yellow Ball:
            Picture.Report:
            Picture.Box:
            Picture.Blue Ball;

RESOURCES:  bank clerk,Capacity(2),,,,COST(0.0,0.0,0.0),CATEGORY(Resources),,AUTOSTATS(Yes,,);

REPLICATE,  1,,MinutesToBaseTime(40320),Yes,Yes,,,,,24,Minutes,No,No,,,Yes,No;

ENTITIES:   customer,Picture.Report,0.0,0.0,0.0,0.0,0.0,0.0,AUTOSTATS(Yes,,);
```

Figure 8A.2 Arena SIMAN experimental file code listing

events. Figure 8A.3 shows the debugger used to provide a trace of the code executed as the simulation runs. To cancel the trace running, press the ESC key and use the trace cancel command CAN TRACE. To run the simulation with no trace until a set time, use the GO UNTIL (for example, go until 500) command. The SHOW command can be used to find the number of customers in all the queues (for example, show nq(*)). The VIEW command can show the attributes of the entities in a queue (for example, view queue process 2.queue).

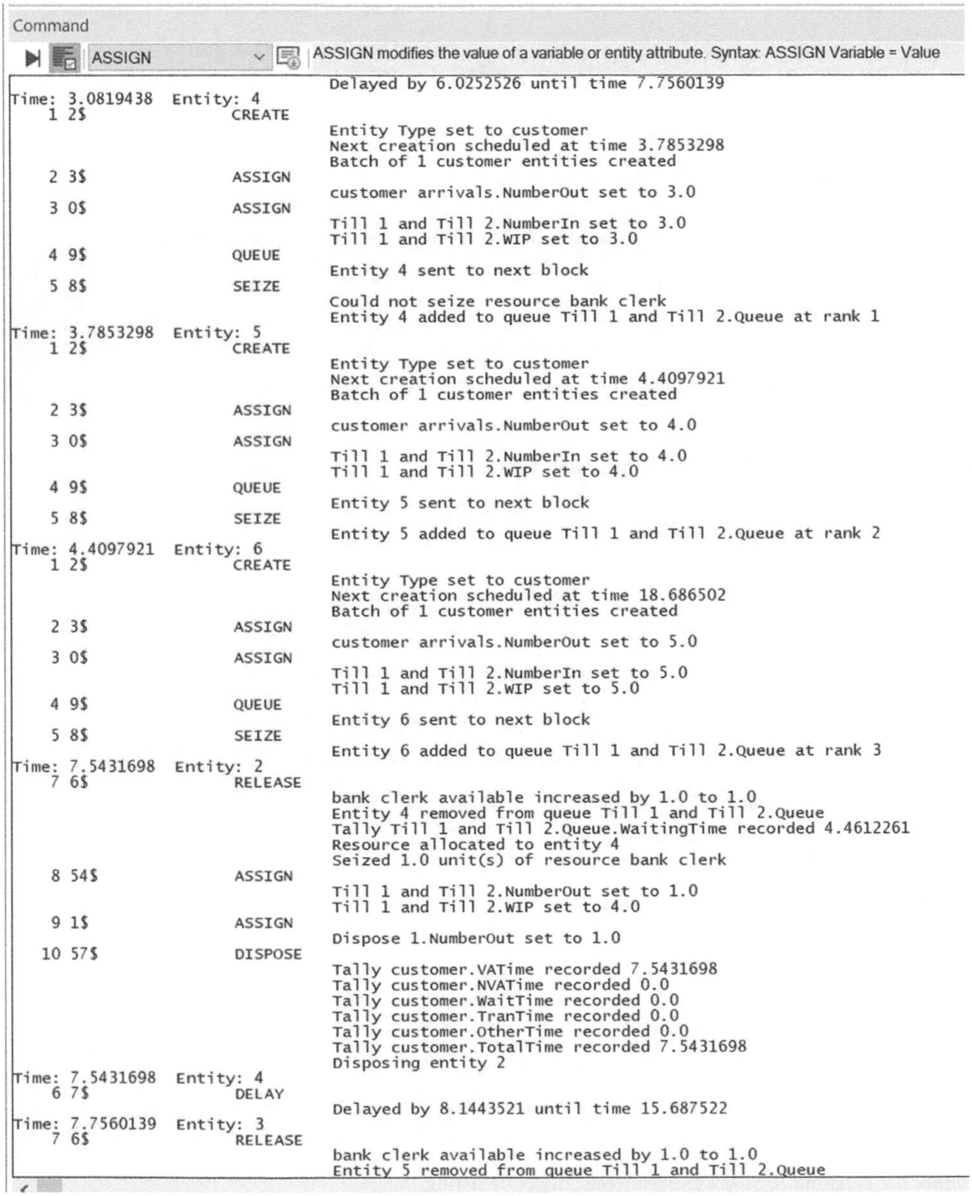

```
Command
ASSIGN          ASSIGN modifies the value of a variable or entity attribute. Syntax: ASSIGN Variable = Value
                                          Delayed by 6.0252526 until time 7.7560139
Time: 3.0819438  Entity: 4
   1 2$               CREATE
                                          Entity Type set to customer
                                          Next creation scheduled at time 3.7853298
                                          Batch of 1 customer entities created
   2 3$               ASSIGN
                                          customer arrivals.NumberOut set to 3.0
   3 0$               ASSIGN
                                          Till 1 and Till 2.NumberIn set to 3.0
                                          Till 1 and Till 2.WIP set to 3.0
   4 9$               QUEUE
                                          Entity 4 sent to next block
   5 8$               SEIZE
                                          Could not seize resource bank clerk
                                          Entity 4 added to queue Till 1 and Till 2.Queue at rank 1
Time: 3.7853298  Entity: 5
   1 2$               CREATE
                                          Entity Type set to customer
                                          Next creation scheduled at time 4.4097921
                                          Batch of 1 customer entities created
   2 3$               ASSIGN
                                          customer arrivals.NumberOut set to 4.0
   3 0$               ASSIGN
                                          Till 1 and Till 2.NumberIn set to 4.0
                                          Till 1 and Till 2.WIP set to 4.0
   4 9$               QUEUE
                                          Entity 5 sent to next block
   5 8$               SEIZE
                                          Entity 5 added to queue Till 1 and Till 2.Queue at rank 2
Time: 4.4097921  Entity: 6
   1 2$               CREATE
                                          Entity Type set to customer
                                          Next creation scheduled at time 18.686502
                                          Batch of 1 customer entities created
   2 3$               ASSIGN
                                          customer arrivals.NumberOut set to 5.0
   3 0$               ASSIGN
                                          Till 1 and Till 2.NumberIn set to 5.0
                                          Till 1 and Till 2.WIP set to 5.0
   4 9$               QUEUE
                                          Entity 6 sent to next block
   5 8$               SEIZE
                                          Entity 6 added to queue Till 1 and Till 2.Queue at rank 3
Time: 7.5431698  Entity: 2
   7 6$               RELEASE
                                          bank clerk available increased by 1.0 to 1.0
                                          Entity 4 removed from queue Till 1 and Till 2.Queue
                                          Tally Till 1 and Till 2.Queue.WaitingTime recorded 4.4612261
                                          Resource allocated to entity 4
                                          Seized 1.0 unit(s) of resource bank clerk
   8 54$              ASSIGN
                                          Till 1 and Till 2.NumberOut set to 1.0
                                          Till 1 and Till 2.WIP set to 4.0
   9 1$               ASSIGN
                                          Dispose 1.NumberOut set to 1.0
  10 57$              DISPOSE
                                          Tally customer.VATime recorded 7.5431698
                                          Tally customer.NVATime recorded 0.0
                                          Tally customer.WaitTime recorded 0.0
                                          Tally customer.TranTime recorded 0.0
                                          Tally customer.OtherTime recorded 0.0
                                          Tally customer.TotalTime recorded 7.5431698
                                          Disposing entity 2
Time: 7.5431698  Entity: 4
   6 7$               DELAY
                                          Delayed by 8.1443521 until time 15.687522
Time: 7.7560139  Entity: 3
   7 6$               RELEASE
                                          bank clerk available increased by 1.0 to 1.0
                                          Entity 5 removed from queue Till 1 and Till 2.Queue
```

Figure 8A.3 Arena trace listing

Test Runs

To enable testing, set up appropriate conditions in the model such as forcing events and extreme conditions. Check the performance of the model using Arena's model reporting facilities.

Sensitivity Analysis

See Rossetti (2016:372) for sensivity analysis using the Process Analyzer.

Summary

Arena provides a number of facilities for model verification and validation. This chapter has covered the conversion of the model into simulation language coding and the debugging and trace facility.

Reference

Rossetti, M.D. (2016) *Simulation Modeling and Arena*, 2nd edition, John Wiley & Sons Ltd.

8B: Verification and Validation with Simio

Introduction

Simio provides a number of facilities for model verification and validation.

Structured Walthrough

A structured walkthrough can be achieved by reading through the computer model code to check that the correct data and logic have been entered. These should be checked against the conceptual model specification.

Animation Inspection

The animation facilities provide a powerful tool in aiding understanding of model behaviour and enable us to observe the flow of entities. To check the logic of the model, run the model slowly and watch how each element of the model behaves.

Trace Analysis

To assist with trace analysis and debugging, Simio offers trace facilities. From the Run tab, select the Model Trace option. A window will appear at the bottom of the screen and will show trace information as the simulation runs (figure 8B.1).

Test Runs

To enable testing, set up appropriate conditions in the model such as forcing events and extreme conditions. Check the performance of the model using Arena's model reporting facilities.

Sensitivity Analysis

Simio provides an inbuilt tool to undertake response sensitivity analysis. This first requires that input parameters such as those for interarrival times and service times are defined in the Input Parameters option found on the Data tab. From here select the Distribution option in the ribbon and enter the parameters for the distribution. Figure 8B.2 shows the customer interarrival and figure 8B.3 shows the customer service distributions entered for the single-queue bank clerk simulation model. Note for each input parameter, Simio displays a chart at

Figure 8B.1 Simio Trace display

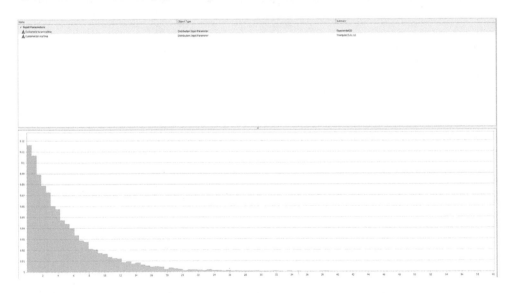

Figure 8B.2 Customer interarrival distribution shape for the blank clerk simulation

the bottom of the screen showing the shape of the distribution for the modeller to check the range and shape is are appropriate. This display is created by Simio based on 10,000 random draws from the defined distribution.

The name for each input parameter distribution should now be used in the bank clerk model instead of the original values. In the Properties Window for Source1, assign the

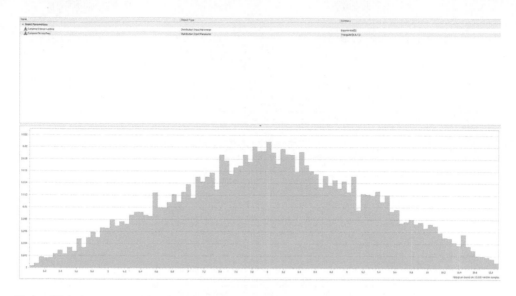

Figure 8B.3 Customer service time distribution shape for the blank clerk simulation

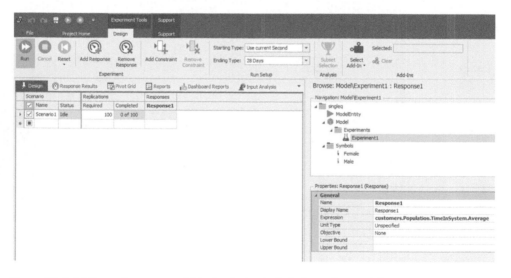

Figure 8B.4 Adding a Response variable for the bank clerk simulation model

Interarrival Time to the CustomerInterarrivalTime input parameter, and in the Properties Window for Server1, assign the Processing Time to the CustomerServiceTime input parameter. In the experimental screen, select the Design tab and choose the Add Response option from the menu. Enter customer.population.timeinsystem.average for the response expression (figure 8B.4).

After running the bank clerk simulation for 100 replications, move to the input analysis tab and select the response sensitivity option to the left of the screen. Simio displays a

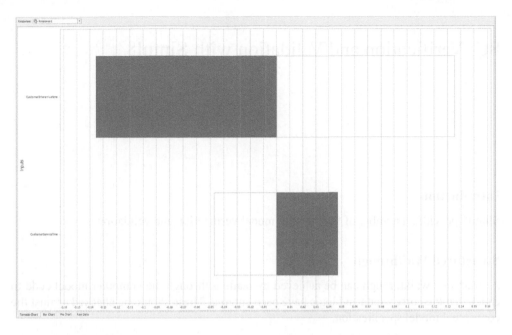

Figure 8B.5 Simio response sensitivity analysis for bank clerk simulation model

tornado chart of each input parameter sensitivity in terms of the target response defined as customer time in the system. Figure 8B.5 shows the chart with the parameters ordered by sensitivity from the top of the chart to the bottom. What the chart is showing is the sensitivity of the response (time in the system) to a change in the input parameter of 1 unit (in this case, 1 minute) while holding all other input parameters constant. It is clear that the 'time in the system' metric is more sensitive to interarrival time and, to a lesser extent, customer service time. The blue bars indicate a negative relationship between the interarrival time and the time in the system and a positive relationship between the service time and time in the system. Thus, the chart shows that decreased interarrival times and increased service times will increase the time in the system and will provide a useful validation check to see that these positive and negative relationships would be intuitively expected. This result of greater sensitivity to interarrival times than customer service times implies that if you wish to collect additional data to improve the input distributions and thus improve the accuracy of the model, then this effort should be focused around interarrival times as they affect the results the most in terms of time in the system.

Summary

Simio provides a number of facilities for model verification and validation.

8C: Verification and Validation with Simul8

Introduction

Simul8 provides a number of facilities for model verification and validation.

Structured Walthrough

A structured walkthrough can be achieved by reading through the computer model code to check that the correct data and logic have been entered. These should be checked against the conceptual model specification.

Animation Inspection

The animation facilities provide a powerful tool in aiding understanding of model behaviour and enable us to observe the flow of entities. To check the logic of the model, run the model slowly and watch how each element of the model behaves.

Trace Analysis

Load a Simul8 model and then select the Advanced tab on the menu and select the Monitor Simulation option. Enlarge the monitor window and select the History tab. Select the Play button, and the trace listing will appear in the Monitor (figure 8C.1). Select pause to stop the simulation, and then you can browse through the listing. Any events that have been placed on the future event calendar can be displayed by selecting the Future tab.

If you wish to search through the trace listing, select the options tab, and the menu will appear (figure 8C.2).

Test Runs

To enable testing, set up appropriate conditions in the model such as forcing events and extreme conditions. Check the performance of the model using Arena's model reporting facilities.

Sensitivity Analysis

Sensitivity analysis can be undertaken in Simul8 by observing the output measure of interest with data set to levels above and below the initial set level for the data. A graph may be used

Figure 8C.1 Simul8 Monitor

Figure 8C.2 Monitor options menu

to show model results for a range of data values if detailed analysis is required. If the model output does not show a significant change in value in response to the sensitivity analysis, then we can judge that the accuracy of the estimated value will not have a significant effect on the result

Summary

Simul8 provides a number of facilities for model verification and validation.

9 Experimentation

Simulation Output Analysis

Introduction

This chapter covers the procedure for obtaining accurate results from a single simulation model. To do this, we need to determine the nature of the simulation output, deal with initial bias, ensure enough data has been collected and use appropriate measures of performance. Chapter 10 extends the analysis covered in this chapter to investigate and compare multiple model designs.

Obtaining Accurate Results for Simulation

When conducting simulation experimentation, we are concerned with the following issues that will affect the accuracy of our model results and the nature of the how we report the performance of the system:

* Determining the Nature of the Simulation Output

    The type of system (terminating or non-terminating) and the nature of the simulation output (transient or steady-state) will determine how we ensure the accuracy of the model results and how performance will be reported.

* Dealing with Initial Bias

    At the beginning of a simulation run, the system will normally be empty with a consequent effect on performance measures such as queue times. Dealing with the effect of this start-up period is particularly relevant to the accuracy of model results when measuring the steady-state performance of a non-terminating system.

* Obtaining Enough Data

    In discrete-event simulation, you cannot treat successive output values as independent observations; for example, you might be able to do in traditional statistical sampling applications, such as surveys. This is because in queuing systems, the queuing time of entities in the queue will be affected by other entities in the queue. For example, your waiting time in a queue will be longer if the person in front of you (or the person in front of them) takes a long time to service. This behaviour leads to what is termed auto-correlated data and requires an extended amount of data collection in order to achieve a reasonable picture of the system behaviour. We need to generate a large enough sample of data to obtain what we can consider a good estimate of the mean of our measure of performance. This allows us to obtain a sufficiently

DOI: 10.4324/9781003124092-9

narrow confidence interval around the mean estimate when we report our model performance.

- Measuring Performance

  The main method used to measure performance is to construct a confidence interval around the grand mean (mean of all the replications) for the metric of interest. This provides a measure of central tendency. We can also measure variability using range and percentile measures.

Simulation Output Analysis and Accuracy

It should be noted that when conducting simulation output analysis, accuracy relates to the statistical accuracy we are reporting and does not necessarily mean that the model is accurate in the sense of being representative of the real system (that is, the role of verification and validation). To be an accurate representation of the real system will depend to some extent on our domain knowledge. This kind of uncertainty is difficult to quantify and relates to the topic of model validity and emphasises that it is unlikely that a model will be wholly valid. It may be that during output analysis, we find that the simulation will require additional modelling work before it can provide an accurate representation of the real system; this reflects the fact that there will be an iterative approach to the execution of the simulation study stages. However, the model will always be a simplification of reality, and the model results should not be viewed in isolation but interpreted by people with the required knowledge of the model (its assumptions, simplifications and scope) and knowledge of the real system that is being modelled.

Why We Need Statistical Analysis of Simulation Output

Although we can simply use the animation facilities of our simulation to view future behaviour of our system, we also need to undertake the statistical analysis outlined in this chapter. This is because we need to consider the simulation results over an extended time period to provide a representative view of behaviour. One reason for this is termed serial autocorrelation, which is typically seen in the queuing system that is represented by DES. For example, the serve time for a customer in a shop will impact the queue time for the customer after them, and their queue time will impact the queue time of the customer after them. This means that the successive queue times for these customers cannot be treated as independent observations, and a small sample of these times may not provide a representative value of measures such as average queue times. Another issue when observing simulation output is the bias in results that can be introduced when the simulation commences its run from an empty state. During this initial time period, we are likely to observe lower than normal values for our measures, such as average queue time. This chapter provides a number of approaches for dealing with autocorrelation and initial bias in our simulation output.

Determining the Nature of the Simulation Output

How we deal with the issues of initial bias and ensuring enough data will depend on the nature of the simulation output, and so we address this issue now. Firstly, the type of system is defined in the categories of terminating and non-terminating, as each type requires a different method of output analysis.

Terminating Simulations

Terminating simulations run between predefined states or times where the end state matches the initial state of the simulation. Most service organisations tend to be terminating systems that close at the end of each day with no in-process inventory (i.e. people waiting for service) and thus return to the 'empty' or 'idle' state they had at the start of that day. For example, a simulation of a retail outlet from opening to closing time. Thus, terminating systems have an obvious endpoint, such as a day's operation in a service operation or a production cycle in a manufacturing system. Note that what might be considered a terminating system, such as an office which is in operations 8 hours a day, might actually be non-terminating in that some aspects as work in the office may be carried over to the next day. Thus, another way of defining terminating simulations is that they do not keep entities in the system from one cycle to the next or that they contain an event which specifies when the simulation has finished.

Non-Terminating Simulations

Non-terminating simulations may have no obvious endpoint (unlike terminating simulations); examples include continuous (24/7) service operations like hospitals and manufacturing systems. Most manufacturing organisations are non-terminating as they contain inventory in the system that is awaiting a process. Thus, even if the facility shuts down temporarily, it will start again in a different state from the previous start state (i.e. the inventory levels define different starting conditions). Thus, another way of defining non-terminating simulations is that if they do have an endpoint, they keep entities in the system from one cycle to the next.

Transient and Steady-State Simulation Output

Simulation output can be either transient or steady-state. Transient output is when the distribution of the output is not stable and is constantly changing. Most terminating simulations show this behaviour at the start, during and at the end of the run (figure 9.1).

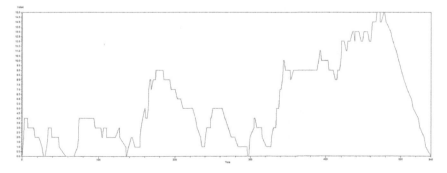

Figure 9.1 A terminating simulation showing transient behaviour

Steady-state output is when the distribution of the output is stable. This indicates the mean output level and the variability around this mean level remain constant. Most non-terminating simulations have a transient period during the start of the run and then enter a steady state during the run (figure 9.2).

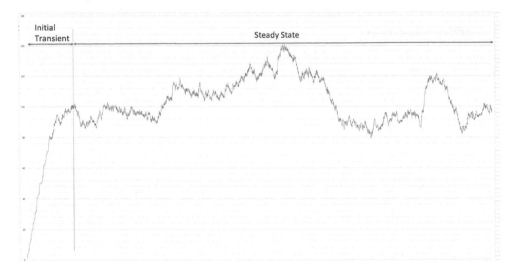

Figure 9.2 A non-terminating simulation showing transient and steady-state behaviour

Some terminating simulations show transient output at the start and end of the run with steady-state output during the run (figure 9.3).

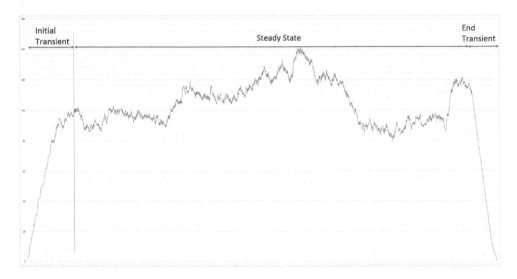

Figure 9.3 A terminating simulation showing transient and steady-state behaviour

Table 9.1 Simulation Output by Simulation Type

	Simulation Output	
Simulation Type	**Transient**	**Steady-State**
Terminating	Always at start and end and usually through all the run	Sometimes in the middle of the run
Non-Terminating	Always at the start of the run period	Usually after the initial start period

Table 9.1 shows the relationship between simulation type and simulation output.

Note that apart from the starting conditions, non-terminating simulations may be in a transient state, such as when moving from one production cycle to another. Also, some non-terminating simulations may not ever reach a steady state. Steady-state cycle simulation output repeatedly moves between transient and steady-state phases. This can be caused by demand patterns that are defined by timeslots, such as hour, shift, day, week and month. Thus, there is a transition when moving from one time slot to the next. A heuristic technique for identifying the shifts in the mean of a time series is applied to the output data from simulation models with known shifting steady-state behaviour in Robinson et al. (2002)

Concept Drift

When observing simulation output, note that there may be a shift from one steady-state to another due to external factors such as new product introduction or a change in staff levels. This reflects the fact that the system environment, although not part of the system, if modified, can produce a change in the state of the system itself. Normally these external factors are held at a constant level for the duration of the simulation run or treated as scenario variables outside of the model. However, when conducting real-time simulation with continuous data streams, it is important to distinguish between the natural random variation in data and external factors that change the context of the data. This has been recognised as an important aspect in process mining applications and is given the term concept drift (Bose et al., 2011). Figure 9.4 shows a process in terms of transient and steady-state behaviour. For this non-terminating simulation, there is a warm-up period represented by an initial transient phase where the system fills with products from empty. The system then quickly reaches a steady-state phase in which values with approximately the same distribution fluctuate around a mean value. An outside event – in this case, an equipment breakdown event – causes the process to enter a transient phase. Shortly after the transient phase, actions are taken to recover from the loss of output which involves running the system at a higher rate of output. This represents a new steady-state level that is caused by what can be termed concept drift as the system is operating in a different manner than before. Finally, normal operating procedures are reinstated, and thus, the process returns to its long-run steady-state operation.

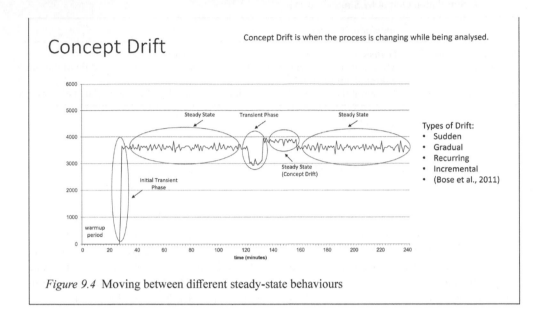

Figure 9.4 Moving between different steady-state behaviours

Dealing with Initial Bias (Terminating Simulations)

Because we are considering the performance of the system over the full cycle in a terminating simulation, we do not normally need to consider dealing with initial bias. Also, our initial condition of our terminating system (say, a customer service system) is usually empty (at the start of a day's operation). What we may need to do is ensure that our system returns to its initial state. For example, in a retail system, at the end of the day's service, no customers should remain in the system. In practice, this may mean running the simulation for an extended period after the official closing time to clear the system. The system terminates when the final customer leaves the system, but this time will vary as it depends on the period of time it takes to process the remaining customers. An extended time of 30 minutes when no new customers are permitted to enter the system should be sufficient for a typical customer service operation to clear the system, but this should be checked to ensure the system is actually empty at the end of each run. Too long an extended run length should be avoided as the empty system after the final customer has left the system may bias some of our performance measures, such as the average number of customers in the system over the run length.

Dealing with Initial Bias (Non-Terminating Simulations)

A non-terminating simulation generally goes through an initial transient phase and then enters a steady-state phase for the performance measure when its value is independent of the simulation starting conditions. A simulation analysis will be directed toward measuring the performance of output values during their steady-state phase and avoiding measurements during their initial transient phase. Thus, for a non-terminating simulation, the effect of the initial conditions on the performance measures should be considered. The following methods of achieving this are discussed.

Extended Run

This approach simply consists of running the simulation for an extended run length, thus reducing the bias introduced on output variables in the initial transient phase. This represents a simple solution to the problem and can be applied in combination with one or both of the other approaches. The main issue with using the extended run length approach is to determine how long the run should be to ensure the initial bias is reduced to an acceptable level. This approach is becoming more feasible as the speed of execution of simulation software makes long runs quicker to execute.

Setting Initial Conditions

This approach involves specifying start conditions for the simulation that will provide a quick transition to steady-state conditions for the relevant performance measures. Most simulations are started in an empty state for convenience, but by using knowledge of steady-state conditions for the performance measures (e.g. stock levels), it is possible to reduce the initial bias phase substantially. The disadvantage of this approach is the effort in initialising simulation variables, of which there may be many, and when a suitable initial value may not be known. It is unlikely that the initial transient phase will be eliminated entirely, so it may be necessary to set initial run conditions and then run for a short warm-up period method.

Warm-up Period

Instead of manually setting initial conditions, this approach uses the simulation software to discard all measurements collected on a performance variable before a predetermined time (the warm-up period) in order to ensure that no data is collected during the initial phase. The point at which data is discarded must be set late enough to ensure that the simulation has entered the steady-state phase for the performance measure but not so late that insufficient data points can be collected for a reasonably precise statistical analysis.

The time-series inspection method is a popular method of choosing the discard point by visually inspecting the simulation output behaviour of the performance measure over time. It is important to ensure that the model is inspected over a time period which allows infrequent events (e.g. machine breakdowns) to occur a reasonable number of times. If our simulation has a number of performance measures, we may need to determine the warm-up period for each of these performance measures of interest and use the longest of these warm-up periods for the simulation analysis. Another approach is to choose a value such as WIP, which can provide a useful measure of overall system behaviour. In a manufacturing setting, this could relate to the amount of material within the system at any given time. In a service setting, the WIP measure may be represented by the number of customers in the system. To ensure the correct estimation of the warm-up period, we should undertake multiple replications as the steady-state period will commence at different times for different runs. This approach is also useful for noisy data when it is difficult to ascertain the beginning of a steady state. Plotting the averages of the replications aids the visual inspection by smoothing the time-series data. Figure 9.5 shows the cumulative average graphs for four replications.

There are a number of other methods for determining the warm-up period, including the use of a heuristic method known as the marginal standard error rule (MSER), as shown by Kelton et al. (2015) and Robinson (2014). An adaption of MSER named MSER-5 is detailed by Hoad et al. (2010).

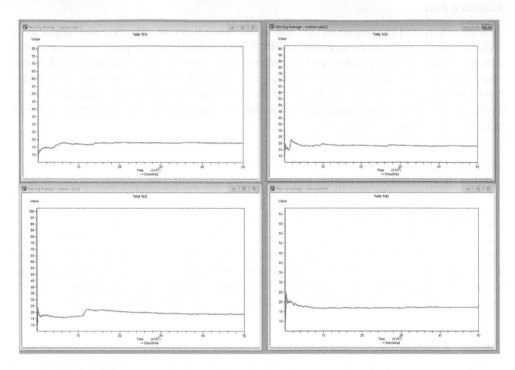

Figure 9.5 Cumulative moving average (four replications)

Obtaining Enough Data (Terminating Simulations)

For a terminating simulation, our run length will be determined by when the simulation terminates. This could be at the end of a day's operation in a service system or the completion of a production schedule in a manufacturing department. We may need to consider extending the simulation runtime to empty the system and thus make it a true terminating system (see initial bias section). For a terminating simulation, we will use multiple replications (simulation runs) to obtain sufficient data to report accurate results.

Multiple Replications

We use multiple replications because although we can obtain results from a single run of the simulation, say for one day's operation, that will only provide measures based on a specific stream of random numbers generated by the simulation software. The random number stream is used to generate values for the theoretical distributions, such as the exponential distribution, we are employing in our model. In effect, we have produced a single sample of the results of the simulation. We generate multiple samples by running the model multiple times, each time changing the random number stream (this is done automatically by the simulation software). Using separate runs for each of our samples means that we will generate statistics that are statistically independent of one another. This is important because one of the basic requirements for our statistical analysis is that observations are independent. We can use the methods of estimation, the graphical method and the confidence interval method to determine the number of replications required.

• *Estimation*

We need to determine the number of replications that are required for the desired precision in the performance measure. This calculation is a trade-off between the effort in time and money in running many replications against the risk of an incorrect decision made as a consequence of inaccurate results. However, the need to take measures to minimise the number of replications has decreased as simulation software has become increasingly fast. As a guide, 20 replications may be considered a minimum, but 50 or 100 replications can usefully be performed. Remember that increasing replications increases the statistically precision of the model results but does not relate to the accuracy of the model's representation of the real-world system.

• *Graphical Method*

This approach plots the cumulative means of output data over a number of replications. As the number of replications increases, then the cumulative graph should become a flat line which denotes the number of replications required.

• *Confidence Interval Method*

In general, when determining the number of replications needed, we are guided by what we consider to be the precision required in our performance measures in relation to the study objectives. This precision can be expressed as a confidence interval, which is a measure of the error in our measurement due to the size of the sample (number of replications) we have used (we would need an infinite number of replications to eliminate this error). In this method, we measure precision by observing the deviation of the confidence interval from either side of the cumulative mean. Figure 9.6 shows how the confidence interval narrows after more and more replications have occurred. We can construct a spreadsheet to perform the calculations using the following Excel formulae:

Cumulative mean   = average(first data point: current data point)
Standard deviation = stdev.s(first data point: current data point)
Confidence interval = confidence.t(significance level, standard deviation, replication no.)
Lower interval   = cumulative mean − confidence interval/2
Upper interval   = cumulative mean + confidence interval/2
% deviation   = (confidence interval/2) / cumulative mean
Note for a 95% confidence interval the significance level is 0.05 divided by 2 (0.025).

We can also use the simulation software to determine the number of replications using the confidence interval method; for example, we can use model logic to check for a target confidence interval at runtime in Arena (see chapter 9A), and in Simul8, we can use the Trials calculator (see chapter 9C).

Antithetic Variates

The number of replications may be decreased by using the variance reduction technique (VRT) of antithetic variates. This method could, for example, generate a low value whenever the original random number stream had generated a high value and so ensure that the system is being investigated under a variety of different scenarios. See Law (2015) for more details.

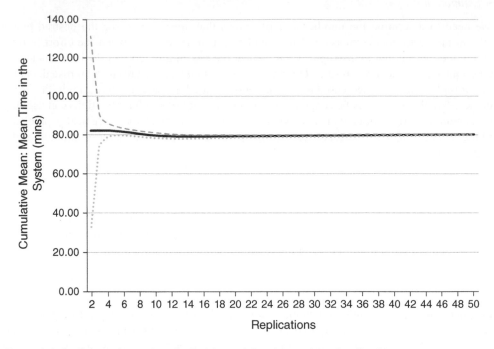

Figure 9.6 Confidence interval method of determining the number of replications

Obtaining Enough Data (Non-Terminating Simulations)

For a terminating simulation, we have a set run length, and so we only have the option of undertaking multiple replications to obtain enough data. With a non-terminating simulation, we can also adjust the run length as well as determine the number of replications. The following are the options.

Multiple Replications

We need to make sure initial bias has been dealt with, and then we can make multiple replications for a terminating system. As for a terminating simulation, we can use estimation (say, 20 replications), the graphical method or the confidence interval method to determine the number of replications required (see terminating simulations section).

Run Length (Multiple Replications)

For run length, we should consider what might represent a steady output; this could be a week, month or year, for example. The run length should take into account how certain we are that initialisation bias has been removed (see earlier sections on removing bias). In general, it is better to have as long a run length as possible within the time constraints of model execution time. A guide is to have a run length of 10 times the warm-up period.

Run Length (One Long Run)

It may be that in order to deal with initial bias, we have specified an extended warm-up period for our simulation. To avoid repeatedly discarding data during this initial transient phase for each run when undertaking multiple replications, an alternative approach allows all data to be collected during one long run. To determine the one long-run length, we can employ the method of Robinson (2014:190), which uses the cumulative means of output data which are compared over three replications of the model. If the cumulative means converge to a target value of less than 5%, then this can be considered acceptable. Figure 9.7 shows the cumulative means for a simulation run over 500 days. We can construct a spreadsheet to perform the following calculations:

Cumulative mean = average(first data point: current data point)
Convergence = (max(data points for 3 replications) − min(data points for 3 replications))/
min(data points for 3 replications)

Batch Means

An issue with using one long run is that there will be auto-correlation across the run, which makes it difficult to calculate confidence intervals. To deal with this, we can make use of the batch means method, which consists of making one very long run of the simulation and collecting data at intervals during the run. Each interval between data collection is termed a batch. Each batch is treated as a separate run of the simulation for analysis, and so confidence

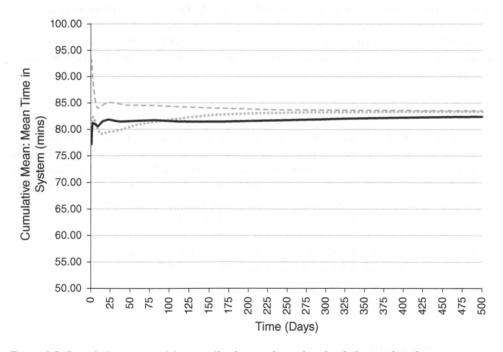

Figure 9.7 Cumulative means of three replications to determine simulation run length

interval analysis can be employed as described for terminating systems. The main issue with the batch means method is determining the size of the batch. More information on the batch means method is provided by Law (2015).

Note that if sufficient data has been collected, the batch means method is undertaken automatically when conducting a single run in simulation software such as Arena and Simio, so confidence intervals can be estimated of the steady-state value. More details on the algorithms used in the Simio batch means method are contained in the work of Joines and Roberts (2015:179). It should be noted that the batch means method undertaken for a single replication in the simulation software is only for steady-state analysis and so should be ignored for transient output (usually terminating simulations).

Measuring Performance

For terminating simulations, if we conduct output analysis over the complete terminating cycle (such as a day's operation in a retail shop), then the analysis may be considered transient phase analysis. In this case, average measures may not be appropriate performance measures as they may be skewed by the transient phases. For example, average customer queueing times over a day's operation may seem reasonable but may mask unacceptable queuing times at peak periods of customer demand during the day. Thus, measures such as maximum queue times, maximum lead times and counters such as customers served may be more appropriate performance measures. However, terminating simulations can also go through steady-state periods during the day where average queue times may be an appropriate measure.

Before a non-terminating simulation is analysed, the bias introduced by the non-representative starting conditions (for example, an empty factory that will never return to its empty state) should be eliminated to obtain steady-state conditions from which a representative statistical analysis can be undertaken. Performance can then be measured during the steady-state period using average and maximum performance of measures, such as queues, lead times and throughput rates.

Confidence Intervals

The main approach for measuring performance in a simulation is to measure the range within which the true mean of performance is expected to lie using a confidence interval. To assess the precision of our results, we can compute a confidence interval or range around the sample mean that will include, to a certain level of confidence, the true mean value of the variable we are measuring. Thus, confidence intervals provide a point estimate of the expected average (average over an infinite number of replications) and an idea of how precise this estimate is. A 95% confidence interval means that if the experiment was repeated many times, then 95% of those confidence intervals would contain the true value of the parameter.

The formula for the confidence interval involving the t-distribution is as follows:

$$CI = \bar{x} \pm t_{n-1,\alpha/2} \times s / \sqrt{n}$$

where
CI = confidence interval
$\bar{x}$ = sample mean (from the replications)
$t_{n-1,\alpha/2}$ with n-1 degrees of freedom and $\alpha/2$ = significance level

s = standard deviation (from the replications)
n = number of replications

Both the confidence interval analysis and the t-tests assume the data measured is normally distributed. This assumption is usually acceptable if measuring an average value for each replication as the output variable is made from many measurements, and the central limit theorem applies. However, the central limit theorem applies to a large sample size, and the definition of what constitutes a large sample depends partly on how close the actual distribution of the output variable is to the normal distribution. A histogram can be used to observe how close the actual distribution is to the normal distribution curve.

Figure 9.8 shows a confidence interval graph produced by the Output Analyzer of the Arena software (see chapter 9A). The display shows the mean (vertical line), the confidence interval (thick horizontal line) and the minimum and maximum values observed (thin horizontal line).

Prediction Intervals

When we compute a confidence interval for the mean, if we were to repeat the simulation experiment (across replications) and compute a confidence interval using the same methods many times, then 95% of the confidence intervals would include the true but unknown mean. In other words, we actually computed only one of these intervals, but we can be 95% sure that the interval is one of the 95% of intervals that includes the true mean. Thus, the confidence interval gives you both a point estimate of the mean and an idea of how precise the estimate is.

Thus, a confidence interval is a measure of error – a confidence interval of 95% tells us how much we can trust the interval to actually bound the error between our performance

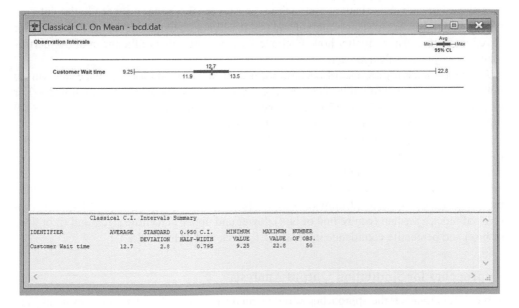

Figure 9.8 Arena confidence interval analysis using the Output Analyzer

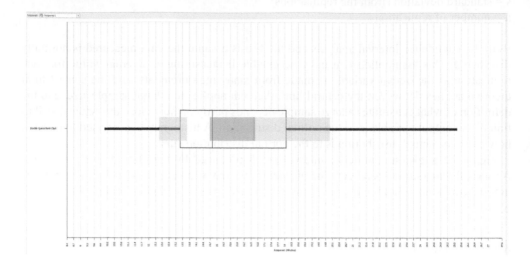

Figure 9.9 Simio SMORE plot of simulation output

measure and our estimate of it based on our simulated sample. We can increase our sample size by increasing the number of replications so the error will converge to zero as the number of replications goes to infinity.

An alternative measure sometimes called a prediction interval specifies a most likely range of values for the performance measure. This can be achieved by computing percentiles which are values within which a specified percentage of the generated data for an output fall.

Thus a prediction interval is a measure of risk – it measures what a particular performance measure might be at a particular point in time. This means that generally a prediction interval will be wider than a confidence interval and that it will not go to zero as replications increase to reflect the fact that no matter how much we simulate, the value of the mean of our performance measure will always vary.

Prediction intervals are useful because mean measures around a confidence interval do not indicate the spread of values that could occur or what values are likely and unlikely. For example, although our 95% confidence interval may indicate a mean stock level of 100 ± 20 units, it may be that there is a 30% chance of a stockout occurring.

In order to provide a measure of risk the Simio software incorporates the use of SMORE (Simio Measure of Risk and Error) plots (Smith et al., 2018) which display lower and upper percentile values (points at or below which are that per cent of the summary responses across the replications). These are based on the MORE (Measure of Risk and Error) plots developed by Nelson (2008). Figure 9.9 shows a SMORE plot with the mean (dot), confidence interval (central block), median (centre line of box), lower and upper percentiles (left and right lines of box) and percentile confidence intervals (left block and right block).

Approaches for Simulation Output Analysis

Table 9.2 summarises the approaches to output analysis that can be taken for terminating and non-terminating simulations. Terminating simulations require an analysis of performance

Table 9.2 Obtaining Accurate Results for Terminating and Non-Terminating Simulations

	Dealing with Initial Bias	Obtaining Enough Data	Nature of Output Measurement
Terminating	Normally not required	Multiple replications	Mean performance over transient
Non-Terminating	Extended run Set initial conditions Warm-up	Multiple replications Run length One long run	Mean performance at steady-state

over the transient. For non-terminating simulations, the analysis requires both dealing with the initial bias introduced into the results from the initial transient period and data from the system during a steady-state period, which does not reach a natural endpoint. Because techniques for non-terminating simulations involve more complex analysis than for a terminating simulation, consideration should be given to treating the model as a terminating simulation if at all possible. Note also that in terms of measuring performance, the results for the non-terminating simulation generally relate to the steady-state performance of the system, while the results for a terminating simulation generally relate to the performance of the system from its start point to its endpoint.

Summary

This chapter has covered the procedure for obtaining accurate results from a single simulation model. To do this, we have provided an overview of the nature of the simulation output, dealing with initial bias, ensuring enough data has been collected and using appropriate measures of performance.

Exercises

Two types of customers arrive at an airport with an exponential interarrival time distribution of five minutes. The first type of customer (accounting for 80% of total customers) proceeds to the check-in desk, goes through customs and x-ray and proceeds to the gate. The second type of customer (accounting for 20% of customers) goes to the ticket counter to purchase tickets and then proceeds as type 1 customers. The process times for ticket buying are exponential with a mean of five minutes. The time for check-in is triangular with parameters of two, four and five minutes. The time for customs and x-ray is exponentially distributed with a mean of one minute. Run the model for 2,400 minutes and collect statistics on resource utilisation at each process, queue sizes and time in the system for each customer type. Present and interpret the results of the simulation.

Change the scenario described in the exercise (output analysis chapter) so that the check-in and ticket-buying desks are combined (with two staff). Compare the results of this model over ten replications with the original using appropriate statistical techniques. Present and interpret the results of the simulation.

A dentist operates with one dentist with a customer mean arrival rate of 20 minutes with a Poisson distribution. The time for a check-up varies uniformly between 10 and 20 minutes. The dentist has five waiting spaces for customers. If a customer arrives and all these spaces are taken, then they will leave and then return after 10 minutes with a 30% probability or simply leave and not return with a 70% probability. The dentist opens at 7:00 a.m. and serves all customers that arrive before 5.30 p.m. Develop an ARENA model that estimates the following:

- The average waiting time for customers and the proportion of arriving customers who receive service.
- The average waiting time for customers and the proportion of arriving customers who receive service if the dentist adds an additional waiting space.
- The average waiting time for customers and the proportion of arriving customers who receive service if the dentist adds two additional waiting spaces.

The dentist expands its operation and now has two dentists. The additional dentist works with a checkup time that varies uniformly between 15 and 30 minutes. Due to a marketing campaign, customers now arrive with a Poisson rate of five customers per hour. Sixty per cent of customers choose the original dentist, and 40% of customers choose the new dentist. Six waiting spaces are now provided, and 30% of arriving customers who find all the spaces taken will return after a delay of 10 minutes (the rest just leave without returning). The dentist opens at 7:00 a.m. and serves all customers that arrive before 5:30 p.m. Develop an Arena model that estimates

- the average waiting time for customers, the proportion of arriving customers who receive service and the utilisation of each dentist.

On further investigation, it was found that, in fact, 30% of customers have no preferences for either dentist, 50% prefer the original dentist and 20% prefer the new dentist. If a customer prefers a particular dentist, then they will wait until their preferred dentist is available. However, all customers are served on a strict FCFS basis, so a customer with no preference will be served by either dentist before a waiting customer if they are in the queue. Develop an Arena model that estimates

- the average waiting time for customers, the proportion of arriving customers who receive service and the utilisation of each dentist.

It was found that a customer's preference for a dentist would end if it meant an extended wait for that dentist of between 30 and 60 minutes uniformly distributed. Develop an Arena model that estimates

- the average waiting time for customers, the proportion of arriving customers who receive service and the utilisation of each dentist.

Modify the dentist model so that it investigates the check-up in terms of an x-ray, teeth check, and teeth clean. The same dentist performs all these three stages with service times of uniform (3,6), uniform (5,12) and uniform (2,6), respectively. However, 25% of customers miss the x-ray stage, and 40% miss the teeth-cleaning stage. All customers have a teeth check. Develop an Arena model that estimates

- the average waiting time for customers, the proportion of arriving customers who receive service and the utilisation of each dentist when the dentist has five and six waiting spaces.

References

Bose, R.P.J.C., van der Aalst, W.M.P., Žliobaitė, I. and Pechenizkiy, M. (2011) *Handling Concept Drift in Process Mining*, CAiSE, LNCS 6741, 391–405.

Hoad, K., Robinson, S. and Davies, R. (2010) Automating warm-up length estimation, *Journal of the Operational Research Society*, 61, 1389–1403.

Joines, J.A. and Roberts, S.D. (2015) *Simulation Modeling with SIMIO: A Workbook*, 4th edition, SIMIO LLC.

Kelton, W.D., Sadowski, R.P. and Zupick, N.B. (2015) *Simulation with Arena*, 6th edition, McGraw-Hill Education.

Law, A.M. (2015) *Simulation Modeling and Analysis*, 5th edition, McGraw-Hill Education.

Nelson, B.L. (2008) The MORE plot: Displaying measures of risk and error from simulation output, *Proceedings of the 2008 Winter Simulation Conference*, 413–416.

Robinson, S. (2014) *Simulation: The Practice of Model Development and Use*, 2nd edition, Palgrave Macmillan.

Robinson, S., Brooks, R.J. and Lewis, C.D. (2002) Detecting shifts in the mean of a simulation output process, *Journal of the Operational Research Society*, 53, 559–573.

Smith, J.S., Sturrock, D.T. and Kelton, W.D. (2018) *Simio and Simulation: Modeling, Analysis, Applications*, 5th edition, Simio LLC.

9A: Arena Output Analysis

Introduction

We will now outline procedures for measuring performance for a terminating and non-terminating simulation using Arena. The analysis will cover the use of multiple replications and one long run. Performance measures will be reported using confidence intervals.

Terminating Simulation Analysis for Arena

Arena can be used to analyse the double-queue bank clerk simulation constructed in chapter 7A. However, before the analysis can begin, an adjustment to the model must be made to ensure that the simulation is a true terminating system. At present, the simulation starts from empty and then customers arrive at the bank until the simulation run is completed. To be a true terminating system, the simulation must return to its starting condition (i.e. empty system) at the end of its run. To achieve this, we can stop the simulation from receiving new customers after a certain time period and then service any remaining customers in the system. This will ensure the system ends the run empty, thus returning to its starting state.

To update the double-queue bank clerk simulation (see chapter 7A) to a terminating system, load the simulation into Arena. Double-click on the Decide module and copy the current queue select expression onto the clipboard by dragging the mouse over it and selecting the edit/copy menu option. Change the type field from 2-way by condition to N-way by condition. Click on the Add button, select Expression for the If field and enter the expression TNOW.GT.480. TNOW is an Arena variable containing the current simulation time. This command will redirect customers to a Dispose module if the current time is greater than 480 minutes (simulating that customers will be turned away after the bank has been opened for 480 minutes). Click on the Add button again and select Expression for the If field and paste the queue select expression to the Value field by clicking on the field and selecting the menu/paste option (figure 9A.1).

Drag the Dispose module block (from the Discrete Processing panel template) onto the model window. Use the connect button on the toolbar to connect the 'GT.480' decision node on the decision module to the Dispose module and name the Dispose module 'bank closed'. Also, use the connect button to connect the queue select option on the decision module block to the Till1 module block and the else decision node to the Till2 module. The simulation should be as shown in figure 9A.2.

In order to save information to a data file for analysis, we use the Output module from the Input Output template. Click on the Output module to obtain the spreadsheet view. Double-click to add a new row. To collect statistics on the average time it takes a customer

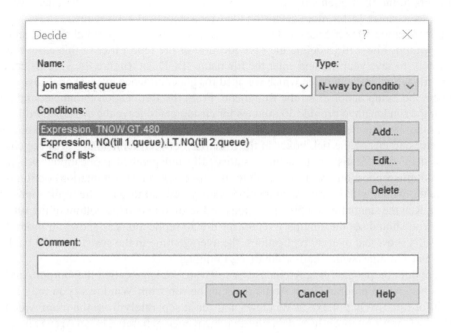

Figure 9A.1 Decide module for bank clerk terminating system

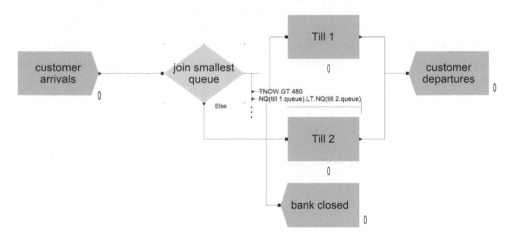

Figure 9A.2 Arena bank clerk terminating simulation model

to pass through the system, enter TAVG(Customer.TotalTime) in the expression box. TAVG(Customer.TotalTime) is an Arena expression to collect the average time of a tally variable over a simulation replication. In this case, the variable customer.Totaltime represents the time it takes for a customer to pass through the system. You can use the Arena simulation report to identify more variables to report and use the Arena help system to find other Arena expressions for data collection. For example, to collect statistics on the maximum time for customers in the till 1 queue, the following would be entered TMAX(Till1.queue.Waiting-Time). See chapter 7A for more details on the Arena statistical expressions.

Enter 'Average Time in System Double Queue' in the 'Name/Report Label' cell, and click in the 'Output File' cell to define the save location of the report file. In this case, move to a directory to save your file and enter the file name 'BCD.dat' (figure 9A.3). This creates a binary file with a. dat extension which we need for the confidence interval analysis.

Select the Setup option from the Run menu. From the Replication Parameters tab, enter 510 for the run length to provide 30 minutes for customers to leave the system after the closing at time 480 minutes. Set Hours per Day to 8. Enter 50 for the Number of Replications parameter and ensure the tick boxes in the initialize between replications area are checked for 'System' and 'Statistics' to achieve statistically independent replications. When running multiple replications, you may wish to use the batch run (no animation) option on the Run menu, which will disable the animation display and run through the replications much quicker. Run the simulation for 50 replications and scroll down to the bottom of the summary report. You should see the summary report for the 50 replications as shown in figure 9A.4. The results show that over 50 replications, the average time in the system for the bank customers is 16 minutes with a half-width of 1.24 minutes.

To conduct output analysis, Arena uses a software package called the Output Analyzer. This is a separate program from Arena that can be run from Windows (you may need to search for the file Output.exe in Windows and run it separately from the main Arena system). The Output Analyzer uses data files that have been generated by an Arena simulation run. If you require an output file for a specific period, you can define a DStats or Frequency statistic with the required replication length to collect this data. You can examine the data in a data file by using the Data Files, Export option of the File menu to generate an ASCII file. All output data files contain a file header followed by a series of pairs of numbers. The first number in each pair is the time at which an observation (for example, a tallied value or a change in a DStats variable) was recorded. The second number is the observed value at that time. Special data pairs with a negative first value indicate the end

	Name/Report Label	Output File	Expression	Comment
1 ▸	Average Time in System Double Queue	C:\Users\greaslea\Desktop\Sim Book 2E\chapter 10 output analysis\ch 10 Arena output analysis\bcd.dat	TAVG(customer.TotalTime)	

Double-click here to add a new row.

Figure 9A.3 Entering the output module parameters

OUTPUTS

Identifier	Average	Half-width	Minimum	Maximum	# Replications
Average Time in System Double Queue	16.014	1.2365	10.233	31.736	50
customer.NumberIn	103.20	3.2361	79.000	124.00	50
customer.NumberOut	102.86	3.1832	79.000	123.00	50
bank clerk2.NumberSeized	57.060	.85294	47.000	61.000	50
bank clerk2.ScheduledUtilization	.89690	.01254	.74208	.97450	50
bank clerk1.NumberSeized	40.140	2.2442	25.000	53.000	50
bank clerk1.ScheduledUtilization	.62970	.03565	.37848	.86528	50
System.NumberOut	102.86	3.1832	79.000	123.00	50

Simulation run time: 0.12 minutes.
Simulation run complete.

Figure 9A.4 Bank clerk terminating system model summary report for 50 replications

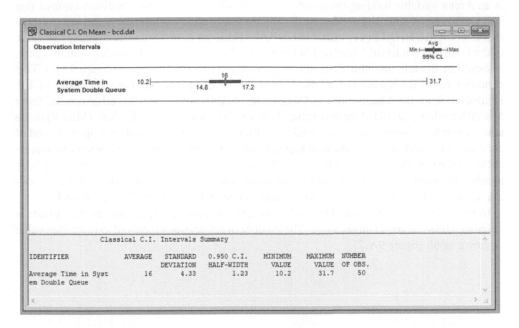

Figure 9A.5 Arena confidence interval on mean analysis for terminating system (50 replications)

of replications; a value of −1 for the second value in an end-of-replication pair marks the end of the data file.

Run the Output Analyzer program and select the Analyze/Confidence Interval on Mean/ Classical menu option. Add the file BCD.DAT and select 'lumped' from the pull-down menu for the replications parameter. Data from the 50 replications are now presented together to compute the confidence interval. Leave the default confidence interval at 0.95 (95%). Click on OK. The analysis, as shown in figure 9A.5, will appear.

Using the Arena Output Analyzer processor, the results show the confidence interval as the thick horizontal line. The graphs show that the average time in the system for customers in the double-queue model is 16 minutes with a half-width of 1.23 minutes.

Establishing Confidence Intervals at a Given Half-Width Using Arena

Normally a fixed number of replications are made (say, 50) without knowing the size of the confidence intervals of the values we are measuring. We can use Arena to check a particular confidence interval value after each simulation run and automatically stop running when this target value is reached. To do this, we need some additional modules to control the simulation run behaviour.

Load in the terminating double-queue bank clerk simulation file. Add a Create, Decide, Assign and Dispose module to the simulation screen away from the main model. Double-click on the Create module and enter type constant, first arrival at 0 and 1 for max arrivals to create one entity at the beginning of each simulation replication. Double-click on the Decide module. Select the N-way by condition type. Add the expression NREP <= 2. NREP is an Arena variable holding the number of replications made. This condition ensures that at least two replications have been made, and thus, a confidence interval is formed. Add the expression ORUNHALF(1) > 1.0. ORUNHALF(1) is an Arena variable holding the value of the confidence interval 1 (defined in the number field of the outputs module – in this case, it should be the tally variable defined using the outputs module shown in figure 9A.3). This condition runs the simulation until the defined half-width is less than the target value of 1.0. Double-click on the Assign module. Click on the Add button. Select the other option. Enter MREP for other and NREP for new value. This sets the number of replications (MREP) to the current number of replications executed (NREP), causing the simulation to stop at the end of the current replication. From the Run menu, select Setup, choose the Replication Parameters option and enter 99,999 for the Number of Replications parameter. This is an arbitrarily high number, the replication number in this case being controlled by the confidence interval coding. Connect the modules using the connect button as in figure 9A.6. Run the model.

In this case, the confidence interval for the double-queue average time in the system is given as 0.988 (below 1) target value. The number of replications required to reach this value is shown as 68 (figure 9A.7).

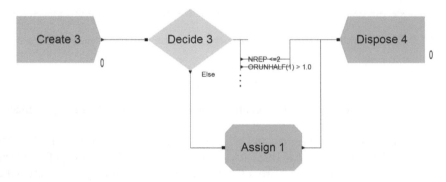

Figure 9A.6 Arena logic for establishing confidence intervals at a given half-width

```
                              OUTPUTS

Identifier                      Average   Half-width Minimum   Maximum # Replications
_____

Average Time in System Double Queue  15.641    .98801    10.233    31.736      68
Entity 1.NumberIn                1.0000    .00000    1.0000    1.0000      68
Entity 1.NumberOut               1.0000    .00000    1.0000    1.0000      68
customer.NumberIn                102.63    2.6955    79.000    124.00      68
customer.NumberOut               102.36    2.6554    79.000    124.00      68
bank clerk2.NumberSeized         56.911    .73516    47.000    63.000      68
bank clerk2.ScheduledUtilization  .89557    .01086    .74208    .98415      68
bank clerk1.NumberSeized         39.852    1.8787    25.000    55.000      68
bank clerk1.ScheduledUtilization  .62366    .02978    .37848    .86528      68
System.NumberOut                 103.36    2.6554    80.000    125.00      68

Simulation run time: 0.08 minutes.
Simulation run complete.
```

Figure 9A.7 Bank clerk terminating simulation results at target confidence interval half-width of 1

Non-Terminating Simulation Analysis for Arena

The main options for the analysis of a non-terminating simulation in Arena are the following:

- Redefine the model as terminating.
- If the warm-up period is relatively short, determine the warm-up period, discard this period from the results and perform multiple replications (see warm-up period estimation using Arena).
- If the warm-up period is relatively long, then undertake an extended run using the batch means method (see batch means using Arena).

Warm-up Period Estimation Using Arena

To demonstrate a method of determining the warm-up period in Arena, load the non-terminating (original) version of the double-queue bank clerk simulation in Arena developed in chapter 7A. We will use a tally of the customer time in the system as the performance measure in this case. We should undertake this procedure for all of the performance measures we plan to utilise (both tally and time-persistent) and determine the longest warm-up time from our analysis. Note time-persistent data should be filtered into batches for processing (Rossetti, 2016). In order to collect the tally results, add an Assign module after the Create module and a Record module before the Dispose module in the Arena model (figure 9A.8).

In the Assign module, add an attribute called arrivaltime and set the attribute value to TNOW. In the Record module, add a Statistic definition and set the type to Time Interval and the attribute name to arrivaltime. In the Statistic module, change the type from Output to Tally for the current definition. The Tally name should be Tally 1 for the Record module. Set the file name to be BCDNOTERM.DAT and save it in a file directory. Select run/setup/project parameters from the menu bar. Enter 4 for the Number of Replications parameter and enter 50,000 for the replication length. Ensure the tick boxes (in the 'Initialize between replications' area) are checked for 'System' and 'Statistics' to achieve statistically independent replications. Their replication length should be set by trial and error as it needs to be long enough to determine the warm-up period, which is, of course, the length of time we are attempting to determine. Select the fast-forward button to run the model to create the data file (BCDNOTERM.DAT).

Ideally, we would like to plot the time series over a number of replications to smooth out any outliers, but if we use the Output Analyzer, we can only plot individual replications. Now run the separate Output Analyzer software. Click on the Graph tab and then the Moving

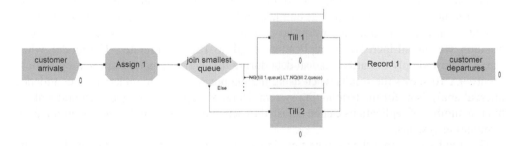

Figure 9A.8 Arena double-queue model with Assign and Record modules

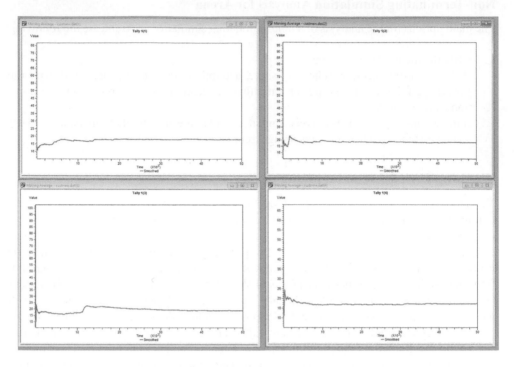

Figure 9A.9 Cumulative moving average of customer time in the system (four replications)

Average option. Add the filename BCDNOTERM.dat. Choose the replication All option and choose the Cumulative option for the Averaging Type. Untick Plot Individual Data Points. Click on OK. The graphs generated are a plot of the results of the time in the system over the 50,000 minutes with the associated cumulative moving average line (figure 9A.9).

From figure 9A.9, we can see from the flat moving average line that a steady-state behaviour of the performance measure is established after around 15,000 minutes across the four replications. Once a warm-up period has been selected, the value can be entered in the Arena run/setup/replication parameters dialog.

Multiple Replications with Warm-up Period

Once a warm-up period has been defined, the model can then be analysed in the same way as a terminating model simulation as outlined earlier in this chapter. The replication period should be at least ten times the warm-up period, and so for a warm-up period of 15,000 minutes, we should increase the replication length to 150,000 minutes. The model, when run, will now simply discard statistical data during the warm-up period of each replication. Figure 9A.10 shows the results when using the Output Analyzer to undertake a confidence interval analysis as for the terminating system. Here, 50 replications have been undertaken, but the number of replications can be adjusted to achieve a certain half-width as outlined for terminating systems.

The graphs show that the average time in the system for customers in the double-queue non-terminating model is 17.2 minutes with a half-width of 0.0996 minutes. Note that this

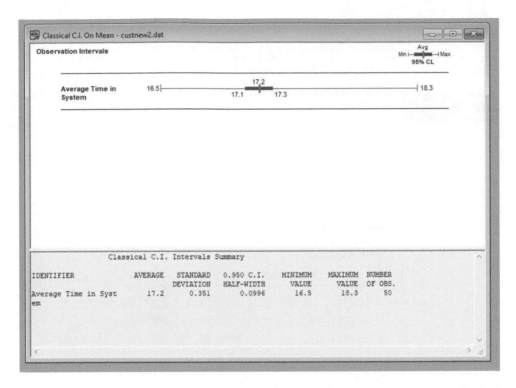

Figure 9A.10 Arena confidence interval on mean analysis for non-terminating system (50 replications)

differs from the terminating results, which give a time in the system of 16 minutes with a half-width of 1.23 minutes. This is to be expected as the terminating results include the start from empty and end-of-day empty periods when the number of customers in the system is lower, and thus, the average time in the system for customers will be likely to be lower than average. For a non-terminating simulation, our analysis is for the steady-state expected performance measures rather than for performance measures that are defined in relation to specific starting and ending conditions (for example, the performance over a day's operation) that we would use for a terminating simulation.

One Long Run Using Batch Means with Warm-up Period

In the batch means method, an initial warm-up period is defined and discarded from the simulation run, and then the remainder of the simulation run is divided into batches. This method thus entails running the simulation for one long run rather than a number of shorter runs (replications) and thus further lessens the effect of any initial conditions over and above the use of a warm-up period. However, it is important to note that the batches are formed within-replication and thus may well be correlated.

Arena automatically calculates 95% confidence intervals using batch means for the means of all output statistics and gives the results as a half-width in the average column for the performance measure for each replication. Note that these data will only be reported if sufficient data has been collected of the performance measure during the run. If insufficient data has

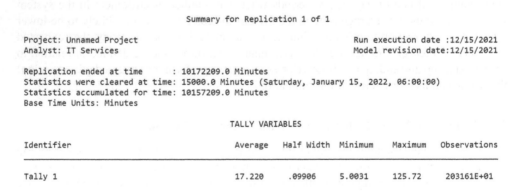

Figure 9A.11 Replication Parameters screen for batch means analysis

Summary for Replication 1 of 1

Project: Unnamed Project   Run execution date :12/15/2021
Analyst: IT Services   Model revision date:12/15/2021

Replication ended at time   : 10172209.0 Minutes
Statistics were cleared at time: 15000.0 Minutes (Saturday, January 15, 2022, 06:00:00)
Statistics accumulated for time: 10157209.0 Minutes
Base Time Units: Minutes

TALLY VARIABLES

Identifier	Average	Half Width	Minimum	Maximum	Observations
Tally 1	17.220	.09906	5.0031	125.72	203161E+01

Figure 9A.12 Arena confidence on interval analysis using one long run.

been collected, 'Insufficient' appears in the output summary report; if the batches tested are correlated, 'Correlated' appears in the output summary report.

To perform the method of batch means using Arena, determine first the warm-up period using the method outlined in the warm-up period section. The run length now needs to be determined in terms of a target half-width for the confidence interval of our performance measure. For the analysis in the warm-up period section, the performance measure is defined as Tally 1 (customer time in the system). So to match the half-width achieved for the 50 replications shown in figure 9A.11 in the run/setup/replication parameters option, set the replication length to Infinite and the replication number to 1, and the terminating condition for the simulation should be THALF(Tally 1) < 0.0996 (figure 9A.11).

In this case, the replication length required to meet the half-width target of 0.0966 minutes will be approximately 10,172,209 minutes (figure 9A.12).

Figure 9A.12 shows the results for Tally 1 (customer time in the system) to have a mean of 17.22 minutes with a half-width of 0.099 minutes.

Summary

This chapter has described procedures for measuring performance for a terminating and non-terminating simulation using Arena. The analysis has covered the use of multiple replications and one long run. Performance measures have been reported using confidence intervals.

Reference

Rossetti, M.D. (2016) *Simulation Modeling and Arena*, 2nd edition, John Wiley & Sons Ltd.

9B: Simio Output Analysis

Introduction

Simio provides a number of facilities in the software package to analyse and display performance measures. Data can also be exported if required for analysis using Excel and other software. We will outline procedures for measuring performance for a terminating and non-terminating simulation.

Terminating Simulation Analysis for Simio

Simio can be used to analyse the double-queue bank clerk simulation constructed in chapter 7B. However, before the analysis can begin, we need to ensure that the simulation is a true terminating system. At present, the simulation starts from empty and then customers arrive at the bank with a runtime specified of 480 minutes. To be a true terminating simulation, the simulation must reach its starting condition (i.e. empty system) at the end of its run. To achieve this, the simulation must stop receiving new customers after a certain time period and then service any remaining customers in the system.

For the Simio double-queue simulation model, the following steps are required to ensure that the simulation is terminating. The first step is to stop new customers from entering the bank after 480 minutes. To do this, click on the Source1 object in the Navigation Window and in the Properties Window enter a maximum time of 480 for the stopping conditions. Next, select the Run tab, and on the ribbon, change the runtime to 510 minutes.

Now we need to define our statistic that we wish to report our confidence interval on. Click on the Project Home tab and select New Experiment from the ribbon. Select the Design tab and click on the Add Response option on the ribbon. We now need to define our performance measure. If we wish to report on the average queue waiting for Server 1, our response variable would be Server1.InputBuffer.Contents.AverageTimeWaiting. In this case, enter Sink1. TimeInSystem.Average as the expression in the Response1 properties menu. This will collect statistics on the average flow time for customers in the bank clerk system. Rename the response as Time_In_System, and set the Unit Type parameter to time and the display units to minutes. Set the Required Replications to 50 in the Scenario (figure 9B.1).

Select Run in the Design tab to run the simulation for 50 replications. Click on the Pivot Grid tab to see the simulation results. Notice that the results now show the average, minimum, maximum and half-width values for the statistics. Click on the Response Results tab to show the box plot of the average time in the system for the bank clerk customers in the terminating simulation. Click on the Rotate Plot option to provide a horizontal confidence interval and box plot display (figure 9B.2).

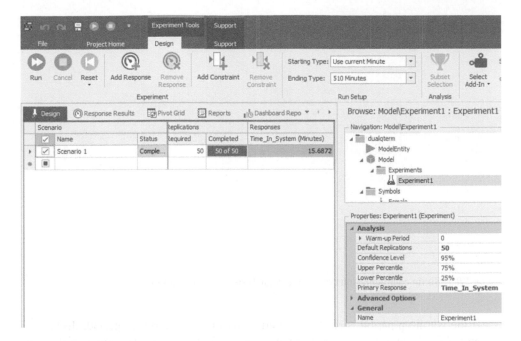

Figure 9B.1 Setting the experiment statistics collection

The confidence interval is shown as a block in the middle of the plot. Click on the dot in the middle of this block, and the confidence interval statistics are displayed. The results show that the average time in the system for the double-queue model bank clerk model is 15.69 minutes with a half-width of 1 minute.

Simio provides SMORE plots that provide a measure of risk. A confidence interval is a measure of error which shows if we have done enough simulation to reach a conclusion from the results (i.e. how confident we are of the average value presented). Note that we can simply generate a narrower confidence interval by increasing the number of replications. The box in the SMORE plot is a measure of future risk, and that is what we often need to support our decision (Nelson, 2008). In figure 9B.2, the SMORE plot shows percentile confidence intervals around the mean for our performance measure. These are wider than the confidence intervals but give a more realistic representation of values that might occur in the future. Thus, if we have performance metrics above or below our mean that we do want to breach, then the SMORE plot may be particularly relevant. The SMORE lower and upper percentile confidence intervals lie at the 5th and 95th percentiles (shown by the box on the plot), so we need to ensure we have sufficient data (replications) in order to estimate these values.

Non-Terminating Simulation Analysis for Simio

The main options for non-terminating analysis in Simio are the following:

•   Redefine the model as terminating.

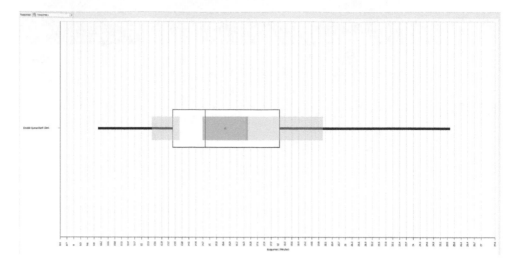

Figure 9B.2 Simio confidence interval on mean analysis (50 replications)

- If the warm-up period is relatively short, determine the warm-up period, discard this period from the results and perform multiple replications (see warm-up period estimation using Simio).
- If the warm-up period is relatively long, undertake an extended run using the batch means method (see batch means using Simio).

Warm-up Period Estimation Using Simio

To demonstrate a method of determining the warm-up period in Simio, load the non-terminating (original) version of the double-queue bank clerk simulation in Simio developed in chapter 7B. From the Run tab, enter 50,000 minutes for the run length. From the Animation tab, add a Status Plot to the Navigation Window. Click on the Plot, and in the Properties Window, enter (Sink1.TimeInSystem.Average)*60 for the Expression. This will plot the average value of the performance measure time in the system in minutes. Run the simulation in normal mode (not fast-forward) but with a high speed setting of 10,000. When run, a plot is generated of the average time in the system for customers over the 50,000 minutes (figure 9B.3).

From figure 9B.3, steady-state behaviour of the performance measure is established after around 5,000 minutes. Thus, we can define a warm-up period for this performance measure of 5,000 minutes for either the analysis by multiple replications or by the batch means method. Ideally, though, we should base this decision on multiple replications of the simulation to ensure any outlier values are smoothed.

Multiple Replications with Warm-up Period

The model with a warm-up period can now be analysed in the same way as a terminating model simulation as outlined earlier in this chapter using the method of independent replications (note this version of the model does not have the stopping condition in the Source1 object). The replication period should be at least ten times the warm-up period, so for a

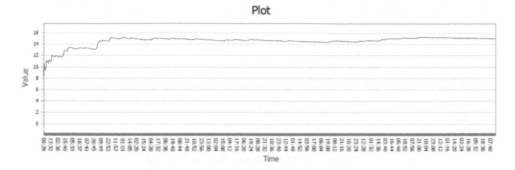

Figure 9B.3 Simio plot of the average customer time in the system (50,000 minutes)

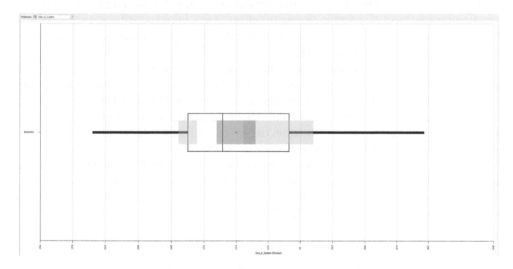

Figure 9B.4 Simio confidence interval on mean analysis for non-terminating system (50 replications)

warm-up period of 5,000 the replication period is set at 50,000 minutes. The model, when run, will now simply discard statistical data during the warm-up period of each replication.

In Simio, in the Project Home tab, select New Experiment. In the Experiment1 Properties Window, define the warm-up period as 5,000 minutes. In the Scenario Window, set the Required Replications to 50. In the Design tab, select Add Response. In the Response1 Properties Window, enter Sink1.TimeInSystem.Average as the Expression. In the Design Tab, select Run. Click on the Response Results tab to show the box plot of the average time in the system for the bank clerk customers in the non-terminating simulation. Click on the Rotate Plot option to provide a horizontal confidence interval and box plot display (figure 9B.4). Here, 50 replications have been undertaken, but the number of replications can be adjusted to achieve a certain half-width.

The confidence interval is shown as a block in the middle of the plot. Click on the dot in the middle of this block, and the confidence interval statistics are displayed. The results show that the average time in the system for the double-queue model bank clerk non-terminating model is 17.4 minutes with a half-width of 0.18 minutes. Note that this differs from the terminating results, which give an average time in the system of 15.69 minutes ± 1 minute. This is to be expected as the terminating results include the start from empty and end-of-day empty periods when the number of customers in the system is lower, and thus, the average time in the system for customers will be likely to be lower than average. For a non-terminating system, our analysis is for the steady-state expected performance measures rather than for performance measures that are defined in relation to specific starting and ending conditions (for example, the performance over a day's operation) that we would use for a terminating simulation.

One Long Run Using Batch Means with Warm-up Period

In the batch means method, an initial warm-up period is defined and discarded from the simulation run, and then the remainder of the simulation run is divided into batches. This method thus entails running the simulation for one long run rather than a number of shorter runs (replications) and thus further lessens the effect of any initial conditions over and above the use of a warm-up period. However, it is important to note that the batches are formed within-replication and thus may well be correlated.

Simio automatically calculates a confidence interval using batch means for the means of user-defined tally and state statistics and also Sink statistics for a Simio experiment having only one replication. All other automatic statistics within the Standard Library objects are custom-generated and do not use StateStatistics or TallyStatistics elements. For users that would like to see a batch means calculation on Server1 utilisation, for example, would need to manually add a StateStatistic to mimic the internal statistic.

To perform the method of batch means using Simio, determine first the warm-up period using the method outlined in the warm-up period section. For the previous example, with a warm-up period of 5,000 minutes and a run length of 50,000 minutes with 50 replications, we will set the replication length to 50,000 × 50 = 2,500,000 minutes. In this case, for a

							Scenario ▲			
Average	Minimum	Maximum	Half Width				Scenario1			
Objec... ▲	Objec... ▲	Data... ▲	Cate... ▲	Data Item ▲	Statistic ▲		Average	Minimum	Maximum	Half Width
ModelEntity	DefaultEntity	[Population]	Content	NumberInSystem	Average		3.4969	3.4969	3.4969	NaN
					Maximum		30.0000	30.0000	30.0000	NaN
			FlowTime	TimeInSystem	Average (Minutes)		17.4525	17.4525	17.4525	NaN
					Maximum (Minutes)		117.9422	117.9422	117.9422	NaN
					Minimum (Minutes)		5.1720	5.1720	5.1720	NaN
					Observations		440,791.0000	440,791.0000	440,791.0000	NaN
			Throughput	NumberCreated	Total		440,798.0000	440,798.0000	440,798.0000	NaN
				NumberDestroyed	Total		440,791.0000	440,791.0000	440,791.0000	NaN
Sink	Sink1	[Destroyed...	FlowTime	TimeInSystem	Average (Minutes)		17.4525	17.4525	17.4525	NaN
					HalfWidth (Minutes)		0.1722	0.1722	0.1722	NaN
					Maximum (Minutes)		117.9422	117.9422	117.9422	NaN
					Minimum (Minutes)		5.1720	5.1720	5.1720	NaN
					Observations		440,791.0000	440,791.0000	440,791.0000	NaN
			InputBuffer	Throughput	NumberEntered	Total	440,791.0000	440,791.0000	440,791.0000	NaN
					NumberExited	Total	440,791.0000	440,791.0000	440,791.0000	NaN

Figure 9B.5 Simio report for a single replication using batch means with one long run (2,500,000 minutes)

2,500,000 minute replication length, the results show that the average time in the system for the double-queue model bank clerk non-terminating model is 17.45 minutes with a half-width of 0.17 minutes (figure 9B.5).

Summary

This chapter has covered the use of Simio to measure performance for a terminating and non-terminating simulation. Performance has been reported using confidence interval analysis.

References

Nelson, B.L. (2008) The MORE plot: Displaying measures of risk and error from simulation output, *Proceedings of the 2008 Winter Simulation Conference*, 413–416.

Rossetti, M.D. (2016) *Simulation Modeling and Arena*, 2nd edition, John Wiley & Sons Ltd.

9C: Simul8 Output Analysis

Introduction

This chapter covers using Simul8 to conduct output analysis for terminating and non-terminating simulations.

Terminating Simulation Analysis for Simul8

Simul8 can be used to analyse the double-queue bank clerk simulation constructed in chapter 7C. Before the analysis can begin, however, an adjustment to the code must be made to ensure the simulation is a true terminating system. At present, the simulation starts from empty, and then customers arrive at the bank with a runtime specified of 480 minutes. To be a true terminating system, the simulation must reach its starting condition (i.e. empty system) at the end of its run. To achieve this, the simulation must stop receiving new customers after a certain time period and then service any remaining customers in the system. From the start point menu, select the Constraints button and enter 480 for the limit of the duration of arriving work items (figure 9C.1).

The next step is to alter the run length to 510 minutes (providing 30 minutes to empty the system). Do this by selecting the Trials/Results Collection Period option from the menu, and enter 510. Select the Trials/Conduct Trials option from the menu, and enter the number of runs as 50. Click on OK, and the simulation will run for 50 replications, and the results screen will appear (figure 9C.2)

The results show that the bank clerk double-queue average time in the system is 15.88 minutes with a half-width of 1.33 minutes.

Simul8 provides MORE plots that provide a measure of risk. A confidence interval is a measure of error which shows if we have done enough simulation to reach a conclusion from the results (i.e. how confident we are of the average value presented). Note that we can simply generate a narrower confidence interval by increasing the number of replications. The box in the MORE plot is a measure of future risk, and that is what we often need to support our decision (Nelson, 2008). In figure 9C.3, the MORE plot shows unlikely values around the mean for our performance measure. These are wider than the confidence intervals (shown by a horizontal line from the mean at the bottom of the plot) but give a more realistic representation of values that might occur in the future. Thus, if we have performance metrics above or below our mean that do want to breach, then the MORE plot may be particularly relevant. The MORE plot unlikely values lie at the 5th and 95th percentiles, so we need to ensure we have sufficient data (replications) in order to estimate these values.

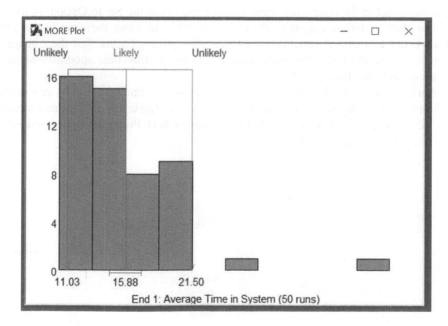

Figure 9C.1 Limiting the duration of arriving work items

Figure 9C.2 Terminating bank clerk double-queue results

Figure 9C.3 MORE plot of double-queue terminating simulation

Non-Terminating Simulation Analysis for Simul8

The main options for the analysis of a non-terminating simulation in Simul8 are the following:

- Redefine the model as terminating.
- If the warm-up period is relatively short, determine the warm-up period, discard this period from the results and perform multiple replications (see warm-up period estimation using Simul8).
- If the warm-up period is relatively long, then undertake an extended run using the batch means method.

Warm-up Period Estimation Using Simul8

To demonstrate a method of determining the warm-up period in Simul8, load the non-terminating (original) version of the double-queue bank clerk simulation in Simul8 developed in chapter 7C. We will record the customer time in the system as the performance measure in this case. We should undertake this procedure for all of the performance measures we plan to utilise and determine the longest warm-up time from our analysis. Note time-persistent data should be filtered into batches for processing (Rossetti, 2016). In order to collect the customer time in the system data, we need to add a dummy activity and associated queue before the End block in the Simul8 model (figure 9C.4).

In the Start Point block, select the Actions button and add a label named entrytime and set it to the timestamp option. In the dummy block, select the Actions button and add a label named leavetime and set it to the timestamp option. In the dummy block, select the Actions button and select the Change Anything button. Select the New button and then select the number option. Enter the name timeinthesystem. Back in the formula editor screen, select the Other Global data option and double-click on the timeinthesystem variable. In the main actions menu, select the timeinthesystem variable and select the Set to Option. In the fixed value box, add leavetime-entrytime (figure 9C.5). This allocates the time in the system for each entity to a global variable named timeinthesystem. Ensure that the Change box has the leavetime and timeinthesystem variables in order (leavetime should be set before timeinthesystem); see figure 9C.5.

We can now record our timeinthesystem values during the simulation run so we can undertake the time series inspection method. Select the Visual Logic tab on the main menu and then select the Time Check VL button. Select the Time Check Properties option and enter 30 for the time interval (figure 9C.6).

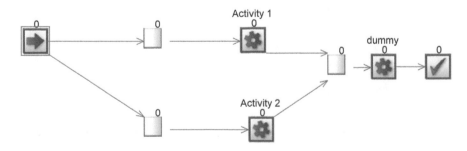

Figure 9C.4 Simul8 double-queue model with Assign and Record modules

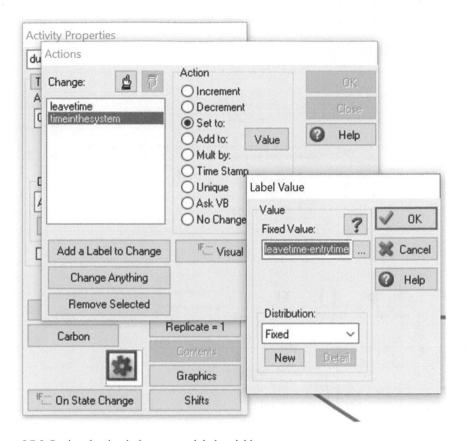

Figure 9C.5 Setting the timeinthesystem global variable

Figure 9C.6 Time Check properties

We will now define the Visual Logic that will be executed at an interval of 30 minutes through the simulation run. Select the Time Check option from the Time Check VL button. Click the right mouse button on the main screen area to add the visual logic. Select the Set to Option from the menu, and enter 'row' for information and 'row+1' for the calculation (figure 9C.7). This increments the row counter for when the data is written to the spreadsheet.

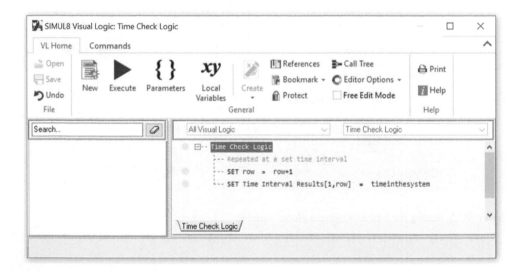

Figure 9C.7 Entering the row increment visual logic

Figure 9C.8 Time Check Logic

Right-click again on the main screen and select the Set to Option. Enter Time Interval Results [1, row] for the information and timeinthesystem for the calculation (figure 9C.8). This writes the timeinsystem value to the Simul8 internal spreadsheet Time Interval Results in the first column, row by row.

On the home menu, set the Run for value to 50,000. Run the simulation until simulation time 50,000. On the Data and Rules menu, select the spreadsheet button and select the Time Interval Results sheet (figure 9C.9).

Drag over all the values in column A and select the Copy icon from the right-hand side of the results screen. Open Excel and paste the values into a sheet at A1. In cell B1, add the formula =AVERAGE($A$1:A1) to calculate+ the cumulative average value. Copy this formula down column B until the values in column A end. In cell C1, add the value 0. In cell c2, add the value = c1 + 30. Copy this formula down column C as for columns A and B. Plot the values in column B using an Excel chart and use the values in column C for the x-axis labels. The chart should look as in figure 9C.10.

Sheet: Time Interval Results

	A	B	C	D	E
1	0				
2	9.5663021				
3	11.060436				
4	17.185799				
5	11.819197				
6	10.104185				
7	13.656023				
8	21.166993				
9	20.465167				
10	9.1603765				
11	8.814281				
12	10.48506				
13	16.075696				

OK
Cancel
Help

☑ Retain Format

Figure 9C.9 timeinthesystem values recorded in the time interval results sheet

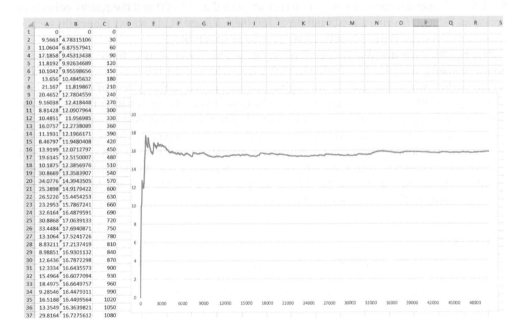

Figure 9C.10 Cumulative average plot for warm-up period

Note that ideally we would like to plot the time series over a number of replications to smooth out any outliers. If you wish to do this, then in the main menu, choose Advanced and select the Random Sampling button. Change the value of the random number stream set value and run the simulation again. Plot the values in the Time Intervals Results sheet to

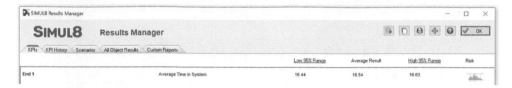

Figure 9C.11 Non-terminating double-queue bank clerk system (50 replications)

separate columns in your spreadsheet. Repeat the procedure for each replication you wish to run. In Excel, calculate the average values over the replications you have made and then undertake the cumulative average plot of the overall average values.

Multiple Replications with Warm-up Period

Once a warm-up period has been defined, the model can then be analysed in the same way as a terminating model simulation as outlined earlier in this chapter. The replication period should be at least ten times the warm-up period, and so for a warm-up period of 15,000 minutes, we should increase the replication length to 150,000 minutes. The model, when run, will now simply discard statistical data during the warm-up period of each replication. Go to the Clock Properties menu and set the warm-up period as 15,000 and the results collection period as 135,000 (to give a total runtime of 150,000). Figure 9C.11 shows the results for the terminating system. Here, 50 replications have been undertaken.

The results show that the average time in the system for customers in the double-queue non-terminating model is 16.54 minutes with a half-width of 0.1 minutes. Note that this differs from the terminating results, which give an average time in the system of 15.88 minutes with a half-width of 1.33 minutes. This is to be expected as the terminating results include the start from empty and end-of-day empty periods when the number of customers in the system is lower, and thus, the average time in the system for customers will be likely to be lower on average. For a non-terminating simulation, our analysis is for the steady-state expected performance measures rather than for performance measures that are defined in relation to specific starting and ending conditions (for example, the performance over a day's operation) that we would use for a terminating simulation.

References

Nelson, B.L. (2008) The MORE plot: Displaying measures of risk and error from simulation output, *Proceedings of the 2008 Winter Simulation Conference*, 413–416.
Rossetti, M.D. (2016) *Simulation Modeling and Arena*, 2nd edition, John Wiley & Sons Ltd.

10 Experimentation

Simulation Scenario Analysis

Introduction

Chapter 9 covered simulation output analysis for obtaining accurate results from a single simulation model (figure 10.1). This can generate descriptive analytics if we are modelling the current state of a system that already exists or predictive analytics if we are modelling a new state of a system or a system that does not exist. This chapter covers comparing the results across two or more versions of our simulation model. Scenario analysis (also termed what-if analysis) involves changing input parameters or the model design and observing the results. This generates predictive analytics, the ability to predict future performance to help plan for the future, and is the type of analysis most associated with simulation (figure 10.1). We can also define targets for output measures and run the simulation with varying input parameters (scenarios) in order to meet this goal. This generates prescriptive analytics in that the simulation recommends a choice of action to reach a goal from predictions of future performance (figure 10.1).

If we have many combinations of input parameters to explore, then we need to search the solution space (the number of possible scenarios required). If we are conducting predictive analytics, we can search the solution space to find the best options using approaches such as experimental design. If we are conducting prescriptive analytics, we can use approaches such as multi-comparison or optimisation software to find the best option for our target performance. We may identify a number of potential best options, and in this case, we may analyse them in more detail using scenario analysis.

Simulation Scenario Analysis

In scenario analysis, we specify the alternative scenarios to compare and conduct statistical tests to judge that an actual change in performance has taken place. Before we begin our analysis, we need to consider issues covered in chapter 9 output analysis when we covered measuring the results of a single model (which is usually our base scenario for the comparisons in this chapter). For non-terminating models, we should consider dealing with an initial bias for each of our scenarios individually as each scenario is, in effect, a different model. However, it may suffice to provide some leeway in our initial conditions based on our base model and use these across all our scenarios to provide faster analysis. For example, we can increase the warm-up period defined for our base model to provide a margin of safety that should cover the other scenarios for comparison. If this approach is undertaken, then the results should be checked to ensure the warm-up period is appropriate for any scenarios of particular interest. In terms of obtaining enough data, the statistical tests in this chapter

DOI: 10.4324/9781003124092-10

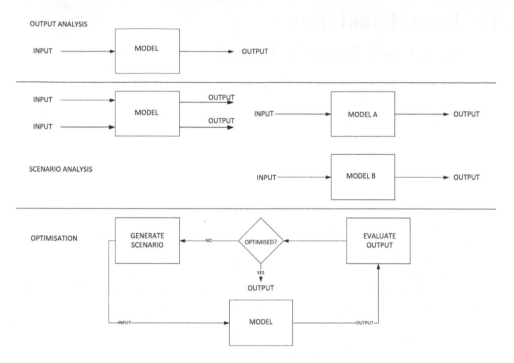

Figure 10.1 Simulation output, scenario and optimisation analysis

generally assume an equal number of replications for each scenario. We can increase the number of replications defined for our base model to give a margin of safety when used across our comparison.

For our scenario analysis, statistical tests are required so that we can judge when comparing model results that a change in performance has taken place. For instance, if we run the simulation (for multiple replications), and the overall mean time in the system is 4.8 minutes and then run the simulation again (for multiple replications), and the mean time in the system is 5.1 minutes, do these results represent a statistically significant difference in performance or are they within the bounds of random variation? Remember that even though we have run multiple replications, our overall mean times will vary as every time we run the simulation, we will obtain different results due to the random number stream used for each replication. What these tests tell us is this. Have we collected enough data (i.e. undertaken enough replications) to enable us to state that there is a statistically significant difference between the results of the scenarios?

When using simulation, we have the advantage of being able to easily increase the sample size by simply increasing the number of simulation replications. What we are really interested in is the magnitude (and direction) of differences in scenario results that impact the performance of the system we are simulating in the real world. Thus, we will then need to make a further judgement of the practical significance, if any, of these results for the client/owner of the real system.

Sensitivity Analysis

As part of our scenario analysis, we may wish to explore the sensitivity of model results to a change in a particular input. This can be to test the effect of assumptions such as a lack of data on the model results and may lead to additional data collection activities. The main purpose of sensitivity analysis, however, is to understand how robust the model results are to changes in input data. In general, we would prefer that the model results are not too sensitive to small changes in input values in order to increase model credibility.

Comparing Two Scenarios

We will now show the use of hypothesis testing and confidence interval analysis to compare two simulated scenarios. The use of common random numbers is also discussed.

Hypothesis Testing

A hypothesis test makes an assumption or a hypothesis (termed the null hypothesis, H0) and tries to disprove it. Acceptance of the null hypothesis implies that there is insufficient evidence to reject it (it does not prove that it is true). Rejection of the null hypothesis, however, means that the alternative hypothesis (H1) is accepted. The null hypothesis is tested using a test statistic (based on an appropriate sampling distribution) at a particular significance level α, which relates to the area called the critical region in the tail of the distribution being used. If the test statistic (which we calculate) lies in the critical region, the result is unlikely to have occurred by chance, and so the null hypothesis would be rejected. The boundaries of the critical region, called the critical values, depend on whether the test is two-tailed (we have no reason to believe that a rejection of the null hypothesis implies that the test statistic is either greater or less than some assumed value) or one-tailed (we have reason to believe that a rejection of the null hypothesis implies that the test statistic is either greater or less than some assumed value).

We must also consider the fact that the decision to reject or not reject the null hypothesis is based on a probability. Thus, at a 5% significance level, there is a 5% chance that H0 will be rejected when it is, in fact, true. In statistical terminology, this is called a type I error. The converse of this is accepting the null hypothesis when it is, in fact, false, called a type II error. Usually, α values of 0.05 (5%) or 0.1 (10%) are used in business applications of simulation. An alternative to testing at a particular significance level is to calculate the p-value, which is the lowest level of significance at which the observed value of the test statistic is significant. Thus, a p-value of 0.045 (indicating a type I error occurring 45 times out of 1,000) would show that the null hypothesis would be rejected at 0.05, but only by a small amount.

Using Statistical Methods to Interpret Simulation Results

All statistical methods make extensive assumptions about how the data was generated and analysed, and so the outcome of any statistical procedure should be one of many considerations that must be evaluated. In particular, statistical significance is not sufficient for determining the scientific or practical significance of a set of observations. The correct interpretation of statistical tests demands examining the size of effect estimates and confidence limits and not just, for example, whether p-values are above or below 0.05 or some other threshold. See Greenland et al. (2016) for more information regarding the misinterpretation of statistical tests.

We will now consider two approaches to hypothesis testing using a paired t-test comparison (when we assume we have the variance reduction technique of common random numbers in operation and it is working) and the two-sample t-test comparison (when we cannot assume common random numbers are working).

Paired t-Test Comparison

This method provides the interval for the difference in means. It assumes that common random numbers are working (reducing variance), allows unequal variances and assumes normally distributed data.

If the scenarios give the same results, then the expected value of the interval is zero. Thus, we can assert with the appropriate confidence level that if the interval does not contain zero, that a difference exists between the two systems. If the interval on the difference does contain zero, the two scenario results are not necessarily the same, but additional replications may be required to discern any difference.

Note that using the paired t approach results in only half the degrees of freedom as it takes differences in results from the two scenarios, thus 'collapsing' the two samples on which the analysis is done to a single sample. Thus, this sample is only half the size of the number of replications that have been made, resulting in a loss of degrees of freedom which increases the confidence-interval half-width. However, the paired t approach is usually preferred as provided the number of replications is a suitable amount (say, above ten replications), then even a small amount of correlation from the use of common random numbers will overcome the disadvantage of the loss of degrees of freedom.

In order to undertake a paired t comparison, we need to calculate the mean, standard deviation and variance for each scenario. Assuming the same number of replications has been performed for both scenarios, the mean difference is calculated using the following equation:

$$\bar{A} = \left(\sum_{j=1}^{n} \left(X_{1j} - X_{2j} \right) \right) / n$$

where
$\bar{A}$ = mean difference between scenarios
X_{1j} = result from scenario 1 and replication j
X_{2j} = result from scenario 2 and replication j
n = number of replications

The standard deviation of the difference is then calculated using the following equation:

$$S_D = \sqrt{ \left(\sum_{j=1}^{n} \left(X_{1j} - X_{2j} - \bar{A} \right)^2 / (n-1) \right) }$$

We can now calculate the confidence interval (CI) for each comparison using the following formula:

$$CI = \bar{A} \pm t_{n-1,\alpha/2} \times S_D / \sqrt{n}$$

where

$t_{n-1,\alpha/2}$ = value from Students t distribution for $\alpha/2$ significance level and $n-1$ degrees of freedom

The rules for interpreting the paired t comparison at the specified confidence level (say 95%) are as follows:

- If the confidence interval is completely to the left of zero, the true mean of scenario 1 is less than the true mean of scenario 2.
- If the confidence interval includes zero, then the true mean of scenario 1 is not statistically different from the true mean of scenario 2.
- If the confidence interval is completely to the right of zero, the true mean of scenario 1 is greater than the true mean of scenario 2.

Figure 10.2 shows a paired t comparison of means test using Arena. Here, the confidence interval includes zero, and so the means of scenario 1 and scenario 2 are not statistically different at the 95% confidence interval. This means, in a statistical sense, we cannot say that the level of the performance measure has changed between the two scenarios.

Two-Sample t-Test Comparison

This approach assumes normally distributed data and equal variances but does not assume common random numbers. It also has double the degrees of freedom of the paired t approach.

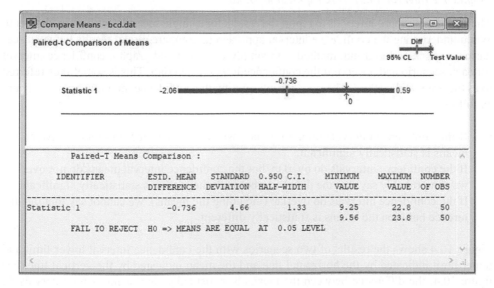

Figure 10.2 Paired t-test comparison

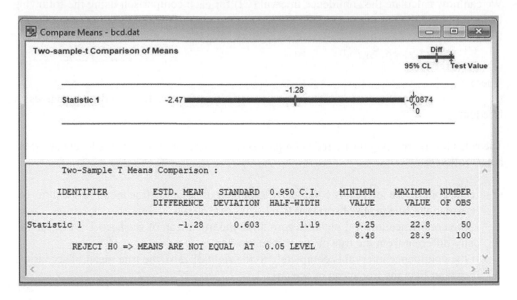

Figure 10.3 Two-sample t-test comparison

The rules for interpreting the Two-sample t comparison are the same as for the paired t comparison. Figure 10.3 shows an example in Arena when the confidence interval is completely to the left of zero, and so in this case, the true mean of scenario 1 is less than the true mean of scenario 2 at the 95% confidence interval.

Confidence Interval Analysis (Graphical Method)

The use of confidence intervals to report the results for a single scenario is given in chapter 9. When undertaking the confidence interval approach to compare model results between scenarios, a quick and informal method is to simply construct and graph a confidence interval for each scenario and observe if the confidence intervals overlap. This is sometimes referred to as the graphical method. The rules for interpreting the confidence intervals graphically are as follows:

- If the confidence intervals do not overlap, we can say that the difference between the means is statistically significant.
- If the confidence intervals do overlap, but the confidence interval means do not overlap, we can probably say that the difference between the means is statistically significant.
- If the confidence intervals do overlap (including the means), we cannot say that the difference between the means is statistically different.

Figure 10.4 shows the results of two scenarios with the confidence interval lower limit and upper limit indicated by the horizontal line and the mean indicated by the vertical line. For figure 10.4, the difference between the means is statistically significant as the intervals do not overlap.

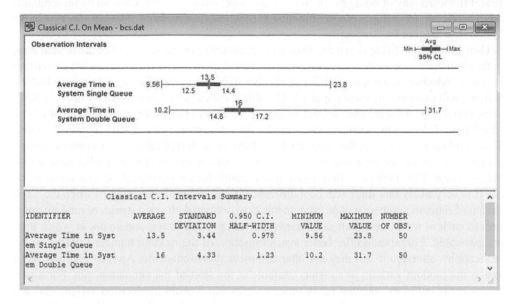

Figure 10.4 Comparing confidence intervals

If the confidence intervals between two scenarios do not overlap, then we can simply compare the results in our results summary for the performance measure that is being presented. Although the difference in performance is significant in a statistical sense, we will need to put the difference in performance into the context of the real system to judge if there is a practical significance in the difference shown by the results.

Interpreting Confidence Intervals

A 95% confidence interval does not predict that 95% of the estimates from future studies will fall inside the observed interval. Ninety-five per cent is the frequency with which other unobserved intervals will contain the true effect (if all the assumptions used to compute the intervals were correct), not how frequently one interval being presented will contain future estimates. In fact, the chance that a future estimate will fall within the current interval will usually be much less than 95%.

Common Random Numbers (CRN)

The probability distributions we have incorporated into our simulation as part of descriptive modelling (chapter 5) will produce random output from our simulation. Thus, there will be variance associated with our simulation output measures, and the greater the variance, the less precise our results. This will present itself as wider confidence intervals of our performance measures. In order to improve the precision of our measures and enable comparison between scenarios, we may wish to reduce variance in our output measures. The most straightforward way of doing this is to simulate more, which can be achieved by undertaking more replications, or for a non-terminating simulation, undertaking a longer run is also an option (see chapter 9).

Using simulation (as opposed to a real-life experiment), we are in control of the randomness in the simulation (see random number generator boxed text), and so we can use what are termed variance reduction techniques (VRTs). A number of VRTs are available; in this introductory text, we will examine the most popular VRT method called common random numbers (CRN). Most simulation software uses a fixed stream of random numbers for each replication of our simulation. This is why when we run a model for replication 1, we usually obtain the same result, and for replication 2, the same result and then for each replication. This means when we compare scenarios, we are using the same random number streams for the replications across our scenarios. This 'default' option is usually acceptable for simple models, but for larger models, it is very likely that there will be a difference in the order of execution of when the fixed stream of random numbers will be used. In this case, we can dedicate a stream of random numbers to each of the places, such as interarrival times, process times, and so on, in which they are generated. This should offer better synchronisation of the random number streams across replications, although it still may not offer complete synchronisation. Another approach is to assign the random variates to an entity attribute at the start of the simulation run. For a particular entity, all of its potential future process times and probability decision assignments are assigned to separate entity attribute values at the start of the simulation run. This disadvantage of this method is the computer memory requirements of multiple entity attributes leading to slower simulation execution speed. These three methods are summarised in table 10.1.

The paired t confidence interval analysis outlined earlier assumes that common random numbers have been used across the scenarios and that they are working. As most simulation software uses common random number streams as a default, we would normally use the paired t approach. To check to see if the common random numbers are working properly, we can check that the variance has been reduced; thus, the variance of the differences in the results from the scenarios should be less than the sum of the individual variances from the results of each scenario.

$$S^2_D < S^2_1 + S^2_2$$

where
S_D = standard deviation of the differences in the results from scenario 1 and scenario 2
S_1 = standard deviation of the results from scenario 1
S_2 = standard deviation of the results from scenario 2

Table 10.1 Common Random Numbers (CRN) Methods

Method	Comments
Use common random number streams (default)	This may be acceptable for simple models but is unlikely to provide synchronisation for larger models.
Dedicated common random number streams for individual variates	This is good for larger models but still may not offer complete synchronisation
Assign attribute values for variates for each entity at the start of each run	This is good for larger models but still may not offer complete synchronisation.

If the common random numbers are not working properly, then we should use the two-sample t confidence interval rather than the paired t confidence interval. This is because the sample t-test compares two independent random samples while the paired t-test compares pairs of correlated variables.

Random Number Generator

Every DES package has a random number generator (technically called a pseudo-random number generator) which is an algorithm that generates an independent random number uniformly distributed between 0 and 1. This number is then used in sampling other random distributions. The sequence of random numbers, called the pseudo-random number stream, can be selected by the simulation modeller.

Multiple-Scenario Analysis – Comparing, Ordering and Optimising

In chapter 3, we defined the changes we make from one model to another as defined by experimental factors, with each factor having a value (termed level). An experimental factor can be quantitative, such as arrival rates or the number of resources. We can also have qualitative factors, such as decision rule logic. For qualitative factors, the level is an option of the factor. A simulation scenario is defined by an experimental factor set to a certain level. We may wish to explore a number of factors set at a number of levels, and so to do this, we will need to run a number of scenarios. In figure 10.5, we show one scenario for three factors set at certain levels (dashed line). Factor 1 and factor 2 are quantitative factors, while factor 3 is a qualitative factor. If we wish to investigate all the levels of each factor in combination with all the levels of our other factors, the number of scenarios required to cover what is termed the solution space is the number of levels for each factor multiplied by the number of levels for the other factors. Thus, for figure 10.5, the solution space would cover $5 \times 3 \times 2 = 30$ scenarios. As can be seen from this example, the solution space can become large as the number of factors and levels increases. Generally, we would attempt to limit our solution space, but if we cannot, there are techniques that we can use, such as experimental design, which aim to reduce the time required to investigate all the possible scenarios.

Will now discuss comparing, ordering and optimising between multiple scenarios. A survey of search experimentation techniques in use for DES is provided in Hoad et al. (2015).

Comparing Multiple Scenarios

When using confidence interval analysis to compare across multiple scenarios, we can compare the base scenario (which will usually be the simulation of the current system) to all other scenarios, and this is termed a comparison to base. If we compare each scenario in turn to all the other scenarios, this is termed a pairwise comparison.

For five scenarios, we can compare to the base scenario using four comparisons, as follows:

Scenario 1 (base) – Scenario 2
Scenario 1 (base) – Scenario 3
Scenario 1 (base) – Scenario 4
Scenario 1 (base) – Scenario 5

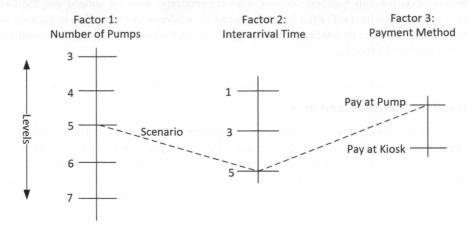

Figure 10.5 Factors, levels and scenarios

We can show the results in a table (table 10.2):

Table 10.2 Comparison to Base for Five Scenarios

Scenario	2	3	4	5
1	S1 – S2	S1 – S3	S1 – S4	S1 – S5

For five scenarios, we can compare to each of the other scenarios with ten comparisons as follows:

Scenario 1 – Scenario 2
Scenario 1 – Scenario 3
Scenario 1 – Scenario 4
Scenario 1 – Scenario 5
Scenario 2 – Scenario 3
Scenario 2 – Scenario 4
Scenario 2 – Scenario 5
Scenario 3 – Scenario 4
Scenario 3 – Scenario 5
Scenario 4 – Scenario 5

We can show the results in a table (table 10.3):

Table 10.3 Pairwise Comparison of Five Scenarios

Scenario	2	3	4	5
1	S1 – S2	S1 – S3	S1 – S4	S1 – S5
2		S2 – S3	S2 – S4	S2 – S5
3			S3 – S4	S3 – S5
4				S4 – S5

The Bonferroni Inequality

When we are comparing scenarios, we need to choose an appropriate confidence level with a value of 90% or 95% usually chosen. However, if we are comparing more than two scenarios, then we need to take account of the Bonferroni inequality and adjust our individual confidence levels for each scenario to obtain the overall confidence level we require for our comparison. The Bonferroni inequality states that the probability of all events in a set occurring is at least one minus the sum of the probability of the individual events occurring. This inequality can be applied to confidence intervals (which are probability statements regarding the chance that the true parameter falls within intervals formed by the procedure). We need to make the following calculation depending on if we are comparing our scenarios to a base scenario or undertaking a pairwise comparison.

For a comparison to base, we will need to adjust the confidence levels as follows.

s = the number of scenarios
c = the number of confidence intervals $(s - 1)$
α = overall significance level $(1 -$ overall confidence level$)$
the individual confidence intervals should be formed with a significance level of α / c.

For example, for five scenarios, the calculation of the individual confidence levels are as follows:

To compare the base scenario to the four further scenarios at an overall confidence level of 90%:

$c = 5 - 1 = 4$
$\alpha = 100\% - 90\% = 10\%$
individual significance level $= 10 / 4 = 2.5\%$; thus, the individual confidence level $= 97.5\%$

For a pairwise comparison, we will need to adjust the confidence levels as follows.

s = the number of scenarios
c = the number of confidence intervals $(s \times (s - 1) / 2)$
α = overall significance level $(1 -$ overall confidence level$)$
The individual confidence intervals should be formed with a significance level of α / c.

For example, for five scenarios, the calculation of the individual confidence levels are as follows:

To compare each scenario to every other scenario at an overall confidence level of 90%:

$c = s \times (s - 1) / 2 = 5 \times (5 - 1) / 2 = 5 \times 2 = 10$
$\alpha = 100\% - 90\% = 10\%$
individual significance level $= 10 / 10 = 1\%$; thus, the individual confidence level $= 99\%$

Note that due to the Bonferroni inequality, because we have increased the individual confidence level (say from 90% to 99%), the individual confidence intervals will become wider, decreasing the precision of our estimates and making comparisons between scenarios more difficult. For these reasons, we can do the following:

- Increase the number of replications to improve precision.
- Limit our analysis to a relatively low number of scenarios.

- Accept an overall lower confidence level.
- Use experimental design to reduce the number of potential scenarios for analysis.
- Use visual analytics to provide an alternative method of analysis.

We will now briefly discuss the use of experimental design and visual analytics.

Experimental Design

Experimental design usually has the purpose of determining which factors have the greatest effect on a response and can thus reduce the size of the solution space. Once we have determined these factors, we can undertake a more detailed investigation using scenario analysis. One approach to experimental design is to use a two-level full-factorial design in which each experimental factor is set at just two (high and low) levels. The levels could be different values of an input variable or different configurations of a model (e.g. different scheduling rules for a queuing system). No rules are provided as to what the levels of the factors should be, but levels need to be set that are different enough to show how the factor affects the response but within normal operating conditions for that factor. For a full-factorial design, each possible combination of factor levels is tested for response. This means for k factors, there are 2^k combinations of low and high factor levels. These possible combinations are shown in an array called the design matrix. A design matrix for a 2^3 factorial design (three factors give 2^3, which equals eight possible combinations of low and high factor levels) is listed in table 10.4.

The advantage of following the full-factorial design approach over varying a single factor at a time is that the effect of interaction effects can be assessed. The ability to assess the impact of one factor change when the level of a second factor changes is important in finding the best system performance because the effect of two factors changing may not be the same as the addition of the effect of each factor change in isolation.

Visual Analytics

Another approach is to use visualisation or visual analytics to simultaneously present simulation results for a number of parameter combinations to the user. Thus, the technique uses the visual display of information and the domain knowledge of the user to observe the results of parameter combinations that may be selected for further investigation. Visual analytics may use analytics techniques such as a clustering algorithm that classifies the simulation experiments as a way of synthesising large amounts of data and helping to reveal patterns

Table 10.4 Two Factorial Design Matrix

Factor Combination	Factor 1	Factor 2	Factor 3	Response
1	−	−	−	R1
2	+	−	−	R2
3	−	+	−	R3
4	+	+	−	R4
5	−	−	+	R5
6	+	−	+	R6
7	−	+	+	R7
8	+	+	+	R8

and relationships between variables that might otherwise be hidden or difficult to find. Clustering methods can be used to explore simulation output data by treating each object in a cluster as a single simulation run allocated on selected parameter results. For example, in a two-dimensional analysis, the variables' cycle time and throughput time may be used. Once the clusters are mapped out visually, analysts can investigate which input settings led to the corresponding systems performance measures that define this cluster. A limitation of visual analytics is that the identification of relationships using visual inspection may be less precise and more open to interpretation than traditional approaches to simulation output analysis. Furthermore, visual analytics may require the training in and use of new analytics software and analysis methods by simulation practitioners. An example of a dedicated visualisation package is the Tableau software (www.tableau.com/products/desktop), which provides dashboard facilities that can be used for the presentation of simulation results (Figure 10.6).

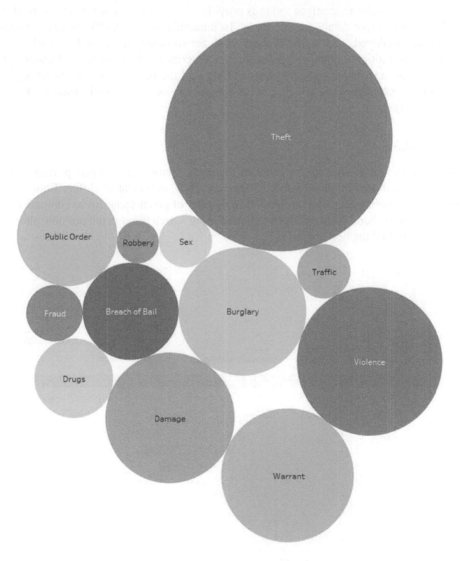

Figure 10.6 Tableau dashboard showing relative cost of simulated arrest types

Process Mining Performance Reporting

Process mining software can also be used to supplement the traditional reports generated by simulation software. The simulation can be developed to generate an event log, which is held in a spreadsheet file. This file is then imported into the process mining software package that provides extensive event-based graphical facilities for model validation and analysis of results (Greasley, 2018). Figure 10.7 reports frequency and 'time in the system' measures for 12 types of arrest.

Ordering Scenarios

One approach to dealing with a relatively large solution space with multiple comparisons is to rank the scenarios in order. Thus, rather than simply comparing the results of the comparisons, we rank the alternatives and thus provide the best solution for a defined goal. Law (2015) provides more details on this topic. To undertake the method in practice, software is normally employed, such as the Process Analyzer software, that is included with Arena, which utilises multiple comparison procedures as described in Goldsman and Nelson (1998). Simio includes a software add-in which can help find the best scenario using an approach based on the KN algorithm, which is a ranking and selection method based on Kim and Nelson (2001).

Optimisation

Optimisation involves finding the value of the input factors (levels) that provide the best outcome for a chosen output measure (response). Thus, optimisation differs from ordering in that when ordering scenarios, we provide a number of given scenarios to compare against (usually no more than 20). In optimisation, we simply search through the possible alternative input levels to find the best scenario.

Figure 10.7 process mining software used to report simulation results (www.minit.io)

Optimisation and Decision-Making

In applications such as defining AGV movement in a factory or supply chain transportation policies, then an optimisation approach can be very useful. However, although optimisation approaches can be useful, in practice decision-makers are concerned with providing what they consider to be a satisfactory answer to a problem. This ensures analysis is not overly extended in search of the 'perfect' answer, but they are also aware that the model does not take into account all aspects of the real system. The limitations of the model mean that the optimum solution provided is only optimal in comparison with the other solutions tried, and there are likely to be other solutions that exist that have not been considered by the optimisation. Also, the decision-maker is unlikely to make a decision solely on the basis of the model solution but is likely to consider other factors outside of the model scope to find a feasible and implementable solution. For example, an analysis to find an optimum work schedule by formulating a number of scenarios based on premises regarding ethical and moral concerns in terms of staff working conditions would be difficult to codify as parameters in an optimisation algorithm.

There are three main approaches to optimisation.

1 Heuristics

In this 'manual' approach, we use the domain knowledge of system experts to reduce the solution space and produce what we hope are optimum results. This approach involves running multiple experiments with different experimental factor settings to find the 'best' option. However, the approach may not find the optimal results, is only feasible for relatively simple optimisation problems and is difficult to scale to complex issues.

2 Optimisation Software

Many simulation software packages incorporate optimisation software such as OptQuest (www.opttek.com) that use what can be termed a meta-heuristic approach using, for example, the machine-learning technique of genetic algorithms. When optimising using software, the following four elements should be defined by the simulation user:

Controls – these are input parameters such as the capacities of resources that you define.
Responses – these are output parameters such as queuing statistics that you define.
Constraints – these are the limitations imposed on the variables (controls and responses), such as minimum and maximum values.
Objectives – sometimes referred to as the criterion function, this is a statement of the goals of the system and how they are to be measured. (This may be expressed as the maximisation of a variable, such as profit level or minimisation of a variable, such as cost.)

Optimisation software can be applied to more complex problems with a large solution space but may not always find the optimal results.

3   Reinforcement Learning

An alternative to optimisation software is to use a reinforcement learning (RL) algorithm. This approach can handle a large solution space and multiple contradictory objectives. Traditional optimisers are static in that they optimise over a simulation run. A key advantage of the RL approach is that it can be triggered to dynamically optimise during the simulation run. The simulation can be used to train the algorithm, and the optimised policy can then be adopted by the model. For more information on the use of RL to optimise simulation models, see www.pathmind.com.

Dealing with the Solution Space

Suppose we had to model a supermarket store and car park, and our experimental factors are the number of checkouts, number of trolleys and number of parking spaces, and we could have up to 36 checkouts, 300 trolleys and 250 spaces. This gives a solution space of 2,700,000 scenarios! In order to deal with this very large solution space, we would need to use multi-comparison software, visual analytics, experimental design or optimisation.

Summary

This chapter has covered comparing two scenarios using hypothesis testing and confidence interval analysis. The comparison of more than two scenarios is considered for a base comparison and a pairwise comparison. The need to consider the Bonferroni inequality is then discussed. For experiments with a large solution space, then further techniques may be considered, such as experimental design and visual analytics. Ordering scenarios and optimisation are then outlined.

Exercise

Compare the university car park system described in the exercises in chapter 7 with a system that allows both staff and students to use either car park. Is there a statistically significant difference in the length of time either car park is full in both scenarios? Present and interpret the results of the simulation.

References

Goldsman, D. and Nelson, B.L. (1998) Statistical screening, selection, and multiple comparison procedures in computer simulation, *Proceedings of the 30th Winter Simulation Conference*, 159–166.

Greasley, A. (2018) An assessment of the simulation capabilities of process mining, *Proceedings of the 6th International Conference on Business Analytics and Intelligence (ICBAI)*, IEEE.

Greenland, S., Senn, S.J., Rothman, K.J., Carlin, J.B., Poole, C., Goodman, S.N. and Altman, D.G. (2016) Statistical tests, P values, confidence intervals, and power: A guide to misinterpretations, *European Journal of Epidemiology*, 31, 337–350.

Hoad, K., Monks, T. and O'Brien, F. (2015) The use of search experimentation in discrete-event simulation practice, *Journal of the Operational Research Society*, 66, 1155–1168.

Kim, S. and Nelson, B.L. (2001) A fully sequential procedure for indifference-zone selection in simulation, *ACM Transactions on Modeling and Computer Simulation*, 11, 251–273.

Law, A.M. (2015) *Simulation Modeling and Analysis*, 5th edition, McGraw-Hill Education.

10A: Arena Scenario Analysis

Introduction

This chapter covers scenario analysis using the Arena simulation software. Two systems are compared using the Arena Output Analyzer to undertake a visual inspection of confidence interval graphs and the use of a paired t-test. For comparison across multiple systems, the use of the Process Analyzer is demonstrated for multiple-scenario comparison and scenario ordering. Finally, the Arena OptQuest application is shown for optimisation.

Comparing Two Systems with Arena

We will compare two systems with Arena using the visual inspection (graphical) method to compare confidence intervals and the use of a hypothesis test. To undertake these methods, we will use the Output Analyzer application that is bundled with the Arena software. The Output Analyzer is a separate application from Arena, so it must be run from Windows (search for Output Analyzer in the Windows search box).

Arena Comparison of Confidence Interval Analysis

In chapter 9A, in order to undertake confidence interval analysis of a single model, we made changes to the double-queue bank clerk model to make it a 'true' terminating system. Here, we will compare the performance of the double-queue system to the single-queue bank clerk system, so we need to repeat the changes to the double-queue system for the single-queue system. To do this load, the single-queue bank clerk simulation (see chapter 7A) into Arena. You will need to add a Decide module before the Process module in your model and direct all customers after 480 minutes to an additional Dispose module (figure 10.1). The replication length for this version of the model is 510 minutes. Save the time in the system data to the file BCS.DAT.

Run both the double-queue and single-queue simulations for 50 replications to create new BCD.dat and BCS.dat files for use by the Output Analyzer. Run the Output Analyzer and select the Analyze/Confidence Interval on Mean/Classical menu option. Add the file BCD. DAT and select 'lumped' from the pull-down menu for the replications parameter. Click on OK. Add the file BCS.DAT. Select 'lumped' from the pull-down menu for the replications parameter. Click on OK. Leave the default confidence interval at 0.95 (95%). Click on OK. The analysis, as shown in figure 10.2, will appear.

Using the Arena output processor, the results show the confidence intervals as the blue lines. The graphs show that we can be 95% confident that the average time in the system

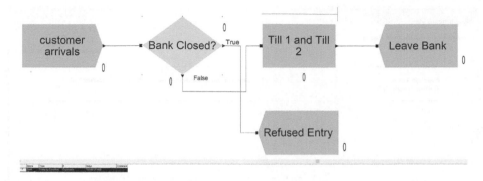

Figure 10A.1 Module connections for single-queue bank clerk terminating system

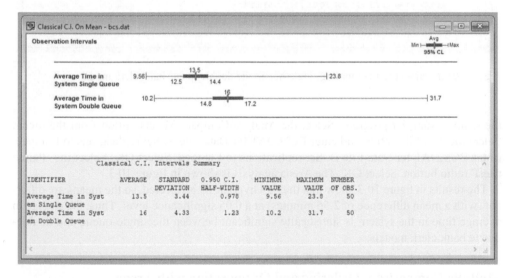

Figure 10A.2 Arena comparison of confidence interval analysis

for the double-queue model is between 14.8 and 17.2 minutes and the average time in the system for the single-queue system is between 12.5 and 14.4 minutes. We can use a visual inspection method of comparing the confidence intervals and say that as the two confidence intervals (blue lines on the graph) do not overlap, then there is a statistically significant difference between the time in the system for customers between the single-queue and double-queue bank clerk models. Note that multiple (more than two) confidence intervals may be compared on the same graph by adding additional. dat files.

Arena Hypothesis Testing

The paired t-test calculates the difference between the two alternatives for each replication. It tests the hypothesis that if the data from both models are from the same distribution, then the mean of the differences will be zero. In Arena, undertake the paired t-test analysis by running

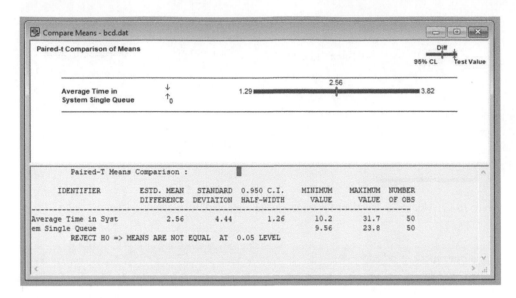

Figure 10A.3 Paired t-test comparing single-queue and double-queue bank clerk models

the Output Analyzer program. Select the Analyze/Compare Means option from the menu. Select the Add File option and enter BCD.DAT for Data File A. Set replications to Lumped. Enter BCS.DAT for Data File B. Set replications to Lumped. Select OK. Select the 'Paired t-test' radio button. Select OK. The Arena analysis is shown in figure 10.3.

The results in figure 10.3 show that the null hypothesis is rejected, so the means are different (with a mean difference of 2.56 minutes) at a 0.05 significance level. Thus, the change in average time in the system is statistically significant between the single-queue and double-queue bank clerk models.

Multiple Comparison, Ordering and Optimisation with Arena

In this section, we will conduct multiple comparisons and ordering using the Arena Process Analyzer and optimisation using the Arena OptQuest. Both these applications are available from the Tools menu in Arena.

Arena Multiple-Scenario Comparison

In order to demonstrate the multiple-scenario analysis, we will use the petrol station model from chapter 7A. Note we should extend the run of the model (as we have the bank clerk simulation earlier in this chapter) in order to achieve a terminating system. However, because there is almost no queuing in this version of the model, it is near empty at run completion, so we will proceed directly to the scenario comparison analysis.

Open the petrol station Arena model from chapter 7A. Select the Process Analyzer from the Arena Tools menu tab. Select the File/New option to display the Scenario Properties screen. A scenario consists of a set of controls, a set of responses and a compiled model file (with file extension. p). To generate the. p file for the petrol station model, select Check

Model from the Run menu tab. Double-click where it is indicated to add a new scenario. A menu will appear in which you can enter a name for the scenario. Browse for the petrol station. p file and select OK. To add your controls, select Insert from the menu and select the Control option. You are then presented with a menu of potential control variables. Enter the resources manual pump, pay pump and payment till in turn. Now enter the response variables of profit, driveaways and Entity 1.TotalTime. Select the Run tab and select Go. The results for one replication are shown in figure 10.4.

The results for the response variables (average time in the system = 9.4 minutes, profit = 4,600, driveaways = 50) correspond with those for the single run shown in chapter 7A.

To perform multiple replications, select the Insert Menu tab and then select Controls, System, Num Reps. This will create an additional column in the main screen in which you can change the number of replications. Change the number of replications to 30 and rerun the scenario. You will see the responses change value accordingly.

We will now enter a number of scenarios and compare the results across the response variables. Currently, we have two manual pumps, two pay pumps and one payment till. If we could allocate two additional units across the three resources, which allocation of resources would lead to the highest profit? First, we need to define the possible scenarios across our controls, so adding two resources provides six scenarios (table 10A.1).

To enter these scenarios into the Process Analyzer right-click on the current scenario and select the Duplicate Scenario option. Repeat this until six scenarios are showing. You can now rename them Scenario 1 to Scenario 6 in the name column. Select all the scenarios by clicking on them and holding the CTRL key. Select Run then Go to run the scenarios and the results should be like figure 10A.5.

We can see from figure 10A.5 that scenario 1 has the highest profit, but we know there will be variability in the response variables, so we can plot the responses on a box-whisker chart to enable us to compare the distribution of the responses across the scenarios. To do

Figure 10A.4 Process Analyzer scenario run

Table 10A.1 Six Scenarios Possible When Allocating Two Additional Resources

	Manual Pump	*Pay Pump*	*Payment Till*
Scenario 1	2	4	1
Scenario 2	3	3	1
Scenario 3	2	3	2
Scenario 4	4	2	1
Scenario 5	3	2	2
Scenario 6	2	2	3

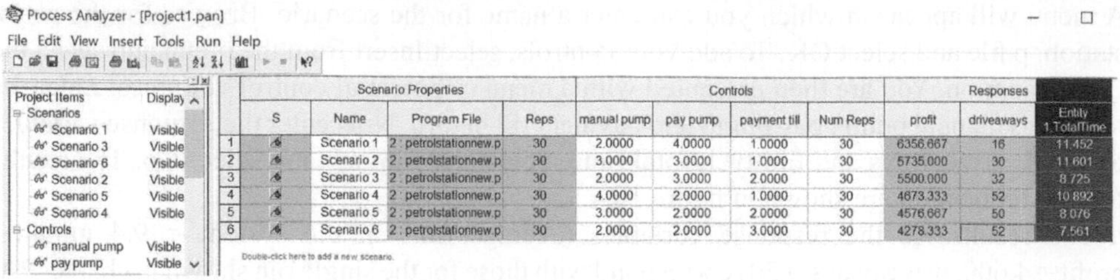

Figure 10A.5 Running a multiple-scenario comparison

this, right-click on a responses column and select the Insert Chart icon from the menu. Select the Chart objective button to 'Compare the average values of a response across scenarios' and select the Box and Whisker Chart Type. Select Next, and then choose profit from the use responses box, ensure all six scenarios are indicated in the across these scenarios box and then select Next. Select Next again. Click on the Identify Best Scenarios box and ensure that the setting is 'Bigger is Better'. Select Finish, and the chart as in figure 10A.6 should display.

The chart shows the high-low values (line) and the 95% confidence interval (box) for each scenario. You can display the numeric figures for these values by right-clicking on the chart and selecting Chart Options. The best scenario is also indicated (in this case, scenario 1).

Note that for multiple comparisons of scenario results to a predetermined overall confidence level, we need to take account of the Bonferroni inequality and adjust the individual confidence levels for each scenario (see chapter 10 for more details). However, the Process Analyzer takes care of this complication for us, and to identify the best scenario, the Process Analyzer uses a method based on multiple comparison procedures described in Goldsman and Nelson (1998). Furthermore, we can control the number of best scenarios and thus control our screening strategy by adjusting the error tolerance value when we construct the chart.

Arena Scenario Ordering

To show the scenarios in order using the Process Analyzer, simply right-click on the column for the response to order by and select the sort ascending or sort descending icon on the menu. When the chart is constructed, it will show the scenarios in order.

Arena Optimisation

While the Arena Process Analyzer can assist when investigating scenarios that we define, optimisation allows us to define response targets, and the optimisation software adjusts the control values to attempt to find the best option. In Arena, we can use the OptQuest application, which is available from the Tools menu.

Load in the petrol station model from chapter 7A. Then from OptQuest, select the File/New option and then select the OptQuest optimisation icon from the screen. The screen will display all the variables you have defined as reported statistics in your Arena model under the Control summary.

At the petrol station there is room for expansion to increase to 6 manual pumps, 6 pay at pumps and 4 payment tills. There is a target of fewer than 5 cars to drive away each day, and

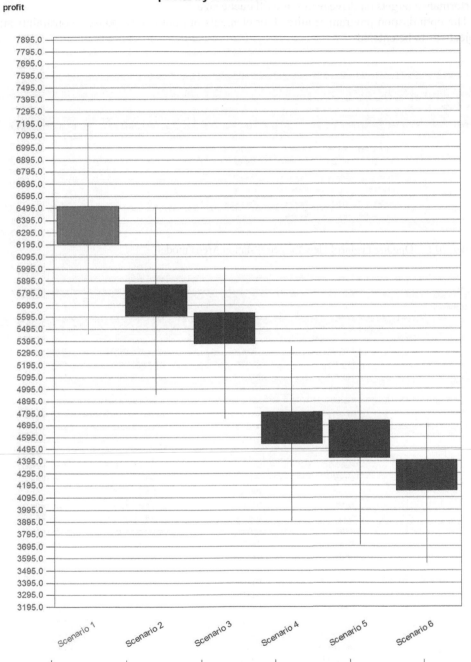

Figure 10A.6 Petrol station scenario profit confidence interval graph

the average number of customers waiting at the till should be less than 5. Management wish to know the best combination of pumps and tills to maximise profit per day and meet their performance targets on driveaways and till queue size.

The optimisation program requires four elements of controls, responses, constraints and objectives to be entered.

Optimization 1*

Controls

	Included	Category	Name	Element Type	Type	Low Bound	Suggested	High Bound	Step
	☐	User Specified	income	Variable	Continuous	0	0	0	N/A
	☑	Resources	manual p...	Resource	Discrete	2	3	6	1
	☑	Resources	pay pump	Resource	Discrete	2	3	6	1
	☑	Resources	payment till	Resource	Discrete	1	2	4	1
	☐	User Specified	profit	Variable	Continuous	0	0	0	N/A
	☐	User Specified	totalcost...	Variable	Continuous	0	0	0	N/A

Figure 10A.7 OptQuest control view for petrol station Arena model

Optimization 1*

Responses

	Included	Category	Data Type	Name	Response Type
	☐	Resource	Usage Cost	pay pump.UsageCost	Output Value
	☐	Resource	Utilization	pay pump.Utilization	DStat Average
	☐	Resource	Busy Cost	payment till.BusyCost	Output Value
	☐	Resource	Idle Cost	payment till.IdleCost	Output Value
	☐	Resource	Number Busy	payment till.NumberBusy	DStat Average
	☐	Resource	Number Scheduled	payment till.NumberScheduled	DStat Average
	☐	Resource	Number Seized	payment till.NumberSeized	Output Value
	☐	Resource	Scheduled Utilization	payment till.ScheduledUtilization	Output Value
	☐	Resource	Usage Cost	payment till.UsageCost	Output Value
	☐	Resource	Utilization	payment till.Utilization	DStat Average
	☐	System	NVA Cost	All Entities.NVACost	Output Value
	☐	System	Other Cost	All Entities.OtherCost	Output Value
	☐	System	Total Cost	All Entities.TotalCost	Output Value
	☐	System	Tran Cost	All Entities.TranCost	Output Value
	☐	System	VA Cost	All Entities.VACost	Output Value
	☐	System	Wait Cost	All Entities.WaitCost	Output Value
	☐	System	Busy Cost	All Resources.BusyCost	Output Value
	☐	System	Idle Cost	All Resources.IdleCost	Output Value
	☐	System	Total Cost	All Resources.TotalCost	Output Value
	☐	System	Usage Cost	All Resources.UsageCost	Output Value
	☐	System	Number Out	System.NumberOut	Output Value
	☐	System	Total Cost	System.TotalCost	Output Value
	☑	User Specified	Count	drive aways	Counter Value
	☐	User Specified	Variable	income	Variable Value
	☐	User Specified	Variable	income Value	DStat Average
	☑	User Specified	Variable	profit	Variable Value
	☐	User Specified	Variable	profit Value	DStat Average
	☐	User Specified	Variable	totalcostperday	Variable Value

Figure 10A.8 OptQuest responses selection

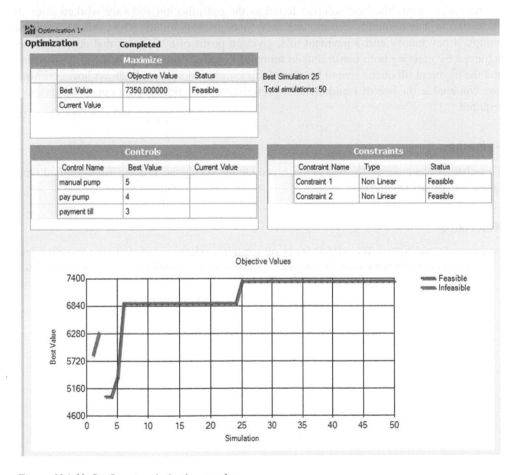

Figure 10A.9 OptQuest add constraints

Figure 10A.10 OptQuest add objectives

Figure 10A.11 OptQuest optimisation results

For the controls, you need to select the resources of the pay pump, manual pump and payment till from the controls list by ticking the Include box. Adjust the upper bounds for the pumps to 6 and for the payment till to 4 as specified for the experiment (figure 10A.7).

For the responses, click on the responses folder in the Editor Explorer at the bottom left of the screen. Select the 'driveaway' and the 'profit' variables from the list (figure 10A.8).

Now right-click on the Constraints folder in the Editor Explorer and select the Add option. From the table that appears, double-click on the Expression row and the Expressions menu will appear (figure 10A.9).

Select the expressions you wish to add by clicking on them, and they will appear in the expression box at the bottom of the menu. Add the constraint to the variable name. For example, amend the expression [driveaways] to [driveaways] < 5. This limits the number of driveaways to less than 5 for a single 8-hour run. Add a second constraint for the number of customers in the till queue to 5 [till service.Queue.NumberInQueue] < 5 (see figure 10A.9).

For the objective, right-click on the Objectives folder and select the Add option. Double-click on the Expression row and select the Profit variable in the Expressions menu. Make sure that the maximise option is selected for the profit objective (figure 10A.10).

Run the optimisation by selecting the go arrow on the top menu bar. The following analysis is displayed by clicking on the optimisation folder (figure 10A.11).

The graph shows the best solution found as the optimisation software worked through 50 scenarios. The optimum scenario that maximises profit is found to be a mix of 5 manual pumps, 4 pay pumps and 3 payment tills, giving a profit of £7,350 for that day. This was achieved by meeting both constraints in terms of keeping driveaways below 5 on that day and the payment till queue size to less than 5 customers. This example shows how optimisation can enable the use of simulation for prescriptive analytics when a course of action is required.

Summary

This chapter has covered the use of the Arena Output Analyzer, Process Analyzer and OptQuest for scenario analysis.

Reference

Goldsman, D. and Nelson, B.L. (1998) Statistical screening, selection, and multiple comparison procedures in computer simulation, *Proceedings of the 30th Winter Simulation Conference*, 159–166.

10B: Simio Scenario Analysis

Introduction

This chapter covers scenario analysis using the Simio simulation software. Two systems are compared by undertaking a visual inspection of confidence interval graphs. For comparison across multiple systems, a multiple-scenario comparison is demonstrated, and the Simio OptQuest application is shown for optimisation.

Simio Comparison of Confidence Interval Analysis

In chapter 9B, in order to undertake a confidence interval analysis of a single model, we made changes to the double-queue bank clerk model to make it a 'true' terminating system. Here, we will compare the performance of the double-queue system to the single-queue bank clerk system.

To do this, load the double-queue terminating bank clerk simulation (see chapter 9B) into Simio. Make sure no new customers enter the bank after 480 minutes. To do this, click on the Source1 object in the Navigation Window, and in the Properties Window, enter a time of 480 for the stopping conditions. Next, select the Run tab, and on the ribbon, change the runtime to 510 minutes.

We can now enter the single-queue version of the bank clerk simulation on the same Facility window (see instructions in chapter 7B). Make this model terminating using the source object Navigation Window as for the double-queue model described previously. The two models should be displayed on the Facility window as in figure 10B.1.

Now we need to define our statistic that we wish to report our confidence interval on. Click on the Project Home tab and select New Experiment from the ribbon. Select the Design tab and click on the Add Response option on the ribbon. We now need to define our performance measures. In this case, enter DefaultEntity.Population.TimeInSystem.Average as the expression in the Response1 properties menu. This will collect statistics on the average flow time for customers in the bank clerk system. Rename the response as Time_In_System and set the Unit Type parameter to time and the display units to minutes. We will need to set two scenarios to record the performance for each of the two versions of the bank clerk model. Enter 'Double-Queue Bank Clerk Model' for the name of the first scenario. Set the required Replications to 50. Enter 'Single-Queue Bank Clerk Model' for the name of the second scenario. Set the required replications to 50. The screen should be as in figure 10B.2.

We will now run each model in turn and compare the results. Return to the Facility window and click on the source object (Source2) for the single-queue version, and set the entities per arrival in the Properties Window to 0. Return to the experiment window and ensure the

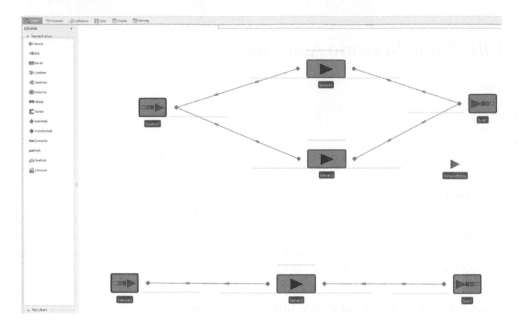

Figure 10B.1 Simio display of double-queue and single-queue terminating bank clerk models

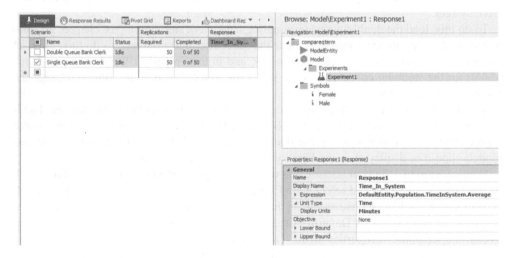

Figure 10B.2 Experiment to compare the results of the single-queue and double-queue bank clerk model

tick box is selected for scenario 1 only. Run the scenario, and the results for the double-queue model should appear. Return to the Facility window and select the entities per arrival as 0 for the double-queue version and 1 for the single-queue version. Return to the experiment and untick the double-queue scenario and tick the single-queue scenario. Run the experiment, and the results for the single-queue model should appear (figure 10B.3).

Design	Response Results	Pivot Grid	Reports	Dashboard Reports

Scenario			Replications		Responses
■	Name	Status	Required	Completed	Time_In_System ...
☑	Double Queue Bank Clerk	Comple...	50	50 of 50	15.5941
☐	Single Queue Bank Clerk	Comple...	50	50 of 50	15.0459
✳ ■					

Figure 10B.3 Results for single-queue and double-queue

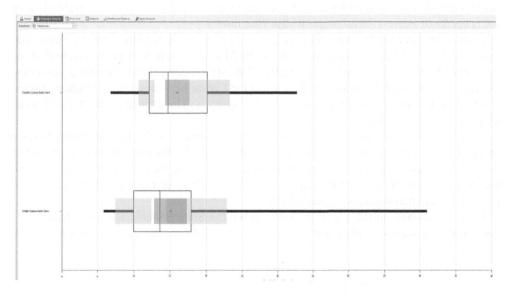

Figure 10B.4 Comparison box plot chart for single-queue and double-queue

Make sure both scenarios are ticked, and then click on the Response Results tab to show the box plots of the average time in the system for the bank clerk customers for single-queue and double-queue scenarios. Click on the Rotate Plot option to provide a horizontal confidence interval and box plot display (figure 10B.4).

The confidence interval is shown as a brown block in the middle of the plot. Click on the dot in the middle of the brown block, and the confidence interval statistics are displayed. The graphs show that we can be 95% confident when the average time in the system for the double-queue model is between 14.58 and 16.6 minutes and the average time in the system for the single-queue system is between 13.68 and 16.4 minutes. We can use a visual inspection method of comparing to compare the confidence intervals and say that as the two confidence intervals overlap, then there is no statistically significant difference between the time in the system for customers between the single-queue and double-queue bank clerk models.

Multiple Comparison and Optimisation with Simio

In this section, we will conduct multiple comparisons and optimisation using Simio.

Simio Multiple-Scenario Comparison

In order to demonstrate the multiple-scenario analysis, we will use the Petrol Station model from chapter 7B. Note we should extend the run of the model in order to achieve a terminating system. However, because there is almost no queuing in this version of the model, it is near empty at run completion, so we will proceed directly to the scenario comparison analysis.

When conducting scenario analysis, each scenario has a set of control variables and output responses. The control variables are the values assigned to the properties of the associated model. Before adding an experiment, you typically add properties to the main model that you wish to serve as the controls that you will change for each scenario. The main model properties may be referenced by the properties of objects within your model. The easiest way to simultaneously add the main level properties and create the reference to it is to right-click on the property of interest for an object within your model.

In this case, our control variables are the capacities of the resources in the Petrol Station model. In the Facility window, click on the Manual_Pump_Service server, and in the Properties Window, right-click on the Initial Capacity property. From the menu, select the Set Referenced Property option and then select the Create New Referenced Property option from the bottom of the menu list. A referenced property will be created for the Initial Capacity property (figure 10B.5).

Now create the referenced property for the Initial Capacity at the Pay_at_Pump_Service server. Go to the Properties View and set the Initial Capacity for both referenced properties to 3. We can now undertake our experimentation. Click on the New Experiment button from the Project Home button, and the experiment design will be displayed with the referenced properties shown as controls (figure 10B.6).

For the responses in the Elements View, define the State Statistic Element Driveaway_ Tally with the state variable name DriveAways. Also, define the Tally Statistics Element

Properties: Manual_Pump_Service (Server)	
▲ **Process Logic**	
Capacity Type	Fixed
Initial Capacity	↱ **Manual_Pump_Service_InitialCapacity**
Ranking Rule	First In First Out
Dynamic Selection Rule	None
▸ Transfer-In Time	0.0
Process Type	Specific Time
▸ Processing Time	**Random.Triangular(4,6,10)**
Off Shift Rule	Suspend Processing

Figure 10B.5 Setting the initial server capacity to a referenced property

	Design	Response Results	Pivot Grid	Reports	Dashboard Reports	Input Analysis	
Scenario			Replications		Controls		
✓	Name	Status	Required	Completed	Manual_Pump_Service_InitialCapacity	Pay_at_Pump_Service_InitialCapacity	
▸ ✓	Scenario1	Idle	10	0 of 10	4	4	

Figure 10B.6 Initial experiment screen showing the defined control variables

Profit_Tally. Now click on the add response button on the Design ribbon. In the Properties Window, enter Till_Service.InputBuffer.Contents.AverageNumberWaiting in the expression property and Till_NumberInQ in the name property. Enter a response for driveaways with the expression Driveaway_Tally.LastRecordedValue and a response for Profit with the expression Profit_Tally.LastRecordedValue. Add another scenario and set the manual pump initial capacity to 4 and the pay at pump initial capacity to 3. Run the experiment, and the screen should be as in figure 10B.7.

Click on the Response Results tab, choose the rotate plot option from the menu and choose the TillNumberinQ response from the pull-down menu. The following graph should be displayed (figure 10B.8).

We can see the confidence intervals (dark bars) overlap. Click on the dot or use the Pivot screen to obtain the actual confidence interval results. In this case, the results for scenario 1 are the mean across the ten replications for the average number of customers waiting in the till service queue is 0.7073 with a half-width of 0.2378. For scenario 2, the figures are a mean of 1.2413 and a half-width of 0.4624.

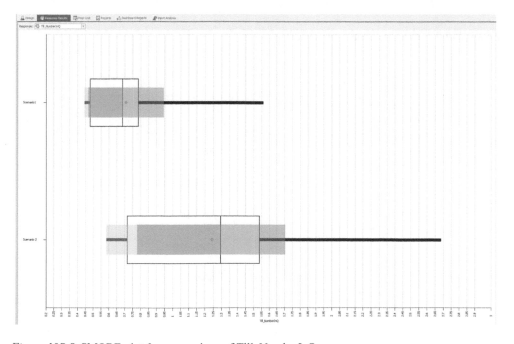

Figure 10B.7 Experiment screen with controls and responses

Figure 10B.8 SMORE plot for comparison of Till_NumberInQ

Optimisation with Simio

While the Simio Experiment tools can assist when investigating scenarios that we define. Optimisation allows us to define response targets and the optimisation software adjusts the control values to attempt to find the best option. In Simio, we can use the OptQuest application, which is available from Add-In options on the menu.

Load in the petrol station model from chapter 7B and select the OptQuest add-in from the menu. At the petrol station, there is room for expansion to increase to 6 manual pumps, 6 pay at pumps and 4 payment tills. There is a target of fewer than 5 cars to drive away each day, and the average number of customers waiting at the till should be less than 5. Management wish to know the best combination of pumps and tills to maximise profit per day and meet their performance targets on driveaways and till queue size. The optimisation program requires four elements of controls, responses, constraints and objectives to be entered. Select the Add-In button on the experiment Design ribbon and choose OptQuest for Simio from the

Properties: Manual_Pump_Service_InitialCapacity (Control)	
◢ **Manual_Pump_Service_InitialCapacity**	
Description	
◢ **OptQuest for Simio - Parameters**	
Include in Optimization	**Yes**
Minimum Value	**1**
Maximum Value	**6**
Increment	**1**

Figure 10B.9 Setting the control parameters

Properties: Profit (Response)	
◢ **OptQuest for Simio - Parameters**	
Weight	**1**
◢ **General**	
Name	**Profit**
Display Name	Profit
◢ Expression	**Profit.LastRecordedValue**
Units	USD
◢ Unit Type	**Currency**
Display Units	**USD**
Objective	**Maximize**
◢ Lower Bound	
Units	**USD**
◢ Upper Bound	
Units	**USD**

Figure 10B.10 Setting the profit response

☑ Name	Status	Required	Completed	Manual_Pump_Service_InitialCapacity	Till_Service_InitialCapacity	Pay_at_Pump_Service_InitialCapacity	Drive_Aways	Profit (... ▾	Till_NumberInQ
☑ 014	Comple...	6	6 of 6	5	3	3	3.66667	6408.33	1.25884
☑ 017	Comple...	6	6 of 6	6	3	3	1.5	6316.67	1.10978
☑ 012	Comple...	6	6 of 6	5	3	4	1.83333	6283.33	1.32013
☐ 007	Comple...	6	6 of 6	5	3	2	8.33333	6250	0.963737
☑ 005	Comple...	6	6 of 6	5	3	5	1.83333	6208.33	1.32051
☑ 020	Comple...	6	6 of 6	6	3	4	1	6125	1.03637
☑ 013	Comple...	6	6 of 6	5	3	6	1.5	6116.67	1.31997
☐ 019	Comple...	6	6 of 6	4	3	3	6	5975	0.701907
▸ ☐ 001	Comple...	6	6 of 6	4	3	4	6.83333	5975	0.813824
☑ 003	Comple...	6	6 of 6	6	3	6	0.833333	5933.33	1.04119
☐ 016	Comple...	6	6 of 6	3	3	3	16.6667	5858.33	0.197023
☐ 018	Comple...	6	6 of 6	3	3	4	16	5791.67	0.182059
☐ 023	Comple...	6	6 of 6	4	3	6	6.83333	5775	0.813824
☐ 008	Comple...	7	7 of 7	3	3	6	13.5714	5678.57	0.190036
☐ 021	Comple...	6	6 of 6	3	3	2	20	5466.67	0.154195
☐ 022	Comple...	6	6 of 6	2	3	4	38.1667	4625	0.0086065
☐ 015	Comple...	6	6 of 6	2	3	2	48.1667	4600	0.0136245
☐ 004	Comple...	6	6 of 6	2	3	3	40.6667	4600	0.00743333
☐ 010	Comple...	6	6 of 6	2	3	5	37.8333	4500	0.00883776
☐ 009	Comple...	7	7 of 7	1	3	4	71.5714	3121.43	0
☐ 002	Comple...	6	6 of 6	1	3	2	76.1667	3033.33	0
☐ 011	Comple...	8	8 of 8	1	3	5	71	3000	0
☐ 006	Comple...	8	8 of 8	1	3	6	71	2900	0

Figure 10B.11 OptQuest optimisation results

list. Additional properties will appear relating to the OptQuest for Simio in the Properties Window. Click on each of the Control Name tabs in turn and set the upper bounds (maximum value) for the pumps to 6 and for the payment till to 4 as specified for the experiment (figure 10B.9).

For the responses, select the Objective as maximise for the profit response (figure 10B.10).

With the Personal Edition of Simio, the optimisation is limited to 2 controls and 2 constraints and a maximum of 20 scenarios run. To work within these limits, set the default value for the Till_Service_InitialCapacity parameter to 3. Select the Till_Service_InitialCapacity control and select the No option for inclusion in the optimisation. Run the optimisation by selecting the Design tab on the ribbon and clicking on the run arrow. The analysis that is displayed when the 20 scenarios are run is shown in figure 10B.11.

The graph shows the best solution found as the optimisation software worked through 20 scenarios. The scenarios are displayed in order of profit maximisation. The optimum scenario that maximises profit is found to be a mix of 5 manual pumps, 3 pay pumps and 3 payment tills, giving a profit of £6,408 for that day. This was achieved by meeting both constraints in terms of keeping drive aways to no more than 5 on that day (3.67) and the payment till queue size to no more than 5 customers (1.26).

10C: Simul8 Scenario Analysis

Introduction

This chapter covers scenario analysis using the Simul8 simulation software. Systems are compared using the visual inspection of confidence interval graphs and the use of a paired t-test.

Simul8 Comparison of Confidence Interval Analysis

In chapter 9C, in order to undertake a confidence interval analysis of a single model, we made changes to the double-queue bank clerk model to make it a 'true' terminating system. Here, we will compare the performance of the double-queue system to the single-queue bank clerk system, so we need to repeat the changes to the double-queue system for the single-queue system. To do this, load the single-queue bank clerk simulation (see chapter 7C) into Simul8. From the start point menu, select the Constraints button and enter 480 for the limit of the duration of arriving work items. Select the Trials/Results Collection Period option from the menu, and enter 510.

To export the simulation results, create a new spreadsheet file in Excel. The quickest way to export the 'time in the system' measure is to run the model and click on the relevant block (End block) and select the results button. Click on the histogram icon, and a graph will be displayed in a new window. Right-click on the graph and select the copy to clipboard option from the pull-down menu. Go to Excel and paste the values on the sheet. The simulation time and 'time in the system' measures will be displayed in the spreadsheet.

To export any performance measure, select the Export Results button from the home menu and select the Export to Excel option. Click on the browse button and locate a spreadsheet file you have created. Enter a sheet name which matches a sheet name in the spreadsheet, such as sheet1. Tick on the Every Run box in the exports results section (figure 10C.1).

We can undertake a paired t-test using the Data Analysis option on the Data menu in Excel. If the Data Analysis option does not appear, it should be available as an add-in from the options menu. Select the t-test: Paired Two Sample for Means option from the list. The t-test menu appears (figure 10C.2). Select the mean 'time in the system' values (previously exported to an Excel sheet) for each of the 5 runs for the double-queue simulation as the variable 1 range. Select the single-queue values for the variable 2 range. Enter the alpha value as 0.1 and enter a cell for the top-left of the range of cells in which the results will appear.

The results are shown in figure 10C.3. From figure 10C.3, the t stat value of 3.256 is greater than the t critical value (two-tail) of 2.131, so we reject the null hypothesis and accept there is a difference in the average time in the system for each scenario.

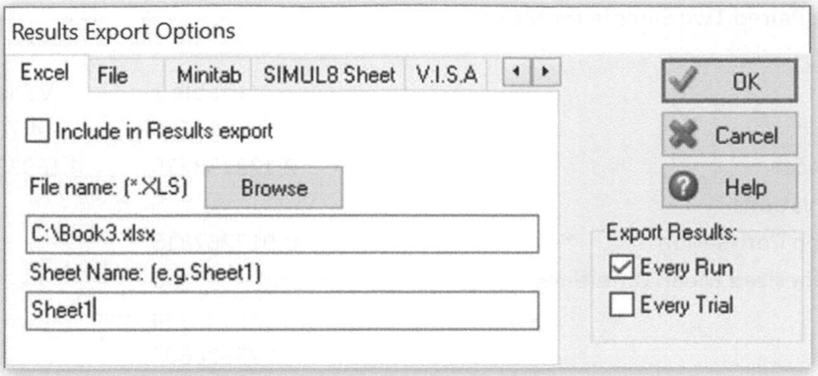

Figure 10C.1 Exporting results to a spreadsheet file

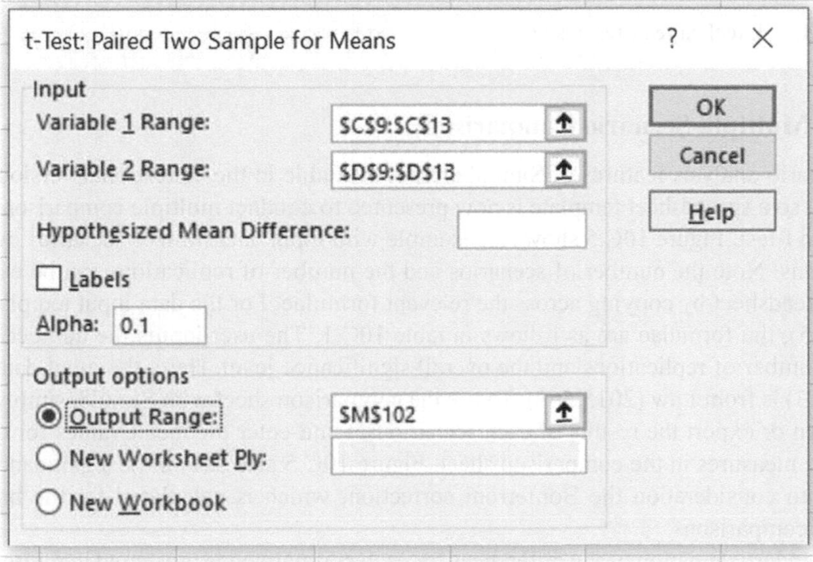

Figure 10C.2 t-test menu

Alternatively, we undertake a comparison of the paired t confidence intervals (figure 10C.4). More details on the spreadsheet used for this are contained in the next section covering multiple-scenario analysis.

Both methods confirm that the average time in the system for the double-queue simulation is higher than for single-queue simulation. This is to be expected as the available capacity in the double-queue simulation may be wasted if customers are queuing in one queue while the other queue is empty.

t-Test: Paired Two Sample for Means		
	Variable 1	Variable 2
Mean	16.617606	14.766484
Variance	8.122158275	4.169237701
Observations	5	5
Pearson Correlation	0.917267815	
Hypothesized Mean Difference	0	
df	4	
t Stat	3.25626604	
P(T<=t) one-tail	0.015595276	
t Critical one-tail	1.533206274	
P(T<=t) two-tail	0.031190553	
t Critical two-tail	2.131846786	

Figure 10C.3 Excel paired t-test results

Simul8 Multiple-Scenario Comparison

The scenario analysis features of Simul8 are not available in the educational version of the software, so a spreadsheet template is now presented to conduct multiple comparisons using the paired t-test. Figure 10C.5 shows an example with input data for five scenarios over five replications. Note the number of scenarios and the number of replications can be extended in the spreadsheet by copying across the relevant formulae. For the data input template (figure 10C.5), the formulae are as follows in table 10C.1. The user inputs the number of scenarios, number of replications and the overall significance level. Here, the input data (from C9 to G13) is from Law (2015:561). To use the comparison sheet with Simul8, simply either note down or export the results of each scenario run and enter the mean values for the performance measures in the comparison sheet. Figure 10C.5 also shows the significance level taking into consideration the Bonferroni correction, which is calculated for the base and pairwise comparisons.

The standard deviation of the differences for each comparison is presented in figure 10C.6.

For the calculation of the standard deviation of the differences to base (figure 10C.6), the formulae are in table 10C.2.

The paired t confidence intervals for the comparison to base and incorporating the Bonferroni correction are shown in the template in figure 10C.7. The rules for interpreting the paired t comparison at the specified confidence level (say 95%) are as follows:

- If the confidence interval is completely above zero, the true mean of scenario A is greater than the true mean of scenario B.
- If the confidence interval includes zero, then the true mean of scenario A is not statistically different from the true mean of scenario B.
- If the confidence interval is completely below zero, the true mean of scenario A is less than the true mean of scenario B.

▲	A	B	C	D
1	SCENARIOS	2		
2	REPLICATIONS	5		
3	SIGNIFICANCE (OVERALL)	0.90		
4	BONFERRONI CORRECTION			
5	α (BASE)	0.100		
6	α (PAIRWISE)	0.100		
7			SCENARIOS	
8	REPLICATIONS		S1 (BASE)	S2
9		1	13.319	12.023
10		2	15.906	13.910
11		3	20.641	17.617
12		4	15.043	15.068
13		5	18.179	15.214
14		6		
59				
60	MEAN		16.618	14.766
61	ST. DEV.		2.850	2.042
62	VARIANCE		8.122	4.169
63	HALF WIDTH		2.717	1.947
64	**Mean and Standard Deviation Differences (Comparison to B**			
65			S2	
66	MEAN DIFFERENCE	S1	1.851	
67	ST. DEV. DIFF.	S1	1.271	
68				
69	**Paired-t Confidence Intervals for Mean Differences (Bonferr**			
70			S2	
71	CONFIDENCE INTERVAL	S1	0.64	3.06
72				
73	**Paired-t Confidence Intervals Comparisons (Bonferroni Cor**			
74			S2	
75		S1	S1>S2	

Figure 10C.4 Paired t-test confidence intervals

◢	A	B	C	D	E	F	G
1	SCENARIOS	5					
2	REPLICATIONS	5					
3	SIGNIFICANCE (OVERALL)	0.90					
4	BONFERRONI CORRECTION						
5	α (BASE)	0.025					
6	α (PAIRWISE)	0.010					
7			SCENARIOS				
8	REPLICATIONS		S1 (BASE)	S2	S3	S4	S5
9		1	126.970	118.210	120.770	131.640	141.090
10		2	124.310	120.220	129.320	137.070	143.860
11		3	126.680	122.450	120.610	129.910	144.300
12		4	122.660	122.680	123.650	129.970	141.720
13		5	127.230	119.400	127.340	131.080	142.610
14		6					
59							
60	MEAN		125.570	120.592	124.338	131.934	142.716
61	ST. DEV.		2.000	1.939	3.903	2.964	1.366
62	VARIANCE		4.001	3.761	15.234	8.787	1.866
63	HALF WIDTH		3.127	3.032	6.101	4.634	2.135

Figure 10C.5 Input data for five scenarios

Table 10C.1 Cell Formulae for Multiple Comparisons Using the Paired t-Test

Cell	Formula	Description
B1		Scenarios
B2		Replications
B3		Overall significance (0 → 1)
B5	=(1-B3)/(B1-1)	Significance (base)
B6	=(1-B3)/(B1*(B1-1)/2)	Significance (pairwise)
C9:G58		Data for up to 50 replications and for up to five scenarios
C60 → G60	=AVERAGE(C9:C58)	Mean
C61 → G61	=STDEV.S(C9:C58)	Standard deviation
C62 → G62	=C61*C61	Variance
C63 → G63	=T.INV.2T($B$5,$B$2–1)*C$61/SQRT($B$2)	Half-width

114			ST. DEV DIFFERENCES (BASE)			
115	REPLICATIONS		S1-S2	S1-S3	S1-S4	S1-S5
116		1	14.304	24.681	2.870	9.157
117		2	0.789	38.963	40.909	5.779
118		3	0.560	23.406	9.822	0.225
119		4	24.980	4.937	0.895	3.663
120		5	8.134	1.801	6.320	3.119
121		6				
166						
167	ST. DEV. DIFFERENCE		3.492	4.842	3.899	2.342

Figure 10C.6 Calculation of the standard deviation differences for comparison to base

Table 10C.2 Formulae for the Calculation of the Standard Deviation of the Differences

Cell	Formula	Description
B116 → E120	=($C9-D9-C$66)*($C9-D9-C$66)	Std. dev. differences calculation
B167 → E167	=SQRT(SUM(B116:B165)/($B$2–1))	

64	Mean and Standard Deviation Differences (Comparison to Base)				
65			S2	S3	S4	S5
66	MEAN DIFFERENCE	S1	4.978	1.232	-6.364	-17.146
67	ST. DEV. DIFF.	S1	3.492	4.842	3.899	2.342
68						
69	Paired-t Confidence Intervals for Mean Differences (Bonferroni Correction) (Comparison to Base)					
70			S2	S3	S4	S5
71	CONFIDENCE INTERVAL	S1	-0.48 10.44	-6.34 8.80	-12.46 -0.27	-20.81 -13.48
72						
73	Paired-t Confidence Intervals Comparisons (Bonferroni Correction) (Comparison to Base)					
74			S2	S3	S4	S5
75		S1	no diff	no diff	S1<S4	S1<S5

Figure 10C.7 Comparison to base

Table 10C.3 Formulae for the Comparison to Base

Cell	Formula	Description
C66, E66, G66, I66	=C60-D60	Mean difference
C67, E67, G67, I67	=B167	St. dev. difference
C71, E71, G71, I71	=$C$66-T.INV.2T($B$5,$B$2–1)*$C$67/SQRT($B$2)	Lower CI
D71, F71, H71, J71	=$C$66+T.INV.2T($B$5,$B$2–1)*$C$67/SQRT($B$2)	Higher CI
C75, E75, G75, I75	=IF(AND(C71<=0,D71>=0),"no diff", IF(C71<0,"S1<S2","S1>S2"))	Comparison to base

114	ST. DEV DIFFERENCES (PAIRWISE)									
115	S1-S2	S1-S3	S1-S4	S1-S5	S2-S3	S2-S4	S2-S5	S3-S4	S3-S5	S4-S5
116	14.304	24.681	2.870	9.157	1.407	4.360	0.572	10.719	3.771	1.774
117	0.789	38.963	40.909	5.779	28.665	30.338	2.298	0.024	14.730	15.936
118	0.560	23.406	9.822	0.225	31.203	15.070	0.075	2.904	28.217	13.018
119	24.980	4.937	0.895	3.663	7.706	16.419	9.511	1.628	0.095	0.937
120	8.134	1.801	6.320	3.119	17.590	0.114	1.179	14.869	9.660	0.560
121										
166										
167	3.492	4.842	3.899	2.342	4.652	4.071	1.846	2.745	3.757	2.838

Figure 10C.8 Calculation for the standard deviation of the differences pairwise

Thus in figure 10C.7, the confidence intervals are displayed (row 71) with the result of the comparison in row 75.

For the comparison to base (figure 10C.7), the formulae are as in table 10C.3.

For the standard deviation of the differences pairwise (figure 10C.8), the formulae are as in table 10C.4.

The paired t confidence intervals for the pairwise comparison and incorporating the Bonferroni correction are shown in the template in figure 10C.9.

Table 10C.4 Formulae for the Calculation of the Standard Deviation of the Differences

Cell	Formula	Description
G116 → P120	=($C9-D9-C$66)*($C9-D9-C$66)	Std. dev. differences calculation
G167 → P167	=SQRT(SUM(B116:B120)/($B$2-1))	

	A	B	C	D	E	F	G	H	I	J
78	**Mean and Standard Deviation Differences (Pairwise Comparison)**									
79			S2		S3		S4		S5	
80	MEAN DIFFERENCE	S1	4.978		1.232		-6.364		-17.146	
81		S2			-3.746		-11.342		-22.124	
82		S3					-7.596		-18.378	
83		S4							-10.782	
84										
85	ST. DEV. DIFFERENCE	S1	3.492		4.842		3.899		2.342	
86		S2			4.652		4.071		1.846	
87		S3					2.745		3.757	
88		S4							2.838	
89										
90	**Paired-t Confidence Intervals for Mean Differences (Bonferroni Correction) (Pairwise Comparison)**									
91			S2		S3		S4		S5	
92	CONFIDENCE INTERVAL	S1	-2.21	12.17	-8.74	11.20	-14.39	1.66	-21.97	-12.32
93		S2			-13.32	5.83	-19.72	-2.96	-25.93	-18.32
94		S3					-13.25	-1.94	-26.11	-10.64
95		S4							-16.63	-4.94
96										
97	**Paired-t Confidence Intervals Comparisons (Bonferroni Correction) (Pairwise Comparison)**									
98			S2		S3		S4		S5	
99		S1	no diff		no diff		no diff		S1<S5	
100		S2			no diff		S2<S4		S2<S5	
101		S3					S3<S4		S3<S5	
102		S4							S4<S5	

Figure 10C.9 Pairwise comparison

For the pairwise comparison (figure 10C.9), the formulae are as in table 10C.5.

Note that for the results shown in the spreadsheet template, we should check to see if variances are reduced if using the paired t-test. The results show that the comparison S1–S4 to base is significant, but for pairwise, the same comparison has no significant difference. This is due to the different significance levels used for the base and pairwise comparisons.

We can use the graphical method to compare the confidence intervals by inserting an XY graph onto the Excel sheet. To construct the graph, follow these steps:

1   Select the mean values on the sheet you wish to plot (row 60).
2   Select the XY graph type.
3   Select Series in Columns.
4   Select Finish to add the graph to the sheet.
5   Double-click on one of the data points in the graph.
6   On the Format Data Series menu, select the Y Error Bars menu.
7   In Display, select Both.
8   In Error Amount, select Custom.
9   Add and subtract the error bounds using the half-width values from your sheet (row 63).

Table 10C.5 Pairwise Comparison Formulae

Cell	Formula	Description
C80, E80, G80, I80, E81, G81, I81, G82, I82, I83	=C60-D60	Mean difference
C85, E85, G85, I85, E86, G86, I86, G87, I87, I88	=G167	St. dev. difference
C92, E92, G92, I92, E93, G93, I93, G94, I94, I95	=$C$80-T.INV.2T($B$6,$B$2-1)*$C$85/ SQRT($B$2)	Lower CI
D92, F92, H92, J92, F93, H93, J93, H94, J94, J95	$C$80+T.INV.2T($B$6,$B$2-1)*$C$85/ SQRT($B$2)	Higher CI
C99, E99, G99, I99, E100, G100, I100, G101, I101, I102	=IF(AND(C92<=0,D92>=0),"no diff", IF(C92<0,"S1<S2","S1>S2"))	Pairwise comparison

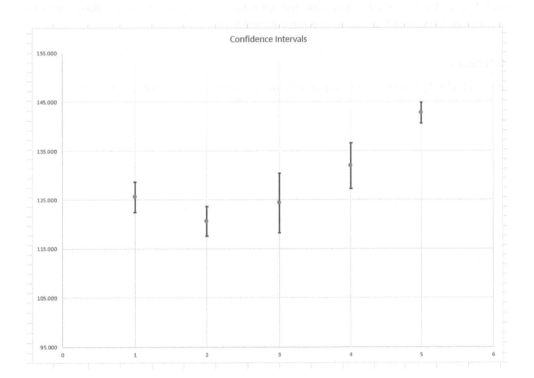

Figure 10C.10 Plot of five confidence intervals

The sheet should be as shown in figure 10C.10.

By observing figure 10C.10. we obtain the following results for the base comparisons using the graphical method:

S1–S2: probably a significant difference
S1–S3: no significant difference
S1–S4: probably a significant difference
S1–S5: a significant difference

This compares to the paired t-test results in row 75.

S1–S2: no significant difference
S1–S3: no significant difference
S1–S4: a significant difference
S1–S5: a significant difference

The difference in results between the graphical method and the paired t-test method reflects that the graphical method has a 'probably' option when the confidence intervals overlap (but not the means).

Simul8 Optimisation

Simul8 uses the OptQuest application for optimisation, but this is not available with the educational version of Simul8, so it is not covered here.

Reference

Law, A.M. (2015) *Simulation Modeling and Analysis*, 5th edition, McGraw-Hill Education.

11 Implementing and Introducing Simulation

This chapter covers the issue of ensuring the implementation of a simulation study and the changes recommended as a consequence of simulation study results. It requires the use of a project management approach in addition to managerial and operational involvement in the implementation. The steps required to introduce a simulation modelling capability in the organisation are discussed.

Simulation Project Management

The use of simulation to address an organisational issue can be approached as a project activity, and the ideas of project management can be employed in order to manage the resources and skills needed to implement a simulation analysis. In order to use simulation successfully, a structured process must be followed. This section aims to show that simulation is more than just the purchase and use of a software package, but a range of skills is required by the simulation practitioner or team. These include project management, client liaison, statistical skills, modelling skills and the ability to understand and map out organisational processes.

Firstly, an important aspect of the project management process is identifying and gaining the support of personnel who have an interest in the modelling process. The simulation developer(s), in addition to the technical skills required to build and analyse the results from a model, must be able to communicate effectively with people in the client organisation in order to collect relevant data and communicate model results. Roles within the project team include the following:

- Client: The sponsor of the simulation project – usually a manager who can authorise the time and expenditure required.
- Model user: A person who is expected to use the model after completion by the modeller. The role of the model user will depend on the planned level of usage of the model. A model user will not exist for a problem definition exercise but will require extended contact with the developer if the model is to be used for ongoing decision-support to ensure all options (e.g. menu option facilities) have been incorporated into the design before handover.
- Data provider: Often, the main contact for information regarding the model may not be directly involved in the modelling outcomes. The client must ensure that the data provider feels fully engaged with the project and is allocated time for liaison and data collection tasks. In addition, the modeller must be sensitive to using the data provider's time as productively as possible.

DOI: 10.4324/9781003124092-11

The simulation project proposal should contain the simulation study objectives and a detailed description of how each stage in the simulation modelling process will be undertaken. This requires a definition of both the methods to be used and any resource requirements for the project. It is important to take a structured approach to the management of the project as there are many reasons why a project could fail. These include the following:

• The simulation model does not achieve the objectives stated in the project plan through a faulty model design or coding.
• Failure to collect sufficient and relevant data means that the simulation results are not valid.
• The system coding or user interface does not permit the flexible use of the model to explore scenarios defined in the project plan.
• The information provided by the simulation does not meet the needs of the relevant decision-makers.

These diverse problems can derive from a lack of communication leading to failure to meet business needs to technical failures, such as a lack of knowledge of statistical issues in experimentation, leading to invalid model results. For these reasons, the simulation project manager must have an understanding of both the business and technical issues of the project.

The project management process can be classified into four areas: estimation, scheduling/planning, monitoring and control, and documentation.

Estimation

This entails breaking down the project into the main simulation project stages (data collection, modelling input data, etc.) and allocating resources to each stage. The time required and skill type of people required along with the requirement for access to resources such as simulation software. These estimates will allow a comparison between project needs and project resources available. If there are insufficient resources available to undertake the project, then a decision must be made regarding the nature of the constraints on the project. A resource-constrained project is limited by resources (i.e. people/software) availability. A time-constrained project is limited by the project deadline. If the project deadline is immovable, then additional resources will need to be acquired in the form of additional personnel (internal or external), overtime or additional software licenses. If the deadline can be changed, then additional resources may not be required as a smaller project team may undertake the project over a longer time period.

Once a feasible plan has been determined, a more detailed plan of when activities should occur can be developed. The plan should take into account the difference between effort time (how long someone would normally be expected to take to complete a task) and elapsed time which takes into account availability (actual time allocated to the project and the number of people undertaking the task) and work rate (skill level) of people involved. In addition, a time and cost specification should be presented for the main simulation project stages. A timescale for the presentation of an interim report may also be specified for a larger project. Costings should include the cost of the analyst's time and software/hardware costs. Although an accurate estimate of the timescale for project completion is required, the analyst or simulation client needs to be aware of several factors that may delay the project completion date.

The most important factor in the success of a simulation project is to ensure that appropriate members of the organisation are involved in the simulation development. The simulation provides information on which decisions are made within an organisational context, so involvement is necessary of interested parties to ensure confidence and implementation of model results. The need for clear objectives is essential to ensure the correct systems components are modelled at a suitable level of detail. Information must also be supplied for the model build from appropriate personnel to ensure important detail is not missing and false assumptions regarding model behaviour are not made. It is likely that during the simulation process, problems with the system design become apparent that require additional modelling and/or analysis. Both analyst and client need to separate between work for the original design and additional activity. The project specification should cover the number of experimental runs that are envisaged for the analysis. Often, the client may require additional scenarios to be tested, which again should be agreed upon at a required additional time/cost.

Scheduling/Planning

Scheduling involves determining when activities should occur. Steps given in the simulation study are sequential, but in reality, they will overlap – the next stage starts before the last one is finished – and are iterative (e.g. validate part of the model, go back and collect more data, model build, validate again). This iterative process of building more detail into the model gradually is the recommended approach but can make judging project progress difficult.

Monitoring and Control

A network plan is useful for scheduling overall project progress and ensuring on-time completion, but the reality of iterative development may make it difficult to judge actual progress.

Documentation

Interim progress reports are issued to ensure the project is meeting time and cost targets. Documents may also be needed to record any changes to the specification agreed by the project team. Documentation provides traceability. For example, data collection sources and content should be available for inspection by users in order to ensure validation. Documentation is also needed of all aspects of the model, such as coding and the results of the simulation analysis.

Project Report

For each simulation study, the simulation model should be accompanied by a project report outlining the project objectives and providing the results of experimentation. Discussion of results and recommendations for action should also be included. Finally, a further work section will communicate to the client any possible developments and subsequent results it is felt could be obtained from the model. If there are a number of results to report, an appendix can be used to document detailed statistical work, for example. This enables the main report to focus on the key business results derived from the simulation analysis. A separate technical document may also be prepared, which may incorporate a model and/or model details, such as key variables and a documented coding listing. Screenshots of the model display can also be used to show model features. The report structure should contain the following elements:

- Introduction
- Description of the Problem Area
- Model Specification
- Simulation Experimentation
- Results
- Conclusions and Recommendations
- Further Studies
- Appendices: Process Logic, Data Files, Model Coding

A good way of 'closing' a simulation project is to organise a meeting of interested parties and present a summary of the project objectives and results. Project documentation can also be distributed at this point. This enables discussion of the outcomes of the project with the client and provides an opportunity to discuss further analysis. This could be in the form of further developments of the current model ('updates' or 'new phase') or a decision to prepare a specification for a new project.

Strengthening the Reporting of Empirical Simulation Studies (STRESS) Guidelines

The STRESS guidelines provide a template for the reporting of empirical simulation studies for DES models (STRESS-DES), ABS models (STRESS-ABS) and SD models (STRESS-SD). Details are provided in Monks et al. (2019).

Project Implementation Plan

It is useful to both the simulation developer and client if an implementation plan is formed to undertake recommendations from the simulation study. Implementation issues will usually be handled by the client, but the simulation developer may be needed to provide further interpretation of results or conduct further experimentation. Changes in the system studied may also necessitate model modification. The level of support at this time from the developer may range from a telephone hotline to further personal involvement specified in the project report. Results from a simulation project will only lead to the implementation of changes if the credibility of the simulation method is assured. This is achieved by ensuring each stage of the simulation project is undertaken correctly.

The Organisational Context of Implementation

A simulation modelling project can use extensive resources both in terms of time and money. Although the use of simulation in the analysis of a one-off decision, such as investment appraisal, can make these costs low in terms of making the correct decision, the benefits of simulation can often be maximised by extending the use of the model over a period of time.

It is thus important that during the project proposal stage, elements are incorporated into the model and the implementation plan that assist in enabling the model to provide ongoing decision support. Aspects include the following:

- Ensure that simulation users are aware at the project proposal stage that the simulation is to be used for ongoing decision support and will not be put to one side once the immediate objectives are met.
- Ensure technical skills are transferred from simulation analysts to simulation users. This ensures an understanding of how the simulation arrives at results and its potential for further use in related applications.
- Ensure communication and knowledge transfer from simulation consultants and industrial engineers to business managers and operational personnel.

The needs of managerial and operational personnel are now discussed in more detail.

Managerial Involvement

The cost associated with a simulation project means that the decision of when and where to use the method will usually be taken by senior management. Thus, an understanding of the potential and limitations of the method is required if correct implementation decisions are to be made.

Operational Involvement

Personnel involved in the day-to-day operation of the decision area need to be involved in the simulation project for a number of reasons. They usually have a close knowledge of the operation of the process and thus can provide information regarding process logic, decision points and activity durations. Their involvement in validating the model is crucial in that any deviations from operational activities seen from a managerial view to the actual situation can be indicated. The use of process maps and a computer-animated simulation display both provide a means of providing a visual method of communication of how the whole process works (as opposed to the part certain personnel are involved in) and facilitates a team approach to problem-solving by providing a forum for discussion.

Simulation can be used to develop involvement from the operational personnel in a number of areas. It can present an ideal opportunity to change from a top-down management culture and move to greater involvement from operational personnel in change projects. Simulation can also be a strong facilitator for communicating ideas up and down an organisation. Engineers, for example, can use simulation to communicate reasons for taking certain decisions to operational personnel who might suggest improvements. The use of simulation as a tool for employee involvement in the improvement process can be a vital part of an overall change strategy. The process orientation of simulation provides a tool for analysis of processes from a cross-functional as opposed to a departmental perspective.

It is important to remember that the use of a simulation model in a business context is to support decision-makers in the organisation by providing descriptive, predictive and prescriptive analysis. To be successful in this role, the simulation model developer should ensure the steps in the simulation development, such as data collection, model building and experimentation, are undertaken well but should also remember that the end purpose of the study should lead to the implementation of a decision. From the perspective of simulation used for decision-making:

- The decision-maker will need to recognize a problem and the ability of simulation to provide insight that can lead to a better decision.
- The decision-maker will be most interested in the usefulness of the model for decision-making rather than the sophistication of the model itself.
- The simulation model should meet the needs of the decision-maker in terms of providing them with confidence in its results and have been developed in a cost-effective manner.
- Confidence in the model from a decision-maker's perspective will be focused on comparing its behaviour to the real-world system more than on statistical tests of validity.
- The cost-effectiveness of the simulation will be judged by comparing the cost of development of the model with the importance of the decision.
- The model developer must be able to explain the model results clearly and simply to the decision-maker avoiding excessive use of jargon and statistical references.
- The decision-maker will use the model results in combination with their own experience and intuition when making the decision.

Case Study: Simulation in the Organisation

The study concerns an autonomous division of a major UK-based manufacturer of railway rolling stock and equipment. The plant manufactures a range of bogies, which are the supporting frame and wheelsets for rail vehicles. The company has a history of supplying the passenger train market in the UK, but over a period of time, low demand and increased competition had led it to enter new markets, including European inner-city transport and the supply of freight bogies to Far East countries. The need to compete on a global basis led the company to re-evaluate its manufacturing facility with particular emphasis on the need to increase output, reduce lead times and increase flexibility. To meet these demands, management had identified areas where substantial investment was required. The focus of the study was on the product layout design, with the main objective being to ensure that the performance of the whole manufacturing system would meet the required output levels. The output level was converted into a target cycle time (i.e. the time between the manufacture of products or output rate). The product layout consists of six main stages, with the product passing through each stage in turn. This means that the effective cycle time for the whole system is determined by the stage with the longest cycle time. The simulation study was to ensure that any investment in a particular production stage would not be nullified by a longer cycle time elsewhere. The simulation would provide an analysis tool to signal any process improvement activities needed before the installation took place. The objective was to obtain a balanced line (i.e. all cycle times equal), which would enable smooth parts to flow through the production stages. This would facilitate the introduction of a pull-type just-in-time (JIT) production control system to replace the present push materials requirement planning (MRP) make-to-stock system.

The project team for the study included the production manager, an industrial engineer, an internal consultant (from another site) with some experience in simulation, and the author acting as an external consultant. In the event that the objectives had been agreed upon, most contact was made between the author and the industrial engineer based at the facility. Information was supplied by the industrial engineer on components flows, setup and process times and other relevant information. Most of the data was gathered from the MRP control system in use.

It was clear that the simulation model achieved its aim in terms of providing a tool for management in improving system operation before the introduction of the proposed machinery. However, within the case company, there was a lack of awareness of the potential benefits of simulation, which are discussed in the following sections.

Use as a One-Off Project

The research found that there was still a perception among the industrial engineers and management involved in the project that the simulation study was a one-off project. Once the simulation was used and the decision made regarding the introduction of machinery, the simulation model was put to one side. On questioning whether there would be any further use for the model, one manager said that 'the simulation had done its job and paid for itself'. There was no attempt by any of the project group to see if the simulation model could be extended and used in another area or as part of the training and education process. It was seen as a decision-making tool, and once the decision was made, then it was redundant.

Expertise Transfer

The lack of awareness of the scope of the method was found to be connected to other findings within the case study. In particular, the lack of technical skills and understanding in applying and interpreting the results of the simulation. The author acted as a consultant on the model-building stage of the project and was surprised at the lack of understanding of the simulation method. Only the internal consultant had some knowledge, but he was situated on a different site. The project group seemed unwilling to try and learn how simulations worked, and instead of training and educating their own staff with the necessary skills which could be drawn upon at any time, they preferred the use of consultants. This has a number of effects in not only achieving a superficial understanding of the simulation process but a lack of appreciation of the potential for simulation in other areas. Without understanding it, they will not be able to adopt it, for example, in the training area of the change process. This is combined with the observation that even those who do know how to use simulation become experts within a technically oriented environment. This means that those running the business do not fully understand the method, which could impact their decision to use it or go with the decisions. Thus, the point of using simulation as a decision-making tool for managers is becoming lost within the computerised technical sphere of a small number of individuals.

Communication Tool

A further finding from the case study was the lack of involvement from the shop floor in the development of the simulation model and the subsequent decision. The company was going through a period of organisational change, not only in the way they manufactured the product but also in their approach towards human resources. They were attempting to move away from adversarial labour relations with a multi-union site to a single union agreement and a reorganisation of the management hierarchy to a much flatter system with managers reporting directly to the managing director. Within this context of change, the company could have used the simulation project to develop involvement from the shop floor in a number of areas. When requiring information on the current configuration of machinery, the industrial engineers and management were not inclined to ask the shop floor. If they were unsure, a guess was made between the group rather than approach those on the shop floor. Although this probably reflects the traditional nature of the organisation, it was an ideal opportunity in the current climate of change to break the traditional mould and move to shop floor input on the project. Simulation can be a strong facilitator for communicating ideas up and down an organisation. Engineers, for example, could have used the simulation to communicate the reasons for taking certain decisions to shop-floor personnel who might suggest improvements. Thus, the use of simulation as a tool for employee involvement in the improvement process could be a vital part of the overall change strategy.

Extract from Greasley (2004)

Determining the Level of Usage of the Simulation Model

The objective of the simulation method is to aid decision-making by providing a forum for problem definition and providing information on which decisions can be made. Thus, a simulation project does not necessarily require a completed computer model to be a success. However, for many complex and interacting systems (most business systems), the model will be able to provide useful information which will aid the decision-making process. The focus of the simulation project implementation will be dependent on the intended usage of the model as a decision-making tool (table 11.1). As the level of usage moves from a stand-alone to an integrated tool for decision-making, the focus moves towards a data-driven approach that allows for real-time and adaptable models.

The level of usage categories are defined as follows.

Table 11.1 Levels of Usage of a Simulation Model

	Level of Usage				
	Problem Definition	Demonstration	Scenarios	Ongoing Decision Support	Real-Time Integrated
Level of development	Process map	Animation	Experimentation	Decision support system	Ongoing decision support
Level of interaction	None	Simple menu	Menu	Extended menu	Automated
Level of integration	None	Stand-alone	Stand-alone Excel files	Integrated with Company database	Fully integrated as a digital twin
Analytic outcome	None	Descriptive	Predictive and prescriptive	Predictive and prescriptive	Predictive and prescriptive

Problem Definition

One of the reasons for using the simulation method is that its approach provides a detailed and systematic way of analysing a problem in order to provide information on which a decision can be made. It is often the case that ambiguities and inconsistencies are apparent in the understanding of a problem during the project proposal formulation stage. It may be that the process of defining the problem may provide the decision-makers with sufficient information on which a decision can be made. In this case, model building and quantitative analysis of output from the simulation model may not be required. The outcome of this approach will be a definition of the problem and possibly a process map of the system.

Demonstration

Although the decision-makers may have an understanding of system behaviour, it may be that they wish to demonstrate that understanding to other interested parties. This could be to internal personnel for training purposes or to external personnel to demonstrate the capability to perform to an agreed specification. The development of an animated model provides a powerful tool for communicating the behaviour of a complex system over time. An example of this could be a train manufacturer who is bidding for the manufacture of a number of train carriages. Associated with this contract is the delivery of a train maintenance service. If the company has experience in train manufacture, then they can demonstrate this to the client. If the company have no experience in delivering train maintenance operations, then they can develop a simulation of a proposed train maintenance operation with animation to demonstrate the capability to the client. These models are associated with a descriptive capability to help in understanding.

Scenarios

The next level of usage involves the development of a model and experimentation in order to assess system behaviour over a number of scenarios. The model is used to solve a number of predefined problems but is not intended for future use. For this reason, the use of a menu system allowing change to key variables is appropriate. The simulation may use internal data files or limited use of external data held in spreadsheets. These models are associated with a predictive capability for scenario analysis and if used to direct action with a prescriptive capability.

Ongoing Decision Support

This option provides decision support for a number of problems over time and requires that the model be adapted to provide assistance to new scenarios as they arise. An extended menu system will need to provide the ability to change a range of variables for ongoing use. The level of data integration may require links to company databases to ensure the model is using the latest version of data over time. Animation facilities should be developed to assist in understanding cause-and-effect relationships and the effect of random events such as machine breakdowns. The technical hardware and software capability issues relevant to an integrated system need to be addressed at the project proposal stage to ensure a successful implementation. If it is envisaged that the client will perform modifications to the simulation model after delivery, then the issue of model reuse should be addressed. Reuse issues include ensuring detailed model code documentation is supplied and detailed operating procedures are provided. Training may also be required in model development and statistical methods. In general, this type of simulation will be largely data-driven, with most of the data held external to the model in spreadsheets and company databases. These models are associated with a predictive and prescriptive analytics capability.

Real-Time Integrated

Here the model adapts automatically in response to real-time data. The purpose of these models should be distinguished from a traditional DES application in that they are real-time adaptive models that work on historical and current data to provide a replication of the real system for applications such as digital twins. These models will often be able to direct actions automatically in the real system and are associated with a predictive and a prescriptive analytics capability.

We can also look at the usage of simulation in terms of its relationship with time (figure 11.1). A descriptive simulation using historical data can be used for checking for conformance to a level of performance or used in a demonstration mode to enable learning and understanding of how the system works. Real-time simulations can be used to monitor current performance and provide a copy (i.e. digital twin) of the real system, which can be used for predictive purposes. The most common use for simulation is to predict the future to enable design options to be tested under predicted conditions.

Introducing Simulation in the Organisation

The use of simulation is both a technical issue involving model development and analysis and a process of the implementation of organisational change. This section discusses

Figure 11.1 The role of simulation in the past, present and future

technical issues, such as the selection of simulation software, and organisational issues, such as the selection of personnel and the acquisition of resources required to provide the capability to undertake a simulation project. It is important that the full costs of introducing simulation are considered, including user time and any necessary training activities. The potential benefits of simulation must also be estimated. One of the reasons that simulation is not used more widely is the benefits from making better decisions as a result of a simulation study can be difficult to quantify.

We should be aware that simulation may not always be the appropriate tool. As well as providing a positive cost-benefit analysis, it should be compared to alternative approaches to solving the problem. Solutions such as spreadsheet analysis and the use of analytical methods may be faster and cheaper. It may be that the organisation lacks the infrastructure to provide the necessary data required by the simulation model. Also, some aspects of the organisation, such as human behaviour and social interactions, may be too complex to represent as a model.

The steps in introducing simulation in the organisation are outlined as follows:

1   Select a simulation sponsor.
2   Estimate the benefits of simulation.
3   Estimate the costs of simulation.
4   Select the simulation software.

1. Select a Simulation Sponsor

If the organisation has not utilised the simulation method previously, then it may be necessary to assign a person with responsibility for investigating the relevance and feasibility of the approach. This person will ideally have both a managerial understanding of the process change that simulation can facilitate and knowledge of data collection and statistical interpretation issues which are required for successful analysis. The development of training schemes for relevant personnel should be investigated, so the required mix of skills and experience is present before a project is commenced. It may be necessary to use consultancy experience to guide staff and transfer skills in initial simulation projects.

2. Estimate the Benefits of Simulation

Often the use of simulation modelling can be justified by the benefits accruing from a single project. However, due to the potentially high setup costs in terms of the purchase of simulation software and user training needs, the organisation may wish to evaluate the long-term benefits of the method across a number of potential projects before committing resources to the approach. This assessment would involve the simulation project sponsor and relevant personnel in assessing potential application areas and covering the following points:

- Do potential application areas contain the variability and time-dependent factors which make simulation a suitable analysis tool?
- Do the number and importance of the application areas warrant the investment in the simulation method?
- Is there existing or potential staff expertise and support to implement the method?
- Are sufficient funds available for aspects such as software, hardware, training and user time?

- Is suitable simulation software available which will enable the required skills to be obtained by staff within a suitable timeframe?
- Will sufficient management support in the relevant business areas be forthcoming in the areas of the supply of data and implementation of changes suggested by the method?
- Are there opportunities for integration with other process improvement tools such as activity-based costing (ABC)?
- Does the level of uncertainty/risk in change projects increase the usefulness of simulation as a method to accept change and increase confidence in implementing new practices?

Although not always easy to do, simulation can be treated just like any other investment, and its desirability can be measured by the level of the return on investment (ROI) it can provide. One way to do this is to estimate the potential savings made through analysis of a problem using simulation as opposed to alternatives such as a spreadsheet analysis. When making substantial investment decisions, the detailed information contained in simulation results are likely to prove their worth over the static analysis of a spreadsheet. For example, a client may wish to know the quantity of equipment required when planning a new manufacturing plant to meet a certain output capacity. If each unit of capacity costs £500,000, then a £25,000 expenditure on a simulation to obtain the correct amount of capacity represents a high ROI for simulation. Savings might also be estimated through the reduction in cost elements such as increased staff efficiency or a reduction in the use of inventory. Improvements in other aspects of performance, such as speed and flexibility, will need to be translated into monetary terms in order for the ROI benefit to be estimated.

As well as an ROI calculation, there are other intangible benefits that can be considered. For example, the simulation study process requires a detailed approach to system design that can increase understanding of how the business works, which may lead to improvements. This benefit may be achieved at the conceptual modelling stage without the need to build the simulation model. Another aspect is that the simulation animation facilities can also increase understanding of processes and be used as a marketing tool to demonstrate capability. Even if the simulation results do not lead to changes in policy, the simulation can increase confidence that planned actions will lead to certain outcomes and so can be seen as a risk management tool.

3. Estimate the Costs of Simulation

The main areas to consider in terms of resource requirements when implementing simulation are as follows.

Software

Most simulation software has an initial cost for the package and an additional cost for an annual maintenance contract which supplies technical support and upgrades. It is important to ensure that the latest version of the software is utilised as changes in software functionality can substantially enhance the usability of the software and so reduce the amount of user development time required.

Hardware

Most software runs on a PC under Windows (although software for other operating systems is available). Specifications for PC hardware requirements can be obtained from the software vendors.

Staff Time

This will be the most expensive aspect of the simulation implementation and can be difficult to predict, especially if simulation personnel are shared with other projects. The developer time required will depend on both the experience of the person in developing simulation models, the complexity of the simulation project and the number of projects it is intended to undertake. Time estimates should also factor in the cost of the time of personnel involved in data collection and other activities in support of the simulation team.

Training

To conduct a simulation modelling project successfully, the project team should have skills in the following areas.

General Skills for All Stages of a Simulation Project

- Project management (ensure the project meets time, cost and quality criteria)
- Awareness of the application area (e.g. knowledge of manufacturing techniques)
- Communication skills (essential for the definition of project objectives and data collection and implementation activities)

Skills Relevant to the Stages of the Simulation Study

- Data collection (ability to collect detailed and accurate information)
- Process analysis (ability to map organisational processes)
- Statistical analysis (input and output data analysis)
- Model building (simulation software translation)
- Model validation (ability to critically evaluate model behaviour)
- Implementation (ability to ensure results of the study are successfully implemented)

In many organisations, it may be required that one person acquires all these skills. Because of the wide-ranging demands that will be made on the simulation analyst, it may be necessary to conduct a number of pilot studies in order to identify suitable personnel before training needs are assessed. Training is required in the steps in conducting a simulation modelling study as presented in this text, as well as training in the particular simulation software that is being used. Most software vendors offer training in their particular software package. If possible, it is useful to be able to work through a small case study based on the trainees' organisation in order to maximise the benefit of the training. A separate course of statistical analysis may also be necessary. Such courses are often run by local university and college establishments. Training courses are also offered by colleges in project management and communication skills. A useful approach is to work with an experienced simulation consultant on early projects in order to ensure that priorities are correctly assigned to the stages of the simulation study. A common mistake is to spend too long on the model-building stage before adequate consultation has been made, which would achieve a fuller understanding of the problem situation. The skills needed to successfully undertake a simulation study are varied, and one of the main obstacles to performing simulation in-house is not cost or training but the lack of personnel with the required technical background. This need for technical skills has meant that most simulation project leaders are systems analysts, in-house simulation developers or external consultants rather than people who are closer to the process, such as a shop-floor supervisor. However, the need for process owners to be involved in the simulation study can be important in ensuring ongoing use of the method and that the results of the study are implemented.

4. Selecting the Simulation Software

Historically DES systems were built using general-purpose computer languages, such as FORTRAN, C and C++. Later, languages such as Java were employed, and there are also implementations using the Visual Basic for Applications (VBA) language to employ the method on a spreadsheet platform. There are also a number of specialist computer languages developed specifically for constructing DES models, including SIMAN, SIMSCRIPT, SLAM and GPSS. However, for most applications for decision-making in an organisational setting, the use of Windows-based software, sometimes referred to as Visual Interactive Modelling systems (VIMS), is employed. These software packages include Arena, Simio, AnyLogic, Witness, Simul8 and the Tecnomatix Plant Simulation. These packages are based on the use of graphic symbols or icons which reduce or eliminate the need to code the simulation model. A model is instead constructed by placing simulation icons on the screen which represent different elements of the model. Data is entered into the model by clicking with a mouse on the relevant icon to activate a screen input dialog box. Animation facilities are also incorporated into these packages. For most business applications, these systems are the most appropriate, although the cost of the software package can be high. These systems use graphical facilities to enable fast model development and animation facilities. However, these systems do not release the user from the task of understanding the building blocks of the simulation system or understanding statistical issues.

When selecting simulation software, the potential user can read the software tutorial papers from the Winter Simulation Conference available at www.informs-cs.org/wscpapers. html. Additional information can be obtained from both vendor representatives (especially a technical specification) and established users on the suitability of software for a particular application area.

Vendors of simulation software can be rated on aspects, such as the following:

- Quality of vendor (current user base, revenue, length in business)
- Technical support (type, responsiveness)
- Training (frequency, level, on-site availability)
- Modelling services (e.g. consultancy experience)
- Cost of ownership (upgrade policy, runtime license policy, multi-user policy)

A selection of simulation software supplier details is presented in table 11.2.

Simulation software can be bought in a variety of forms, including single-user copies and multi-user licenses. Some software allows runtime models to be installed on unlicensed machines. This allows the use of a completed model, with menu options that allow the selection of scenario parameters. Runtime versions may not allow any changes to the model code or animation display. It is also possible to obtain student versions (for class use in universities) of software which contain all the features of the fully licensed version but are limited in some way, such as the size of the model or have disabled save or print functions.

Simulation is associated with planning and scheduling software. Here, schedules can be analysed using a probabilistic analysis incorporating variability to estimate the underlying risks associated with the schedule. Risk measures generated can include the probability of meeting defined targets with expected, pessimistic and optimistic results.

Table 11.2 Simulation Software Vendors

Vendor	Software	Web Address
Simul8 Corporation	Simul8	www.simul8.com
Adept Scientific	Micro Saint Sharp	www.adeptscience.co.uk/products/mathsim/microsaint
ProModel Corporation	ProModel	www.promodel.com/products/ProModel
Lanner Group Ltd.	Witness Horizon	www.lanner.com/en-gb/technology/witness-simulation-software.html
Siemens PLM	TecnoMatix	www.plm.automation.siemens.com/global/en/products/tecnomatix/
The AnyLogic Company	AnyLogic	www.anylogic.com
Simio LLC	Simio	www.simio.com
Rockwell Software Inc.	Arena	www.arenasimulation.com

Table 11.3 ABS Vendors

Vendor	Software	Web Address
The AnyLogic Company	AnyLogic	www.anylogic.com
Center for Connected Learning and Computer-Based Modeling (CCL), Northwestern University	Netlogo	https://ccl.northwestern.edu/netlogo
Repast Organization for Architecture and Development (ROAD)	Repast	https://sourceforge.net/projects/repast/files

Table 11.4 SD Vendors

Vendor	Software	Web Address
isee systems	Stella	www.iseesystems.com/store/products/stella-simulator.aspx
Ventana Systems, Inc.	Vensim	https://vensim.com

Commercial software includes Dropboard (by Systems Navigator, www.systemsnavigator.com/dropboard) and Planning and Scheduling with Simio Enterprise (by Simio LLC, www.simio.com/software/production-scheduling-software.php).

Tools such as Visio (by Microsoft, www.microsoft.com) can be used to develop the simulation process map, which can then be imported into simulation software such as Arena or Simio to form the basis of the simulation model. Tools such as AutoCAD (www.autodesk.co.uk) can be used to create background schematics and drawings that can be imported into simulation software such as Arena and Simio. There is also optimisation software associated with simulation. Of the commercial software available, one of the most popular is the OptQuest software (by OptTek Systems Inc., www.opttek.com).

Hybrid Simulation involves the use of DES with either or both ABS and SD software (see chapter 12). For hybrid simulation, the following ABS (table 11.3) and SD vendors (table 11.4) are provided.

Hybrid modelling involves the use of DES with other analytic techniques (see chapter 13). For hybrid modelling a selection of process mining software that has been used with

Table 11.5 Process Mining Software Vendors

Vendor	Software	Web Address
Open-Source (Eindhoven University of Technology)	ProM	www.promtools.org
Fluxicon BV	DISCO	https://fluxicon.com/disco
Minit	Minit	www.minit.io

Table 11.6 Machine Learning Software Vendors

Vendor	Software	Web Address
RapidMiner	RapidMiner	https://rapidminer.com
IBM	IBM SPSS Modeler	www.ibm.com/products/spss-modeler
MathWorks	MatLab	https://uk.mathworks.com/products/matlab.html
Open-Source (R Foundation)	R	www.r-project.org
Viscovery	Viscovery SOMine	www.viscovery.net/somine
Open-Source (University of Waikato)	Massive Online Analysis (MOA)	https://moa.cms.waikato.ac.nz

simulation is provided in table 11.5 and a selection of machine learning software that has been used with DES is provided in table 11.6.

Summary

This chapter has covered project management for a simulation study. The steps required to introduce a simulation modelling capability in the organisation have been described.

Exercises

- Search the web at the addresses given for simulation vendors and evaluate their claims for simulation.
- List the stakeholders involved in a simulation project and write a brief description of their roles.
- What benefits and disadvantages does each of the following simulation usage levels provide?

  - Problem definition
  - Demonstration simulation
  - Stand-alone scenario simulation
  - Ongoing decision support system
  - Real-time integrated digital twin

- Develop a simulation project plan for the analysis of a telephone call centre.
- The simulation modeller needs to take into account the needs of management and operational personnel to ensure successful project implementation. What are these needs?

- Discuss the advantages and disadvantages of employing a specialist simulation modeller or conducting simulation studies using end-user personnel.

References

Greasley, A. (2004) The case for the organisational use of simulation, *Journal of Manufacturing Technology Management*, 15(7), 560–566.

Monks, T., Currie, C.S.M., Onggo, B.S., Robinson, S., Kunc, M. and Taylor, S.J.E. (2019) Strengthening the reporting of empirical simulation studies: Introducing the STRESS guidelines, *Journal of Simulation*, 13(1), 55–67.

12 Hybrid Simulation
(Combining DES, ABS and SD)

Introduction

Chapter 1 covered the main simulation methods of discrete-event simulation (DES), agent-based simulation (ABS) and system dynamics (SD). In many circumstances, it may be that one of these methods is appropriate to address a problem situation. The decision on which method to use will be determined by the experience and preferences of the modeller, as well as the problem situation to be addressed. It may also be appropriate to use a combination of these methods. This chapter covers different design options for combining these methods and then examines their characteristics to show when they might be applied to a particular problem situation.

Defining Hybrid Simulation

There are many definitions of hybrid simulation, but here, we take a broad view of hybrid simulation as the use of multiple SD, DES and ABS models and/or multiple SD, DES and ABS methods that are used for different aspects of the same simulation study. This definition is based on Morgan et al. (2017), who define the use of a combination of DES and SD. The different modes of interaction between DES and SD, which here are extended to include ABS, are presented in table 12.1.

Isolationism is the use of a single method and model, such as a DES model. The remaining five design options are categorised under the hybrid simulation approach. A parallel design uses more than one of the SD, DES and ABS models to provide complementary insight into the same system under investigation. A sequential design covers studies when the use of one model, such as an SD model, is followed by the use of an additional model, such as a DES model, when it was decided that more detailed modelling was required in a particular area of the system. An enrichment design is when a base model is enriched with elements of a second method. An example is using SD to model continuous processes within a DES model. An interaction design is when two models using different methods exchange data between them. An integration design is when more than one method is applied in the same model and to the same problem situation, producing a single model with characteristics of both methods.

Characteristics of SD, DES and ABS

SD, DES and ABS are covered in chapter 1. Here, table 12.2 provides a review of the characteristics of the simulation methods of DES, SD and ABS to provide a guide to their individual

DOI: 10.4324/9781003124092-12

Table 12.1 Hybrid Simulation Designs (Adapted from Morgan et al., 2017)

Design	Hybrid Simulation					
	Isolationism	*Parallel*	*Sequential*	*Enrichment*	*Interaction*	*Integration*
View	Single view of system	Two possible representations of the same system	Need to capture different parts/ behaviours of the same system	Need to capture different parts/ behaviours of the same system	Need to capture different parts/ behaviours of the same system	Need to capture different parts/ behaviours of the same system
Justification	Tried, tested and trusted methodology	Complementary insight into the system to reveal a plausible explanation of behaviour	Allows for emergent insights as knowledge of the system improves	Benefit from characteristics of a second method without a second model	Capture interactive influences within the system while being grounded in each method	Capture interactive influences; present one concise and coherent view
Models/Methods	1 / 1	More than 1 / more than 1	More than 1 / 1 or more	1 / more than 1	More than 1 / more than 1	1 / more than 1
Comments	Modeller should remain open to adopting another method as the project progresses	Same system modelled by each method (at least 2) for complementary insight	Each part captures different parts of the system or at a different level of detail	Frequency of interaction and whether it is triggered or regular depends on the master method	Models developed can operate independently but work together to contribute to the problem	Methods function together as a single model

Table 12.2 Characteristics of System Dynamics, Discrete-Event Simulation and Agent-Based Simulation

Factor	System Dynamics	Discrete-Event Simulation	Agent-Based Simulation
Purpose	Investigate patterns of behaviour in systems	Investigate operational performance of processes	Directly represent agents and their behaviour
Determination of Behaviour (Emergence)	Feedback: System behaviour determined by feedback and accumulation structures	Structure: System behaviour determined by the stochastic nature and interdependency of processes	Individual actions: System behaviour determined by the interaction of autonomous components
Aggregation Level	The system can be modelled with elements aggregated into flows.	Each element can be modelled with a set of attributes.	Each element can be modelled with a set of attributes and operations.
Conceptual Model Notation Representation	Influence diagram, causal loop diagrams, stocks and flows	Process flow diagram, activity diagram, entities and resources	State charts, Unified Modelling Language (UML), agents
Presentation of Results	Statistics showing system performance; plots showing behaviour patterns and feedback loops	Statistics showing system performance; animation showing individual process routing	Statistics showing system performance; visualisations and animations of individual elements
Software Tool	Stella, iThink, Vensim	Simio, Arena, Simul8	AnyLogic, NetLogo, Repast
Software Coding	Flow diagrams	Visual interactive modelling interface	Java, NetLogo

and combined application. For an overview of current trends in the application of hybrid simulation to the design and operation of manufacturing systems, see Mourtzis (2020).

- In terms of *purpose*, SD aims to investigate the patterns of behaviour in the system. DES is focused on the operational performance of processes in terms of flow rate and flow time. ABS is focused on representing individual agent behaviour and how that leads to system behaviour.
- In terms of the *determination of behaviour*, SD explains behaviour due to feedback by employing systems theory and emphasises the role of feedback and accumulation structures. DES explains behaviour due to uncertainty by combining an explanatory modelling approach in the mapping of interdependent processes with a descriptive modelling approach in describing the stochastic nature of systems. ABS explains behaviour due to emergence by describing the interaction of autonomous components.
- In terms of the *aggregation level*, the difference in the approach of SD, DES and ABS can be demonstrated by an example of a simulation of a new product development process. Here, SD can model the quantity sold during a time period. The discrete-event approach is able to model each customer purchase and thus model individual purchase decisions through the ability of DES to carry information regarding each entity (customer) in the system. ABS could be employed to model individual customer behaviour when making a purchase decision.
- In terms of *conceptual model notation*, each method employs different methods. Influence and causal diagrams map out the relationships in SD, DES employs process flow diagrams and activity diagrams, and ABS employs state charts and other diagramming methods associated with the Unified Modelling Language (UML) standard.
- In terms of *representation*, the SD method models the real system using stocks and flow elements, the main representation in DES are entities and resources, and ABS employs an agent representation. There is, however, a relationship between the concepts of stocks in SD with queues in DES and a relationship between flows in SD with processes in DES. Agents in ABS can be related to entities in DES, which have self-contained decision logic.
- In terms of *presentation of results*, all three methods provide statistical reports and graphical plots of variables over time. DES and ABS generally also provide animation of individual entities or agents.
- In terms of *software tools*, a number are available particularly for DES. AnyLogic provides a tool for hybrid simulation of DES, SD and ABS (figure 12.1). More details of software tools for DES are provided in chapter 11.
- Unlike SD, which employs a flow diagram interface, and DES, which often employs visual interactive modelling systems (VIMS) interface, ABS usually requires *software coding* in either a specialist ABS language, such as NetLogo, or a general-purpose language, such as Java.

Determining the Use of ABS, DES and SD in a Hybrid Simulation

When developing a hybrid simulation, we need to relate the characteristics of the three simulation methods with the characteristics of the system we are modelling. This activity could take place after the overall conceptual model has been developed (i.e. at the modelling stage). However, Eldabi (2021) suggests attempting to establish whether a hybrid simulation model

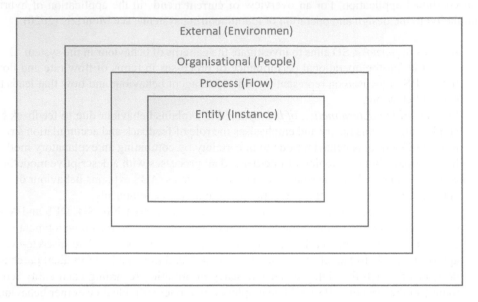

Figure 12.1 Simulation model context levels

may be required or not at an earlier stage of the simulation study and presents a framework which includes the following steps:

- Identify the overall objective of the study: Define the problem situation and objectives and the need for hybridisation.
- Systemic review: Identify characteristics of the system and map them onto the three simulation approaches of SD, DES and ABS. Identify what the simulation modelling requirements are in the different parts of the system leading to specific modules.
- Model conceptualisation for each module: Draw up the conceptual models for each simulation approach within each module.

One way of determining when to use ABS, DES and SD in hybrid simulation is to consider the context level of the process being simulated (figure 12.1). Four main context levels can be defined, moving from a narrow to a wide context. Different simulation approaches are relevant as the context level in the process is expanded from entity to process to organisational to external.

The different context levels and the simulation methods associated with them are now defined.

Entity (Instance)

At the entity level, the consideration is for a single instance of an entity moving through the process, and here, the attributes of the entity are considered. For example, customers (entities) of different customer types (attribute) may take different process flow paths through the process model. This implies we need to define the customer type attribute in our entity definition, but other customer attributes such as customer age may not be in the scope of the model. DES and ABS are associated with modelling at the instance level.

Process (Flow)

At the process level, the consideration is the interaction between the entities in the process. This can be due to the design of the process flow, the nature of arrivals and the resource capacity availability. At the process level, we consider that it is unlikely that a single entity is processed in isolation, but many entities may be moving through the process at the same time. This means that how the entity is processed will be determined by its interaction with other entities, such as the need to share resources. If insufficient resource capacity is available, then inventory may occur. DES is most associated with modelling at the flow level.

Organisational (People)

At this context level, we can take account of business policies and goals which may constrain our process and of people's behaviour in the organisation and how they will impact the process. This includes people's work priorities, skill levels, teamwork and motivation. Thus, at the organisational level, consideration is made that people work on a variety of tasks in different ways and how they organise their work and their productivity will affect how the entity is processed. See the section on using SD, DES and ABS to model people's behaviour for more details on this topic.

External (Environment)

Here, we consider external factors. For an organisational process, this may include customers, suppliers, finance, government actions, weather conditions or any other factors. At the external level, there are a number of factors, such as supplier actions that may affect the process performance. These factors may be within the scope of our model if we are interested in the interactions between organisations, such as in supply chain models. ABS, DES or SD may be used to model environment factors.

Using SD, DES and ABS to Model People's Behaviour

To provide a realistic basis for decision support, people's behaviour may need to be included in simulation studies if they are to be effective tools. Many of the systems that we would like to understand or improve involve human actors, either as customers of the system or as people performing various roles within the system. Modelling passive, predictable objects in a factory or a warehouse, however, is very different from trying to model people. Modelling people can be challenging because people exhibit many traits to do with being conscious sentient beings with free will. Human beings can be awkward and unpredictable in their behaviour, and they may not conform to our ideas about how they should behave in a given situation. This presents a practical challenge to model builders in terms of when and how we represent human behaviour in our simulation models. The use of SD, DES and ABS to model human behaviour is now discussed.

- One method is to model humans as a group which behaves like a flow. The type of simulation used for implementation of the flow method is usually SD, although some DES software is able to model continuous flows. The level of abstraction means that this approach does not possess the ability to carry information about each individual through the system being modelled. This means the simulation of human behaviour in areas such as customer-processing applications in which we would like to measure individual queuing times may not be feasible using this approach.
- One way of modelling human behaviour is to model a person as a resource, such as a unit of equipment that is either 'busy' or 'idle'. In this approach, variations in process durations due to individual performance levels can be modelled. DES is associated with this method. Human performance modelling is implemented using rules governing the behaviour of the attributes of human behaviour. This method is particularly associated with the MicroSaint DES software.
- Finally, we can model how humans actually behave based on individual attributes, such as perception and attention. The approach is where objects are not only self-contained units combining data and functions but are also able to interact with one another. ABS is most associated with modelling people in this way.

More details on this topic can be found in the work of Greasley and Owen (2016).

Implementing Hybrid Simulation

As can be seen from table 12.2, each of the three methods of SD, DES and ABS provides a different modelling perspective, and modellers tend to specialise in one of the three methods. These methodological differences go some way to explaining their different user backgrounds. For example, ABS is widely used for complex systems that we cannot conceptualise well, so we build a model based on our theory of what governs that model (at an individual level) and observe what behaviour emerges from this theory. In DES, we have a firmer definition of how the system operates (at a system level) based on empirical data and wish to observe the system behaviour under future scenarios. Only a minority of simulation practitioners are skilled in more than one of these methods, and thus, one of the aims of hybrid simulation is to encourage simulation education and training to span all three approaches. Hoad and Kunc (2018) provide a case study of teaching SD and DES together.

For all but parallel hybrid simulation design, there is likely to be required a mechanism for data exchange between models. Chapter 13 covers software architectures for the combination of DES and machine learning. These architectures can also be applied to the combined use of DES, SD and ABS. The three main architectures are a manual (offline) interface in which data is transferred between models by saving data to a file such as an Excel spreadsheet. The second architecture is an automated (online) interface of the DES, SD and ABS models, which may allow a real-time exchange of data between the models. Finally, there is the integrated architecture which allows different methods to be used within a single model.

In terms of software tools, the AnyLogic software package provides a multimethod modelling platform that allows the three simulation methods to be combined and is the most

Table 12.3 A Comparison of DES and ABS and the ABS Capability of Simio

DES	ABS	Simio DES (ABS Capability)
A top-down modelling approach focused on the process (flow) level	A bottom-up modelling approach focused on the entity (instance) level	An approach that could be adopted using Simio object modelling
Input modelling primarily based on descriptive modelling using empirical data	Input modelling primarily based on theories of individual behaviour	An approach that could be adopted using Simio object modelling
Algorithms representing decision-making are primarily embedded at the process (flow) level	Algorithms representing decision-making are embedded at the entity (instance) level	The Simio object modelling capability permits algorithms to be embedded at the entity level
Entities flow through a predefined system of queues and resources	System behaviour from the decision-making of individual entities	It is not necessary to model queues within Simio or in a DES model generally (for example, see Robinson, 2015)
Spatial movement of entities is predefined.	Spatial movement is not predefined and can be an important part of the interpretation of model results.	The Simio FreeSpace capability allows spatial movement across x, y, and z axes.

widely used computer simulation package in hybrid simulation (Brailsford et al., 2019). In AnyLogic, there is a clear delineation between the DES, SD and ABS components, and so AnyLogic models are classified as enabling an interaction hybrid simulation design (Brailsford et al., 2019). Another aspect of AnyLogic is that it usually requires Java programming, which may be a barrier to DES modellers only experienced in using VIMS platforms.

A potential software tool for providing a platform for an integrated hybrid simulation design for DES and ABS is Simio which provides an object orientation as its main paradigm (although a process orientation and event orientation are also supported). This means that instead of the traditional approach of having passive entities that are acted upon by the model processes, in Simio, the entities can have intelligence and control their own behaviour (Pegden, 2007). This is a key criterion for an ABS, and if we look at table 12.3, we can see that the Simio DES software provides capabilities in terms of permitting the embedding of algorithms (process logic) within the entity definition and provides a spatial display that permits free movement of entities. These object-oriented capabilities are built into the modelling environment rather than an object-oriented programming environment which means that the skills required to define and add new objects to the system are modelling skills, not programming skills (Pegden, 2007). To demonstrate this capability, Greasley (2019) outlines the implementation of a simple ABS model in Simio (summarised in the boxed text 'Conducting ABS Using the Simio Software Package').

Conducting ABS Using the Simio Software Package

The Simio model for the turtles application consists of 2 source nodes which are used to create the blue turtles and red turtles as separate arrival streams. An Entity object instance is also defined and named as ModelEntity1. One initial batch of turtles is

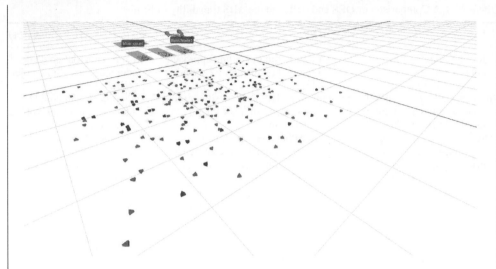

Figure 12.2 Simio DES implementation of ABS turtles model

created at the start of the simulation run and when they enter the BasicNode point, an add-on process is triggered that defines the behaviour of each turtle as it moves around the grid. This defines the actions of the token associated with the entity object that is represented as a turtle in the model. Actions here include placing the turtle on the screen display, moving the turtle from one coordinate to another and procedures for creating and destroying turtles. Turtles are created using the create block which creates an entity object instance which is associated with the entity object that triggered the process. These new turtles automatically inherit their properties from the entity (turtle) that is associated with them. The turtle model implemented using Simio is shown in Figure 12.2. The display shows the model in a 3D view although only movement in 2 planes is defined in this case. The turtles move around the grid by the use of the Travel command which defines a subsequent random location in relation to the current coordinates.

Extract from Greasley, A. (2019)

Summary

This chapter has covered hybrid simulation – the use in combination of two or three of the main simulation methods of DES, ABS and SD. There has been increasing interest in combining SD, DES and ABS and using their different capabilities in a complementary way, and there is a small but growing number of practitioners who express a preference for developing hybrid simulations (Padilla et al., 2018). Possible uses of hybrid simulations include the combination of DES and SD when SD is being used to understand the problem situation or to understand the reasons (causal relationships) that are leading to the DES results. DES and ABS could be combined to benefit from a process flow defined in the DES with the ability of ABS to model individual entity logic (to represent human behaviour, for example).

Exercises

- Compare and contrast the capabilities of DES, SD and ABS.
- What are the advantages and disadvantages of hybrid simulation?
- What are the major barriers to the increased use of hybrid simulation?

References

Brailsford, S.C., Eldabi, T., Kunc, M., Mustafee, N. and Osorio, A.F. (2019) Hybrid simulation modelling in operational research: A state-of-the-art review, *European Journal of Operational Research*, 278, 721–737.

Eldabi, T. (2021) Systemic characteristics to support hybrid simulation modelling, *Proceedings of the 2021 Winter Simulation Conference*, IEEE.

Greasley, A. and Owen, C. (2016) Behavior in models: A framework for representing human behavior, in M. Kunc, J. Malpass, and L. White (eds.) *Behavioral Operational Research: Theory, Methodology and Practice*, Palgrave Macmillan.

Greasley, A. (2019) Simulating Business Processes for Descriptive, Predictive and Prescriptive Analytics, DeGruyter Press.

Hoad, K. and Kunc, M. (2018) Teaching system dynamics and discrete event simulation together: A case study, *Journal of the Operational Research Society*, 69(4), 517–527.

Morgan, J.S., Howick, S. and Belton, V. (2017) A toolkit of designs for mixing discrete event simulation and system dynamics, *European Journal of Operational Research*, 257, 907–918.

Mourtzis, D. (2020) Simulation in the design and operation of manufacturing systems: State of the art and new trends, *International Journal of Production Research*, 58(7), 1927–1949.

Padilla, J.J., Diallo, S.Y., Lynch, C.J. and Gore, R. (2018) Observations on the practice and profession of modeling and simulation: A survey approach, *Simulation*, 94(6), 493–506.

Pegden, C.D. (2007) Simio: A new simulation system based on intelligent objects, *Proceedings of the 2007 Winter Simulation Conference*, 2293–2300.

Robinson, S. (2015) Modelling without queues: Adapting discrete-event simulation for service operations, *Journal of Simulation*, 9(3), 195–205.

13 Hybrid Modelling

(Combining Model-Driven and Data-Driven Analysis)

Introduction

While hybrid simulation is the combined use of the simulation methods of SD, ABS and DES, hybrid modelling can refer to the use of simulation in combination with other analytical methods. Bell et al. (2019) define a hybrid modelling approach as one in which simulation models are extended, utilising methodologies, standards, tools and software from the field of computer science, applied computing, industrial engineering, and data science. This could include the use of simulation in combination with other analytical methods such as data envelopment analysis (DEA) (Greasley, 2005). When examining the relationship between simulation and analytical methods, such as machine learning, we can consider the use of a model-driven approach using simulation compared to data-driven analysis usually associated with the use of large data sets termed big data and computer programs running algorithms to process that data. Understanding the different approaches to the prediction of model-driven and data-driven approaches will help us to understand what each method can and cannot do. This chapter covers model-driven and data-driven perspectives for the analysis of business processes, including the possibility of using these approaches in combination (i.e. hybrid modelling). This chapter also covers the use of simulation to facilitate a digital twin.

Model-Driven Analysis

The approach of simulation modelling is to tackle the prediction problem by the use of a theory (our understanding of how something works) about the problem itself. This involves people deriving a mental model of the problem area that incorporates the underlying structure of how the elements of the problem area fit together. Thus, we define, using our knowledge, the cause-and-effect relationships between the incoming data stream and the predictions.

The main steps in using a model-driven analysis for prediction are shown in figure 13.1. Here, the real world is transformed into a conceptual model, which is then realised as a computer model. The computer model generates data that we can use for prediction.

Model-driven analysis is a way of understanding the world based on a systems approach in which a real system is simplified into its essential elements (its processes) and relationships between these elements (its structure). Thus, in addition to input data, information is required on the system's processes, the function of these processes and the essential parts of the relationships between these processes. These models are called explanatory models as they represent the real system and attempt to explain the behaviour that occurs. This means that the effect of a change on the design of the process can be assessed by changing the structure

DOI: 10.4324/9781003124092-13

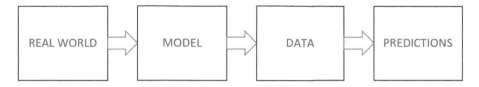

Figure 13.1 Model-driven analysis

of the model. These models generally have far smaller data needs than data-driven models because of the key role of the representation of structure. For example, we can represent a supermarket by the customers that flow through the supermarket and the processes they undertake – collecting groceries and paying at the till. However, most real systems are very complex – a supermarket has many different staff undertaking many processes using differ-ent resources – the collection and unpacking of goods, keeping shelves stocked, heating and ventilation systems and so on. It is usually not feasible to include all the elements of the real system, so a key part of modelling is making choices about which parts of the system should be included in the model in order to obtain useful results. This simplification process may use statistics in the form of mathematical equations to represent real-life processes (such as the customer arrival rate) and a computer program (algorithm) in the form of process logic to represent the sequence of activities that occur within a process. An example of a model-driven analysis method is the approach of simulation modelling covered in this book.

Data-Driven Analysis

The approach of data-driven analysis is to tackle the prediction problem by measurement. A stream of data from the real world is transformed by a mathematical model into a predic-tion of future behaviour. The approach makes associations between the data we have selected and the measures we are trying to predict. Thus, a data-driven analysis approach aims to derive a description of behaviour from observations of a system so that it can describe how that system behaves (its output) under different conditions or scenarios (its input). Because they can only describe the relationship between input and output, they are called descriptive models. One approach is to use pattern recognition as a way to build a model that allows us to make predictions. The idea of pattern recognition is based on learning relationships through examples. Pattern recognition is achieved through methods such as associations, sequences, classification and clustering of the data. These methods are implemented in models that use equations, logical statements and algorithms to find the patterns. In essence, this approach produces a model that imitates real behaviour based on past observations of that behaviour. This imitation can be achieved by defining a relationship that relates model input to model output. Generally, the more data (observations) that can be used to form the description, the more accurate the description will be and thus the interest in big data analytics that uses large data sets.

The main steps in using data-driven analysis for prediction are shown in figure 13.2. Here, the real world is represented as a data set which is then used to create a model (algorithm) that can be used for prediction.

In general terms, there are many analysis methods that can be considered as data-driven methods, including regression analysis, econometric modelling, time-series experiments and

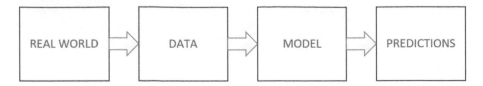

Figure 13.2 Data-driven analysis

yield management. However, data-driven methods considered here are most often associated with big data analytics. These methods relate to those that are used for the analysis of large-scale data sets termed big data. A brief description follows each of the main categories of big-data-driven analytics methods.

Data Mining

In a general sense, data mining can be defined as identifying patterns in complex and ill-defined data sets. Particular data mining methods include the following:

- Identifying associations involves establishing relationships about items that occur at a particular point in time (e.g. what items are bought together in a supermarket).
- Identifying sequences involves showing the sequence in which actions occur (e.g. click-stream analysis of a website).
- Classification involves analysing historical data into patterns to predict future behaviour (e.g. identifying groups of website users who display similar visitor patterns).
- Clustering involves finding groups of facts that were previously unknown (e.g. identifying new market segments of customers or detecting e-commerce fraud).

There are various categories of mining depending on the nature of the data that is being analysed. For example, there is text mining for document analysis and web mining of websites.

Machine Learning

Machine learning (ML) uses an iterative approach for the analysis of data in order to produce an analytical model. This model may be in the form of a mathematical equation, a rule set or an algorithm. Thus, ML does not refer to actual learning by a machine (computer) but the use of algorithms that, through iteration, provide an ability to predict outcomes from a data set. The main steps involved in ML are pre-processing of the data set, creating a training set (usually 80% of the data) and a test set (usually 20% of the data) and selecting a learning algorithm to process the data.

Supervised ML relates to learning algorithms that build models that can be used to make predictions using classification and regression methods, while unsupervised ML relates to identifying similar items using clustering methods. In supervised ML, our training data sets have values for both our input (predictor) and output (outcome) variables that are known to us so that we can use classification methods such as support vector machines (SVMs) and regression methods, such as linear regression, decision trees (DTs) and neural networks for prediction. In unsupervised learning, our training data sets have values for our input (predictor) variables but not for our output (outcome) variables, so this approach involves examining the attributes of a data set in order to determine which items are most similar to one another. This clustering function can be achieved using methods such as K-means algorithms and neural networks.

When compared to simulation, ML can be seen as the construction of a model that predicts outputs from inputs. Supervised learning looks at several input values with associated output values (termed labels), then, through learning, generates a model to predict outputs from inputs. Unsupervised learning looks at several input values of a random input value, then, through, learning generates a model in the form of a probability distribution that predicts outputs from inputs (figure 13.3).

In addition to the categories of supervised and unsupervised ML, reinforcement learning is a subfield of ML that uses learning algorithms that explore options and, when they achieve their aim, deduce how to get to that successful endpoint in the future. A reinforcement approach can be implemented by the use of a reward and penalty system to guide a choice from a number of random options. Simulation is particularly relevant for this type of ML as it can provide a virtual environment in which reinforcement training can take place safely and far quicker than in a real system.

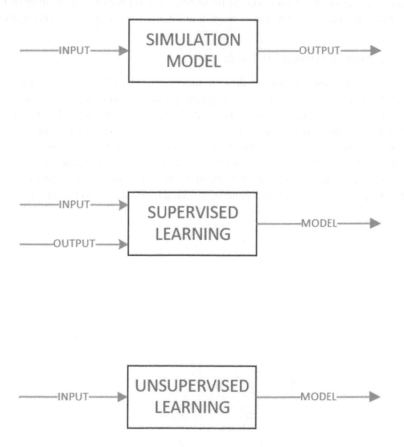

Figure 13.3 Simulation modelling, supervised learning and unsupervised learning

Some examples of ML algorithms used are as follows:

- Association rules mining (ARM) uses a rules-based approach to finding relationships between variables in a data set.
- Decision trees (DT) generate a rule set that derives the likelihood of a certain outcome based on the likelihood of the preceding outcome. DTs belong to a class of algorithms that are often known as CART (classification and regression trees). Random forest DTs are an extension of the DT model in which many trees are developed independently, and each 'votes' for the tree that gives the best classification of outcomes.
- Support vector machines (SVM) are a class of ML algorithms that are used to classify data into one or another category.
- k-Means is a popular algorithm for unsupervised learning that is used to create clusters and thus categorise data.
- Neural networks, or artificial neural networks, represent a network of connected layers of (artificial) neurons. These mimic neurons in the human brain that 'fire' (produce an output) when their stimulus (input) reaches a certain threshold. They have become a popular approach due to the development of the backpropagation algorithm, which makes it possible to train multilayered neural networks. Multilayered neural networks have one or more intermediary ('hidden') layers between the input and output layers to enable a wider range of functions to be learnt. Neural networks with three or more hidden layers are generally known as deep neural networks or deep learning systems.

How Data-Driven Supervised ML Works

Figure 13.4 summarises the role of data in supervised ML. Data is collected and then is processed, which consists of data cleaning and labelling. Labelling can be considered as acquiring input values which are then associated with output values. The data is then split into training data and testing data. Supervised learning tasks are divided into classification (predicting a discrete class label output from an input) and regression (predicting a continuous quantity output from an input). The error in the training set is termed the training error. To check that the model will predict outside of the training data set, we test the model using labelled testing data. This is termed generalisation, and the aim is to minimise the test error.

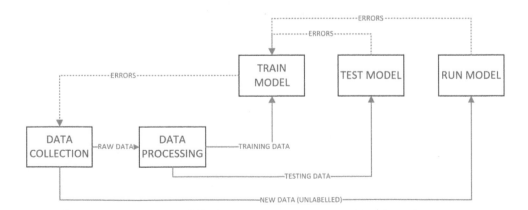

Figure 13.4 Data flow in supervised machine learning

When satisfied, we can run the model on new, unlabelled data. Deployment errors may be corrected by returning to the train model stage. One reason that errors occur in deployment is if, in non-stationary environments, there is a shift in the nature of the data over time. The model can be adapted (retrained) either manually or automatically to take account of this.

Comparing the Stages of Simulation and ML When Using for Decision-Making

A comparison of the stages of simulation and ML is shown in table 13.1. The conceptual modelling process in simulation has a focus on domain knowledge to abstract exploratory and descriptive models from a real-world problem situation. ML requires domain knowledge to choose appropriate types of algorithms and other experimental features such as hyperparameters (values set before the training begins, which has an influence on the eventual parameters, such as coefficients or weights, that are updated from the training process). Data collection in simulation has a focus on collecting quantitative sample data for descriptive modelling and qualitative data for exploratory modelling. In supervised ML, the emphasis is on the collection of relatively large data sets that can be labelled in order to provide training and test material for the ML algorithm. Building the model in simulation involves the use of simulation software and is usually a manual task undertaken by the modeller. Building the model in ML is an automated training cycle in which the ML algorithm (e.g. neural network, decision tree) finds a function that maps the training set examples to labels. Verification in simulation is checking the computer model meets the conceptual model specification. In ML, it is achieved by deploying the ML algorithm against a test data set which has been previously labelled, thus allowing any discrepancies between the function and the test data. In simulation, validation is checking the model results against real-world behaviour – taking into consideration the assumptions and simplifications made in the modelling process. In ML, validation is made when checking model performance on new unlabelled data outside the test and train data set. Simulation results are delivered by output and scenario analysis. This is usually undertaken manually. ML results are delivered by the execution of the ML algorithm when presented with input data. This will usually take place automatically and quickly. When implementing a decision using simulation or ML, then domain knowledge should be used to interpret the results of the analysis before implementation of any solutions indicated by the two methods.

Interpretability of ML Models

A major issue with ML models is the concept of interpretability. Simulation models are constructed by simulation modellers, and so with appropriate documentation, including a statement of assumptions and simplifications, results from a simulation study should be understood and derived from an understanding of how the simulation model works. We may

Table 13.1 Comparison of Stages in Using Simulation and Machine Learning for Decision-Making

Simulation	Machine Learning
Conceptual modelling	Choose an algorithm, hyperparameters, etc.
Data collection	Collect data
Build model	Train model
Verification	Test model
Validation	Validate model
Output and scenario analysis	Run model
Implement decision	Implement decision

find, though, that this causality is difficult to define for large and complex models. In the context of ML models, the term 'interpretability' refers to how we can explain the predictions from these models. ML models are often associated with a lack of interpretability, with the term 'black box' being used to indicate models that lack transparency and cannot be understood by humans. Not all ML models are 'black box', however, and different ML model types have different levels of interpretability. For example, Morocho-Cayamcela et al. (2019) suggest the following types of ML algorithms in decreasing levels of interpretability:

- Classification rules
- Linear regression
- Decision trees
- k-Nearest neighbours
- Support vector machines
- Random forest
- Neural networks

So generally, neural networks have a low level of interpretability and represent non-linear and non-smooth relationships. Classifications rules have a high level of interpretability and represent linear and smooth relationships and are relatively easy to compute. However, it may be the case that a small neural network is more interpretable than a very large decision tree (Lipton, 2018) and Liu et al. (2006) state that causal relationships may sometimes be inferred from such approaches as regression trees and Bayesian neural networks.

When discussing interpretability, we need to consider the differing definitions of what interpretability actually means. Lipton (2018) defines interpretability in two categories of transparency (how does the model work?) and post hoc explanations (what else can the model tell me?). In terms of transparency, this can be considered for the whole model (simulatability), individual components (decomposability) and the training algorithm (algorithmic). Post hoc interpretability encompasses text explanations, visualisation, local explanations and explanation by example. Post hoc interpretability has the advantage of being able to interpret opaque models after the fact without sacrificing predictive performance.

Because of these different definitions of interpretability, we should ensure that any statement regarding the interpretability of an ML algorithm should specify in detail what kind of interpretability is meant and provide evidence as to how this has been demonstrated. A lack of interpretability should not necessarily be used as a pretext to preclude the use of a model that can match or surpass human abilities in complex tasks. On the other hand, we should be wary of post hoc interpretations that can present misleading but plausible explanations. For more details on aspects of interpretability, see Lipton (2018). Because of the issue of the lack of transparency of black-box algorithms, a discipline termed explainable artificial intelligence (XAI) has recently become popular and aims to make AI-derived decisions reconstructable and comprehensible (Adadi and Berrada, 2018). Feldkamp (2021) provides an overview of XAI methods and shows how these methods can be used for the output analysis of simulation data farming projects.

Using ML for Prediction in an Organisational Context

Here are a number of challenges to the use of ML for prediction in an organisational context:

- Although the prediction algorithm is generated, the learning algorithm and training method must be devised to enable this. This task can be challenging.

- We often do not understand how the prediction algorithm has arrived at its prediction. Thus, algorithms based on approaches such as neural networks are usually considered 'black box' and are thus difficult to validate. This might not be an issue with applications such as pattern recognition, but when analysing organisational systems, we are usually interested in knowledge around the causality of effects when dealing with human behaviours. Model credibility in simulation often depends on being able to explain how the results were generated.
- The data used to train and test the algorithm is based on a fixed period of time (i.e. a sample) and thus may not cover all required learning examples – this is termed incompleteness.
- The data used to train and test the algorithm is based on a historical period of time and therefore may be biased to human behaviour in the past that has now changed.
- There is a need to distinguish natural variation in the data from changes in the data due to rare or infrequent behaviour not representative of typical behaviour – this is termed noise.
- The data used for to train and test the algorithm may have been chosen for its accessibility rather than its appropriateness for an accurate prediction. Choosing the correct input data requires the user to employ domain knowledge to think deeply about what data is needed.
- As the context of the prediction widens, the number of potential variables impacting the prediction increases vastly. Thus, there is a need for increasingly massive data sets to cover the 'state space' of the effects of these variables. One example of these difficulties in action is self-driving cars, which can become confused by unexpected road markings or irrational behaviour by humans around them. Humans themselves seem to be able to navigate through complex environments like road systems and usually take suitable actions when confronted with new and unforeseen events. Humans do this by the use of models – mental models using representations and analogies. Mordue et al. (2020) discuss the issues of transferring the responsibility of decision-making affecting the operation of a vehicle away from the driver.

Predictive Accuracy in ML

Predictive accuracy in ML is not enough for prediction systems (Lisboa, 2013). A powerful predictive model may base its predictions on structural artefacts (noise) that cannot be generalised to future data. A popular example is image recognition based on the non-blurred parts of a photograph rather than the objects of interest within the images themselves. This could lead to fictional generalisation accuracy and, when presented with fully focused images, would fail. This implies that domain knowledge in the interpretation of predictions for decision-making made by ML algorithms should be considered.

The Role of Simplification in Simulation and Machine Learning

In the area of data-driven ML, the terms 'overfitting' and 'underfitting' are used to describe the simplification process. Overfitting is when the learning algorithm 'tries too hard' to fit the data, approximating nearly all the points in the data set. This means there is a lack of generalisation and the algorithm only explains behaviour that directly derives from the training data. In this case, any noise such as missing or incorrect data in the test data set will cause a misleading prediction. The algorithm will produce a number of different mistakes, termed high variance. Underfitting is when the algorithm is 'not trying hard enough' to fit the data, leading to the same mistakes repeated, termed high bias. This means there is too much generalisation, and the algorithm predicts behaviour that does not derive from the training data. The solution to overfitting is to try a less flexible learning algorithm or to obtain more data. The solution to underfitting is to try a more flexible learning algorithm or try a different learning algorithm. The issue of simplification in ML is about guiding the learning algorithms to provide a balance between underfitting and overfitting the data, which is a difficult task.

In the area of model-driven simulation, simplification is about providing a specification for a conceptual model that contains a suitable level of detail to meet the predictive needs of the model. Too little simplification will lead to an overly complex model, which may hinder understanding of the effects being studied. Too much simplification will lead to inaccurate results as important elements of the system that have an effect on the predictive metrics of interest have been omitted from the model.

In data-driven ML, the simplification process is coded into the design of the learning algorithm by the data scientist, whereas in model-driven simulation, the simplification process is achieved using the domain knowledge of the modeller. Both approaches need careful application of the model and interpretation of model results by personnel with the requisite technical (quantitative) and domain knowledge (qualitative) skillsets.

Correlation and Machine Learning

The statistical approach of ML can only provide a correlation for prediction. As is often quoted, correlation is not causation; we cannot use the strength of correlation between observed and predicted data to infer that a model's prediction is valid. We may also have issues with the use of correlation as a measure in itself. For example, if a model systematically under or over-predicts by a roughly constant amount, no matter how large, then the correlation will be unaffected. Also, if there is a lag in the timing of the prediction, the correlation will be low, even if the magnitude of the prediction is reasonably accurate. Finally, very different data can give exactly the same correlation coefficient, and the use of visual inspection of model outcomes is recommended. Despite this, however, correlation analysis may provide all the information we need, and we may even take our correlation as a sign of causation in certain circumstances. Also, we may be attempting to predict aspects such as human behaviour that may be difficult or impossible to codify in a simulation model.

Process Mining

The use of process mining involves obtaining and extracting event data to produce an event log and transforming the event log into a process model termed process discovery. The process model can then be used to check the conformance of the system with the process design and to measure the performance of the process. In terms of event log construction, the data required to make an event log can come from a variety of sources, including collected data in spreadsheets, databases and data warehouses or directly from data streams. The minimum data required to construct an event log consists of a list of process instances (i.e. events), which are related to a case identification number and, for each event, a link to an activity label. Activities may reoccur in the event log, but each event is unique, and events within a case need to be presented in order of execution in the event log so that causal dependencies can be derived in the process model. It is also usual for there to be a timestamp associated with each event in the event log. Additional attributes associated with each event may also be included, such as the association of a resource required to undertake the event and the estimated cost of the event.

Once we are satisfied that the process model does provide a suitable representation of behaviour, then we can use the model in a normative mode and judge discrepancies in terms of deviations from the ideal behaviour shown by the model. Undesirable behaviour is when deviations occur due to unwanted actions (for example, not obtaining authorisation for a purchase), and desirable deviations occur when actions occur that are outside normal parameters but show flexibility in meeting the process objectives (for example, providing additional customer service). Conformance checking of processes against a normative model is a major use of process mining. In addition to conformance checking, process mining can be used to assess performance across a number of dimensions by providing additional information in the event log, which is subsequently incorporated into the process model. For example, performance can be reviewed by associating resources with the people undertaking the activities. The interactions between people can be mapped in a social network to provide an organisational perspective. In addition, a cost perspective can be achieved by associating costs with activities.

Visual Analytics

The basic idea of visual analytics is to present large-scale data in some visual form, allowing people to interact with the data to understand processes better. In order to facilitate a better understanding of data, software that provides a visual representation of data is available in the form of applications such as spreadsheets, dashboards and scorecards. In conjunction with their statistical and forecasting capabilities, spreadsheets are particularly useful at providing graphical displays of trends such as sales for analysis by an organisation. To meet the needs of managers who do not use computers frequently, a graphical interface, called a dashboard (or a digital dashboard), permits decision-makers to understand statistics collated by an organisation. A dashboard display is a graphical display on the computer presented to the decision-maker, which includes graphical images such as meters, bar graphs, trace plots and text fields to convey real-time information. Dashboards incorporate drill-down features to enable data to be interrogated in greater detail if necessary. Dashboards should be designed so that the data displayed can be understood in context. For example, sales figures can be displayed against sales figures for the previous time period or the same time period in the previous year. Figures can also be compared against targets and competitors. For example, quality performance can be benchmarked against best-in-class competitors in the same industry. The visual display of data can also be used to show the amount of difference between performance and targets both currently and the trend over time. Visual indicators, such as traffic lights, can be used to show when performance has fallen below acceptable levels (red light), is a cause for concern (amber light) and is acceptable (green light). While dashboards are generally considered to measure operational performance, scorecards provide a summary of performance over a period of time. Scorecards may be associated with the concept of the balanced scorecard strategy tool and examine data from the balanced scorecard perspectives of finances, customers, business process, and learning and growth.

Data Farming

Data farming is the purposeful generation of data from computer-based models, including simulation models. Large-scale simulation experiments can be initiated by varying many input variables, examining many different scenarios or both. Data farming offers the possibility of using simulation to generate big data, with the advantage that the data generated is under the control of the modeller. Data farming can be used to train ML algorithms (although care must be taken that the trained algorithms are not just mimicking the algorithm (model logic) within the simulation!).

The implementation of data farming may require the use of simulation software with a relatively fast execution speed. When using data farming to generate big data, Feldkamp et al. (2017) provide an example of the infrastructure used at these high-volume data levels:

- Half a million simulation runs are performed using the Siemens Plant Simulation (DES) parallelised on ten machines.
- Output data is streamed in small blocks of files to a dedicated Apache Hadoop Distributed File System (HDFS) server.
- Data is then clustered using the k-means package from the Apache Spark Computing Framework.
- Data is then used to train a decision tree model using the Hoeffding Tree Implementation on the Massive Online Analysis software framework (MOA).

An aim of generating these large amounts of data from a simulation is to provide insights such as showing previously hidden relationships in a system. This can be achieved using data mining methods alongside suitable visualisation and interactive methods from the farmed simulation data (Feldkamp, 2021).

People Analytics

Some of the pitfalls around data-driven analytics are shown by the use of people analytics in organisations. People analytics deals with perceptual data and data based on intangible variables rather than the factual data used in finance, for example. Historically, data on people within a business has been used for applications such as workforce modelling in order to match the supply of people and skills to the planned workload. Performance measurement of people has also taken place in the context of the business itself. The use of big data to drive analytics has seen the development of people analytic models that provide measurement based on data gathered on a massive scale. The idea is that the sheer scale of data will improve the accuracy of the analytical process and allow fact-based decisions to be made on people at the individual level.

However, as Cathy O'Neil (2016) found, the complexity of people has led to a number of pitfalls with the use of people analytic methods, including the following:

- Proxy measures are used to attempt to measure complex human behaviours that may not be an accurate representation.
- The algorithms have inbuilt feedback loops that reinforce the assumptions of the model leading to self-fulfilling results.
- There is an inbuilt bias by model builders reflecting their viewpoint on people's behaviours.
- There is a lack of transparency in the workings of the models leading to a lack of knowledge around the limitations of the results of the models and a lack of accountability regarding the model's validity.

Data-Driven Analysis and Model-Driven Analysis with Simulation and Analytics

So far, we have defined data-driven and model-driven approaches to the analysis of business processes. We can categorise analytics as a data-driven approach and simulation as a model-driven approach. There are instances, however, of the use of analytics methods that are driven by data generated from a model that will be termed model-driven analytics and simulations that are data-driven, termed data-driven simulation. Each of these combinations attempts to codify the real world into a computer model that can be used for understanding and predicting the real system. This reality will usually be based on knowledge of only a part of all the data that exists (or ever existed) about the real system. The relationship between data-driven and model-driven analytics and simulation is presented in this context. Figure 13.5 shows how the four combinations of simulation and analytic analysis can be represented by four types of reality that reflect their different emphasis in terms of the use of a subset of all the data that exists that is related to a system.

The categories in figure 13.5 cover the following.

	DATA-DRIVEN	MODEL-DRIVEN
ANALYTICS	SELECTED REALITY Data (Raw)	FARMED REALITY Data (Simulated)
SIMULATION	DIGITAL REALITY Data (Analysed)	SIMPLIFIED REALITY Data (Sampled)

Figure 13.5 Data- and model-driven analysis with simulation and analytics (Greasley and Edwards, 2021)

Data-Driven Analytics

These methods that use raw data to learn from the past to represent a *selected reality* based on the variables and observations included. This is the data-driven approach described earlier in this chapter and is represented by analytics methods such as data mining, machine learning and process mining. Data-driven analytics represent a selected reality in that no matter how large the data sets used for analysis, they will only present a selected view of all the data generated by a process over time.

Model-Driven Simulation

These methods use sampled data from the past to represent a *simplified reality*. This is the model-driven approach described earlier in this chapter and is represented by the method of simulation. This is termed a simplified reality as the modelling process employs a simplification of reality by removing elements that are not considered relevant to the study objectives.

Model-Driven Analytics

These methods use simulated data to drive analytics methods to provide a *farmed reality*. This enables simulation to be used for training and testing ML algorithms and facilitating the use of analytic methods for future system behaviours and for systems that do not currently exist. This is termed a farmed reality in reference to the term data farming, which refers to the use of a simulation model to generate synthetic data.

One example of model-driven analytics is the use of simulation to generate data to train and test ML algorithms. For example, in scheduling manufacturing systems, a simulation can compare the scheduling performance of the trained ML-based algorithms against traditional scheduling rules, such as the shortest process time. Using simulation in this way offers the possibility of its use for training algorithms for current and planned systems and for systems that do not currently exist. However, this approach of using synthetic data generated by the simulation is not always appropriate as the ML algorithm may simply learn the rules with which the simulator was programmed. Thus, the ML algorithm will not reflect the unobservable features of the real world that could be learnt from real data. Thus, real-world experience cannot be replaced by learning in simulations alone, and at some stage, the algorithms must be tested in the real world to ensure validity (Kober et al., 2013).

Data-Driven Simulation

These methods use analysed data to drive simulation to provide a *digital reality*. These applications allow data, which may be processed through analytic methods such as process mining, data mining and machine learning, to advance the capability of simulation model development and experimentation. The use of a data-driven approach to provide model-building capabilities and thus enable recoding of the model to reflect the actual state of a system is a particularly important advance represented by the use of applications such as digital twins. This is termed digital reality as the approach and is used to construct a real-time digital replica of a real-world object.

Usually, a simulation model will take some time to develop with a custom model built for each application and collection of data over a period of time by methods such as observation and interviews with personnel involved in the process. This relatively long development time and use of historical data can limit the use of simulation to medium- to long-term decisions. To enable simulation for short-term operational decision-making, there is a need for continuous updating of both the data that is used by the model and, in some instances, of the model itself.

This can be now be achieved in a number of ways, including the following:

- The use of historical process data from factories such as those provided using the manufacturing execution systems (MES) standard to provide automated collection and faster updating of data values to configure a simulation model.
- Real-time information on the status of machines and production schedules in the factory to provide automated model regeneration to reflect changes in the physical system as they occur.
- Data from the simulation model is used in conjunction with ML analytics to flow back to the physical system to control its actions.

All three of these options could be referred to as data-driven simulations, and their use should be based on the complexity of the system being modelled and the objectives of the simulation study. In terms of the use of historical process data, MES systems are used to track and control production systems and provide a scheduling capability. For example, the Simio simulation software package provides facilities to extract data directly from an MES and build and configure a Simio model from that data. Simio includes a feature to auto-create model components and their properties based on the contents of the imported tables, which can then be used to build complete models from external data. These models would normally provide a base model, which could then be refined if necessary. This option provides the ability to generate a model much faster than traditional simulation approaches. More details of data driven models in Simio are by Smith et al. (2018:231).

When combining simulation with analytic methods to undertake data-driven simulation and model-driven analytics, the simulation methodology employed in this book is extended as shown in figure 13.6.

Figure 13.6 shows the use of the analytic methods of process mining, machine learning, data mining and visual analytics to facilitate stages of the simulation methodology. At the process-mapping stage, process mining can be used to generate a process map. At the input modelling stage, machine learning and data mining can be used to cluster data and determine decision logic. At the 'building of the model' stage, ML algorithms can be used to facilitate digital twins. At the output analysis and scenario analysis stage, machine learning and data mining can be used to facilitate simulation experimentation, for example, in optimisation, and visual analytics is relevant in providing analysis of large-scale simulation experiments through methods such as clustering. The large data sets required for these methods are derived at the data collection phase through sources such as sensors. Alternatively, the simulation can generate large data sets, known as data farming. Examples of the combined use of DES and big data analytics techniques can be found in Greasley and Edwards (2021). One area is the use of ML algorithms as a supplement to traditional simulation descriptive modelling methods, with Cavalcante et al. (2019) stating that with the advent of big data, model abstractions can be replaced by an ML model.

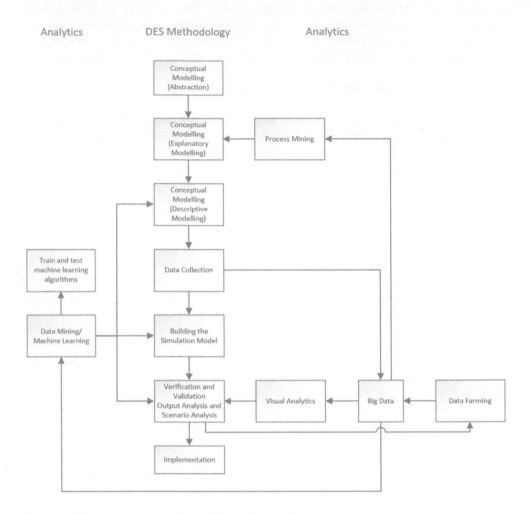

Analytics   DES Methodology   Analytics

Figure 13.6 Combining simulation with big data analytics

Simulation and Industry 4.0

Industry 4.0 (I4.0) is considered a new socio-technical paradigm that depends on further development, access, and integration of information and communication technologies (ICT) with automation technologies to promote end-to-end systems integration across the entire value chain (Kagermann et al., 2015). Simulation tools are considered a key component of the success of I4.0 (Posada et al., 2015).

In their review of simulation in I4.0, de Paula Ferreira et al. (2020) found the following:

- Simulation can aid companies in evaluating the risks, costs, implementation barriers, impact on operational performance, and roadmap towards I4.0.

- The extensiveness wherein I4.0 principles are captured varies according to each simulation-based approach. In this regard, hybrid simulation and digital twin stand as the most promising approaches for I4.0 because they are able to capture most principles of I4.0. However, traditional simulation approaches such as DES are still valid and will continue to evolve, driven by I4.0.
- Data-driven and real-time simulations: incorporating real-time data or big data into the simulation models and developing real-time optimised simulations is a research trend that can advance I4.0 towards its vision of real-time self-optimised production systems. In this regard, there are several opportunities to integrate artificial intelligence methods (e.g. genetic algorithms, artificial neural networks, reinforcement learning) as well as other machine learning and deep learning methods into simulation models.

Simulation and the Smart Factory

De Paula Ferreira et al. (2020) define the smart factory as consisting of a network of smart objects or interconnected cyber-physical systems, and its main features include comprehensive connection, deep convergence, and reliance on data-driven simulation optimisation (Kusiak, 2018; Wang, Wan, Li et al., 2016, Wang, Wan, Zhang et al., 2016). Benotsmane et al. (2019) discuss the role of simulation tools and AI in improving the efficiency of the smart factory. Simulation is used to predict, evaluate and validate system behaviour to transform the basic concepts of the smart factory into reality.

Software Architectures for Combining Simulation and Machine Learning

At a technical level, when combining simulation and ML, there is a choice of an offline architecture in which the simulation and ML software exchange data manually through an intermediate data file or an online architecture in which data is exchanged in real-time through a data interface. While the offline approach is appropriate for activities such as simulation input modelling, the online approach is needed for real-time factory simulation as associated with I4.0 applications (de Paula Ferreira et al., 2020). An online approach is also required to enable the use of digital twins, which are discussed later in this chapter.

When undertaking simulation and analytics in combination, the following approaches are possible. For data-driven simulation, a non-integrated approach involves the use of analytics to process input data for further use in a simulation model. For example, ML algorithms can be used to generate decision trees that can be codified within the simulation, which then runs independently of the analytics application. An integrated approach embeds the analytics methods within the simulation model. One approach is to 'call' previously trained algorithms from the simulation during runtime. However, in order for the context of the simulation and analytics algorithms to be synchronised, it may be necessary to undertake the training of algorithms simultaneously with each simulation run. This can be undertaken during the warm-up period of the simulation (before execution of the main simulation experiment) or during the simulation run itself through the use of real-time data streams such as may be used by a digital twin. For model-driven analytics applications, the simulation can either generate data files that are subsequently used by the analytics application or, in an integrated approach, provide the environment around which the analytics application operates. An example of this approach could be the use of simulation to provide the transport environment in which the analytics algorithms are trained to direct delivery vehicles.

Figure 13.7 shows how software architectures are employed to enable synthetic data generated by a DES to be used by an ML algorithm and the use of an ML algorithm to provide decisions for a simulation. These two roles are combined in architectures 3, 6 and 7, where simulation data is used by an ML algorithm which is subsequently used to generate decisions for a simulation model. Each of the seven architectures will now be described in more detail.

- Architecture 1 uses synthetic data generated by a simulation and held in a data file that is then used by ML algorithms. These algorithms are used stand-alone and are not employed in the simulation model.
- Architecture 2 enables the use of ML as an alternative to the traditional DES input modelling method of sampling data for theoretical distributions and deriving decision rules from domain knowledge (documents, interviews, etc.).
- Architecture 3 uses simulation to generate synthetic data that is used by ML algorithms, which are subsequently employed in the simulation. If this option is chosen, then a data file may be used for offline analysis.
- Architecture 4 enables an online version of architecture 1.
- Architecture 5 enables an online version of architecture 2, in which ML algorithms generate decisions for a simulation model.
- Architecture 6 provides real-time online interaction between simulation software, which generates data for ML software, which in turn communicates decisions back to the simulation software as it executes over simulated time.
- Architecture 7 is implemented by codifying the ML algorithms directly in the DES software. This option provides an online capability without the need for a data interface between the DES and ML software.

When combining the use of DES and ML offline approaches involve using intermediate data files to pass data between the DES and ML software. This is found to be suitable for applications such as the training and testing of ML algorithms with the use of synthetic data generated by the simulation. It is then possible to either codify the ML algorithms within the simulation or to provide an interface between the simulation and trained algorithm. However, the offline architecture is not suitable for methods that require continuous online learning, such as RL, or for real-time applications, such as digital twins.

Architectures that use an online approach may be facilitated by a wrapper interface or the use of a server, but these options require technical knowledge to implement. Recent developments in DES provide them with an online interface through the use of APIs but require knowledge in programming languages such as C# and Java. All of the aforementioned offline and online options require the ability to use ML software such as MatLab and R, apart from architecture 7, that use the facilities of a DES package to integrate an ML capability embedded in the simulation process logic. The advantage of this approach is that it requires coding in the DES process logic with which the DES practitioner is familiar and does not require the use of an intermediate interface or knowledge of external ML software.

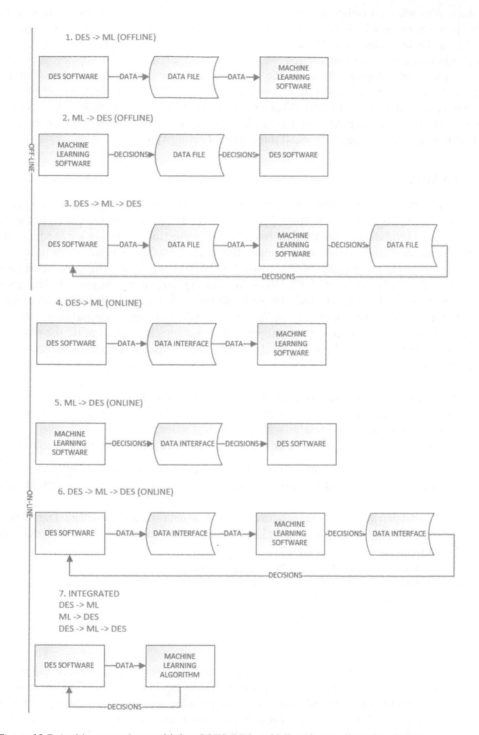

Figure 13.7 Architectures for combining COTS DES and ML software (Greasley, 2020a)

Examples using an online mode in which the ML algorithms are supplying data to the simulation at runtime include where sensors installed in machines obtain data from the real system and process this using ML algorithms to form the basis of a digital twin. Also, neural networks and a number of supervised ML algorithms have been used to implement simulation decision rules during runtime. In the context of the online examples, the data interface between the DES and ML software is achieved using Wrapper, Server or API methods. For example, the Simio software offers Visual C# user extensions in areas such as user-defined model selection rules, and AnyLogic offers Java user extensions that can make use of Java-based libraries such as Deeplearning4j (https://deeplearning4j.org).

Digital Twins

A type of data-driven simulation is a digital twin. The first work that refers to using simulation as a digital twin was published in 1993 (Katz and Manivannan, 1993), but since then, various terms have been used to describe the connection of simulation models with real systems and processes to support operational decisions such as near real time, real time, cyber-physical systems, semi-physical simulation and symbiotic simulation (dos Santos et al., 2021). Negri et al. (2019) define a digital twin as an integrated simulation of a complex product/system that, through physical models and sensor updates, mirrors the life of its corresponding twin. Tao et al. (2018) state that a digital twin consists of three parts: physical product, virtual product and connected data that tie the physical and virtual product. Based on Tao et al. (2018), the following are characteristics of a digital twin:

- Real-time reflection: Two spaces exist in a digital twin, the physical space and the virtual space. The virtual space is the real reflection of the physical space, and it can keep ultra-high synchronisation and fidelity with the physical space.
- Interaction and convergence: This characteristic can be explained from three aspects.

    - Interaction and convergence in the physical space: A digital twin is fully integrated so the data generated in various phases in the physical space can connect with each other.
    - Interaction and convergence between historical data and real-time data: Digital twin data not only depends on expert knowledge but also collects data from all deployed systems in real time.
    - Interaction and convergence between physical space and virtual space: The physical space and virtual space are not isolated in the digital twin with connection channels between the two spaces.

- Self-evolution: A digital twin can update data in real time by comparing virtual space with physical space in parallel.

Simulation can help understand what may happen in the real world. Digital twins help understand not only what may happen but also what is happening in the real world (Taylor et al., 2021). Thus, simulation as digital twins is of most use when an object is changing over time, thus making the initial model of the object invalid, and when measurement data that can be correlated with this change can be captured (Wright and Davidson, 2020). In the guise of a digital twin, this implies that simulation requires an ongoing capability in areas such as model updates, verification, validation and experimentation activities.

One distinction is between a digital twin that automatically commands changes in the physical system (termed autonomous) and those that suggest actions to a human decision-maker. Autonomous systems are associated with the smart factory concept. In terms of the data connection between the simulation and the real system, this can be through process management systems (such as ERP), company databases, sensors and IoT devices such as Bluetooth, RFID and GPS. Connections can be direct or through intermediate systems.

Data flows between the simulation and the real system may be in the following areas:

- Model realisation data is required when the simulation model is defined and updated as a consequence of data from the real system. This is often referred to as a data-driven simulation. However, a purely data-driven model within a digital twin of a physical system is often not advisable as the data-driven model is only reliable within the region of input parameter space from which the data used to construct the model was taken. Using data-driven models for extrapolation without imposing any constraints based on physical knowledge is a dangerous approach (Wright and Davidson, 2020).
- Model validation data is needed to ensure that changes in the real system are reflected in the simulation model. Checks for validity can be undertaken at periodic intervals over time.
- Model experimentation data is needed in a sufficient quantity in order to update the simulation model parameters, but if there are high levels of data processing, then data reduction methods may be used in order to ensure timely processing is feasible.

Synchronisation refers to the updating of the simulation model in response to changes in the real system. Real-time (RT) update of the model is when the updation is synchronised with any changes to the real system. Neal-real-time (NRT) is when there is a periodic update of the model. The choice of RT or NRT should depend on the timeliness of the decision-making required. RT applications are often used in process control applications. Dos Santos et al. (2021) found that currently the majority (72%) of implementations use the NRT approach. RT or NRT synchronisation issues can occur with large and complex simulation models that are required to undertake lengthy analyses, such as optimisation. One approach to dealing with this issue is to use the relatively fast execution speeds of ML algorithms in conjunction with the simulation model. Cao et al. (2021) outline optimisation undertaken using the combination of a low-fidelity neural network metamodel with a high-fidelity discrete-event simulation. Table 13.2 summarises some of the challenges from a simulation perspective of implementing a digital twin capability and possible solutions.

Digital twins can be used in the context of supply chains or even cities. In the context of the organisation, the scope of a digital twin can be at the product, process and enterprise level.

• *Digital Twins of Products*

This type of digital twins relates to the emulation of physical objects such as machines, vehicles, people and energy. They can be considered as an extension of computer-aided design (CAD) and computer-aided engineering systems, which capture data that can then be used to detect issues and generate information that can be used to improve performance. They often have a focus on improving the efficiency of product-life-cycle management, which is important for successful product-as-a-service business models. Digital twins allow the monitoring of multiple products and resources in different operating conditions and different geographic locations.

Table 13.2 Simulation Requirements for a Digital Twin Application

Simulation Requirement	Simulation Solution
Fast execution speed	Distributed simulation: Parallel or multiple simulations on a grid (network) and/or a cloud platform (Taylor, 2019)
Real-time model adaption	DDDAS: Adaptable simulation model (Fujimoto et al., 2019)
Interaction between the physical and simulated systems	Symbiotic simulation: Acquisition analysis of high volumes of data in real time. Interface to the physical system by decision-maker or actuator. Use of big data analytic techniques, such as ML to learn from past performance (Onggo et al., 2018).

- **Digital Twins of Processes**

These emulate processes over time, and so require a dynamic simulation engine based on methods such as DES. One application area is smart maintenance scheduling. An example is predictive maintenance for a welding machine. Here, a simulation provides a virtual representation in real time of the manufacturing process through data connections over the IoT. The current status of the welding machine is known by the digital twin. An ML algorithm is used to provide a prediction of the remaining useful life of the manufacturing equipment based on its current usage and historical data of the process. The digital twin can be run into the future and predict machine failure based on its current status and scheduled future usage. The digital twin can then communicate back to the equipment to instigate a maintenance operation at the appropriate time. The digital twin thus provides an intelligent and automated predictive maintenance capability. Other applications include smart assembly, where individual parts are chosen for assembly based on optimal performance in order to reduce scrap rates.

- **Digital Twins of Enterprises**

At the enterprise level, enterprise simulations aim to evaluate decisions made anywhere in the company on the performance of the whole business (Barton et al., 2001). The objective of a digital twin is to capture the business-operating model for control and management purposes. Enterprise digital twins can be implemented by using multiple digital twins that are in use at the process level. Applications include the connection of the digital twin to an enterprise resource planning system in order to improve factory scheduling to reduce waste and management of inventory.

Level of Integration

In terms of the level of data integration, there are three possible levels of integration between the simulation and its real-world object counterpart (table 13.3). When there is no automated data exchange between the simulation and the real-world object which is a standard simulation application. When there is an automated one-way data flow from the real-world object which leads to a change in the state of the simulation. These one-way digital twins may be referred to as Digital Shadows (Marquardt et al., 2021). When data flows fully integrated into both directions the term Digital twin indicates a requirement for a two-way data flow to provide a monitoring and control capability to take action in response to predicted behaviour. Corrective actions are often implemented

Table 13.3 Level of Integration of a Digital Twin

Onggo et al. (2018)	Kritzinger et al. (2018)	Description
	No way	A copy but not updated in real-time (i.e. a simulation).
Type 1 (DSS) Type 3 (OpenLoop)	One way	Physical system sends data to the simulation. For type 1, a decision-maker controls the physical system.
Type 2 (Control)	Two ways	Data flow in both directions. The simulation controls the physical system with an actuator.

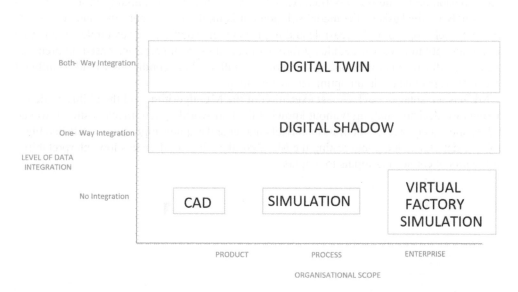

Figure 13.8 Level of data integration and organisational scope of a digital twin

using analytics methods based on ML algorithms that provide appropriate methods of process control actuation. The development of digital twins with fully integrated data flows in both directions is complex and is still in its infancy.

By combining the classification of digital twins by the level of data integration and organisational scope, we can see that the application of the concept covers a wide range of applications (figure 13.8). A key consideration between these different applications is the complexity implied in the application, with a full (both-way) digital twin of the enterprise representing the most complex.

Components of a Digital Twin

The context for many digital twin implementations is the development of I4.0 initiatives and, in particular, the move to greater automation of processes. To enable automated and flexible systems ideally requires the digital twin to make the best decisions in real time. Simulation, ML and mathematical optimisation algorithms can be employed in combination to meet this challenge (Li et al., 2021). Each component has strengths and weaknesses in terms of meeting this objective, but utilised together, the weaknesses may be overcome. Figure 13.9 summarises some of their complementary features.

Optimisation methods provide fast execution and will find the 'best' option from the solution space. There are however challenges when using optimisation for prediction in an organisational. Although optimisation approaches can be useful, in practice decision makers are concerned with providing what they consider to be a satisfactory answer to a problem. This ensures analysis is not overly extended in search of the "perfect" answer, but they are also aware that the model does not take into account all aspects of the real system. The limitations of the model mean that the optimum solution provided is only optimal in comparison with the other solutions tried and there are likely to be other solutions that exist that have not been considered by the optimisation. Also, the decision maker is unlikely to make a decision solely on the basis of the model solution but is likely to consider other factors outside of the model scope to find a feasible and implementable solution. For example, an analysis to find an optimum work schedule by formulating a number of scenarios based on premises regarding ethical and moral concerns in terms of staff working conditions would be difficult to codify as parameters in an optimisation algorithm.

ML has advantages, such as fast execution of the ML algorithm and the ability to define outputs for decision-making without knowing the real-world system mechanism. However, ML cannot easily predict out of its historical data set and requires high-quality data and high-volume data for training and testing the ML algorithm. It also often has low interpretability of the model connecting inputs to outputs.

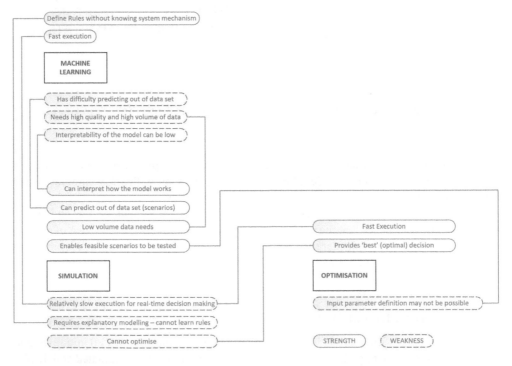

Figure 13.9 The complementary use of machine learning, simulation and optimisation

Simulation models are constructed by simulation modellers and so with appropriate documentation including a statement of assumptions and simplifications, results from a simulation study should be understood derived from an understanding of how the simulation model works. We may find though that this causality is difficult to define for large and complex models. However, simulation has a relatively slow execution speed particularly for large complex models with complex experimentation needs. It also requires an exploratory model to be defined by the modeller and cannot find the optimum 'best' decision directly.

Thus, the combination of simulation with ML and optimisation algorithms can provide the best solution from a number of alternatives. In particular, ML algorithms and simulation can be used in conjunction with optimisation software to find the best outcomes for NRT or RT analysis. In addition, simulation can be used to provide a fast way of training the ML algorithms used in these systems.

The End of Theory

Anderson's famous article in *Wired* magazine (Anderson, 2008) put forward the argument that due to the advent of big data, this meant computers could find relationships between data. Our theories were being exposed for what they were – oversimplifications of reality. We'd stop looking for the cause of things and be satisfied with correlations. This was a challenge to theory in general but also to the deductive approach of simulation. In some ways, these statements make sense – using inductive approaches, such as ML, we are not constrained by theory; we are deriving our answers from the real world with all its complexity enabled by big data, which allows us to incorporate enough experience of the real world. There are, however, limitations to approaches such as ML. For instance, we can never collect all the data about everything, so the data we do use (select) can be biased, and any analysis of data needs to be guided and lead to action to be useful. Thus, we still need human knowledge to select and set up the training of the algorithms and to interpret and use the results.

In terms of simulation, though, when the emphasis is on the prediction of future behaviour over time, the obvious disadvantage of ML approaches is that although it allows interpolation (it can predict the future if the future is similar to the past), we can't extrapolate (look at new situations) because we don't have a theory to do that; what we have is based on learned patterns that mimic complex behaviour. Simulation starts with a theory (our simplification of reality). This means our answers are based on a theory (why behaviour happens), and so we can, within reason, predict what might happen under different circumstances assuming our theory holds. There are limitations to simulation, too, though. Because our theory is a simplification of reality, it does not reflect the complexity of the real world. There are many aspects of reality for which we have no theory, such as aspects of human behaviour, and so simulation may not be a feasible option.

Case Study: Using a Hybrid Modelling Approach

This study provides an example of hybrid modelling in which a simulation provides a virtual environment for the training of a reinforcement learning (RL) algorithm. The algorithm is used to find the best path to direct robot movement around a factory. The simulation represents the process of offloading and collection at pickup points and the robot movement between pickup points (based on robot acceleration, deceleration and speed parameters).

Conceptual Model Building

Figure 13.10 shows the conceptual model of the train and move robot processes. Training commences in order to find an (approximate) best route to a destination location. When training is complete, the move robot process moves the robot from its current position to its destination along the path determined by the RL algorithm. The train and move process is repeated for each movement required.

The elements that implement the RL algorithm are now outlined in greater detail in terms of the observation space, action space and reward structure of the factory and the agents (robots) that move within it (Sartoretti et al., 2019).

Observation Space

The approach involves placing an agent on a grid made up of cells termed a grid-world which covers a full map of the environment within which the robot will travel. An alternative configuration is to have a partially observable grid-world, where agents can only observe the state of the world in a limited field of vision (FOV) centred around themselves. This might be utilised when reducing the input dimension to a neural network algorithm, for example, but still requires the robot agent to acquire information on the direction (unit vector) and Euclidean distance to its goal at all times (Sartoretti, 2019). In this study, the observation space is based on a layout for an AGV system presented in Seifert et al. (1998) which incorporates ten pick and delivery stations, numbered 1 to 10. In the original configuration in Seifert et al. (1998), the AGV routing is confined to nodes at each station connected by direct path arcs. In this implementation, the grid system permits more flexible movement of the autonomous robot. The observation space represents a

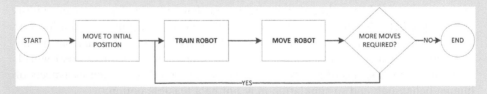

Figure 13.10 Conceptual model of train and move robot processes

relatively challenging operating area for the robots as there is only a narrow opening between two areas of the factory. This makes it difficult for a simple step-by-step algorithm to direct efficient movement around the factory, but this problem can be avoided by pre-computing complete paths (Klass et al., 2011), which is the approach taken here.

Action Space

Robot agents in the grid-world can move one cell at a time in any of eight directions (to orthogonal and diagonal adjacent neighbours) representing a Moore neighbourhood. This is used rather than the four-direction von Neumann neighbourhood to represent the autonomous and free moving capabilities of the robots and provide a greater level of locally available information. Robot agents are prevented from moving into cells occupied by predefined static objects and will only move when a feasible cell is found. The action space of the factory layout is represented by a 20 × 10 grid-world, with each robot occupying a single grid cell at any one time. The grid-world is implemented in the simulation by a 20 × 10 two-dimensional array which is populated with a '0' value for cells that are available to travel and a '1' value for cells which contain a static object and thus must be avoided. The action space is easily increased in size in the model by increasing the size of the array holding the cell values. In this example, a cell in the grid-world represents $1m^2$ of factory floor space, and a robot travels at a constant speed of 0.6m/s between cells.

Reward Structure

An RL algorithm has to explore and try out different possibilities until it works out how to get the answer right. In terms of action selection, a number of options are available, but the most recognised ones are as follows:

Greedy: Pick the action with the highest value to always exploit current knowledge.

ϵ – greedy: Same as greedy but with a small probability ϵ to pick some other action at random, thus permitting more exploration and potentially finding better solutions.

Soft-max: A refinement of the ϵ – greedy option in which the other action is chosen in proportion to their estimated reward, which is updated whenever they are used.

The reinforcement learner is trying to decide on what action to take in order to maximise the expected reward into the future, where the expected reward is known as the value. In this case, we implement a type of reinforcement learning using the method of Q-learning (Watkins and Dayan, 1992), which repeatedly moves the agent to an adjacent random cell position and provides a reward if that moves the agent closer to our intended destination cell. A large reward is allocated when the agent finds the target cell. Each cell is allocated a Q value as the agent moves to it, which is calculated by the Bellman equation:

$$Q(s, a) = r + \gamma(max(Q(s', a')))$$

The Bellman equation expresses a relationship between the value of a state and the values of its successor states. Thus, the equation calculates the discounted value of the expected next state plus the reward expected along the way. This means the Q value for the state 's' taking the action 'a' is the sum of the instant reward 'r' and the discounted future reward. The discount factor 'γ' determines how much importance you give to future rewards and is set to a default value of 0.8 in this study. The Q values are held in a two-dimensional array (termed the Q-matrix or transition matrix) that matches the size of the action space array and holds a Q value for each available cell in the factory layout. The following algorithm implements the RL method using the greedy action selection:

1   Initialise the Q-matrix to zeros. Set the start position and target position for the robot.
2   Move the robot to the start position.
3   The robot makes a random move to an adjacent cell (which is available and not an obstacle).
4   The reward 'r' is calculated based on the straight-line distance between the new cell position and the target cell position.
5   The maximum future reward $max(Q(s', a'))$ is calculated by computing the reward for each of the eight possible moves from the new cell position (which are available and not an obstacle). The future reward value is discounted by the discount factor 'γ'.
6   The Q value for the new cell position is calculated using the Bellman equation by summing the reward and discounted future reward values.
7   If the target cell has been reached, end. Otherwise, repeat from step 3.

When the target cell is reached, this is termed a learning pass. The robot is then placed back at the starting cell, and the process is repeated from step 2. After a number of learning passes, the Q values in each grid cell should be stabilised, and so the training phase can be halted. The robot can now follow the (approximate) shortest path by choosing adjacent cells with the highest Q values in turn as it travels to the destination. The number of learning passes required will be dependent on the size and complexity (number of obstacles and position of obstacles) of the grid-world. When the robot is required to move from its new position, it enters training mode again, and the algorithm is implemented from step 1.

Computer Implementation

A simulation was built using the Simio v11 DES software using an object modelling approach. This means numeric values can be associated with an entity (termed attributes in Arena or labels in Simul8), but in Simio, process definitions can also be embedded within the entity definition. This enables autonomous behaviour of individual entities and allows capabilities associated with agent-based modelling approaches to be achieved. Simio allows the use of object constructs in the following way. An object definition defines how an object behaves and interacts with other objects and is defined by constructs such as properties, states and events. An object instance is an instantiation of an object definition that is used in a particular model. These objects can be specified by setting their properties in Simio. An object runspace is an object that is created during a simulation run based on the object instance definition. An example in Simio is ModelEntity1[25], which represents the entity with an instance identification number of 25. In this case, an instance of the Simio entity object definition is defined in the Facility window as ModelEntity1, which is associated with a robot animation symbol. A source node is used to create a robot arrival stream, and each robot then enters a BasicNode and is then transferred into what is termed FreeSpace in Simio. The separate arrival streams permit a schedule of pickup/dropoff station moves to be allocated to each robot. When the robot entities transfer to FreeSpace, no route pathways are defined, but the robot entities move in either 2D or 3D space using x, y and z coordinates at a defined heading, speed and acceleration. This allows flexible routing to be specified without the need for a predefined routing layout. This provides a second capability that is not usually associated with DES software, which usually animates entities between fixed points (for example, the fixed points are termed stations in Arena). Thus, Simio permits both simulation through time but also through space; thus, spatial simulation models are possible.

The mechanism by which entities incorporate both attribute values and process definitions and can thus have their own behaviour is by the use of an entity token approach. Here, a token (or 'dummy' entity) is created as a delegate of the robot entity in order to execute a process associated with that entity. Tokens and thus processes can be triggered by events, such as the movement of entities into and out of objects or by other processes. In this case, what Simio terms Add-on Processes are incorporated into the ModelEntity1 (Robot) object definition, allowing data and processes to be encapsulated within each entity definition within the simulation. This means each entity (robot) runspace object simulated in the model will have its own process execution and data values associated with it. The process logic (algorithms) for the simulation contained in the add-on processes trains and moves each robot through a number of predefined pick and deliver locations. The hierarchy for the robot object definition is shown in figure 13.11. In this implementation, the 'Train and Move Robot', 'Train Robot' and 'Move Robot' subroutines are defined at the Model level to allow a grid matrix to be defined with the current position of each robot. This matrix can then be used to track the relative position of the robots and be used for

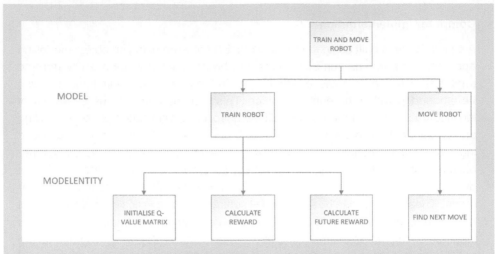

Figure 13.11 The Simio add-on process hierarchy for the robot object definition

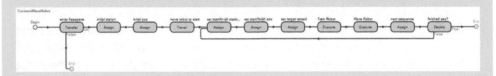

Figure 13.12 The Train and Move Robot add-on process

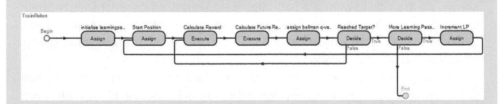

Figure 13.13 The Train Robot add-on process

collision detection purposes. The 'Initialise Transition Matrix', 'Calculate Reward', 'Calculate Future Reward' and 'Find Next Move' subroutines are embedded at the ModelEntity level, so the individual training and movement of each autonomous robot are defined within each robot definition. This means a unique grid-world defining the factory layout, and no-go areas can be associated with each robot.

The Train and Move Robot process definition is shown in figure 13.12. This assigns the start station for each robot, transfers the robot to FreeSpace and repeatedly trains and moves the robot between the sequence of load and unload station defined by the user.

The Train Robot process definition is shown in figure 13.13. Here, the RL algorithm is called until the target location has been reached, representing a learning

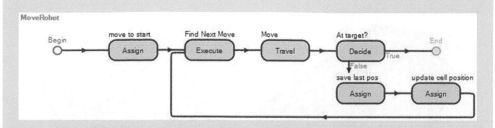

Figure 13.14 The Move Robot add-on process

pass. The robot is then returned to its start position, and this is repeated until the number of defined learning passes has been made.

When using RL, one decision to be made is to specify the number of learning passes or attempts that the robots will make to find an efficient path between two stations. Here, a maximum learning pass figure of 50 was chosen. However, in this case, the number of steps required to move between the stations quickly converges from an initial value of 100 to around 15 steps for this routing in around five learning passes. This is an indication of how quickly the RL algorithm 'learns' the 'shortest' route between the two stations.

The Move Robot process definition is shown in figure 13.14. Here, the robot moves from its start point by checking the Q value at each adjacent grid cell and choosing the grid cell to move to with the highest Q value. When the target grid cell has been reached, the process terminates.

Validation

The main method used for validating the RL algorithms in Simio was to project the Q value transition matrix for a robot onto the Simio animation display of the factory. The user can then observe the Q values updating on each learning pass and confirm the path derived from the RL algorithm and ensure that the robot moves along this path.

Experimentation

With verification and validation complete, the model can be run with the training mode operating in the background and the animation showing the movement of the trained robots between pick and deliver stations. Figure 13.15 shows the final Simio simulation display with two robots moving between stations following routes based on the RL algorithm.

The model provides a testbed to explore a number of scenarios, such as the following:

- In terms of the operation of the RL algorithm by investigating the effect of adjusting the discount factor and number of learning passes on the generation of an approximate best route strategy.

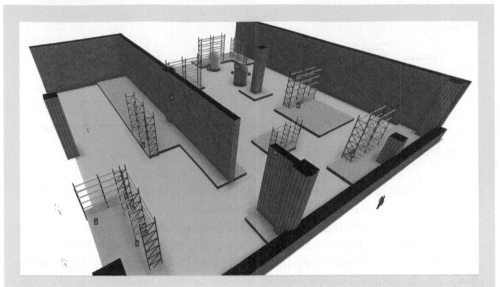

Figure 13.15 Simio 3D display of two robots following routes based on reinforcement learning

- The use of different action selection rules such as soft-max could also be investigated.
- In terms of the model design, the effect of robot travel speed (which can vary according to loading) and the incorporation of acceleration and deceleration of the robot could be investigated.
- The model could also be tested for larger industrial applications that require a larger grid-world and a greater number of robots and thus place higher processing demands on the simulation.

Discussion

A barrier to the growth in hybrid modelling is the different backgrounds and skillsets of simulation and analytics practitioners. Simulation practitioners typically combine the technical knowledge required to undertake simulation, such as model building and statistical methods, with an understanding of an application domain such as manufacturing or healthcare. In a business setting, analytics may be undertaken by teams consisting of data scientists with data, statistical and IT skills, business analysts with deep domain knowledge and IT professionals to develop data products. Many simulation practitioners began their simulation careers coding models in simulation languages, such as SIMAN, and using languages, such as FORTRAN, for file processing. However, in the light of the development of drag and drop interfaces in such tools as Arena, recent users may find it a particular challenge to adapt to the need for coding when developing an ML algorithm in Matlab, R or Python. One way of addressing this issue may be to emphasise the need for training simulation practitioners in data science methods and the adoption of a multidisciplinary approach to research and training. This case study shows how using the object-oriented and visual display capabilities of the Simio software can enable the incorporation of ML algorithms within a DES without the need for coding in ML languages or an interface with external ML software.

Extract from Greasley (2020b).

Summary

This chapter provides an introduction to model-driven analysis adopted by simulation and data-driven analysis adopted by methods such as ML. The strengths and weaknesses of both approaches are examined in the context of their use to assist decision-making in organisations. The model-driven and data-driven analysis approaches can be considered complementary. The model-driven approach of simulation encapsulates a theory about how the system works and enables causation to be established, assisting in the understanding of model prediction. The data-driven approach of ML provides a pattern matching and correlation capability that can provide a prediction when a model-driven approach may not be feasible. The combined use of simulation and ML in applications such as digital twins suggests that the development and importance of simulation models as part of hybrid models will continue to increase in the coming years. Hybrid modelling is an exciting area which is sure to see many developments in the future.

Exercises

- Compare and contrast model-driven analysis and data-driven analysis.
- Compare and contrast simulation and ML as tools for decision-making.
- What are the main components of a digital twin?
- Discuss potential applications of hybrid modelling.

References

Adadi, A. and Berrada, M. (2018) Peeking inside the black-box: A survey on explainable artificial intelligence (XAI), *IEEE Access*, 6, 52138–52160.

Anderson, C. (2008) The end of theory: The data deluge makes the scientific model obsolete, *Wired Magazine*.

Barton, J.A., Love, D.M. and Taylor, G.D. (2001) Evaluating design implementation strategies using enterprise simulation, *International Journal of Production Economics*, 72, 285–299.

Bell, D., Groen, D., Ozik, J., Mustafee, N. and Strassburger, S. (2019) Hybrid simulation development – Is it just analytics? *Proceedings of the 2019 Winter Simulation Conference*, IEEE.

Benotsmane, R., Kovács, G. and Dudás, L. (2019) Economic, social impacts and operation of smart factories in industry 4.0: Focusing on simulation and artificial intelligence of collaborating robots, *Social Sciences*, 8(143).

Cao, Y, Currie, C., Onggo, B.S. and Higgins, M. (2021) Simulation optimization for a digital twin using a multi-fidelity framework, *Proceedings of the 2021 Winter Simulation Conference*, IEEE.

Cavalcante, I.M., Frazzon, E.M., Fernando, A. and Ivanov, D. (2019) A supervised machine learning approach to data-driven simulation of resilient supplier selection in digital manufacturing, *International Journal of Information Management*, 49, 86–97.

de Paula Ferreira, W., Armellini, F. and De Santa-Eulalia, L.A. (2020) Simulation in industry 4.0: A state-of-the-art review, *Computers and Industrial Engineering*, 149.

dos Santos, C.H., Montevechi, J.A.B., de Queiroz, J.A., de Carvalho Miranda, R. and Leal, F. (2021) Decision support in productive processes through DES and ABS in the Digital Twin era: A systematic literature review, *International Journal of Production Research*, 1–20.

Feldkamp, N. (2021) Data farming output analysis using explainable AI, *Proceedings of the 2021 Winter Simulation Conference*, IEEE.

Feldkamp, N., Bergmann, S. and Strassburger, S. (2017) Online analysis of simulation data with stream-based data mining, *Proceedings of the 2017 ACM SIGSIM Conference on Principles of Advanced Discrete Simulation*, 241–248.

Fujimoto, R., Barjis, J., Blasch, E., Cai, W., Jin, D., Lee, S. and Son, Y-J. (2018) Dynamic data application systems: Research challenges and opportunities, *Proceedings of the 2018 Winter Simulation Conference*, IEEE, 664–678.

Greasley, A. (2020a) Architectures for combining discrete-event simulation and machine learning, in F. De Rango, T. Oren, M. Obaidat, M. Obaida, and M. Obaidat (eds.) *Proceedings of the 10th International Conference on Simulation and Modeling Methodologies, Technologies and Applications*, SciTePress, 47–58.

Greasley, A. (2020b) Implementing reinforcement learning in simio discrete-event simulation software, *Simulation Series*. 52(3), 314–324.

Greasley, A. (2005) Using DEA and simulation in guiding operating units to improved performance, *Journal of the Operational Research Society*, 56(5), 727–731.

Greasley, A. and Edwards, J.S. (2021) Enhancing discrete-event simulation with big data analytics: A review, *Journal of the Operational Research Society*, 72(2), 247–267.

Kagermann, H. (2015) Change through digitization – Value creation in the age of industry 4.0, *Management of Permanent Change*, 23–45.

Katz, D. and Manivannan, S. (1993) Exception management on a shop floor using online simulation, *Proceedings of the 1993 Winter Simulation Conference*, 888–896.

Klass, A., Laroque, C., Fischer, M. and Dangelmaier, W. (2011) Simulation aided, knowledge-based routing for AGVs in a distribution warehouse, *Proceedings of the 2011 Winter Simulation Conference*, IEEE, 1668–1679.

Kober, J., Bagnell, J.A. and Peters, J. (2013) Reinforcement learning in robotics: A survey, *The International Journal of Robotics Research*, 32(11), 1238–1274.

Kritzinger, W., Karner, M., Traar, G., Henjes, J. and Sihn, W. (2018) Digital twin in manufacturing: A categorical literature review and classification, *IFAC PapersOnLine*, 1016–1022.

Kusiak, A. (2018) Smart manufacturing, *International Journal of Productions Research*, 56(1–2), 508–517.

Li, H., Cao, X., Jin, X., Lee, L.H. and Chew, E.P. (2021) Three carriages driving the development of intelligent digital twins – simulation plus optimization and learning, *Proceedings of the 2021 Winter Simulation Conference*, IEEE.

Lipton, Z.C. (2018) The mythos of model interpretability, *Communications of the ACM*, 61(10), 36–43.

Lisboa, P.J.G. (2013) Interpretability in machine learning – principles and practice, *Proceedings of the International Workshop in Fuzzy Logic Applications*, 15–21.

Liu, C., Rani, P. and Sarkar, N. (2006) An empirical study of machine-learning techniques for affect recognition in human-robot interaction, *Pattern Analysis and Applications*, 9(1), 58–69.

Marquardt, T., Morgan, L. and Cleophas, C. (2021) Indolence is fatal: Research opportunities in designing digital shadows and twins for decision support, *Proceedings of the 2021 Winter Simulation Conference*, IEEE.

Mordue, G., Yeung, A. and Wu, F. (2020) The looming challenges of regulating high level autonomous vehicles, *Transportation Research Part A*, 132, 174–187.

Morocho-Cayamcela, M.E., Lee, H. and Lim, W. (2019) Machine learning for 5G/B5G mobile and wireless communications: Potential, limitations, and future directions, *IEEE Access*, 7, 137184–137206.

Negri, E., Fumagalli, L., Cimino, C. and Macchi, M. (2019) FMU-supported simulation for CPS digital twin, in *International Conference on Changeable, Agile, Reconfigurable and Virtual Production*, Procedia Manufacturing, vol. 28, 201–206.

O'Neil, C. (2016) *Weapons of Math Destruction: How Big Data Increases Inequality and Threatens Democracy*, Allen Lane.

Onggo, B.S., Mustafee, N., Juan, A.A., Molloy, O. and Smart, A. (2018) Symbiotic Simulation System: Hybrid systems model meets big data analytics, *Proceedings of the 2018 Winter Simulation Conference*, IEEE, 1358–1369.

Posada, J., Toro, C., Barandiaran, I., Oyarzun, D., Stricker, D., de Amicis, R., Pinto, E.B., Eisert, P., Dollner, J. and Vallarino, I. (2015) Visual computing as a key enabling technology for industrie 4.0 and industrial internet, *IEEE Computer Graphics & Applications*, 35(2), 26–40.

Sartoretti, G., Kerr, J., Shi, Y., Wagner, G., Kumar, T.K.S., Koenig, C. and Choset, H. (2019) PRIMAL: Pathfinding via reinforcement learning and imitation multi-agent learning, *IEEE Robotics and Automation Letters*, 4(3), 2378–2385.

Seifert, R.W., Kay, M.G. and Wilson, J.R. (1998) Evaluation of AGV routeing strategies using hierarchical simulation, *International Journal of Production Research*, 36(7), 1961–1976.

Smith, J.S., Sturrock, D.T. and Kelton, W.D. (2018) *Simio and Simulation: Modeling, Analysis, Applications*, 5th edition, Simio LLC.

Tao, F., Cheng, J., Qi, Q., Zhang, M., Zhang, H. and Sui, F. (2018) Digital twin-driven product design, manufacturing and service with big data, *The International Journal of Advanced Manufacturing Technology*, 94, 3563–3576.

Taylor, S.J.E. (2019) Distributed simulation: State-of-the-art and potential for operational research, *European Journal of Operational Research*, 273, 1–19.

Taylor, S.J.E., Johansson, B., Jeon, S., Lee, L.H., Lendermann, P. and Shao, G. (2021) Using simulation and digital twins to innovate: Are we getting smarter? *Proceedings of the 2021 Winter Simulation Conference*, IEEE.

Wang, S., Wan, J., Li, D. and Zhang, C. (2016) Implementing smart factory of industrie 4.0: An outlook, *International Journal of Distributed Sensor Networks*, 12(1), 1–10.

Wang, S., Wan, J., Zhang, D., Li, D. and Zhang, C. (2016) Towards smart factory for industry 4.0: A self-organized multi-agent system with big data based feedback and coordination, *Computer Networks*, 101, 158–168.

Watkins, C.J.C.H. and Dayan, P. (1992) Q-learning, *Machine Learning*, 8(3–4), 279–292.

Wright, L. and Davidson, S. (2020) How to tell the difference between a model and a digital twin, *Advanced Modeling and Simulation in Engineering Sciences*, 7(13), 1–13.

Index